2015

AFFORDABLE CARE ACT

Law, Regulatory Explanation and Analysis

Wolters Kluwer, CCH Editorial Staff Publication

Access the Latest Tax Legislation Developments

A special webpage created by Wolters Kluwer, CCH will keep you up-to-date with key federal tax law developments occurring after publication of the **Affordable Care Act—Law, Regulatory Explanation and Analysis** book. Visit *CCHGroup.com/TaxUpdates* to find the information you'll need to keep Wolters Kluwer, CCH as your first source for practical tax guidance.

Wolters Kluwer

This publication is designed to provide accurate and authoritative information in regard to the subject matter covered. It is sold with the understanding that the publisher is not engaged in rendering legal, accounting, or other professional service. If legal advice or other expert assistance is required, the services of a competent professional person should be sought.

ISBN 978-0-8080-3993-8

4025 W. Peterson Ave.
Chicago, IL 60646-6085
800 248 3248
CCHGroup.com

Printed in the United States of America

Certified Chain of Custody
Product Line Contains At Least
20% Certified Forest Content
www.sfiprogram.org
SFI-00756

Patient Protection and Affordable Care Act, as amended by the Health Care and Reconciliation Act of 2010

Health Care Reform and Related New Taxes

The Patient Protection and Affordable Care Act (PPACA) (P.L. 111-148), as amended by the Health Care and Education Reconciliation Act of 2010 (P.L. 111-152) (2010 Reconciliation Act), was meant to expand the number of insured individuals to near-universal levels, increase the quality and affordability of health insurance, and reduce the costs of health care. The legislation phases many of its changes in over several years, and the federal departments overseeing implementation of the law (the Departments of Treasury, Health and Human Services, and Labor) have provided extensive transition relief due to the complicated nature of the reform. See ¶105 for a timeline of the implementation of health care reform.

To meet its goals, the legislation requires that most individuals obtain qualified health care coverage and that large employers offer qualified health care coverage to employees and their dependents. Failure to do so will result in additional tax. The legislation also makes credits and subsidies available to help lower-income individuals, as well as some middle-class families, purchase health care coverage at one of the health insurance marketplaces that were required to be established in every state. To help pay for these and other reforms, the legislation included over $400 billion in revenue raisers and new taxes.

The Internal Revenue Code plays several key functions in achieving the goals of health care reform, ranging from providing "carrots" and "sticks" as incentives to extend health care coverage, raising revenue to help pay for these programs, placing new requirements on insurance providers, and enforcing the legislation. Thus, the IRS is responsible for overseeing a significant part of the reform, and has provided a slew of guidance on most aspects of the PPACA.

About This Work

Following the release of guidance implementing the Patient Protection and Affordable Care Act (P.L. 111-148) and the Health Care and Education Reconciliation Act of 2010 (P.L. 111-152), Wolters Kluwer, CCH is providing practitioners with a single integrated law and explanation of the tax provisions of these Acts. This resource includes IRS regulations and other regulatory decrees executing the many aspects of health care reform. It explains the regulations enforcing the individual mandate and the proposed regulations that outline the employer mandate as it is currently envisioned, along with other guidance relevant to individuals and businesses. This work clarifies the new information reporting requirements for employers and insurers, the required reforms to health care plans, and the new taxes imposed on individuals and certain entities. As always, Wolters Kluwer, CCH Tax and Accounting remains dedicated to responding to the needs of tax professionals in helping them quickly understand and work with these new laws as they take effect. Other products and tax services relating to the new legislation can be found at *tax.cchgroup.com*.

October 2014

Wolters Kluwer, CCH Tax and Accounting
EDITORIAL STAFF

Joshua Braunstein, *Vice President, Research and Learning*
Elizabeth Albers, *Director, Books and Production*
Mark L. Friedlich, J.D., *Director, International and Accounting*
Grace Hong, *Vice President, Strategic Product Development*
Jennifer M. Lowe, J.D., *Director, State Tax*
Sarah Stevens, J.D., LL.M., M.B.A., *Director, Federal Tax*

Explanation and Analysis

Jeff Baxendale, J.D.

David Becker, J.D.

Dan Billings, J.D.

Glenn L. Borst, J.D., LL.M.

Anne E. Bowker, J.D., LL.M.

John Buchanan, J.D., LL.M.

Mildred Carter, J.D.

James A. Chapman, J.D., LL.M.

Tom Cody, J.D., LL.M., M.B.A.

Casie Cooper

Jennifer R. Cordaro, J.D.

Donna J. Dhein, C.P.A.

Kurt Diefenbach, J.D.,
Managing Editor

Liliana Dimitrova, LL.B., LL.M.

Karen Elsner, C.P.A.

Alicia C. Ernst, J.D.

Elena Eyber, J.D.

Shannon Jett Fischer, J.D.

Donna M. Flanagan, J.D.

Mary Jo Gagnon, C.P.A.

Brant Goldwyn, J.D.

Bruno L. Graziano, J.D., M.S.A.

Joy A. Hail, J.D., LL.M.

Michael Henaghan, J.D., LL.M.,
Managing Editor

Kathleen M. Higgins

Caroline L. Hosman, J.D., LL.M.

David M. Jaffe, J.D.

George G. Jones, J.D., LL.M.,
Managing Editor

Thomas K. Lauletta, J.D.

Adam R. Levine, J.D., LL.M.

Laura M. Lowe, J.D.,
Managing Editor

Mark A. Luscombe, J.D., LL.M,
C.P.A.,
Principal Analyst

Jerome A. Maes, J.D.

Chantal M. Mahler

Sheri Wattles Miller, J.D.

Ellen Mitchell, EA

Robert A. Morse, J.D., LL.M.

Jonathan Mosier, J.D.

John J. Mueller, J.D., LL.M.,
Managing Editor

Jean T. Nakamoto, J.D.

Jerome Nestor, J.D., M.B.A., C.P.A.,
Managing Editor

Karen A. Notaro, J.D., LL.M.,
Portfolio Managing Editor

Lawrence A. Perlman, J.D., LL.M.,
C.P.A.

Deborah M. Petro, J.D., LL.M.

Robert Recchia, J.D., M.B.A., C.P.A.

Betty Ross, J.D.

John W. Roth, J.D., LL.M.

Carolyn M. Schiess, J.D.

Michael G. Sem, J.D.

James Solheim, J.D., LL.M.

Raymond G. Suelzer, J.D., LL.M.

Kenneth L. Swanson, J.D., LL.M.

Mary P. Taylor, J.D.

Laura A. Tierney, J.D.

James C. Walschlager, M.A.

Kelley Wolf, J.D., LL.M.

George L. Yaksick, Jr., J.D.

Ken Zaleski, J.D.

Susan M. Zengerle, J.D., LL.M.,
Managing Editor

Washington News Staff

Jeff Carlson, M.A.

Stephen K. Cooper

Kathryn Hough

Rosalyn Johns-Thomas

Joyce Mutcherson-Ridley

William Pegler

¶3 Detailed Table of Contents

Taxpayers Affected

1

PATIENT PROTECTION AND AFFORDABLE CARE ACT AS AMENDED BY HEALTH CARE AND RECONCILIATION ACT OF 2010

PATIENT PROTECTION AND AFFORDABLE CARE ACT AS AMENDED BY HEALTH CARE AND RECONCILIATION ACT OF 2010

¶105 Timeline and Implementation

The reorganization of America's health care system enacted in the Patient Protection and Affordable Care Act (PPACA) (P.L. 111-148), as amended by the Health Care and Education Reconciliation Act of 2010 (P.L. 111-152) (2010 Reconciliation Act), was deliberately designed to be spread out over several years. Additionally, certain reforms have been delayed beyond their intended effective dates, while other provisions were repealed before coming into effect.

A few high-profile adjustments were put in place in 2010. These are the availability of a small business tax credit (see ¶310) and the implementation of several market reforms, such as the option for adult children under age 27 to be included on their parent's insurance (see ¶220) and the elimination of preexisting conditions for children under age 19 (the elimination of preexisting conditions for all other individuals occurs in 2014). Also, additional requirements were imposed on charitable hospitals (see ¶355), and a Patient-Centered Outcomes Research Trust fund was established (see ¶545), with fees imposed on insurers and self-insurers (see ¶550) starting in 2012 to help pay for it.

2011 saw only a few provisions go into force. The cost of most over-the-counter medicines could no longer be excluded from an individual's gross income when paid for from a tax-favored health account, the penalty for non-qualified distributions from health savings accounts and Archer MSAs was increased to 20 percent, and an annual fee on drug manufacturers and importers was imposed (see ¶352).

The Administration decided to delay from 2011 to 2012 the requirement that employers disclose the aggregate cost of health coverage on each employee's Form W-2, and certain small employers are able to further postpone this disclosure until further notice. See ¶405. Also beginning in 2012, small employers were allowed to provide simple cafeteria plans for employees under which the normal nondiscrimination rules were deemed to be satisfied. See ¶330. Additionally, some individuals started to receive medical loss ratio rebates from their insurers in response to the requirement that insurers spend a certain percentage of premium dollars on activities to improve health care quality. See ¶555.

Several revenue-raising provisions came into effect in 2013 and 2014. Beginning in 2013, a controversial 3.8 percent tax was imposed on the net investment income of high-income individuals (see ¶605) as well as estates and trusts (see ¶610), and a 0.9 percent additional Medicare tax was imposed on certain wages and self-employment income (see ¶620). In addition, the deduction for medical expenses became less valuable and harder to obtain (see ¶215), the deduction for contributions to flexible spending arrangements offered through a cafeteria plan was limited to $2,500 (adjusted for inflation after 2013) (see ¶325), and the deduction for federal subsidies for certain retiree prescription drug program was eliminated (see ¶335). Also in 2013 (although applicable to compensation paid after 2009), health insurance companies could no longer deduct compensation in excess of $500,000. See ¶340. Beginning in 2014, an annual fee was imposed on health insurance providers (see ¶545) and an excise tax was applied to sales of medical devices (see ¶350).

The so-called individual mandate, requiring most individuals to either obtain qualified health care coverage or pay a penalty, went into effect January 1, 2014. See ¶205. Tax credits and subsidies became available for low- and middle-income individuals purchasing insurance through a health care marketplace. See ¶505. Relevant to certain small employers, cafeteria plans may offer insurance through an exchange. See ¶320. Also in 2014, many of the PPACA's market reforms and improvements to coverage came into effect (see ¶540), although grandfathered health plans are exempt from certain requirements (see ¶535).

The employer mandate, requiring large employers to either offer qualified health care coverage to employees and their dependents or pay a penalty, was originally intended to be effective in the same year as the individual mandate, but the Administration has delayed implementing the provision for one year, until January 1, 2015, and the requirements for the mandate were eased for 2015. See ¶305. Tied to the employer mandate is the requirement that employers report whether their employees (and their dependents) are offered the opportunity to enroll in minimum essential coverage. See ¶410. Insurers are subject to a similar requirement. See ¶415. These reporting obligations have likewise been delayed until 2015.

In 2018, an excise tax will apply to certain "Cadillac" health plans. See ¶345.

Self-insured plans are subject to certain nondiscrimination requirements, and the PPACA subjected group plans to similar rules. This extension of the nondiscrimination requirements has been delayed by the Administration until further notice, however. See ¶540.

Certain provisions of the PPACA were repealed before they came into effect. These include the CLASS Act program, which would have created a government-run long-term care insurance program and the free-choice voucher program, which would have allowed employees to receive vouchers to help pay for insurance from one of the state-run marketplaces.

¶108 Taxpayers Affected

Although the primary thrust of the Patient Protection and Affordable Care Act (P.L. 111-148) as amended by the Health Care and Reconciliation Act of 2010 (P.L. 111-152) is health insurance reform, the Internal Revenue Code plays several key functions in achieving that goal. First, the Internal Revenue Code provides "carrots" to lower income individuals and small businesses in the form of tax breaks for health care expenses in order to help work toward the goal of universal health coverage. Second, the Internal Revenue Code also provides "sticks" in the form of penalties imposed on individuals and businesses that do not obtain health coverage for themselves or their employees. Third, the Internal Revenue Code is used to raised revenue to help pay for the overall cost of health insurance reform. Fourth, many requirements are placed on health insurance providers. Fifth, many additional burdens are placed on the IRS to help enforce the components of this legislation.

INDIVIDUALS

¶109 Effect on Individuals Generally

The Patient Protection and Affordable Care Act (P.L. 111-148), as amended by the Health Care and Reconciliation Act of 2010 (P.L. 111-152), is designed to encourage all individuals to be covered under a health care plan providing at least minimum essential coverage. The Acts accomplish this objective by requiring many of the 40 percent of Americans not previously covered under an employment-based plan to purchase insurance either from a private insurer or through one of the new Exchanges. Those who can afford such coverage, but do not purchase it, are subject to a penalty. Those who cannot afford coverage may be eligible for premium assistance credits and/or subsidies.

The Health Care and Reconciliation Act of 2010 broadens the definition of dependents to include children under age 27 for purposes of the general exclusion for reimbursements for medical care expenses under an employer-provided accident or health plan, and certain other purposes. Beginning in 2012 (later for those employed by small employers), individuals whose employers offer health insurance coverage see the total cost of such coverage reported on their W-2 wage statements.

To help offset the cost of these changes, higher income employees and self-employed individuals are subject to an additional hospital services insurance (Medicare) tax. In addition, a 3.8 percent tax is imposed on net investment income beginning in 2013. Itemized medical expenses are generally deductible only to the extent they exceed ten percent of adjusted gross income

Starting in 2013, an FSA is not a qualified benefit under a cafeteria plan unless the plan provides for a $2,500 maximum salary reduction contribution to the FSA (adjusted annually for inflation starting in 2014).

¶111 Effect on Individuals Without Health Care Coverage

Mandatory coverage.—An important objective of the Patient Protection and Affordable Care Act is to require the 40-50 million individuals living in the U.S. who currently do not have health coverage, but who annually receive more than $116 billion worth of health care, to purchase minimum essential coverage. Beginning in 2014, individuals who do not have minimum coverage for themselves and their dependents become liable for a shared responsibility payment civil penalty. Certain individuals are exempt from the penalty, however.

For 2014 the monthly penalty cannot exceed the greater of $285 ($95 × 3) (the "flat dollar amount") or 1 percent of household income over the filing threshold (the "percentage of income"), with the flat dollar amount increasing to $975 in 2015 and $2,085 and 2016, and the percentage of income increasing to 2% in 2015 and 2.5% in 2016. After 2016, the flat dollar amount is increased for inflation. Household income is defined for this purpose as modified adjusted gross income increased by foreign earned income and tax-exempt interest. (¶205).

Prisoners, undocumented aliens, health care sharing ministry members and those certified as being opposed to having coverage on religious grounds are exempt from the requirement. The penalty does not apply to individuals who fall below the filing threshold, are members of an Indian tribe, have only a short-term gap in coverage, establish hardship, or live outside the U.S.

¶112 Effect on Individuals With Health Care Coverage

Any person who provides minimum essential health care coverage to an individual during a calendar year is required to file a return reporting such coverage in the form and manner described by the Secretary of the Treasury. Individuals with health care coverage will annually receive a written statement from the provider of such coverage detailing the contents of the informational return (¶410).

¶113   Effect on Lower Income Individuals

Premium assistance credit for low income individuals.—Individuals whose incomes are up to four times the federal poverty line (or up to approximately $95,400 for a family of four in 2014), are not receiving Medicare, Medicaid, military or Peace Corp health coverage, and cannot otherwise afford to purchase health insurance may benefit from the Patient Protection and Affordable Care Act's refundable health insurance premium assistance credit. Such low income individuals will be eligible for a premium credit if they purchase one of four levels of qualified health plan coverage accessed through the new state American Health Benefit Exchanges (AHBE).

To be eligible for the credit, lower income individuals are required to pay between two and 9.5 percent (adjusted annually) of their annual incomes for health insurance premiums (¶210).

¶114   Effect on Higher Income Individuals

Hospital services insurance tax.—As one of the revenue offsets against expenditures resulting from the Patient Protection and Affordable Care Act, and to help finance Medicare, the employee portion of the Medicare payroll tax and the total Medicare tax imposed on self-employed individuals increased from 2.9 percent to 3.8 percent on wages and self-employed income in excess of $200,000 ($250,000 for joint filers, $125,000 in the case of a married taxpayer filing separately) (¶620).

¶115   Effect on Individuals With Investment Income

Net investment income tax—The Health Care and Reconciliation Act of 2010 imposes an annual 3.8 percent tax annually beginning in 2013 on the lesser of: (1) net investment income from interest, dividends, annuities, royalties, rents and certain other income and gains not generated in the ordinary course of an active trade or business, or which is generated in a trade or business of trading financial instruments or commodities or (2) modified adjusted gross income (which includes, for this purpose, foreign earned income net of certain expenses) in excess of $200,000 ($250,000 for joint filers and surviving spouses, $125,000 in the case of married taxpayers filing separately) (¶605).

The definition of net investment income excludes distributions from most qualified plans and amounts subject to self-employment tax. In the case of the disposition of a partnership interest, or stock in an S corporation, net investment income includes gain or loss only if it would be taken into account by the partner or shareholder had the entity sold all its properties for fair market value immediately before the disposition. Thus, only net gain or loss attributable to property held by the entity, and not attributable to an active trade or business, is included (¶615).

Similar rules apply to estates and trusts with respect to their undistributed net investment income. They become subject to a 3.8 percent tax on the lesser of: (1) their undistributed net investment income or (2) the excess of their adjusted gross income over the dollar amount at which the highest income tax bracket applicable to an estate or trust begins (¶610).

¶117 Effect on Individuals Covered by an Employer-Sponsored Plan

The W-2 Wage and Tax Statements employees receive will, starting in 2012 (later for small employers) show the full cost (both the employer and the employee paid portions) of employer sponsored health care coverage. This will not include any long-term care coverage, accident or disability insurance coverage or salary reduction contributions to flexible spending arrangements, Health Savings Accounts or Archer Medical Savings Accounts (¶405).

¶122 Effect on Individuals With Young Adult Children

The Health Care and Reconciliation Act of 2010 provides that children under age 27 are considered dependents of a taxpayer for purposes of the general exclusion from gross income for reimbursements for medical care expenses of an employee, spouse, and dependents under an employer-provided accident or health plan, the deduction for the health insurance costs of a self-employed person, spouse, and dependents, the rule that allows a qualified pension or annuity plan to provide benefits for sickness, accident, hospitalization, and medical expenses to retired employees, spouses, and dependents, and the rule that treats a voluntary employee benefits association that provides sick and accident benefits to its members and their dependents as a tax-exempt organization (¶220).

¶123 Effect on Itemizers of Medical Expense Deductions

Ten percent threshold for itemized medical expenses.—While the Patient Protection and Affordable Care Act is designed to encourage obtaining health care coverage, it reduces the ability to deduct any unreimbursed medical care expenses. Starting in 2013, the threshold for the itemized deduction of such expenses increases from 7.5 percent to 10 percent of adjusted gross income. For AMT purposes, the threshold remains at 10 percent. For 2013-2016 the increased threshold will not apply to taxpayers or their spouses who are age 65 or older before the end of the applicable tax year (¶215).

¶125 Effect on Health Account Holders

An FSA can no longer be a qualified benefit under a cafeteria plan unless the plan provides for a $2,500 maximum salary reduction contribution to the FSA. Beginning in 2014 the $2,500 limitation is adjusted annually for inflation (¶325).

BUSINESSES

¶133 Effect on Businesses Generally

Employers are given many responsibilities in the Patient Protection and Affordable Care Act (P.L. 111-148) to help achieve health insurance reform. These range from providing greater health insurance coverage and helping to pay for that coverage to providing the information necessary to enforce the requirements of the new legislation. Health insurance providers also have many new requirements imposed by the legislation, including limits on executive compensation, taxes and fees, and reporting obligations.

¶135 Effect on Employers

Penalty taxes.—A penalty tax is imposed on employers with 50 or more full-time employees for failure to offer full-time employees an opportunity to enroll in minimum essential coverage under an employer-sponsored health plan. A penalty tax is also imposed if employees qualify for a premium tax credit or cost-sharing reductions or if employees are subject to extended waiting periods (¶305).

Medicare tax withholding.—Employers are required to withhold additional Medicare tax on high-income taxpayers (¶620).

Excise tax on "Cadillac" plans.—Employers are required to calculate the excise tax applicable to high coverage "Cadillac" health plans and report amounts to the IRS and each coverage provider. A penalty is provided for calculation errors (¶345).

Expanded W-2 reporting.—Employers are required to include on Form W-2 the total cost of employer-sponsored health insurance coverage (¶405).

Minimum coverage report.—Large employers are required to report to the IRS and to the individuals involved whether they offer minimum essential coverage. A large employer is defined as an employer with an average of at least 50 full-time employees. Penalties are provided for failure to correctly report (¶415).

Limits on FSAs.—Health flexible spending arrangements (FSAs) must limit contributions through salary reductions to $2,500, adjusted for inflation for tax years after December 31, 2013 (¶325).

Children under age 27 dependents.—Children under age 27 are considered dependents for purposes of the general exclusion for reimbursed employee medical expenses and medical expenses of retirees under qualified pension or annuity plans (¶220).

Business deduction to consider retiree drug subsidy.—Employers, as plan sponsors, may no longer disregard the value of any qualified retiree prescription drug plan subsidy in calculating the employer's business deduction for retiree prescription drug costs (¶335). For many employers, this may significantly increase the expense of self-insuring retiree prescription drug costs.

¶137 Effect on Small Employers

A small employer with 25 or fewer full-time employees and average compensation of $50,000 or less may be eligible for up to a credit for premiums paid toward employee health coverage. The credit percentage was originally set at 35 percent, but was increased to 50 percent after 2013. Also for years beginning after 2013, the credit is available only for employers participating in an insurance exchange, and can only be claimed for two years (¶310). A five-percent owner and related individuals are not considered employees for this purpose.

An employer must be a qualified employer for purposes of the exchange in order for an employer cafeteria plan to include a health plan. (¶320).

An employer that, during either of the two preceding years, employed an average of 100 or fewer employees on business days may choose to provide a simple cafeteria plan for employees that permits greater flexibility under the nondiscrimination rules (¶330).

¶139 Effect on Seasonal Employers

Special rules apply to determine whether seasonal employers qualify for the small employer health insurance credit (¶310) and whether reporting on health insurance coverage is required (¶415).

¶141 Effect on Self-Employed Persons

Self-employed coverage under any group health plan is subject to the excise tax on employer-sponsored health coverage if a deduction is allowable under Code Sec. 162(I) for any portion of the cost of the coverage (¶345).

Self-employed persons and related individuals are not considered an employee for purposes of the small employer health insurance credit (¶310).

Self-employed persons are subject to the additional Medicare tax on high-income individuals (¶620).

Children under age 27 are considered dependents for purposes of the deduction for self-employed health insured costs (¶220).

¶143 Effect on Agricultural Employers

Agricultural employers are subject to special rules in determining whether they are liable for the shared responsibility penalty tax (¶305).

¶144 Effect on Construction Industry Employers

Construction industry employers are subject to special rules in determining whether they are liable for the shared responsibility penalty tax (¶305).

¶145 Effect on Corporations

Controlled groups of corporations are treated as a single employer for purposes of the shared responsibility penalty tax (¶305), the small employer health insurance credit (¶310), and the excise tax on high coverage "Cadillac" health plans (¶345).

¶147 Effect on S Corporations

A two-percent shareholder of an S Corporation and related individuals are not considered employees for purposes of the small employer health insurance credit (¶310).

Passive trade or business activities in an S Corporation may be subject to the net investment income tax (¶615).

¶149 Effect on Partnerships

Partners of partnerships and members of Limited Liability Companies (LLCs) are subject to the additional Medicare tax on high-income individuals (¶620).

Controlled groups of partnerships are treated as a single employer for purposes of the shared responsibility penalty tax (¶305), the small employer health insurance credit (¶310), and the excise tax on high coverage "Cadillac" health plans (¶345).

Passive trade or business activities in a partnership may be subject to the net investment income tax (¶615).

¶151 Effect on Real Estate Investment Trusts (REITs)

Special rules for calculating the small business health insurance credit apply to Real Estate Investment Trusts (REITs) (¶310).

¶153 Effect on Regulated Investment Companies (RICs)

Special rules for calculating the small business health insurance credit apply to Regulated Investment Companies (RICs) (¶310).

¶155 Effect on Controlled Groups

Controlled groups of corporations, partnerships and proprietorships under common control, and affiliated service groups are treated as a single employer for purposes of the shared responsibility penalty tax (¶305), the small employer health insurance credit (¶310), and the excise tax on high coverage "Cadillac" health plans (¶345).

¶157 Effect on Health Insurance Providers

Deduction limit on compensation.—A $500,000 deduction limitation is placed on employee and director remuneration paid by certain health insurance providers. For tax years beginning after December 31, 2012, health insurance providers are subject to the restrictions only if not less than 25 percent of the gross premiums from providing health insurance coverage is from essential health benefits coverage. There is also a limitation for deferred compensation (¶340).

Excise tax on "Cadillac" plans.—A 40 percent excise tax is imposed on health insurers if the aggregate value of coverage of an employer-sponsored health plan exceeds certain threshold amounts – a "Cadillac" plan. The threshold amounts are increased for certain high cost states. There are also additional annual limits for certain retirees and high risk professions. Health insurance providers may include plan administrators and employers in the case of contributions to an employer-sponsored Health Savings Account (HSA) or Archer Medical Savings Account (MSA) (¶345).

Fees on net premiums.—New annual fees are imposed on the net premiums written by certain U.S. health insurance providers (¶543). A partial exclusion is provided for certain exempt activities.

Coverage reporting.—Any person who provides minimum essential health care coverage is required to file a return reporting such coverage to the IRS and to the individual (¶410).

¶159 Effect on Health Insurance Policy Issuers

Fees are imposed on health insurance policy issuers to fund a new Patient-Centered Outcomes Research Trust Fund (PCORTF) for competitive effectiveness research (¶545).

¶161 Effect on Sponsors of Self-Employed Health Plans

Fees are imposed on sponsors of self-employed health plans to fund a new Patient-Centered Outcomes Research Trust Fund (PCORTF) for competitive effectiveness research (¶550).

¶163 Effect on Group Health Plans

Group health plans are subject to new requirements with respect to coverage, acceptable limits, and rescission (¶540).

¶165 Effect on Manufacturers and Importers of Branded Prescription Drugs

New annual fees are imposed on manufacturers and importers of branded prescription drugs (¶352).

¶167 Effect on Manufacturers and Importers of Medical Devices

New excise taxes are imposed on manufacturers and importers of medical devices (¶350).

¶173 Effect on Estates and Trusts

Estates and trusts must apportion the small business health insurance credit between the estate or trust and its beneficiaries based on the income allocated to each (¶310).

A 3.8 percent tax on a portion of net investment income is imposed on estates and trusts (¶610).

TAX-EXEMPT ENTITIES

¶179 Effect on Nonprofit Health Insurance Issuers and Reinsurers

A partial exemption from the fees imposed on the net premiums of health insurance providers is provided for certain exempt activities (¶543).

¶180 Effect on Voluntary Employee Benefit Associations (VEBAs)

Children under age 27 are considered dependents of the members of Voluntary Employee Benefit Associations (VEBAs) that provide sick and accident benefits (¶220).

¶163

¶181 Effect on Nonprofit Charitable Hospitals

Additional requirements are imposed on hospitals to maintain tax-exempt status. An excise tax is provided for failure to meet the requirements (¶355).

¶182 Effect on Tax-Exempt Trusts

Certain tax-exempt trusts are not subject to the net investment income tax (¶610).

¶183 Effect on Patient-Centered Outcomes Research Trust Fund (PCORTF)

A new Patient-Centered Outcomes Research Trust Fund (PCORTF) for comparative effectiveness research is established and funded (¶545).

GOVERNMENT ENTITIES

¶187 Effect on Government Entities

The Patient Protection and Affordable Care Act imposes many new responsibilities on government bodies. Required returns and statements with respect to health insurance coverage provided by a government unit or agency must be made by the officer or employee who entered into the agreement to provide the coverage or the person otherwise designated (¶410).

¶188 Effect on Government Health Plans

Employer-sponsored health insurance coverage for civilian employees by federal, state and local governments, or any agency thereof, is subject to the excise tax on employer-sponsored coverage (¶345).

Fees are imposed on certain government health plans to fund a new Patient-Centered Outcomes Research Trust Fund (PCORTF) (¶545).

¶189 Effect on Secretary of Treasury and IRS

Penalty taxes.—The Treasury and IRS are given a number of responsibilities under the Patient Protection and Affordable Care Act. The IRS is to administer the penalty imposed on individuals without health insurance, however criminal prosecutions and use of liens and levies are prohibited (¶205). The IRS is also to give notice of, and demand payment for, the shared responsibility penalty tax on larger employers (¶305).

Health insurance credits.—The IRS is authorized to issue any regulations necessary to carry out the premium assistance credit rules (¶210) and the small business health insurance credit (¶310).

Lack of coverage notice.—The IRS, in consultation with Department of Health and Human Services, is required to send notice to each individual return filer who is not enrolled in minimum essential coverage (¶505).

Individuals

2

¶205 Individual Health Insurance Mandate

SUMMARY OF NEW LAW

Beginning in 2014, the individual health insurance mandate requires that individuals must make a "shared responsibility payment" if they do not have minimum essential health insurance for themselves and their dependents.

BACKGROUND

The United States federal government has never provided universal health care, or required individuals to have health insurance. About 60 percent of Americans under the age of 65 have employment-based health insurance, with premiums often paid or subsidized by the employer. Most Americans who are at least 65 years old qualify for Medicare, a social insurance program that is partially financed by special payroll taxes on workers and employers. Many other Americans obtain health insurance through government programs like veterans' care, Medicaid or the State Children's Health Insurance Program (SCHIP). Many millions of Americans remain uninsured, however.

LAW EXPLAINED

Penalty imposed on individuals without health insurance.—Beginning in 2014, a penalty is imposed on applicable individuals for each month they fail to have "minimum essential coverage" for themselves and their dependents (Code Sec. 5000A, as added and amended by the Patient Protection and Affordable Care Act (PPACA) (P.L. 111-148), amended by the Health Care and Education Reconciliation Act of 2010 (P.L. 111-152), amended by the TRICARE Affirmation Act (P.L. 111-159, and amended by P.L.

LAW EXPLAINED

111-173). This penalty is also referred to as a "shared responsibility payment," and the requirement to maintain minimum essential coverage is known as the "individual mandate." The Supreme Court has held that the individual mandate is constitutional under Congress's broad power to "lay and collect taxes" (*National Federation of Independent Business v. Sebelius*, SCt, 2012-2 USTC ¶ 50,423, 132 SCt 2566).

Taxpayers affected. The individual mandate is subject to several exemptions. An exempt individual is not subject to a penalty for failing to maintain minimum essential health coverage for themselves and their dependents.

Affordability exemption. An individual is exempt from the individual mandate for any month in which the individual cannot afford minimum essential health coverage. Coverage is unaffordable for a month if the individual's annual required contribution for coverage for the month would exceed eight percent of the individual's household income for the tax year. For plan years beginning after 2014, the eight-percent-of-household-income limit is replaced by the percentage that reflects the excess of the rate of premium growth between the preceding calendar year and 2013, over the rate of income growth for that period (Code Sec. 5000A(e)(1), as added and amended by PPACA). For 2015, the amount is adjusted to 8.05 percent (Rev. Proc. 2014-37).

Household income is the sum of the individual's modified adjusted gross income (AGI) and the modified AGI of all other members of the individual's family for whom the individual is allowed a dependency exemption under Code Sec. 151 and who were required to file a tax return for the year. Modified AGI is AGI increased by any Code Sec. 911 exclusion for foreign earned income or foreign housing costs and by any tax-exempt interest (Code Sec. 5000A(c)(4), as added by PPACA). Household income for purposes of this exemption must be increased by any required contribution made through a salary reduction agreement and excluded from the individual's gross income (for example, health insurance premiums paid through a cafeteria plan) (Code Sec. 5000A(e)(1)(A), as added by PPACA).

The required contribution for an employee eligible to purchase minimum essential coverage through an eligible employer-sponsored plan is the portion of the annual premium that the employee would pay, through salary reduction or otherwise, for the lowest-cost self-only coverage (Code Sec. 5000A(e)(1)(B), as added by PPACA). The required contribution for an individual related to the employee is determined based on the lowest-cost family coverage that would cover the employee and all individuals in the employee's family who are not otherwise exempt from the individual mandate. A related individual is someone eligible for coverage under an employer-sponsored plan because of a relationship to an employee, and is claimed by the employee as a dependent under Code Sec. 151. An employee or related individual is treated as eligible for coverage under an eligible employer-sponsored plan for a month if the employee or related individual could have enrolled in the plan for any day in that month during an open or special enrollment period, regardless of whether the employee or related individual is eligible for any other type of minimum essential coverage. An employee eligible for coverage under his or her employer's plan is not treated as a related individual for purposes of coverage under another plan, such as a plan offered by the employer of his

LAW EXPLAINED

or her spouse. A former employee or related individual who may enroll in continuation coverage, such as COBRA, or in retiree coverage under an eligible employer-sponsored plan is considered to be eligible for coverage under an eligible employer-sponsored plan only if the individual actually enrolls in the coverage (Reg. § 1.5000A-3(e)(3)). Proposed regulations provide that employer contributions to the employee's health reimbursement account (HRA), as well as incentives provided to the employee for participating in a wellness plan for cutting tobacco use (but not for other wellness plans) count towards determining the overall cost of coverage to the employee (i.e., they reduce the employee's required contribution) (Proposed Reg. § 1.5000A-3(e)(3)(ii)(D), (E)).

> **Comment:** If two or more members of a family are employed and their respective employers offer self-only and family coverage under eligible employer-sponsored plans, each employed individual determines the affordability of coverage using the premium for the self-only coverage offered by the individual's employer. Neither individual may determine the affordability of coverage using the premium for family coverage offered by the other individual's employer. In these cases, each employed individual's self-only coverage may be treated as affordable, even though the aggregate cost of covering all employed individuals may exceed eight percent of the family's household income. The Department of Health and Human Services has issued regulations that would permit families in these circumstances to qualify for a hardship exemption (45 CFR 155.605(g)(5), as added by 78 FR 39494).

> **Comment:** An individual who is eligible to enroll in an eligible employer-sponsored plan by reason of a relationship to an employee, but is not claimed as a dependent by the employee, is not treated as a related individual; the unclaimed dependent's household income is independently determined.

> **Planning Note:** The IRS anticipates that future guidance will address the treatment of employer contributions to health reimbursement arrangements (HRAs) and of wellness program incentives in determining required contributions (T.D. 9632).

The required contribution for self-only coverage under an employer plan may cost less than eight percent of household income, while the required contribution for family coverage under the same plan may cost more than eight percent of household income. In this situation, the employee is required to maintain minimum essential coverage for him or herself, but not for any related individuals (Joint Committee on Taxation, *Technical Explanation of the Revenue Provisions of the Reconciliation Act of 2010, as amended, in combination with the Patient Protection and Affordable Care Act*, JCX-18-10, March 21, 2010; Reg. § 1.5000A-3(e)(3)(ii)(D), Ex. 2).

> **Example 1:** In 2015, Brad and Carla are married, file joint returns, and have two children. Brad is eligible to enroll in self-only coverage under a plan offered by his employer at a cost of $5,000 to Brad. Carla and the two children are eligible to enroll in family coverage under the same plan at a cost of $20,000 to Brad. The family's household income is $90,000. Brad's required contribution is his

LAW EXPLAINED

share of the cost for self-only coverage ($5,000); Brad has affordable coverage during the year because his required contribution ($5,000) does not exceed $7,245 ($90,000 household income × 8.05%). The required contribution for Carla and the children is Brad's share of the cost for family coverage ($20,000); Carla and the children lack affordable coverage because their required contribution ($20,000) exceeds 8.05 percent of their household income ($7,245).

The required contribution for an individual who is not eligible to purchase minimum essential coverage through an eligible employer-sponsored plan is the annual premium for the lowest cost bronze plan available in the individual market through an American Health Benefit Exchange (Exchange) in the rating area in which the individual resides (regardless of whether the individual actually purchases a plan through the Exchange), reduced by the individual's Code Sec. 36B premium assistance credit for the tax year, if any (Code Sec. 5000A(e)(1)(B), as added by PPACA). The required contribution is determined based on the plan that would cover all individuals in the individual's family, other than family members who are otherwise exempt from the individual mandate or who are covered by an employer-sponsored plan. If the relevant Exchange does not offer a bronze plan covering all members of the individual's family, the premiums of multiple plans can be combined. The premium for the applicable plan must take into account the rating factors, such as age and tobacco use, that an Exchange would use to determine cost of coverage. The reduction due to the premium assistance credit is determined as if the individual and all members of the individual's non-exempt family were covered by a qualified health plan offered through the Exchange for the entire tax year (Reg. § 1.5000A-3(e)(4)).

> **Planning Note:** The IRS is considering simplified methods for identifying the premium for the applicable plan for individuals ineligible for coverage under an employer-sponsored plan (T.D. 9632).

> **Comment:** An Exchange is allowed to offer catastrophic health plans to individuals who are certified by the Secretary of Health and Human Services as exempt from the penalty under the affordability exemption (Act Sec. 1302(e)(2)(B) of PPACA).

Filing threshold exemption. An individual is exempt from the individual mandate for the entire tax year if the individual's household income is less than the gross income threshold for filing a federal income tax return for the year (Code Sec. 5000A(e)(2), as added and amended by PPACA, and amended by the 2010 Reconciliation Act).

Household income for this purpose is the sum of the individual's modified AGI and the modified AGI of all other members of the individual's family for whom the individual is allowed a dependency exemption and who were required to file a tax return for the year. Modified AGI is AGI increased by any Code Sec. 911 exclusion for foreign earned income or foreign housing costs and by any tax-exempt interest (Code Sec. 5000A(c)(4), as added by PPACA).

The applicable filing threshold for an individual who is properly claimed as a dependent by another taxpayer is equal to the other taxpayer's applicable filing

LAW EXPLAINED

threshold (Reg. §1.5000A-3(f)(2)(ii)). Thus, if a taxpayer who claims a dependent is exempt from the penalty under this exception, the dependent is also exempt from the penalty.

Individuals are not required to file a return solely to claim the exemption (Reg. §1.5000A-3(f)(3)).

Hardship exemption. The individual mandate does not apply for a month if the Secretary of Health and Human Services (HHS) determines that the individual has suffered a hardship with respect to the capability to obtain coverage under a qualified health plan for the month (Code Sec. 5000A(e)(5), as added by PPACA). An individual is exempt from the penalty for any month that includes a day on which the individual has an effective hardship exemption certificate, as issued by an Exchange under rules provided by HHS, or if the individual may claim a hardship exemption on the individual's return (Reg. §1.5000A-3(h)).

Under final regulations issued by HHS, a hardship exemption certificate may be received in the following circumstances:

- An Exchange must grant an exemption if the Exchange determines that (1) financial or domestic circumstances, including an unexpected natural or human-caused event, caused a significant and unexpected increase in essential expenses that prevented the individual from obtaining coverage under a qualified health plan; (2) the expense of purchasing a qualified health plan would have caused the individual serious deprivation of food, shelter, clothing or other necessities; or (3) other circumstances prevented the individual from obtaining coverage. These hardship exemptions must cover the month(s) the hardship occurs, as well as at least the month before and the month after.

- An Exchange must grant an exemption if it appears, based on projected annual household income, that the individual will be unable to obtain affordable coverage, even if it turns out that available coverage would have been affordable. This exemption is intended to protect individuals who reject coverage because the Exchange projects it will be unaffordable, but whose actual income for the year makes them ineligible for the affordability exemption. The individual must apply for this exemption before the last date on which he or she could enroll in a qualified plan through the Exchange for the month or months of a calendar year for which the exemption is requested. The Exchange must make this exemption available prospectively, and provide it for all remaining months in a coverage year, notwithstanding any change in the individual's circumstances.

- An Exchange must grant an exemption for the calendar year to an individual who would be eligible for Medicaid but for a state's choice not to expand Medicaid eligibility. This exemption is intended to protect individuals who live in states that refuse to implement the expansion of Medicaid eligibility that was originally provided in the PPACA.

- An Exchange must grant an exemption to an Native American who (1) is eligible for services through an Indian health care provider, but is not otherwise eligible for the exemption that applies to members of Indian tribes, or (2) is eligible for services through the Indian Health Service. This exemption is granted each month

LAW EXPLAINED

on a continuing basis, until the individual reports that he or she no longer qualifies for it (45 CFR 155.605(g)(1), (g)(2), (g)(4), and (g)(6), as added by 78 FR 39494; Reg. § 1.5000A-3(h)).

For purposes of the first circumstance outlined above, HHS has clarified that, when determining what constitutes a hardship, federally-run Exchanges may consider whether an applicant:

- has become homeless;
- has been evicted in the past six months, or is facing eviction or foreclosure;
- has received a shut-off notice from a utility company;
- recently experienced domestic violence;
- recently experienced the death of a close family member;
- recently experienced a fire, flood, or other natural or human-caused disaster that resulted in substantial damage to the individual's property;
- filed for bankruptcy in the last six months;
- incurred unreimbursed medical expenses in the last 24 months that resulted in substantial debt;
- experienced unexpected increases in essential expenses due to caring for an ill, disabled, or aging family member;
- is a child who has been determined ineligible for Medicaid and CHIP, and for whom a party other than the party who expects to claim him or her as a tax dependent is required by court order to provide medical support (applicable only during months in which the medical support order is in effect); or
- as a result of an eligibility appeals decision, is determined eligible for enrollment in a qualified health plan through the Exchange, advance payments of the premium tax credit, or cost-sharing reductions for a period of time during which he or she was not enrolled in a such a plan (applicable only during the period of period of time affected by the appeals decision) (HHS Guidance, *Guidance on Hardship Exemption Criteria and Special Enrollment Periods* (June 26, 2013)).

Caution: State-run Exchanges may either rely on these criteria or develop their own.

Comment: If an individual receives a certificate of exemption based on one of these criteria, but during the year he or she loses eligibility for the exemption, the Exchange may allow a special enrollment period during which the individual and his or her dependents may enroll in coverage, even if the normal enrollment period is no longer open.

HHS also announced that individuals whose insurance policies are cancelled and who believe that the other Marketplace plans are not affordable qualify for an exemption. Like other individuals that qualify for exemptions, these individuals are eligible to purchase catastrophic plans. They can fill out the exemption form, and then use this form as evidence of their eligibility to purchase such a plan.

Compliance Note: To prove hardship based on a cancelled policy, the individual must submit the following items to an issuer offering catastrophic coverage in

LAW EXPLAINED

the individual's coverage area: (1) the hardship exemption form, and (2) supporting documentation indicating that the previous policy was cancelled. For example, the individual can submit a cancellation letter or some other proof of cancellation. If the individual is applying for catastrophic coverage from the same issuer that cancelled the previous policy, the issuer may be able to confirm that based on its internal records.

Comment: An Exchange is allowed to offer catastrophic health plans to individuals who are certified by the HHS as exempt from the individual mandate under the hardship exception (P.L. 111-148, § 1302(e)(2)(B)).

The IRS may grant a hardship exemption for a calendar year in the follow circumstances; however instead of receiving a hardship exemption certificate, the taxpayer claims a hardship exemption on his or her return:

- An individual has gross income below the filing threshold who nevertheless files a tax return, claimed a dependent with a filing requirement, and as a result, had household income exceeding the applicable return filing threshold.

- An employed individual can obtain affordable self-only employer-sponsored insurance, but the cost of self-only coverage for all employed individuals in the household would exceed eight percent of household income for the calendar year (45 CFR 155.605(g)(3) and (g)(5), as added by 78 FR 39494; Reg. § 1.5000A-3(h)(3)).

Additionally, under proposed regulations, an individual may claim a hardship exemption without obtaining certification for any of the following months:

- Any month that includes a day on which the individual meets the requirements of 45 CFR 155.605(g)(3) (relating to individuals with gross income below the applicable return filing threshold who filed a return), or 45 CFR 155.605(g)(5) (relating to the affordability of coverage under an eligible employer-sponsored plan for family members);

- The months in 2014 prior to the individual's effective date of coverage, if the individual enrolls in a plan through an Exchange prior to the close of the open enrollment period for coverage in 2014; or

- Any month that includes a day on which the individual meets the requirements of any other hardship for which: (a) The Secretary of HHS issues guidance of general applicability describing the hardship and indicating that an exemption for such hardship can be claimed on a federal income tax return pursuant to guidance published by the Secretary; and (b) the Secretary issues published guidance of general applicability allowing an individual to claim the hardship exemption on a return without obtaining a hardship exemption from an Exchange (Proposed Reg. § 1.5000A-3(h)(3)).

Short lapse exemption. An individual is exempt from the individual mandate for a month if, on the last day of the month, the individual lacked minimum essential coverage for a continuous period of less than three months. Once a period of inadequate coverage meets the three-month threshold, the penalty is imposed for the entire period; thus, the penalty does not apply until a taxpayer goes three consecutive months without adequate coverage, but it is then imposed from the beginning of that

LAW EXPLAINED

three-month period. If the individual has more than one qualified coverage gap during the calendar year, the exemption applies only to the months in the first period (Code Sec. 5000A(e)(4), as added by PPACA).

> **Example 2:** Jason is a calendar-year taxpayer. He is uninsured from January 1 until February 19. On February 20, he obtains health insurance through his new employer. However, he loses his job and his insurance on March 31, and is uninsured from April 1 through July 31. He is insured again from August 1 through September 30, but is uninsured for the rest of the year. The penalty waiver for a short lapse applies to his first uninsured period (January 1 through February 19). It does not apply to his second uninsured period (April 1 through July 31) because it is not a short lapse; thus, the penalty applies for that entire four-month period. The short lapse waiver does not apply to his third uninsured period (October 1 through December 31) because it already applied to a period during the calendar year. Thus, the penalty applies for April, May, June, July, October, November, and December.

An individual who lacks minimum essential coverage for a period no longer than the last two months of a tax year may be eligible for the exemption for that period without regard to whether the individual is covered during the first months of the following tax year. However, the months in the first tax year are taken into account when determining whether a short coverage gap occurred in the following year. Months before January 1, 2014, are disregarded (Reg. § 1.5000A-3(j)(3) and (4), Ex. 4).

> **Example 3:** Frank, an unmarried individual with no dependents, has minimum essential coverage for the period January 1 through October 15, 2015. Frank is subsequently without coverage until enrolling in an eligible employer-sponsored plan effective February 15, 2016. He files his return for tax year 2015 on March 10, 2016. The last two months of tax year 2015 (November and December) are treated as a short coverage gap. However, they are included in the continuous period that includes January 2016. This continuous period for 2016 (November and December 2015 and January 2016) is not less than three months and is not a short coverage gap.

Transition relief exemption. An individual eligible to enroll in a non-calendar year employer-sponsored plan with a plan year beginning in 2013 and ending in 2014 (the 2013-2014 plan year) is exempt from the individual mandate for the months falling in that plan year. Any month in 2014 for which an individual is eligible for the transition relief is not counted in determining whether a short coverage gap exists (Notice 2013-42).

> **Example 4:** Ella is unmarried and has a five-year-old son, Donny. They are both eligible to enroll in a non-calendar year employer-sponsored plan offered by

¶205

LAW EXPLAINED

> Ella's employer, whose plan year begins on August 1, 2013, and ends on July 31, 2014. Neither Ella nor Donny enroll in the employer-sponsored plan for the 2013-2014 plan year. Both are exempt from the individual mandate from January 2014 through July 2014.

Non-U.S. residence exemption. An individual is automatically deemed to have minimum essential coverage during any month that is included in a period qualifying the individual for the foreign earned income exclusion under Code Sec. 911, or during which the individual is a bona fide resident of a U.S. territory (Code Sec. 5000A(f)(4), as added by PPACA).

Comment: Individuals generally qualify for the foreign earned income exclusion if they are bona fide residents of a foreign country or countries during an uninterrupted period that includes an entire tax year, or are present in a foreign country or countries for at least 330 full days during any period of 12 consecutive months (Code Sec. 911(d)(1)). To be a bona fide resident of a U.S. territory for a tax year, an individual must be present in the possession for at least 183 days during the year, must not have a tax home outside that possession during the year, and must not have a closer connection to the United States or a foreign country than to the possession (Code Sec. 937(a)).

Religious exemptions. An individual is exempt from the individual mandate for any month in which the individual for at least one day during the month:

• is certified by an Exchange as a member of, and adherent to the tenets or teachings of, a recognized religious sect that causes him or her to be conscientiously opposed to accepting the benefits of any private or public insurance that makes payments because of death, disability, old age, or retirement, or that makes payments toward the cost of, or provides services for, medical care; or

• is a member of a health care sharing ministry (HCSM) that has been in existence at all times since December 31, 1999, and whose members have shared their medical expenses continuously and without interruption since at least December 31, 1999 (Code Sec. 5000A(d)(2), as added and amended by PPACA; Reg. §1.5000A-3(a) and (b)).

Caution: The religious objection exemption is the same test used for exemption from FICA and self-employment taxes. However, an individual seeking the religious conscience exemption from FICA or self-employment taxes must be certified by the Social Security Administration. Persons seeking a religious conscience exception from the requirement to maintain minimum essential health care coverage must be certified by an Exchange.

For the HCSM exemption to apply, the ministry must satisfy the following tests:

• the HCSM must be a tax-exempt organization under Code Sec. 501(c)(3) (a public charity);

• its members must share a common set of ethical or religious beliefs, and share medical expenses among themselves in accordance with those beliefs and without regard to the state in which a member resides or is employed;

¶205

LAW EXPLAINED

- its members must retain their memberships even after they develop medical conditions;

- it (or a predecessor) must have been inexistence at all times since December 31, 1999, and its members must have shared their medical expenses continuously and without interruption since at least December 31, 1999; and

- it must conduct an annual audit that is performed by an independent certified public accountant (CPA) firm in accordance with generally accepted accounting principles (GAAP), and the audit must be made available to the public upon request (Code Sec. 5000A(d)(2)(B), as added by PPACA).

Other exemptions. An individual is exempt for any month in which the individual for at least one day during the month:

- is not a U.S. citizen or U.S. national and is either a non-resident alien or an undocumented alien;

- is incarcerated, after the disposition of charges, in a jail, prison, or similar penal institution or correctional facility (i.e., not incarcerated pending the disposition of charges); or

- is a member of an Indian tribe for purposes of the Code Sec. 45A Indian employment credit (that is, an Indian tribe, band, nation, pueblo, or other organized group or community that is recognized as eligible for special programs and services provided by the United States to Indians because of their status as Indians) (Code Sec. 5000A(d)(3) and (d)(4), as added and amended by PPACA, and (e)(3), as added and amended by PPACA, and amended by the 2010 Reconciliation Act; Reg. § 1.5000A-3(c), (d), and (g)).

Claiming an exemption. If an individual is applying for an exemption based on coverage being unaffordable, membership in a health care sharing ministry, membership in a federally-recognized tribe, or being incarcerated, the individual can either claim the exemption on his or her tax return or apply for the exemption using the correct form from the marketplace Exchange (IRS Pub. 5172).

If an individual is applying for an exemption based on membership in a recognized religious sect whose members object to insurance, or is eligible for a hardship exemption certificate from a marketplace Exchange, the individual must apply for the exemption using the correct form.

If an individual is applying for an exemption based on his or her filing threshold, a coverage gap, a hardship exemption from the IRS, or residency or citizenship, no application is needed. These will be handled on the individual's tax return; individuals with income below the filing threshold are not required to file a return to claim the exemption.

¶205

LAW EXPLAINED

Applying for Exemption

Exemptions	May only be granted by Marketplace	May be granted by Marketplace or claimed on tax return	May only be claimed on tax return
Coverage is considered unaffordable—The amount the individual would have paid for employer-sponsored coverage or a bronze level health plan (depending on the circumstances) is more than eight percent of actual household income for the year as computed on the individual's tax return. Also see the second hardship listed below, which provides a prospective exemption granted by the Marketplace if the amount the individual would have paid is more than eight percent of the individual's projected household income for the year.			X
Short coverage gap—The individual went without coverage for less than three consecutive months during the year.			X
Household income below the return filing threshold—The individual's household income is below the minimum threshold for filing a tax return.			X
Certain noncitizens—The individual is neither a U.S. citizen, a U.S. national, nor an alien lawfully present in the U.S.			X
Members of a health care sharing ministry—The individual is a member of a health care sharing ministry, which is an organization described in section 501(c)(3) whose members share a common set of ethical or religious beliefs and have shared medical expenses in accordance with those beliefs continuously since at least December 31, 1999.		X	
Members of Federally-recognized Indian Tribes—The individual is a member of a federally recognized Indian tribe.		X	
Incarceration—The individual is in a jail, prison, or similar penal institution or correctional facility after the disposition of charges.		X	
Members of certain religious sects—The individual is a member of a religious sect in existence since December 31, 1950, that is recognized by the Social Security Administration (SSA) as conscientiously opposed to accepting any insurance benefits, including Medicare and Social Security.	X		
Hardships:			
• The individual's gross income is below the filing threshold.			X
• Two or more family members' aggregate cost of self-only employer-sponsored coverage exceeds 8 percent of household income, as does the cost of any available employer-sponsored coverage for the entire family.			X
• The individual purchased insurance through the Marketplace during the initial enrollment period but have a coverage gap at the beginning of 2014.			X
• The individual is experiencing circumstances that prevent him or her from obtaining coverage under a qualified health plan.	X		
• The individual does not have access to affordable coverage based on your projected household income.	X		

¶205

LAW EXPLAINED

Exemptions	May only be granted by Marketplace	May be granted by Marketplace or claimed on tax return	May only be claimed on tax return
• The individual is ineligible for Medicaid solely because the state does not participate in the Medicaid expansion under the Affordable Care Act.	X		
• The individual is an American Indian, Alaska Native, or a spouse or descendant who is eligible for services through an Indian health care provider.	X		
• The individual has been notified that his or her health insurance policy will not be renewed and the individual considers the other plans available unaffordable.	X		

Minimum essential coverage. An individual is considered to be covered by minimum essential coverage for a month if the individual is covered by the insurance for at least one day during the month (Reg. § 1.5000A-1(b)).

Minimum essential coverage is coverage under any of the following:

- A government sponsored program, which means Medicare, Medicaid (except limited benefit coverage for certain family planning services, tuberculosis- related services, pregnancy-related services, and coverage limited to treatment of emergency medical conditions), the Children's Health Insurance Program (CHIP), TRICARE for Life, certain veteran's health care programs, the health plan for Peace Corps volunteers, and the Nonappropriated Fund Health Benefits Program of the Department of Defense.

- An eligible employer-sponsored plan, which is a group health plan or group health insurance coverage (including grandfathered and governmental health plans) offered by, or on behalf of, an employer to an employee through the small or large group market within a state or the District of Columbia, as well as self-insured plans.

- An individual market plan, which is health insurance coverage offered to individuals through the market Exchange (including an Exchange located in a territory of the United States), other than certain short-term limited duration insurance.

- A grandfathered plan, which, generally, is a group health plan or health insurance coverage in effect on March 23, 2010.

- Other coverage that the Secretary of Health and Human Services, in coordination with the Treasury Secretary, recognizes for this purpose (Code Sec. 5000A(f)(1), as added by PPACA, amended by the TRICARE Act, and amended by P.L. 111-173, and (f)(2), as added by PPACA; Reg. §§ 1.5000A-2 and 1.5000A-1(d)(18)).

  Planning Note: The IRS has issued proposed regulations that identify types of limited benefit health coverage provided by government sponsors that do not qualify as minimum essential coverage because they are not sufficiently comprehensive. Under the proposed regulations, limited benefit TRICARE coverage, line of duty coverage for inactive service members, Medicaid coverage for the medically needy, and coverage under HHS demonstration projects do not constitute minimum essential coverage (Prop. Reg. § 1.5000A-2(b)(2)). Transition

LAW EXPLAINED

relief is available for individuals who selected such coverage for 2014. The relief extends to individuals who have limited benefit Medicaid coverage for certain family planning services, tuberculosis- related services, pregnancy-related services, and coverage limited to treatment of emergency medical conditions (Notice 2014-10).

Comment: For 2014, the open enrollment period for purchasing coverage through an Exchange began October 1, 2013, and ended March 31, 2014. Individuals must sign up for coverage by the 15th of a given month in order to be covered in the following month. Although the three-month short lapse exemption would seem to indicate that an individual would be penalized if coverage did not begin by March 31, 2014, and that therefore coverage was required to be purchased by February 15, 2014, the Administration has clarified that simply purchasing qualified coverage by March 31, 2014, allows individuals to avoid a penalty.

The Nonappropriated Fund Health Benefits Program of the Department of Defense is both a government sponsored program and an eligible employer-sponsored plan (Reg. § 1.5000A-2(c)(2)).

Minimum essential coverage does not include health insurance coverage that consists of the following excepted benefits:

- coverage only for accident or disability income insurance, or any combination thereof;
- liability insurance, including general liability insurance and automobile liability insurance, and coverage issued as a supplement to liability insurance;
- workers' compensation or similar insurance;
- automobile medical payment insurance;
- credit-only insurance;
- coverage for on-site medical clinics; or
- other similar insurance coverage, specified in regulations, under which benefits for medical care are secondary or incidental to other insurance benefits (Code Sec. 5000A(f)(3), as added by PPACA; 42 U.S.C. § 300gg–91(c)(1)).

If benefits are provided under a separate policy, certificate, or insurance contract, then excepted benefits also include:

- limited scope dental or vision benefits, benefits for long-term care, nursing home care, home health care, community-based care, or any combination thereof, and other similar, limited benefits as specified in regulations;
- coverage only for a specified disease or illness;
- hospital indemnity or other fixed indemnity insurance; and
- Medicare supplemental health insurance, coverage supplemental to the medical and dental coverage provided to military personnel, and similar supplemental coverage provided to coverage under a group health plan (Code Sec. 5000A(f)(3), as added by PPACA; 42 U.S.C. § 300gg–91(c)(2)-(4)).

¶205

LAW EXPLAINED

Penalty. The penalty for failing to maintain minimum essential coverage is included on the individual's income tax return for the year that includes the month for which the penalty applies. It must be paid upon notice and demand by the IRS, and is generally assessed and collected in the same manner as other assessable penalties. However, an individual will not be subject to any criminal prosecution or criminal penalty for failing to timely pay the penalty. In addition, the IRS cannot file a notice of federal tax lien or levy property to collect an unpaid penalty (Code Sec. 5000A(g), as added by PPACA). The IRS can offset an unpaid penalty against any federal tax refund owed to the individual (Reg. § 1.5000A-5(b)(3)).

> **Caution:** The IRS has a number of tools at its disposal to collect the penalty despite the restrictions placed on its ability to use liens, levies, or criminal penalties. Most importantly, the restrictions do not affect the IRS's authority to offset any refund that the taxpayer would otherwise be entitled to by the amount of the penalty. Also, the restriction on liens only applies to the filing a notice of federal tax lien (i.e., a recorded lien), not to the lien itself. A federal tax lien arises automatically under the Code when the IRS assesses a tax whether it is recorded or not. Thus, because the penalty is treated as an assessable penalty (which is treated as a tax under the Code), the failure to pay the penalty becomes a lien on the taxpayer's property once the IRS assesses the penalty. If the taxpayer dies without having paid the penalty, then his or her heirs, legatees, devisees, and distributees of the taxpayer's estate, as well as the fiduciary, can become liable for the penalty.

> **Comment:** No later than June 30 of each year, the IRS will send a written notification to each individual who is not enrolled in minimum essential coverage and who files an individual income tax return. The notification will contain information on the services available through the Exchange operating in the state in which the individual resides (Act Sec. 1502(c) of PPACA).

Liability for penalty. Married taxpayers who file a joint return are jointly liable for a penalty imposed on either individual for any month during the tax year. Joint liability remains even if one of the spouses is an exempt individual (Reg. § 1.5000A-1(c)(1)(ii)).

If a taxpayer claims an individual as a dependent as defined by Code Sec. 152, then the taxpayer (rather than the dependent) is liable for any penalty that would otherwise be imposed on the dependent during the taxpayer's tax year (Code Sec. 5000A(b)(3), as added by PPACA). A taxpayer is liable for the a penalty imposed with respect to any individual for a month for which a taxpayer may claim an individual as a dependent. Whether the taxpayer actually claims the individual as a dependent for the tax year does not affect the taxpayer's liability for any penalty. If an individual may be claimed as a dependent by more than one taxpayer in the same calendar year, the taxpayer who properly claims the individual as a dependent for the tax year is liable for any penalty. If more than one taxpayer may claim an individual as a dependent in the same calendar year, but no one actually claims the individual, the taxpayer with priority under Code Sec. 152 to claim the individual as a dependent is liable for any penalty (Reg. § 1.5000A-1(c)(2)).

¶205

LAW EXPLAINED

> **Example 5:** Helen is a college student who lives with her father during the year. She is covered by his health insurance as long as she is a full-time student, but when she graduates on May 23, she is dropped from his policy. For several months, she works part-time and temporary jobs that do not offer health insurance, and she does not obtain her own insurance. On October 5, she starts working full-time and obtains insurance through her new employer. Because she was uninsured from June through September, the penalty is imposed for at least those four months. However, if Helen's father claims her dependency exemption on his return for the year, the penalty is imposed on him, rather than on Helen.

If a taxpayer legally adopts a child and is entitled to claim the child as a dependent for the tax year when the adoption occurs, the taxpayer is not liable for a penalty attributable to the child for the months before the adoption. The same rule also applies to foster children (Reg. § 1.5000A-1(c)(2)(ii)(A)).

> **Example 6:** Elaine and Newman, married individuals filing a joint return, initiate proceedings for the legal adoption of a two-year old child, George, in January. On May 15 of that year, George becomes the taxpayers' adopted child and resides with them for the remainder of the year. George meets all of the requirements under Code Sec. 152 to qualify as Elaine and Newman's dependent. Prior to the adoption, George resides with Jerry, an unmarried individual, with Jerry providing all of George's support. Elaine and Newman are not liable for any penalty attributable to George for January through May, but are liable for a penalty, if any, for June through December. Jerry is not liable for a penalty attributable to George for any month during the year, because George is not Jerry's dependent under Code Sec. 152.

If a taxpayer who is entitled to claim a child as a dependent for the tax year places the child for adoption or foster care during the year, the taxpayer is not liable for any penalty attributable to the child for the months after the adoption or foster care placement (Reg. § 1.5000A-1(c)(2)(ii)(B)).

> **Example 7:** The facts are the same as in Example 6, except the legal adoption occurs on August 15, and that George meets all requirements under Code Sec. 152 to be Jerry's, and not Elaine and Newman's, dependent during the year. Jerry is liable for a penalty attributable to George, if any, for January through July, but is not liable for any penalty attributable to George for August through December. Elaine and Newman are not liable for a penalty attributable to George for any month because he is not their dependent under Code Sec. 152.

¶205

LAW EXPLAINED

Amount of penalty. For each month in which the penalty is applied, the penalty is equal to the lesser of:

(1) the monthly national average premium for qualified health plans that offer a bronze-level of coverage, provide coverage for families the size of the taxpayer's family, and are offered through Exchanges for plan years beginning in the calendar year with or within which the tax year ends; or

(2) the monthly penalty based on either a flat dollar amount or the individual's income (Code Sec. 5000A(c)(1), as added and amended by PPACA).

In 2014, the monthly national average premium for qualified health plans that have a bronze level of coverage and are offered through Exchanges is $204 per individual and $1,020 for a family with five or more non-exempt members (Rev. Proc. 2014-46).

The monthly penalty amount for a taxpayer is equal to $1/12$ of the greater of:

(1) a flat dollar amount equal to the applicable dollar amount for each of the individuals who were not properly insured by the taxpayer, up to a maximum of 300 percent of the applicable dollar amount, or

(2) an applicable percentage of income (Code Sec. 5000A(c)(2), as added and amended by PPACA, and amended by the 2010 Reconciliation Act).

The flat dollar amount is the sum of the applicable dollar amounts for each individual lacking minimum essential coverage that the taxpayer was required to insure (Code Sec. 5000A(c)(2)(A), as added and amended by PPACA). The applicable dollar amount is:

- $95 for 2014,
- $325 for 2015,
- $695 for 2016, and
- $695, adjusted for inflation in later years (Code Sec. 5000A(c)(3), as added and amended by PPACA, and amended by the 2010 Reconciliation Act).

For any calendar year, the applicable dollar amount is halved for any month in which the uninsured individual is under the age of 18 at the beginning of the month. However, this adjustment is ignored for purposes of the rule that limits the flat dollar amount to 300 percent of the applicable dollar amount (Code Sec. 5000A(c)(3), as added and amended by PPACA, and amended by the 2010 Reconciliation Act).

Due to the 300 percent limitation, the maximum penalty for purposes of the flat dollar amount is:

- $285 in 2014,
- $975 in 2015, and
- $2,085 in 2016.

The applicable percentage of income is an amount equal to a percentage of the excess of the taxpayer's household income over the taxpayer's filing threshold for the tax year. The percentages are:

- 1 percent for tax years beginning in 2014,
- 2 percent for tax years beginning in 2015, and

¶205

LAW EXPLAINED

- 2.5 percent for tax years beginning after 2015 (Code Sec. 5000A(c)(2)(B), as added and amended by PPACA, and amended by the 2010 Reconciliation Act).

For purposes of this calculation, household income has the same meaning as used in determining the filing threshold exemption from the penalty (Code Sec. 5000A(c)(4)(B), as added and amended by PPACA, and amended by the 2010 Reconciliation Act).

> **Comment:** The way the penalty is calculated in 2014, a single adult with household income below $19,650 would pay the $95 flat rate. A single adult with household income above $19,650 would pay an amount based on the 1 percent rate. If income is below $10,150, no penalty is owed.

Example 8: The Johnsons are married and file a joint return for 2015. They are subject to the penalty for failure to maintain minimum essential coverage. Their household income is $45,000, and assume that their filing threshold is $23,900. They and their four dependents are all uninsured for the entire calendar year. One dependent is an adult, and the other three are under the age of 18 for the entire year. The couple are jointly and severally liable for the penalty for themselves and their four uninsured dependents. The Johnson's total penalty for the year would be $1,462.50 ($325 for each of the three adults, and $162.50 for each of the three children). However, the flat dollar amount is limited to $975, which is 300 percent of the applicable dollar amount, with no adjustment for individuals under 18. The Johnson's household income exceeds their filing threshold by $21,100 ($45,000 − $23,900). Thus, their percentage of income penalty for the year is $422 (2 percent of $21,100). The Johnson's actual penalty for the year is the lesser of: (1) the greater of $975 (their sum of the flat dollar amount) or $422 (their percentage of income penalty), or (2) the average national annual premium for qualified health plans that offer bronze-level of coverage for a family of six through an Exchange. They must include the penalty amount with their 2015 return.

> **Comment:** The more rapid increase in the applicable dollar penalties over the percentage-of-income penalties will increase the disparity between the two amounts. For instance, assume the same facts as in Example 8 above except it is 2016, when the applicable dollar amount is $695. The Johnson's initial penalty for the year would be $3,127.50, their flat dollar amount for the year would be $2,085 (300 percent of $695), and their percentage-of-income penalty for the year would be $527.50. The sum of their monthly penalty amounts would be $2,085. In 2014, in contrast, the Johnson's initial penalty would have been $427.50; their flat dollar amount for the year would have been $285 (300 percent of $95); and their percentage-of-income penalty for the year would have been $211.

▶ **Effective date.** The addition of Code Sec. 5000A applies to tax years ending after December 31, 2013 (Act Sec. 1501(d) of the Patient Protection and Affordable Care Act (PPACA) (P.L. 111-148)). The amendments to Code Sec. 5000A(b)(1), (c), (d)(2)(A) and (e)(1)(C) are effective on March 23, 2010, the date of enactment of PPACA. The amendments to Code Sec. 5000A(c)(2)(B), (c)(3), (c)(4) and (e)(2) are effective on March 30,

LAW EXPLAINED

2010, the date of enactment of the Health Care and Education Reconciliation Act of 2010 (P.L. 111-152). The amendments to Code Sec. 5000A(f)(1)(A)(iv) are effective on March 23, 2010, the date of enactment of PPACA (Act Sec. 2(a) of the TRICARE Affirmation Act (P.L. 111-159)). The amendments to Code Sec. 5000A(f)(1)(A)(v) are effective on March 23, 2010, the date of enactment of PPACA (Act. Sec. 1 of P.L. 111-173). The final regulations under Code Sec. 5000A apply to tax years ending after December 31, 2013.

Law source: Law at ¶5340.

— Act Secs. 1501(b), 10106(b), 10106(c), and 10106(d) of the Patient Protection and Affordable Care Act (PPACA) (P.L. 111-148), adding and amending Code Sec. 5000A;

— Act Sec. 1002(a) of the Health Care and Education Reconciliation Act of 2010 (P.L. 111-152), amending Code Sec. 5000A(c)(2)(B) and (c)(3);

— Act Sec. 1002(b) of 2010 Reconciliation Act, striking Code Sec. 5000A(c)(4)(D) and amending Code Sec. 5000A(e)(2);

— Act Sec. 1004(a) of 2010 Reconciliation Act, amending Code Sec. 5000A(c)(4).

— Act Sec. 2 of the TRICARE Affirmation Act, amending Code Sec. 5000A(f)(1)(A)(iv).

— Act Sec. 1 of P.L. 111-173, amending Code Sec. 5000A(f)(1)(A)(v).

— Act Sec. 1501(d) of PPACA, providing the effective date.

Reporter references: For further information, consult the following reporters.

— Standard Federal Tax Reporter, ¶34,963.01

— Tax Research Consultant, HEALTH: 3,000

— Practical Tax Explanation, § 42,001

¶210 Health Insurance Premium Assistance Refundable Credit

SUMMARY OF NEW LAW

Certain individual taxpayers with household income between 100 percent and 400 percent of the federal poverty line who purchase qualified health care coverage through an insurance exchange are entitled to a refundable tax credit equal to the premium assistance credit amount for tax years ending after December 31, 2013. The credit may not be claimed with respect to coverage purchased for any family member (i.e., the taxpayer, taxpayer's spouse, and dependents) who is eligible for minimum essential coverage other than coverage purchased in the individual market.

BACKGROUND

The Internal Revenue Code provides only three possible tax benefits for taxpayers who pay health insurance premiums. First, individual taxpayers can claim an itemized deduction for medical expenses they pay for themselves, their spouses, and their

BACKGROUND

dependents, to the extent those expenses exceed a certain percentage of their adjusted gross income (AGI) and are not compensated by insurance or otherwise (Code Sec. 213). Deductible expenses include premiums paid for medical insurance. For a discussion of the AGI threshold for claiming itemized deductions of medical expenses, see ¶215.

Second, in calculating their AGI, self-employed individuals can deduct 100 percent of amounts paid for health insurance for themselves, their spouses, and their dependents (Code Sec. 162(l)). The deductible amount is limited to the taxpayer's earned income, which is generally the individual's net earnings from self-employment with respect to a trade or business. No deduction is permitted if the self-employed person is eligible to participate in any subsidized employer-sponsored health plan. Deductible amounts may not be treated as medical expenses for purposes of the AGI threshold for medical expense deductions. For a discussion of who may be claimed as a dependent in deducting health insurance premiums by a self-employed individual, see ¶220.

Finally, a limited group of eligible individuals are allowed a refundable tax credit equal to a percentage of the amount paid during eligible coverage months for qualifying health insurance coverage for themselves and their qualifying family members (Code Sec. 35(a)). This credit, which is referred to as the Health Coverage Tax Credit (HCTC), is available only to individuals receiving trade adjustment assistance (TAA) and retirees age 55 or older receiving benefits from the Pension and Benefit Guarantee Corporation (PBGC). Trade adjustment assistance (TAA) is generally paid to workers who become unemployed due to increases in imports, especially imports from Mexico and Canada, or because of a shift of production to Mexico or Canada. The credit is not available to unemployed individuals paying for health insurance under COBRA who do not fall within one of these two narrow categories.

LAW EXPLAINED

Refundable health insurance premium assistance credit created.—Beginning in 2014, certain individuals who purchase qualified health care coverage through an American Health Benefit Exchange (Exchange) are entitled to the health insurance premium assistance credit (Code Sec. 36B, as added by the Patient Protection and Affordable Care Act (PPACA) (P.L. 111-148)). To be eligible, the individual's household income must be between 100 percent and 400 percent of the federal poverty line (FPL) (Code Sec. 36B(a), as added by PPACA). The credit is refundable and can be paid in advance directly to the insurer, reducing the individual's out-of-pocket premium cost.

> **Comment:** By January 1, 2014, each state may establish an exchange to provide qualified individuals with access to qualified health plans, or the federal government may establish an exchange in states that do not do so. See ¶505. Individuals who are eligible for a premium assistance credit and who purchase silver-level coverage through an exchange may also qualify for cost-sharing subsidies to help pay for out-of-pocket expenses, such as deductibles and copayments, if the individual's household income is at least 100 percent, but not more than 400 percent, of the FPL. Also, for these individuals, the costs of the plan itself may be

¶210

LAW EXPLAINED

decreased if the household income is not more than 250 percent of the FPL. See ¶520.

Caution: According to the Government Accountability Office (GAO), 34 states failed to establish or join an exchange for 2014. As a result, the Centers for Medicare & Medicaid Services (CMS) operate the health insurance exchanges in these states. These federally operated exchanges are also known as federally facilitated exchanges (FFE).

The premium assistance tax credit operates on a sliding scale that begins in 2014 at 2 percent of income for taxpayers at 100 percent of the FPL and phases out at 9.5 percent of income for those at 300-400 percent of the FPL. In 2015, the credit percentage ranges from 2.01 percent to 9.56 percent.

If a taxpayer's marital status changes during the year, the credit requires special allocations.

No deduction (e.g., itemized deduction) is allowed for the portion of premiums paid by the taxpayer for coverage of one or more individuals under a qualified health plan that is equal to the premium assistance tax credit determined for the tax year (Code Sec. 280C(g), as added by PPACA).

Eligibility for health insurance premium assistance tax credit. To be eligible for the health insurance premium tax assistance credit, the taxpayer's household income must be at least 100 percent, but not more than 400 percent, of the FPL for a family of the size involved (Code Sec. 36B(c)(1)(A), as added by PPACA). Family size is based on the number of individuals for whom the taxpayer is allowed a personal exemption for the tax year (Code Sec. 36B(d)(1), as added by PPACA). Family size may include individuals who are not subject to the penalty under Code Sec. 5000A, as added by PPACA, for failing to maintain minimum required insurance (Reg. §1.36B-1(d)). See ¶205.

Household income for this purpose includes the modified adjusted gross income (AGI) of the taxpayer and all individuals for whom the taxpayer can claim a personal exemption and who must file a tax return for the tax year (Code Sec. 36B(d)(2)(A), as added by PPACA). Modified AGI for these purposes is the taxpayer's AGI increased by any:

(1) foreign earned income or foreign housing expenses excluded from gross income under Code Sec. 911;

(2) tax-exempt interest received or accrued; and

(3) title II Social Security benefits or tier 1 Railroad Retirement benefits excluded from gross income under Code Sec. 86 (Code Sec. 36B(d)(2)(B), as added by PPACA).

Comment: Different benefits are available under the Social Security Act. Title II Social Security benefits are a type of disability benefits. Tier 1 Railroad Retirement benefits are a component of a railroad retirement annuity that generally approximates a Social Security benefit.

Affordability and minimum value requirements. As explained in more detail, below, employees eligible for coverage under an employer-sponsored health plan are not

LAW EXPLAINED

eligible for the credit unless the employer's coverage is unaffordable for the employee or fails to provide a minimum value. Additionally, an individual eligible for minimum essential coverage outside the individual market exchange, including certain government programs, is not eligible for the credit (Code Sec. 36B(c)(2)(C), as added by PPACA; Reg. § 1.36B-2(c)(3)).

Married taxpayers. Taxpayers who are married at the end of the tax year generally must file a joint return to claim the credit (Code Sec. 36B(c)(1)(C), as added by PPACA; Reg. § 1.36B-2(b)(2)). If a joint return is not filed, all advance payments must be repaid as an additional tax liability, discussed below (Temporary Reg. § 1.36B-4T(b)(4)). A married taxpayer may file a separate return and remain eligible for the credit if the taxpayer (1) is living apart from the individual's spouse at the time the taxpayer files his or her tax return, (2) is unable to file a joint return because the taxpayer is a victim of domestic abuse or spousal abandonment, and (3) indicates on his or her return in accordance with the relevant instructions that the taxpayer meets these two criteria. Taxpayers may not qualify for this relief from the joint filing requirement for a period that exceeds three consecutive years. Domestic abuse includes physical, psychological, sexual, or emotional abuse, including efforts to control, isolate, humiliate, and intimidate, or to undermine the victim's ability to reason independently. All the facts and circumstances are considered in determining whether an individual is abused, including the effects of alcohol or drug abuse by the victim's spouse. Depending on the facts and circumstances, abuse of the victim's child or another family member living in the household may constitute abuse of the victim. A taxpayer is a victim of spousal abandonment for a tax year if, taking into account all facts and circumstances, the taxpayer is unable to locate his or her spouse after reasonable diligence (Temporary Reg. § 1.36-2T(b)(2); Notice 2014-23).

> **Comment:** The IRS may propose additional exceptions to the prohibition against filing a separate return for spouses who face a particular hardship in filing jointly. The exceptions could cover, for example, incarcerations and pending divorce.

A taxpayer whose marital status changes during the tax year is subject to special rules, discussed below (Code Sec. 36B(c)(1)(C)).

Illegal aliens and incarcerated individuals. Individuals who are not lawfully present in the United States (for example, undocumented aliens) or who are incarcerated (unless the incarceration is pending the disposition of charges) may not enroll for coverage through an exchange. However, the individual may be allowed a tax credit if a family member is enrolled in a qualified health plan through an exchange (Reg. § 1.36B-2(b)(4)).

If an individual not lawfully present in the United States is a member of the taxpayer's household, the taxpayer's household income is computed using (1) a method under which household income is equal to the product of the taxpayer's household income and a fraction, with the numerator being the FPL for the taxpayer's family size excluding the undocumented alien, and the denominator being the FPL for the taxpayer's family size including the undocumented alien, or (2) any comparable method reaching the same result (Reg. § 1.36B-3(l)(2)). An individual not lawfully present for this purpose is any individual who is, and is not reasonably

LAW EXPLAINED

expected to be for the entire enrollment period, a U.S. citizen or national or an alien lawfully present in the United States (Code Sec. 36B(e), as added by PPACA; Reg. §1.36B-1(g)).

Lawfully present aliens ineligible for Medicaid. An alien lawfully present in the United States, but ineligible for Medicaid (Medicaid requires five year residency for lawful aliens), who has household income not greater than 100 percent of the FPL for a family of the size involved is eligible for the premium assistance credit and is to be treated as having a household income equal to 100 percent of the FPL for a family of the size involved (Code Sec. 36B(c)(1)(B), as added by PPACA). The premium assistance amounts for these taxpayers are computed based on actual household income (Reg. §1.36B-2(b)(7)).

Taxpayer claimed as a dependent is not eligible for credit. An individual who can be claimed as another taxpayer's dependent is not eligible for the premium assistance credit (Code Sec. 36B(c)(1)(D), as added by PPACA). If an individual is eligible to enroll in coverage because of the individual's relationship to another individual, such as a 25-year-old child or a domestic partner, but the individual will not be claimed as a dependent, the individual is treated as eligible for minimum essential coverage during the months the individual is enrolled in coverage (Reg. §1.36B-2(c)(4)). Therefore, coverage through a related individual does not prevent the related individual from claiming the credit (Preamble to T.D. 9590).

Computation of Health Insurance Premium Assistance Credit. The amount of the health insurance premium assistance credit for any tax year is the sum of the premium assistance amounts for all of the taxpayer's coverage months during the tax year (Code Sec. 36B(b)(1), as added by PPACA; Reg. §1.36B-3(a)). Coverage months generally do not include any month in which the individual is eligible for minimum essential coverage outside of a state exchange (e.g., through an affordable employer-plan that provides minimum value).

Premium assistance amounts. The premium assistance amount for any coverage month is equal to the lesser of:

(1) the monthly premium for one or more qualified health plans offered in the individual market exchange within a state covering the taxpayer, the taxpayer's spouse, or any dependent of the taxpayer who is enrolled through an exchange established by the state; or

(2) the excess, if any, of the adjusted monthly premium for that month for the benchmark plan with respect to the taxpayer over an amount equal to $1/12$ of the product of the applicable percentage and the taxpayer's household income for the tax year (Code Sec. 36B(b)(2), as added by PPACA; Reg. §1.36B-3(d)).

If a qualified health plan is terminated before the last day of a month and, as a result, the issuer reduces or refunds a portion of the monthly premium, the premium assistance amount for the coverage month is prorated (Proposed Reg. §1.36B-3(d)(2)).

A qualified health plan is a health plan that is certified as eligible to be offered via an exchange, not including a catastrophic plan (Code Sec. 36B(c)(3)(A), as added by PPACA).

¶210

LAW EXPLAINED

Benchmark plan premiums. The benchmark plan is the applicable second-lowest-cost silver plan in the individual market in the rating area where the taxpayer resides that is offered through the same exchange offering the qualified health plan and that provides self-only coverage for single taxpayers with no dependents and for anyone else who actually purchases self-only coverage, and that provides family coverage for all other taxpayers (Code Sec. 36B(b)(3)(B), as added by PPACA; Reg. § 1.36B-3(f)).

> **Example 1:** Jerry is single, has no dependents, and enrolls in a qualified health plan. His applicable plan is the second-lowest-cost silver self-only plan (Reg. § 1.36B-3(f)(7), Ex. 1).

> **Example 2:** The facts are the same as Example 1, except that Jerry, his spouse, and their dependent enroll in a qualified health plan. Jerry's applicable plan is the second-lowest-cost silver plan covering himself, his spouse, and their dependent (Reg. § 1.36B-3(f)(7), Ex. 2).

> **Example 3:** Sam is single and resides with his 24-year-old daughter but may not claim her as a dependent. Sam purchases family coverage for himself and his daughter. His applicable plan is the second-lowest-cost silver plan providing self-only coverage. Sam's daughter may qualify for a premium tax credit for herself if she is otherwise eligible (Reg. § 1.36B-3(f)(7), Ex. 3).

The adjusted monthly premium for an applicable second-lowest-cost silver plan is the monthly premium that would have been charged for the plan if each individual covered under a qualified health plan were covered by that silver plan, and the premium was adjusted only for the age of each individual pursuant to section 2701 of the Public Health Service Act (Code Sec. 36B(b)(3)(C), as added by PPACA). In other words, the adjusted monthly premium is determined as if all members of the coverage family for that month were enrolled in the qualified health plan for the entire month (Proposed Reg. § 1.36B-3(e)).

Under proposed regulations, the premium for the applicable benchmark plan for family members who live in different states and enroll in separate qualified health plans is the sum of the premiums for the applicable benchmark plans for each group of family members living in the same state (Proposed Reg. § 1.36B-3(f)(4)).

If any qualified health plan offers benefits beyond the essential health benefits that it must provide, the portion of the premium that is for the additional benefits is not taken into account in determining the monthly premium or the adjusted monthly premium (Code Sec. 36B(b)(3)(D), as added by PPACA). Under proposed regulations, premiums must be allocated to additional benefits before determining the applicable benchmark plan (Proposed Reg. § 1.36B-3(j)).

¶210

LAW EXPLAINED

If an individual enrolls in both a qualified health plan and a limited scope dental plan that provides pediatric dental benefits, the premium for the dental benefits is treated as a premium payable for a qualified health plan since pediatric dental benefits must be provided by a qualified health plan (Code Sec. 36B(b)(3)(E), as added by PPACA; Reg. § 1.36B-3(k)(3)).

> **Caution:** If any individual for whom a taxpayer can claim a personal exemption is an undocumented alien (including the taxpayer or spouse), the aggregate amount of premiums taken into account for purposes of computing the premium assistance credit must be reduced by the portion of the premiums attributable to the undocumented alien (Code Sec. 36B(e)(1)(A), as added by PPACA).

Applicable percentage. The applicable percentage varies depending on the individual's household income compared to the FPL for that year for the taxpayer's family size. The taxpayer's household income must be between 100 and 400 percent of the relevant FPL (Code Sec. 36B(b)(3)(A)(i), as added by PPACA). For 2014 the FPL (i.e., 100 percent of the FPL) is $11,670 for a single-member family and $4,060 for each additional family member. For 2013 the FPL is $11,490 for a single-member family and $4,020 for each additional family member.

The applicable percentage for any taxpayer whose household income is within a FPL income tier specified in the following tables increases, on a sliding scale in a linear manner, from the initial premium percentage to the final premium percentage specified for that income tier, and is rounded to the nearest one-hundredth of one percent (Temporary Reg. § 1.36B-3T(g)(1); Reg. § 1.36B-3(g)(2)). The initial and final applicable percentages, as in effect for the preceding calendar year, are subject to adjustment to reflect the excess of premium growth over income growth for the preceding calendar year. After 2018, an additional adjustment may be required to reflect any excess of the estimated premium growth over the consumer price index rate of growth for the preceding calendar year. However, the additional adjustment applies to a calendar year only if the aggregate amount of premium assistance credits and cost-sharing reductions exceeds 0.504 percent of the gross domestic product for the preceding calendar year (Code Sec. 36B(b)(3)(A)(i), as added by PPACA).

In 2015, the percentage is:

(1) 2.01 percent for incomes from 100 up to 133 percent of the FPL,

(2) between 3.02 and 4.02 percent for incomes from 133 up to 150 percent of the FPL,

(3) between 4.02 and 6.34 percent for incomes from 150 up to 200 percent of the FPL,

(4) between 6.34 and 8.10 percent for incomes from 200 up to 250 percent of the FPL,

(5) between 8.10 and 9.56 percent for incomes from 250 up to 300 percent of the FPL, and

(6) 9.56 percent for incomes from 300 percent up to 400 percent of the FPL (Rev. Proc. 2014-37).

In 2014, the percentage is:

(1) two percent for incomes from 100 up to 133 percent of the FPL,

(2) between three and four percent for incomes from 133 up to 150 percent of the FPL,

LAW EXPLAINED

(3) between four and 6.3 percent for incomes from 150 up to 200 percent of the FPL,

(4) between 6.3 and 8.05 percent for incomes from 200 up to 250 percent of the FPL,

(5) between 8.05 and 9.5 percent for incomes from 250 up to 300 percent of the FPL, and

(6) 9.5 percent for incomes from 300 percent up to 400 percent of the FPL (Code Sec. 36B(b)(3)(A)(i), as added by PPACA).

Example 4: Kristin's household income is 275 percent of the FPL for her family size in 2015. The initial percentage for a taxpayer with household income of 250 to 300 percent of the FPL is 8.10 and the final percentage is 9.56. Kristin's FPL percentage of 275 percent is halfway between 250 percent and 300 percent. Thus, rounded to the nearest one-hundredth of one percent, her applicable percentage is 8.83, which is halfway between the initial percentage of 8.10 and the final percentage of 9.56 (Reg. § 1.36B-3(g)(3), Ex. 1).

Coverage months. A coverage month is any month in which, as of the first day of the month, the taxpayer, the taxpayer's spouse, or any dependent is covered by a qualified health plan (1) that was enrolled in through an exchange and (2) for which the premium is paid by the taxpayer or through advance payment of the premium assistance credit (Code Sec. 36B(c)(2)(A), as added by PPACA). A month is not a coverage month if the individual's share of premiums is not paid in full by the unextended due date for filing the individual's tax return for the tax year (Reg. § 1.36B-3(c)(1)(ii)). An individual may have a coverage month as long as there is at least one day when the individual is not eligible for other minimum essential coverage (Reg. § 1.36B-3(c)(1)(iii)).

A coverage month does not include any month that the individual is eligible for minimum essential coverage outside the individual market exchange (Code Sec. 36B(c)(2)(B)(i), as added by PPACA). However, an employee is not considered to be eligible for minimum essential coverage outside of the market if the coverage is an employer-sponsored plan, including a grandfathered health plan, and either of these exceptions apply:

(1) The employee's required contribution is unaffordable, meaning that it would exceed 9.5 percent of the employee's household income. This rule also applies to any individual who is eligible to enroll in the employer-sponsored plan by reason of relationship to the employee (Code Sec. 36B(c)(2)(C)(i), as added by PPACA). After 2014, the employee's contribution limit of 9.5 percent is subject to adjustment to reflect the excess of premium growth over income growth for the preceding calendar year (Code Sec. 36B(c)(2)(C)(iv), as added by PPACA). After 2018, an additional adjustment may be required (Code Sec. 36B(b)(3)(A)(ii), as added by PPACA). In 2015, the amount is 9.56 percent (Rev. Proc. 2014-37).

LAW EXPLAINED

(2) The plan does not provide a minimum value by paying for at least 60 percent of the total allowed costs of the employee's benefits. These plans are not considered to provide minimum essential coverage (Code Sec. 36B(c)(2)(C)(ii), as added by PPACA).

An employee uses the employee's cost for self-only coverage to determine whether the coverage is affordable (i.e. if the required contribution would exceed 9.5 percent (9.56 percent in 2015) employee's household income) (Reg. §1.36B-2(c)(3)(v)(A)(1)).

Example 5: In 2015, Ana has household income of $47,000. Ana's employer offers its employees a health insurance plan that requires Ana to contribute $3,450 for self-only coverage (7.3 percent of her household income). Because Ana's required contribution for self-only coverage does not exceed 9.56 percent of household income, the plan is affordable for her, and she is considered to be eligible for minimum essential coverage (and therefore ineligible for the credit) for all months in 2015 (Reg. §1.36B-2(c)(3)(v)(D), Ex. 1).

The affordability of coverage for any related individuals of an employee is also determined by using the employee's cost of self-only coverage (Reg. §1.36B-2(c)(3)(v)(A)(2)).

Example 6: The facts are the same as Example 5, except that Ana is married to Javier and Ana's employer's plan requires her to contribute $5,300 for coverage for herself and Javier for 2015 (11.3 percent of their household income). Because Ana's required contribution for self-only coverage ($3,450) does not exceed 9.56 percent of household income, the plan is affordable for herself and Javier, and they are considered to be eligible for minimum essential coverage for all months in 2015 (Reg. §1.36B-2(c)(3)(v)(D), Ex. 2).

If a non-discriminatory wellness program offers incentives related to tobacco use that affect premiums, and the program is offered by an eligible employer-sponsored plan, then the incentives are treated as earned for purposes of determining an employee's required contribution and the affordability of the plan. Wellness program incentives that do not relate to tobacco use are treated as not earned (Proposed Reg. §1.36B-2(c)(3)(v)(A)(4)). In other words, the affordability of a wellness program is determined by assuming that each employee fails to satisfy its requirements, unless the program is related to tobacco use. The affordability of a plan that charges a higher initial premium for tobacco users is determined based on the premium that is charged to non-tobacco users, or tobacco users who complete the related wellness program, such as attending smoking cessation classes.

Amounts newly made available for the current plan year under a health reimbursement arrangement (HRA) that is integrated with an eligible employer-sponsored plan and that an employee may use to pay premiums are counted toward the employee's required contribution (Proposed Reg. §1.36B-2(c)(3)(v)(A)(5)).

¶210

LAW EXPLAINED

The following examples distinguish between unaffordability at the time of enrollment and unaffordability for the plan year.

Example 7: Murphy is an employee. In November 2014, the Exchange in his rating area projects that his 2015 household income will be $37,000. It also verifies that his required contribution for self-only coverage under his employer's health insurance plan will be $3,700 (10 percent of household income). Consequently, the Exchange determines that the plan is unaffordable. Murphy enrolls in a qualified health plan and not in his employer's plan. In December, the employer pays Murphy a $2,500 bonus. Thus, his actual 2015 household income is $39,500 and his required contribution for coverage under Employer's plan is 9.4 percent of household income.

Based on Murphy's actual 2015 household income, his required contribution does not exceed 9.5 percent of household income and his employer's health plan is affordable. However, affordability is determined at the time of enrollment, not at the end of the plan year, and the plan remains treated as unaffordable for Murphy in 2015 (Reg. § 1.36B-2(c)(3)(v)(D), Ex. 3).

Example 8: The facts are the same as in Example 7, except that Murphy's employer's employee health insurance plan year is September 1 to August 31. The Exchange in his rating area determines in August 2015 that his employer's plan is unaffordable for him based on his projected household income for the year. Murphy enrolls in a qualified health plan as of September 1, 2015. The plan is treated as unaffordable for the entire plan year, so Murphy is treated as not eligible for minimum essential coverage for the coverage months September to December 2015 and January through August 2016 (Reg. § 1.36B-2(c)(3)(v)(D), Ex. 4).

Affordability is determined separately for each employment period that is less than a full calendar year or for the portions of an employer's plan year that fall in different tax years (a part-year period) (Reg. § 1.36B-2(c)(3)(v)(B)).

Example 9: Roger begins working for an employer on May 2015. His employer's employee health insurance plan year is September 1 to August 31. Roger's required contribution for self-only coverage for May through August is $150 per month ($1,800 for the full plan year). The Exchange in his rating area determines his household income for purposes of eligibility for advance credit payments as $18,000. Roger's actual household income for the 2015 tax year is $20,000.

Whether coverage under the plan is affordable for Roger is determined for the remainder of the plan year (May through August). His required contribution for a full plan year ($1,800) exceeds 9.56 percent of his household income

---

LAW EXPLAINED

> (1,800/18,000 = 10 percent). Therefore, the Exchange determines that the coverage is unaffordable for May through August. Although Roger's actual household income for 2015 is $20,000 (and his required contribution of $1,800 does not exceed 9.56 percent of his household income), the plan is treated as unaffordable for Roger for the part of the plan year May through August. Consequently, Roger is not eligible for minimum essential coverage under the plan for the period May through August (Reg. § 1.36B-2(c)(3)(v)(D), Ex. 6).

Neither of the exceptions concerning affordability or minimum value apply if the employee (or any individual eligible for an employer-sponsored plan by reason of relationship to the employee) is actually covered by the employer-sponsored or grandfathered plan (Code Sec. 36B(c)(2)(C)(iii), as added by PPACA). In other words, if an individual actually enrolls in the plan, the individual is treated as eligible for employer-sponsored minimum essential coverage even if the coverage does not meet the affordability or minimum value requirements. However, the individual is not treated as eligible for minimum essential coverage if the individual is automatically enrolled in the plan and terminates coverage before the last day of the second full calendar month of the plan year or other period or any permissible opt-out period (Reg. § 1.36B-2(c)(3)(vii)(B)).

> **Example 10:** Tawnie enrolls in her employer's health plan in 2015. Her required contribution exceeds 9.56 percent of her household income. Even though the coverage is unaffordable, she is treated as having minimum essential coverage for the year because she is actually in the plan (Reg. § 1.36B-2(c)(3)(vii)(C), Ex. 1).

> **Example 11:** The facts are the same as in Example 10, except that Tawnie terminates her coverage on June 30, 2015. She is treating as being eligible for minimum essential coverage under her employer's plan from January through June, but not from July through December (Reg. § 1.36B-2(c)(3)(vii)(C), Ex. 2).

> **Example 12:** The facts are the same as Example 10, except that Tawnie's employer automatically enrolls her in the plan for calendar year 2015. She terminates the coverage on January 15, 2015. She is not eligible for minimum essential coverage under the plan for January (Reg. § 1.36B-2(c)(3)(vii)(C), Ex. 3).

As discussed above, under the minimum value requirement, an eligible employer-sponsored plan provides minimum value only if the plan's share of the total allowed costs of benefits provided to an employee (the minimum value percentage) is at least 60 percent. The minimum value percentage is determined by dividing the cost of certain benefits the plan would pay for a standard population by the total cost of certain benefits

LAW EXPLAINED

for the standard population, including amounts the plan pays and amounts the employee pays through cost-sharing, and then converting the result to a percentage. Several methods are available to determine minimum value: (1) a minimum value calculator, available online; (2) any safe harbors established by the IRS and the Department of Health and Human Services; (3) an actuarial certification; or (4) meeting any of the levels for metal coverage (bronze, silver, gold, or platinum) (Proposed Reg. § 1.36B-6).

Eligibility for minimum essential coverage outside of exchange. A coverage month does not include any month that, for the entire month, the individual is eligible for minimum essential coverage outside the individual market exchange, unless one of the exceptions discussed above is met (Code Sec. 36B(c)(2)(B)(i), as added by PPACA). Thus, an individual is not eligible for premium assistance during any month in which the individual is covered by certain government-sponsored programs, employer-sponsored plans, grandfathered health plans, and certain other benefits.

An individual is not eligible for the premium assistance amount for any month that the individual is eligible for government-sponsored minimum essential coverage. An individual is eligible for government-sponsored minimum essential coverage if the individual meets the criteria for coverage under a government-sponsored program as of the first day of the first full month the individual may receive benefits under the program (Reg. § 1.36B-2(c)(2)(i)). An individual who meets the criteria to obtain government-sponsored coverage must actually complete the requirements to obtain coverage (Reg. § 1.36B-2(c)(2)(ii)).

> **Example 13:** On April 10, Terri applies for coverage under a government-sponsored health care program. Her application is approved on July 12, but her coverage is not effective until September 1. She is eligible for government-sponsored minimum essential coverage on September 1 (Reg. § 1.36B-2(c)(2)(vi), Ex. 1).

If an individual does not complete the requirements by the last day of the third full calendar month following eligibility for government-sponsored coverage, the individual is treated as eligible for minimum essential coverage as of the first day of the fourth calendar month following eligibility for government-sponsored coverage (Reg. § 1.36B-2(c)(2)(ii)).

> **Example 14:** Thomas turns 65 on June 3 and becomes eligible for Medicare. He must enroll in Medicare to receive benefits. He enrolls in Medicare in September, which is the last month of his initial enrollment period, and he may begin to receive Medicare benefits on December 1. Because he completed the requirements necessary to receive Medicare benefits by the last day of September, the third full calendar month after the event that established his eligibility (he turned 65), he is eligible for government-sponsored minimum essential cover-

LAW EXPLAINED

> age on December 1, the first day of the first full month that he may receive benefits under the program (Reg. § 1.36B-2(c)(2)(vi), Ex. 2).

> **Example 15:** The facts are the same as in Example 14, except that Thomas fails to enroll in the Medicare coverage during his initial enrollment period. He is treated as eligible for government-sponsored minimum essential coverage as of October 1, the first day of the fourth month following the event that establishes eligibility (he turns 65) (Reg. § 1.36B-2(c)(2)(vi), Ex. 3).

If an individual receiving advance credit payments is determined to be eligible for government-sponsored minimum essential coverage that is effective retroactively (such as Medicaid), the individual is treated as eligible for minimum essential coverage under that program no earlier than the first day of the first calendar month beginning after the approval (Reg. § 1.36B-2(c)(2)(iv)).

> **Example 16:** Cathy enrolls in a qualified health plan for the year and receives advance credit payments. She loses her part-time employment and applies for Medicaid coverage on April 10. Cathy's application is approved on May 15, and her Medicaid coverage is effective as of April 1. She is eligible for government-sponsored minimum essential coverage on June 1, the first day of the first calendar month after approval (Reg. § 1.36B-2(c)(2)(vi), Ex. 4).

For individuals eligible to be covered by an employer-sponsored plan, the plan is considered to provide minimum essential coverage for a month only if the plan is affordable and provides minimum value. An individual is considered to be eligible for coverage so long as the individual could have enrolled in the plan for the month during an open or special enrollment period, even if the individual did not do so. Waiting periods, before which coverage comes effective, are not taken into account (Reg. § 1.36B-2(c)(3)).

> **Example 17:** Joyce's employer offers its employees a health insurance plan that has a plan year from October 1 through September 30. Employees may enroll during an open season from August 1 to September 15. Joyce does not enroll in the plan for the plan year October 1, 2014, to September 30, 2015. In November 2014, she enrolls in a qualified health plan through an Exchange for calendar year 2015. Joyce could have enrolled in her employer's plan during the August 1 to September 15 enrollment period. Therefore, unless her employer's plan is not affordable for Joyce or does not provide minimum value, she is eligible for minimum essential coverage for the months that she is enrolled in the qualified health plan during her employer's plan year (January through September 2015) (Reg. § 1.36B-2(c)(3)(iii)(C)).

LAW EXPLAINED

An individual who may enroll in continuation coverage required under federal law, such as COBRA coverage, or a state law that provides comparable continuation coverage, is eligible for minimum essential coverage only for months that the individual is enrolled in the coverage (Reg. § 1.36B-2(c)(3)(iv)). Proposed regulations would apply this rule to former employees only, however. Active employees eligible for continuation coverage as a result of reduced hours would be subject to the same rules for eligibility of affordable employer-sponsored coverage offering minimum value as other active employees. The proposed regulations would also add a comparable rule for health coverage offered to retired employees. Accordingly, an individual who may enroll in retiree coverage is eligible for minimum essential coverage under the coverage only for the months the individual is enrolled in the coverage (Proposed Reg. § 1.36B-2(c)(3)(iv)).

The IRS has provided rules for determining whether or when certain individuals are eligible for minimum essential coverage under the Medicaid, Medicare, Children's Health Insurance Program (CHIP), or TRICARE programs for purposes of the premium assistance tax credit. If an individual loses CHIP coverage due to a failure to pay premiums and may not re-enroll in CHIP for a certain period of time, the individual is treated as covered by CHIP and is not eligible for qualified health plan coverage subsidized by the premium tax credit during the lockout period. An individual who is terminated from Medicaid or CHIP for failure to pay premiums is treated as eligible for Medicaid or CHIP during any period for which the individual would be eligible for Medicaid or CHIP except for the failure to pay premiums. If an individual is not allowed to enroll in CHIP during a pre-enrollment waiting period, the individual may be eligible for qualified health plan coverage subsidized by the premium tax credit during this period. If an individual receives a favorable determination of eligible for Medicaid coverage requiring a finding of disability or blindness or for Medicare coverage based solely on a finding of disability or illness, the individual is treated as eligible for minimum essential coverage. Finally, an individual is eligible for minimum essential coverage under the following programs for purposes of the premium tax credit only if the individual is enrolled in the coverage:

(1) Medicare part A coverage requiring payment of premiums;

(2) State high risk pools;

(3) Student health plans; and

(4) The following TRICARE Programs: The Continued Health Care Benefit Program (10 U.S.C. 1078), Retired Reserve (10 U.S.C. 1076e), Young Adult (10 U.S.C. 1110b), and Reserve Select (10 U.S.C. 1076d) (Notice 2013-41).

Computing the premium assistance credit amount. In general, the premium assistance credit amount is the sum of the premium assistance amounts for all coverage months in the tax year for individuals in the taxpayer's family (Code Sec. 36B(b)(1), as added by PPACA). A coverage month is any month in which, as of the first day of the month, the taxpayer, the taxpayer's spouse, or any dependent is covered by a qualified health plan (1) that was enrolled in through an exchange and (2) for which the premium is paid by the taxpayer or through advance payment of the premium assistance credit (Code Sec. 36B(c)(2)(A), as added by PPACA). A coverage month does not include any month that,

LAW EXPLAINED

for the entire month, the individual is eligible for minimum essential coverage outside the individual market exchange (Code Sec. 36B(c)(2)(B)(i), as added by PPACA). A child enrolled in a qualified health plan in the month of the child's birth, adoption, or placement with the taxpayer for adoption or in foster care, is treated as enrolled as of the first day of the month (Proposed Reg. § 1.36B-(c)(2)).

> **Example 18:** Mary is single with no dependents. She enrolls in a qualified health plan for the year and the Exchange approves advance credit payments. On May 15, Mary enlists in the U.S. Army and is eligible immediately for government-sponsored minimum essential coverage. January through May are coverage months for Mary. June through December are not coverage months because she is eligible for minimum essential coverage for those months. Her premium assistance credit amount is the sum of the premium assistance amounts for the months January through May (Reg. § 1.36B-3(c)(3), Ex. 1).

> **Example 19:** Carl has one dependent. The dependent is eligible for government-sponsored minimum essential coverage. Carl is not eligible for minimum essential coverage. He enrolls in a qualified health plan for the calendar year and the Exchange approves advance credit payments. On August 1, Carl's dependent loses eligibility for minimum essential coverage. Carl cancels the qualified health plan that covers only himself and enrolls in a qualified health plan that covers both himself and his dependent for August through December. January through December are coverage months for Carl and August through December are coverage months for himself and his dependent. Carl's premium assistance credit amount for the year is the sum of the premium assistance amounts for these coverage months (Reg. § 1.36B-3(c)(3), Ex. 2).

If a single qualified health plan covers more than one family, each applicable taxpayer covered by the plan may claim a premium tax credit, if otherwise allowable. Each taxpayer computes the credit using that taxpayer's applicable percentage, household income, and the cost of the second-lowest-cost silver plan. In determining whether the amount computed (the premiums for the qualified health plan in which the taxpayer enrolls) is less than the premium of the second-lowest-cost silver plan minus the product of household income and the applicable percentage), the premiums paid are allocated to each taxpayer in proportion to the premiums for each taxpayer's applicable plan (Reg. § 1.36B-3(h)(1)).

> **Example 20:** Donna is Brian's 25-year old child and is not his dependent. Brian, Donna, and Brian's other two children (who are his dependents) enroll in a single qualified health plan. The premium for the plan is $15,000. The premium for the second lowest cost silver family plan is $12,000 and the premium for the second lowest cost silver self-only plan is $6,000.

LAW EXPLAINED

> Both Brian and Donna may claim premium tax credits. Brian computes his credit using his household income, a family size of three, and a applicable plan premium of $12,000. Donna computes her credit using his household income, a family size of one, and applicable plan premium of $6,000.
>
> In determining whether the premiums for the qualified health plan Brian and Donna purchase is less than the applicable plan premium minus the product of household income and the applicable percentage, the $15,000 premiums paid are allocated to Brian and Donna in proportion to the premiums for their applicable plans. Thus, the portion of the premium allocated to Brian is $10,000 ($15,000 × $12,000/$18,000) and the portion allocated to Donna is $5,000 ($15,000 × $6,000/$18,000) (Reg. § 1.36B-3(h)(2)).

Advance payment of health insurance premium assistance credit. The health insurance premium assistance credit is payable in advance by the Treasury Department directly to the insurer, thereby reducing the individual's out-of-pocket expenses. To be eligible for the advanced credit, the individual enrolled in the plan must report his income to the exchange. Based on this information, Treasury will be notified of the individual's eligibility and will subsequently pay the credit directly to the insurance plan in which the individual is enrolled (PPACA § 1412(c)).

> **Comment:** To allow this reconciliation, each exchange must report information to the IRS and to each taxpayer or responsible adult who enrolled, or whose family member enrolled, in a qualified health plan through the exchange (Code Sec. 36B(f)(3), as added by PPACA; Reg. § 1.36B-5). The information must be furnished to individuals annually in a written statement or on Form 1095-A and may be delivered electronically if the individual consents (Reg. § 1.36B-5(f), (g)).
>
> **Comment:** A taxpayer who receives advance credit payments must file an income tax return for that tax year on or before the fifteenth day of the fourth month following the close of the year (Reg. § 1.6011-8). Proposed regulations would instead require the taxpayer to file an income tax return for the year on or before the extended due date (Proposed Reg. § 1.6011-8).

For the 2014 tax year, if the premium assistance received through an advance payment exceeds the amount of the credit to which the individual is entitled, the difference is treated as an increase in tax. However, in the case of an individual with household income less than 400 percent of the FPL, the amount of the increase is limited. If the household income is less than 200 percent of the FPL, the increase can not exceed $600 ($300 for single taxpayers). If the household income is at least 200 percent, but less than 300 percent, the increase can not exceed $1,500 ($750 for single taxpayers). If the household income is at least 300 percent, but less than 400 percent, the increase can not exceed $2,500 ($1,250 for single taxpayers). These amounts are adjusted for inflation after 2014, rounded to the next lowest multiple of $50 if the adjustment is not a multiple of $50 (Code Sec. 36B(f)(2), as added by PPACA and amended by the Comprehensive 1099 Taxpayer Protection and Repayment of Exchange Subsidy Overpayments Act of 2011 (P.L. 112-9); Reg. § 1.36B-4(a)).

¶210

LAW EXPLAINED

If the premium assistance received through an advance payment is less than the amount of the credit to which the taxpayer is entitled, the credit is allowed, but is reduced by the amount of the advance payment (Code Sec. 36B(f)(1)). A taxpayer does not have an advance credit payment for a month if the health plan does not provide coverage (Reg. § 1.36B-4(a)(1)(iii)).

Example 21: Deidre is single and has no dependents. The Exchange in her rating area projects household income for 2014 will be $27,925 (250 percent of the FPL for a family of one, applicable percentage 8.05). She enrolls in a qualified health plan. The annual premium for the applicable plan is $5,200. Deidre's advance credit payments are $2,952 (applicable plan premium of $5,200 less contribution amount of $2,248 (projected household income of $27,925 × 0.0805) = $2,952). Her actual household income for the year turns out to be $33,622, which is 301 percent of the federal FPL for a family of one (applicable percentage 9.5). Consequently, her premium tax credit is $2,006 (applicable plan premium of $5,200 less contribution amount of $3,194 (household income of $33,622 × 0.095)). Because her advance credit payments for the year are $2,952 and her credit is $2,006, she has excess advance payments of $946. Deidre's tax liability is increased by $926 (Reg. § 1.36B-4(a)(4), Ex. 1).

Example 22: The facts are the same as in Example 22, except that Deidre's actual household income for the year is $43,560 (390 percent of the FPL for a family of one, applicable percentage 9.5). Consequently, her premium tax credit for the year is $1,062 ($5,200 premium for the second lowest cost silver plan less contribution amount of $4,138 (household income of $43,560 × 0.095)). Her advance credit payments are $2,952; she has excess advance payments of $1,890. Because Deidre's household income is between 300 percent and 400 percent of the FPL, her additional tax liability for the year is $1,250 (Reg. § 1.36B-4(a)(4), Ex. 2).

Married taxpayers. Taxpayers who are married at the end of the tax year are generally not eligible for the premium credit unless a joint return is filed. Exceptions exist in the case of abuse or abandonment, however, as discussed above (Temporary Reg. § 1.36B-2T(b)(2)). If a joint return is not filed, all advance payments must be repaid as an additional tax liability. Married taxpayers who do not file a joint return must allocate advance credit payments between themselves for any period the plan covers and advance credit payments are made for both taxpayers, only one of the taxpayers and one or more dependents of the other taxpayer, or one or more dependents of both taxpayers. If a plan covers or advance credit payments are made for only one of the taxpayers and no dependents, only one of the taxpayers and one or more dependents of that same taxpayer, or only one or more dependents of one of the taxpayers, the advance credit payments for that period are allocated entirely to that taxpayer. If one or both of the taxpayers is an applicable taxpayer eligible for a premium tax credit for the

LAW EXPLAINED

tax year, the credit is computed by allocating the premiums for the plan in which the taxpayers or their family members enroll equally to each taxpayer, although all of the premiums are allocated to only one of the taxpayers for a period in which a qualified health plan covers only that taxpayer, only that taxpayer and one or more dependents of that taxpayer, or only one or more dependents of that taxpayer. The repayment limitation applies to each taxpayer based on the household income and family size reported on that taxpayer's return. These rules also apply to taxpayers who receive advance credit payments as married taxpayers and file a tax return using the head of household filing status (Temporary Reg. § 1.36B-4T(b)(4)).

Dependents claimed and enrolled by different taxpayers. If a taxpayer enrolls an individual in a qualified health plan and another taxpayer claims a personal exemption deduction for the individual, special rules apply for purposes of computing each taxpayer's premium tax credit and reconciling any advance credit payments. The enrolling taxpayer and claiming taxpayer may agree on any allocation percentage between zero and one hundred percent. If the enrolling taxpayer and claiming taxpayer do not agree on an allocation percentage, the percentage is equal to the number of enrollees claimed as a personal exemption deduction by the claiming taxpayer divided by the number of individuals enrolled by the enrolling taxpayer in the same qualified health plan (Temporary Reg. § 1.36B-4T(a)(1)(ii)(B)).

Example 23: Grace and Harry Wong are divorced and have two children, Joan and Kathy. Grace enrolls herself and her children in a qualified health plan for 2015. The premium for the is $13,000. The Exchange in her rating area approves advance credit payments based on a family size of three, an annual benchmark plan premium of $12,000 and projected 2015 household income of $58,590 (assume 300 percent of the FPL for a family of three, applicable percentage 9.56). Grace's advance credit payments for 2015 are $6,399 ($12,000 benchmark plan premium less $5,601 contribution amount (household income of $58,590 × 9.56%)). Grace's actual household income for 2015 is $58,900.

Kathy lives with Harry for more than half of 2015 and Harry claims Kathy as a dependent. Grace and Harry agree to an allocation percentage of 20 percent. Under the agreement, Harry is allocated 20 percent of the items to be allocated and Grace is allocated the remainder of those items.

If Harry is eligible for a premium tax credit, Harry takes into account $2,600 of the premiums for the plan in which Kathy was enrolled ($13,000 × .20) and $2,400 of Grace's benchmark plan premium ($12,000 × .20). In addition, Harry is responsible for reconciling $1,280 ($6,399 × .20) of the advance credit payments for Kathy's coverage.

Grace's family size for 2015 includes only Grace and John, and assume that Grace's household income of $58,900 is 380 percent of the FPL for a family of two (applicable percentage 9.56). Grace's benchmark plan premium for 2015 is $9,600 (the benchmark premium for the plan covering Grace, John, and Kathy ($12,000), minus the amount allocated to Harry ($2,400). Consequently, Grace's

---

LAW EXPLAINED

> premium tax credit is $3,969 (Grace's benchmark plan premium of $9,600 minus her contribution amount of $5,631($58,900 × 9.56%)). Grace has an excess advance payment of $1,150 (the excess of the advance credit payments of $5,119 ($6,399 - $1,280 allocated to Harry) over the premium tax credit of $3,969) (Temporary Reg. §1.36B-4T(a)(4), Ex. 10).

> **Example 24:** Assume the same facts as in Example 24, except that Grace and Harry do not agree on an allocation percentage. The allocation percentage is 33 percent, computed as follows: the number of shifting enrollees, 1 (Kathy), divided by the number of individuals enrolled by the enrolling taxpayer on the same qualified health plan as the shifting enrollee, 3 (Grace, John, and Kathy). Thus, Harry is allocated 33 percent of the items to be allocated and Grace is allocated the remainder of those items (Temporary Reg. §1.36B-4T(a)(4), Ex. 11).

In computing the credit, the claiming taxpayer is allocated a portion of the premiums for the plan in which the dependent enrollee was enrolled equal to the premiums for the plan times the allocation percentage. The enrolling taxpayer is allocated the remainder of the premiums not allocated to one or more claiming taxpayers (Temporary Reg. §1.36B-4T(a)(1)(ii)(B)(3)).

In reconciling any advance credit payments, the claiming taxpayer is allocated a portion of the advance credit payments for the plan in which the dependent enrollee was enrolled equal to the enrolling taxpayer's advance credit payments for the plan times the allocation percentage. The enrolling taxpayer is allocated the remainder of the advance credit payments not allocated to one or more claiming taxpayers (Temporary Reg. §1.36B-4T(a)(1)(ii)(B)(4)). For this purpose, the claiming taxpayer's benchmark plan premium is the sum of the benchmark plan premium for the claiming taxpayer's coverage family, excluding the dependent enrollee or enrollees, and the allocable portion. The allocable portion is the product of the benchmark plan premium for the enrolling taxpayer's coverage family if the dependent enrollee was a member of the enrolling taxpayer's coverage family and the allocation percentage. If the enrolling taxpayer's coverage family is enrolled in more than one qualified health plan, the allocable portion is determined as if the enrolling taxpayer's coverage family includes only the coverage family members who enrolled in the same plan as the dependent enrollee or enrollees. The enrolling taxpayer's benchmark plan premium is the benchmark plan premium for the enrolling taxpayer's coverage family had the dependent enrollee or enrollees remained a part of the enrolling taxpayer's coverage family, minus the allocable portion. (Temporary Reg. §1.36B-4T(a)(1)(ii)(B)(5)). If advance credit payments are allocated under this provision, the claiming taxpayer and enrolling taxpayer must use this same allocation percentage to calculate their adjusted monthly premiums for the applicable benchmark plan (benchmark plan premiums) when calculating the premium assistance credit amount (Temporary Reg. §1.36B-4T(a)(1)(ii)(B)(1)).

¶210

LAW EXPLAINED

These special rules for dependents do not apply to amounts allocated under Reg. § 1.36B-3 (h) with respect to qualified health plan covering more than one family or if the dependent enrollee or enrollees are the only individuals enrolled in the qualified health plan. A taxpayer who is expected at enrollment in a qualified health plan to be the taxpayer filing an income tax return for the year of coverage with respect to an individual enrolling in the plan has enrolled that individual (Temporary Reg. § 1.36B-4T (a) (1) (ii) (B) (1)).

Individuals for whom no personal exemption deduction is claimed. If advance credit payments are made for coverage of an individual for whom no taxpayer claims a personal exemption deduction, the taxpayer who attested to the marketplace Exchange to the intention to claim a personal exemption deduction for the individual as part of the advance credit payment eligibility determination for coverage of the individual must reconcile the advance credit payments (Temporary Reg. § 1.36B-4T (a) (1) (ii) (C)). The failure to claim the projected number of dependents not only decreases the taxpayer's poverty level (which is based on family size) but also decreases the cost of the benchmark plan (which is also based on family size). As a result advance payments in excess of the credit amount are received and must be repaid (Temporary Reg. § 1.36B-4T (a) (4), Ex. 4).

Example 25: Tom and Edna Nault have two children Fred, age 17, and Clara, age 23 whom they expect to claim as dependents in 2015. The annual premium for the benchmark plan for a family of four is $14,100. Tom and Edna's advance premium payments for 2015 are $8,535 based on a projected household income of $63,388 (assume 275 percent of FPL for a family of four with applicable percentage 8.78 percent ($14,100 – ($63,388 × .0878) = $8,535).

Clara, however, is not claimed as a dependent in 2014 which causes the family size for purposes of the credit to decrease to three individuals. Actual household income is the same as projected. The benchmark plan for a family of three costs $12,000. Household income of $63,388 for a family of three is 332 percent of the FPL with an applicable percentage of 9.56. Tom and Edna's premium credit for 2015 is $5,940 ($12,000 – ($63,388 × .0956)). The excess advance payment is $2,595 ($8,535 – $5,940). However, the repayment limitation applies and the additional tax is limited to $2,500.

Self-employed taxpayers. A self-employed taxpayer who receives advance credit payments and deducts premiums for a qualified health plan under Code Sec. 162(l) must use a special limitation amount. The limitation amount must be determined before calculating the Code Sec. 162(l) deduction and premium tax credit (Temporary Reg. § 1.36B-4T (a) (3) (iii)).

The taxpayer must first determine whether he or she qualifies for the limitation amount applicable to taxpayers with household income of less than 200 percent of the FPL for the taxpayer's family size. If the taxpayer is unable to meet certain requirements for that limitation amount, the taxpayer must next determine whether he or she qualifies for the

¶210

LAW EXPLAINED

limitation applicable to taxpayers with household income of less than 300 percent of the FPL for the taxpayer's family size. If the taxpayer is unable to meet the requirements for taxpayers with household income of less than 300 percent of the FPL for the taxpayer's family size, the taxpayer must next determine whether he or she qualifies for the limitation applicable to taxpayers with household income of less than 400 percent of the FPL line for the taxpayer's family size. If the taxpayer is unable to meet the requirements for any limitation amount, the limitation on additional tax under section does not apply to the taxpayer (Temporary Reg. § 1.36B-4T(a)(3)(iii)).

A taxpayer meets the requirements for a limitation amount if the taxpayer's household income as a percentage of the FPL is less than or equal to the maximum household income as a percentage of the FPL for which that limitation is available. Household income for this purpose is determined by using a Code Sec. 162(l) deduction equal to the sum of the specified premiums for the plan not paid through advance credit payments and the limitation amount in addition to any deduction allowable under Code Sec. 162(l) for premiums other than specified premiums (Temporary Reg. § 1.36B-4T(a)(3)(iii)(C)).

A taxpayer who uses the special limitation amount may have his or her Code Sec. 162(l) deduction limited (Temporary Reg. § 1.162(l)-1T). The deduction may not to exceed the lesser of:

(1) the premiums less the premium tax credit attributable to the premiums; and

(2) the sum of the premiums not paid through advance credit payments and any additional tax imposed after application of the special limitation amount.

For this purpose, the premiums may be for any qualified health plan for which the taxpayer may otherwise claim a deduction under Code Sec. 162(l). The qualified health plan may cover the taxpayer, the taxpayer's spouse, or a dependent of the taxpayer. If a qualified health plan covers individuals other than enrolled family members, the premiums include only the portion of the premiums for the qualified health plan that is allocable to the enrolled family members under rules similar to Reg. § 1.36B-3(h), which provides rules when two families are enrolled in the same qualified health plan (Temporary Reg. § 1.162(l)-1T).

Because the Code Sec. 162(l) deduction is allowed in computing adjusted gross income and because adjusted gross income is necessary for computing the premium tax credit, the taxpayer must know the allowable deduction to compute the premium tax credit. Thus, the amount of the deduction is based on the amount of the premium tax credit, and the amount of the credit is based on the amount of the deduction—a circular relationship. Taxpayers may determine the amounts of the deduction and credit using any method that satisfies the requirements of the applicable law, but the IRS has provided two optional calculations (Rev. Proc. 2014-41).

Under the iterative calculation, the taxpayer follows the following steps:

(1) Determine adjusted gross income, modified adjusted gross income, and household income by taking a Code Sec. 162(l) deduction for the amount of specified premiums after applying the limitation described below.

LAW EXPLAINED

(2) Compute the premium tax credit using the adjusted gross income, modified adjusted gross income, and household income determined in Step 1;

(3) Determine the deduction by subtracting the Step 2 premium tax credit amount from the specified premiums and then applying the limitation described below;

(4) Compute the premium tax credit using the adjusted gross income, modified adjusted gross income and household income determined by taking into account the deduction in Step 3;

(5) Repeat Step 3 by substituting the Step 4 premium tax credit for the Step 2 premium tax credit.

(6) If changes in both the deduction and the premium tax credit from Steps 2 and 3 to Steps 4 and 5 are less than $1, use the deduction and premium tax credit amounts for the specified premiums determined in Steps 4 and 5. If the change in either the deduction or the premium tax credit from Steps 2 and 3 to Steps 4 and 5 is not less than $1, repeat Steps 4 and 5 (using amounts determined in the immediately preceding iteration) until changes in both the deduction and the premium tax credit between iterations are less than $1.

Under the alternative calculation, the taxpayer follows the following steps, claiming the amount of the premium tax credit determined under Step 4 and the amount of the Code Sec. 162(l) deduction for the specified premiums determined under Step 3:

(1) Determine adjusted gross income, modified adjusted gross income, and household income by taking a Code Sec. 162(l) deduction for the amount of specified premiums after applying the limitation described below;

(2) Compute the initial premium tax credit using the adjusted gross income, modified adjusted gross income, and household income determined in Step 1;

(3) Determine the deduction by subtracting the Step 2 premium tax credit amount from the specified premiums and then applying the limitation described below;

(4) Compute the final premium tax credit using the adjusted gross income, modified adjusted gross income and household income determined by taking into account the deduction in Step 3.

The limitation referenced in the calculations is that the Code Sec. 162(l) deduction may not exceed the lesser of the taxpayer's earned income derived by the taxpayer from the trade or business with respect to which the health insurance is established, or the sum of the specified premiums not paid through advance credit payments and the limitation on additional tax for purposes of Code Sec. 36B(f)(2)(B) (Rev. Proc. 2014-41).

If a taxpayer has premium assistance amounts that are not covered by both the deduction and the credit, the taxpayer should complete Step 3 of the alternative calculation, and Step 3 and the corresponding succeeding Steps in the iterative calculation, except substituting "premium tax credit determined in Step 2 but only with respect to months in which specified premiums were paid" for "premium tax credit determined in Step 2" (Rev. Proc. 2014-41).

¶210

LAW EXPLAINED

Change in filing status. Married taxpayers generally must file jointly to qualify for the health insurance premium assistance credit (Code Sec. 36B(c)(1)(C), as added by PPACA). Exceptions exist in the case of abuse or abandonment, however, as discussed above (Temporary Reg. § 1.36B-2T(b)(2)).

A taxpayer whose marital status changes during the tax year computes the premium tax credit by using the second-lowest-cost silver plan (or plans) of the individual market exchange in the rating area where the taxpayer resides for the taxpayer's marital status as of the first day of each coverage month. The taxpayer's contribution amount (household income for the tax year times the applicable percentage) is determined using the taxpayer's household income and family size at the end of the tax year (Reg. § 1.36B-4(a)(2)).

Married taxpayers who divorce and are not married to each other on the last day of the tax year must allocate the premium for the applicable benchmark plan, the premium for the plan in which the taxpayers enroll, and the advance credit payments for the period during which they were married in any proportion so long as the proportion is the same for each of these items. If the taxpayers do not agree on a proportion the IRS will allocate one-half to each. Taxpayers must make the allocation if they are enrolled in the same qualified health plan or if one of the taxpayers has a dependent enrolled in the same plan as the taxpayer's former spouse or enrolled in the same plan as a dependent of the taxpayer's former spouse (Temporary Reg. § 1.36B-4T(b)(3)).

Example 26: Karl and Jill are divorced on June 17, 2015, and obtain separate qualified plans on July 1, 2015. They received a $573 monthly premium credit while married ($3,438 ($573 × 6) in total). Karl and Jill do not agree on an allocation percentage, therefore, the $7,050 premium for their applicable benchmark plan and the $3,438 advance credit payments, for the six-month period during which they were married, are allocated 50/50.

Karl

Assume that for the July - December period Karl received advance credits of $2,148 based on his new benchmark plan (annual premiums of $10,000), projected 2015 household income of $60,000 (assume 314 percent of the FPL, applicable percentage 9.56), and a family size of 3. (Karl will claim their two children as dependents).

Total advance credits.........................$3,867 ($3,438 × 50% + $2,148).

Total benchmark plan premium.........$8,525 (($7,050 × 50%) + ($10,000 × 6/12)).

Contribution amount.........................$5,736 ($60,000 × 9.56%).

Premium credit.................................$2,789 ($8,525 total benchmark plan premium – $5,736 contribution amount).

Additional tax.................................... $1,078 ($3,867 advance credit payments – $2,789 premium credit).

¶210

LAW EXPLAINED

> *Jill*
>
> For the July - December period Jill received advance credits of $2,286 based on her new benchmark plan (annual premiums of $5,200), projected 2015 household income of $16,420 (assume 147 percent of the FPL, applicable percentage 3.82), and a family size of 1.
>
> Total advance credits..........................$4,005 ($3,438 × 50% + $2,286).
>
> Total benchmark plan premium.........$6,125 (($7,050 × 50%) + ($5,200 × 6/12)).
>
> Contribution amount..........................$627 ($16,420 × 3.82%).
>
> Premium credit....................................$5,498 ($6,125 total benchmark plan premium – $627 contribution amount).
>
> Additional refundable credit.............$1,493 ($5,498 premium credit – $4,005 advance payments) (Reg. § 1.36B-4(b)(5), Ex. 6).

Taxpayers who are not married at the beginning of the year, but are married at the end of the year, may use an alternative computation (Reg. § 1.36B-4(b)(2)(i)). The alternative marriage-year credit is the sum of both taxpayers' alternative premium assistance amounts for the pre-marriage months and the premium assistance amounts for the marriage months (Reg. § 1.36B-4(b)(2)(ii)(A)).

▶ **Effective date.** Generally, the amendments made by this provision apply to tax years ending after December 31, 2013 (Act Secs. 1401(e) and 10108(h)(2) of the Patient Protection and Affordable Care Act (PPACA) (P.L. 111-148)). However, the amendments to Code Sec. 36B(b)(3)(A)(ii), (c)(1)(A), (c)(2)(C)(iv) and Code Sec. 6211(b)(4)(A) are effective on March 23, 2010, the date of enactment of the Patient Protection Act. The amendments to Code Sec. 36B(b)(3)(A), (c)(2)(C), (d)(2), and the addition of (f)(3), are effective on March 30, 2010, the date of enactment of the Health Care and Education Reconciliation Act of 2010 (P.L. 111-152). The final and temporary regulations also apply to tax years ending after December 31, 2013. Proposed Reg. § 1.36B-1, Proposed Reg. § 1.36B-2, Proposed Reg. § 1.36B-3, Proposed Reg. § 1.36B-6, and Proposed Reg. § 1.6011-8 are proposed to apply for tax years ending after December 31, 2013. Taxpayers may apply the proposed regulations for tax years ending before January 1, 2015 (Notice of Proposed Rule Making REG-125398-12, published in the Federal Register on May 3, 2013).

Law source: Law at ¶5010, ¶5160, and ¶5390.

— Act Secs. 1401(a), 10105(a), (b) and (c), and 10108(h)(1) of the Patient Protection and Affordable Care Act (PPACA) (P.L. 111-148), adding and amending Code Sec. 36B;

— Act Sec. 1401(b), adding Code Sec. 280C(g);

— Act Secs. 1401(d) and 10105(d), amending Code Sec. 6211(b)(4)(A) and 31 U.S.C. Sec. 1324(b)(2);

— Act Sec. 1001(a) of the Health Care and Education Reconciliation Act of 2010 (P.L. 111-152), amending Code Sec. 36B(b)(3)(A) and (c)(2)(C);

— Act Sec. 1004(a)(1)(A) and (a)(2)(A) of 2010 Reconciliation Act, amending Code Sec. 36B(d)(2);

— Act Sec. 1004(c), adding Code Sec. 36B(f)(3);

— Act Secs. 1401(e) and 10108(h)(2), providing the effective date.

LAW EXPLAINED

Reporter references: For further information, consult the following reporters.
— Tax Research Consultant, HEALTH: 3,300
— Standard Federal Tax Reporter, ¶4197.01
— Practical Tax Explanation, §42,015.05

¶215 Itemized Deduction for Medical Expenses

SUMMARY OF NEW LAW

For tax years beginning after December 31, 2012, the threshold to claim an itemized deduction for unreimbursed medical expenses is increased from 7.5 percent of adjusted gross income (AGI) to 10 percent of AGI for regular income tax purposes.

BACKGROUND

An itemized deduction is allowed for unreimbursed expenses paid for the medical care of the taxpayer or the taxpayer's spouse or dependents (Code Sec. 213(a)). Expenses paid for medical care include amounts paid for the diagnosis, cure, mitigation, treatment, or prevention of disease, and for treatments affecting any part or function of the body (Code Sec. 213(d)). Only payments for legal medical services rendered by physicians, surgeons, dentists, and other medical practitioners qualify as medical expenses. Amounts paid for equipment, supplies, and diagnostic devices may be deductible if needed for medical care. Medical care expenses must be incurred primarily to alleviate or prevent a physical or mental defect or illness and do not include expenses that are merely beneficial to general health, such as vitamins or a vacation. Medical expenses also include premiums paid for insurance that covers the expenses of medical care and amounts paid for transportation to get medical care. Amounts paid for long-term care services and limited amounts paid for any qualified long-term care insurance contract are medical expenses. The cost of medicine and drugs is deductible only for medicine and drugs that require a prescription, except for insulin.

Individuals are allowed an itemized deduction for unreimbursed medical expenses only to the extent that the expenses exceed a certain precentage of their adjusted gross income (AGI) (Code Sec. 213(a)). Historically, this percentage was 10 percent for taxpayers whether they were paying regular income tax or alternative minimum tax (AMT) (Code Sec. 56(b)(1)(B)).

LAW EXPLAINED

Medical expense deduction threshold increased.—The threshold to claim an itemized deduction for unreimbursed medical expenses is increased from 7.5 percent of adjusted gross income (AGI) to 10 percent of AGI for regular income tax purposes, for tax years beginning after December 31, 2012 (Code Sec. 213(a), as amended by the Patient Protection and Affordable Care Act (PPACA) (P.L. 111-148)).

LAW EXPLAINED

> **Example:** Rich has adjusted gross income of $50,000 in 2012 and in 2013. His unreimbursed medical expenses are $5,000 for each year. In 2012, Rich can deduct $1,250 ($5,000 - $3,750 ($50,000 x 7.5 percent)) in medical expenses. In 2013, however, he cannot deduct any of his medical expenses ($5,000 - $5,000 ($50,000 x 10 percent)).

If a taxpayer or the taxpayer's spouse is age 65 or older before the close of the tax year, the taxpayer may continue to use the 7.5 percent AGI floor. This temporary waiver applies to tax years beginning after December 31, 2012, and ending before January 1, 2017 (Code Sec. 213(f), as added by PPACA).

> **Comment:** For taxpayers filing jointly, if they are both under age 65 as of the end of the tax year they must use the 10 percent AGI floor. If, however, the taxpayer or the taxpayer's spouse attains age 65 before the end of the tax year, the 7.5 percent AGI floor applies.

The alternative minimum tax (AMT) treatment of the itemized deduction for medical expenses is not changed. Thus, medical expenses are deductible only to the extent that they exceed 10 percent of AGI, even if the taxpayer (or their spouse) is age 65 or older before the close of the tax year (Code Sec. 56(b)(1)(B), as amended by PPACA).

> **State Tax Consequences:** The increased threshold for the itemized deduction for unreimbursed medical expenses from 7.5 percent of AGI to 10 percent of AGI for regular income tax purposes, will impact states that adopt federal itemized deductions but that do not conform by the time the increase takes effect. Such states may allow a subtraction from federal AGI for the difference between federal and state allowable medical expenses. States, like Indiana and Pennsylvania that do not allow itemized deductions or deductions for medical expenses or states like California, Minnesota, and Oregon that do not adopt Code Sec. 139A, will not be affected by the increase. The increase will also not affect states like Alabama, Arizona, and New Jersey that allow a deduction for medical expenses, but that do not adopt the federal threshold amount.

▶ **Effective date.** The provision applies to tax years beginning after December 31, 2012 (Act Sec. 9013(d) of the Patient Protection and Affordable Care Act (PPACA) (P.L. 111-148)).

Law source: Law at ¶5040 and ¶5130.

— Act Sec. 9013(a) of the Patient Protection and Affordable Care Act (PPACA) (P.L. 111-148), amending Code Sec. 213(a);

— Act Sec. 9013(b), adding Code Sec. 213(f);

— Act Sec. 9013(c), amending Code Sec. 56(b)(1)(B);

— Act Sec. 9013(d), providing the effective date.

Reporter references: For further information, consult the following reporters.

— Standard Federal Tax Reporter, ¶12,543.01

— Tax Research Consultant, INDIV:42,300

— Practical Tax Explanation, §7201

¶215

¶220 Medical Benefits for Children Under Age 27

SUMMARY OF NEW LAW

Beginning in 2010, medical benefits for a taxpayer's child under the age of 27 are treated the same as the benefits for the taxpayer's spouse and dependents for purposes of the general exclusion for reimbursements for medical care expenses under an employer-provided accident or health plan (Code Sec. 105(b)), the deduction for the health insurance costs of a self-employed person (Code Sec. 162(l)), the rule that allows a qualified pension or annuity plan to provide benefits for sickness, accident, hospitalization, and medical expenses to retired employees (Code Sec. 401(h)), and the rule that treats a voluntary employee benefits association (VEBA) that provides sick and accident benefits to its members as a tax-exempt organization (Code Sec. 501(c)(9)).

BACKGROUND

The Internal Revenue Code provides a number of tax benefits related to the provision of medical care to individuals, their spouses, and their dependents. In general, a dependent for these purposes is defined by reference to the rules in Code Sec. 152 relating to dependency exemptions. Under these rules, a child is a dependent for whom a dependency exemption may be claimed only if he or she is a qualifying child (Code Sec. 152(c)) or a qualifying relative (Code Sec. 152(d)).

In general, a qualifying child must:

- have a specified relationship to the taxpayer;

- live with the taxpayer for more than one-half of the year;

- provide only one-half or less of his or her own support;

- be under the age of 19 at the end of the year, or, if a full-time student, under the age of 24; and

- not file a joint return except to claim a refund.

If the preceding requirements for qualifying child status are not satisfied, it may be possible to claim a child as a dependent under the rules for a qualifying relative. To be considered a qualifying relative for whom a dependency exemption may be claimed a child must:

- have a specified relationship to the taxpayer;

- have gross income less than the exemption amount for the year;

- receive over one-half of his or her support from the taxpayer; and

- is not a qualifying child of another taxpayer.

¶220

BACKGROUND

It is not necessary for a qualifying relative to live with the taxpayer and no age restrictions apply. Other requirements for qualifying child and qualifying relative status apply.

Employer-financed accident or health insurance. Employees may exclude from gross income the value of employer-provided health coverage for themselves, their spouses, and their dependents under an accident or health plan (Code Sec. 106). Gross income also does not include amounts received by an employee through employer-financed accident or health insurance for amounts that reimburse the employee for expenses incurred for the medical care of the employee, the employee's spouse, or the employee's dependents (as defined in Code Sec. 152, determined without regard to subsections (b)(1), (b)(2), and (d)(1)(B)). Any child to whom Code Sec. 152(e) applies (relating to special rules for divorced parents) is treated as a dependent of both parents (Code Sec. 105(b)).

Health insurance costs of the self-employed. Self-employed persons may deduct from gross income 100 percent of amounts paid during the year for health insurance for themselves, their spouses, and their dependents (Code Sec. 162(l)(1)).

Pension plan providing medical benefits to retirees. A qualified pension or annuity plan can provide benefits for sickness, accident, hospitalization, and medical expenses of retired employees, their spouses, and their dependents if: (1) the benefits are subordinate to the retirement benefits provided; (2) a separate account is established and maintained for these benefits; and (3) the employer's contributions to the separate account are reasonable and ascertainable. A dependent is a person for whom a dependency exemption may be claimed (Reg. § 1.401-14(b)(4)).

Voluntary employees' beneficiary association. A tax-exempt 501(a) organization includes a voluntary employees' beneficiary association (VEBA) that provides for the payment of life, sick, accident, or other benefits to the members of such association or their dependents or designated beneficiaries, if no part of the net earnings of such association inures (other than through such payments) to the benefit of any private shareholder or individual (Code Sec. 501(c)(9)). Dependent means the member's spouse, any child of the member or the member's spouse who is a minor or a student, any other minor child residing with the member, and any other individual who an association, relying on information furnished to it by a member, in good faith believes a dependency exemption may be claimed (Reg. § 1.501(c)(9)-3).

LAW EXPLAINED

Starting in 2010, tax benefits are extended to medical benefits for children under age 27.—A child who is under the age of 27 is now treated the same as a dependent of a taxpayer for purposes of the general exclusion for reimbursements for medical care expenses under an employer-provided accident or health plan, the self-employed health insurance deduction, the rule that allows a qualified pension or annuity plan to provide benefits for sickness, accident, hospitalization, and medical expenses to retired employees, their spouses, and their dependents, and the rule that treats a voluntary employee benefits association (VEBA) that provides sick and accident benefits to its members and their dependents as a tax-exempt organization (Code Secs.

¶220

LAW EXPLAINED

105(b), 162(l), 401(h), and 501(c)(9) as amended by the Health Care and Education Reconciliation Act of 2010 (P.L. 111-152)).

Exclusion for employer-provided accident and health insurance. The exclusion from gross income for reimbursements made under an employer-provided accident or health insurance plan for medical care expenses of an employee, employee's spouse, or employee's dependents is extended to apply to any child of the employee who as of the end of the tax year has not attained the age of 27 (Code Sec. 105(b), as amended by the 2010 Reconciliation Act).

> **Comment:** Although Code Sec. 106, regarding the exclusion for employer-provided coverage, was not amended along with Code Sec. 105(b), the IRS has historically applied the exclusion rules for employer-provided reimbursements and employer-provided coverage in tandem, and the IRS has indicated that it is doing so with the rule extending the tax benefit for children under age 27 (Notice 2010-38).

> **Comment:** Historically, it was necessary for the child to be the employee's dependent for this exclusion to apply. Now, if the child is age 26 or less at the end of the tax year, the exclusion applies even if the child provides more than one-half of his or her own support, earns more income than the exemption amount, does not live with the taxpayer, or any other restriction applies which would prevent the employee from claiming a dependency exemption for the child either under qualifying child or qualifying relative rules.

The exclusion applies only for reimbursements for medical care of individuals who are not age 27 or older at any time during the tax year. For these purposes, the tax year is the employee's tax year, and employers may assume that an employee's tax year is the calendar year. A child attains age 27 on the 27th anniversary of the date the child was born (for example, a child born on April 10, 1987, attained age 27 on April 10, 2014), and employers may rely on the employee's representation as to the child's date of birth (Notice 2010-38).

> **Comment:** In addition to the change in treatment of adult dependents for certain tax benefits, the Patient Protection and Affordable Care Act of 2010 (PPACA) (P.L. 111-148) requires group health plans that provide coverage for dependent children to continue such coverage until the dependent turns 26 years old. This requirement went into effect in 2010 and applies to grandfathered plans as well as nongrandfathered plans. For plan years starting before 2014, grandfathered plans can exclude a dependent if the dependent is eligible for another group plan. For a discussion of group health plan reforms including the change in treatment of dependents, see ¶540.

A child for purposes of this provision is defined by reference to Code Sec. 152(f)(1). Thus, a child includes:

- a son, daughter, stepson, or stepdaughter of the taxpayer;
- a foster child placed with the taxpayer by an authorized placement agency or by judgment, decree, or other order of any court of competent jurisdiction; and
- a legally adopted child of the taxpayer or a child who has been lawfully placed with the taxpayer for legal adoption.

¶220

LAW EXPLAINED

Employer benefits for the employee taxpayer's dependents are not subject to employment tax or to income tax withholding, and the IRS treats benefits for an employee's child under age 27 the same way. The IRS has provided that benefits for children under age 27 do not violate the rules governing flexible spending accounts (FSA), or health reimbursement accounts. It has stated that it intends to change FSA regulations to permit election changes for non-dependent children under the age of 27, but as yet it has not (Notice 2010-38).

Example 1: Alan's employer provides health insurance coverage for its employees and their spouses and dependents and for any employee's child (as defined in Code Sec. 152(f)(1)) who has not attained age 26. For the 2015 tax year, the employer provides coverage to Alan and to his son Charles. Charles will reach age 26 on November 15, 2015. During the 2015 tax year, Charles is not a full-time student, he has never worked for Alan's employer, and he is not Alan's dependent due to his age. However, Charles is Alan's child and he is under age 26 for at least part of the year, so he qualifies under the employer's plan. Because Charles does not attain age 27 during the 2015 tax year, which is the cut off for the exclusion, the employer's coverage is excludible for the period January 1, 2015, through November 15, 2015 (when Charles attains age 26 and loses coverage under the terms of the plan).

Example 2: Ellen's employer provides health care coverage for its employees and their spouses and dependents and for any employee's child who has not attained age 27 as of the end of the tax year. For the 2015 tax year, the employer provides health care coverage to Ellen and her daughter, Gail. Gail will not attain age 27 until after the end of the 2015 tax year. During the 2015 tax year, Gail earns $50,000 per year and she is not Ellen's dependent. Gail is not eligible for health care coverage from her own employer. Because Gail is Ellen's child and she will not attain age 27 during the 2015 tax year, she qualifies for coverage under Ellen's health plan and the coverage and reimbursements for Gail from Ellen's employer are excludible for the 2015 tax year.

Example 3: Same facts as Example 2, except that Gail's employer offers health care coverage, but she has decided not to participate in her employer's plan. Because Gail is Ellen's child and she will not attain age 27 during the 2015 tax year, the health care coverage and reimbursements for Gail are excludible from Ellen's gross income for the 2015 tax year.

¶220

LAW EXPLAINED

> **Example 4:** Same facts as Example 3, except that Gail is married to Harry. Neither Gail nor Harry is a dependent of Ellen. Gail and Harry have decided not to participate in the health care coverage offered by Gail's employer. Ellen's employer provides health care coverage for both Gail and Harry under Ellen's plan. Because Gail is Ellen's child, and Gail will not attain age 27 during the 2015 tax year, the health care coverage and reimbursements for Gail under the employer's plan are excludible from Ellen's gross income for 2015. The fair market value of the coverage for Harry is includible in Ellen's gross income for the 2015 tax year.

> **Compliance Tip:** Employer-provided coverage for children who have not attained age 27 is not subject to employment tax or income tax withholding (Notice 2010-38).

Self-employed health insurance deduction. The deduction for health insurance costs of a self-employed individual is extended to apply to any child of a taxpayer who is under the age of 27 at the end of the tax year regardless of whether or not such child is a dependent of the taxpayer (Code Sec. 162(l)(1), as amended by the 2010 Reconciliation Act). A child for this purpose is defined by reference to Code Sec. 152(f)(1). However, the self-employed taxpayer may not claim the deduction for the cost of health care insurance if the taxpayer is eligible to participate in any subsidized health plan maintained by any employer of a taxpayer's dependent or a child of the taxpayer who is under age 27 at the end of the tax year (Code Sec. 162(l)(2)(B), as amended by the 2010 Reconciliation Act).

> **Comment:** Formerly, a deduction was not allowed for the health care costs of a self-employed individual if he or she could participate in a health plan maintained by an employer (i.e., the self-employed individual has another job) or an employer of the self-employed individual's spouse. Since 2010, the deduction is also denied if the self-employed individual can participate in a subsidized plan maintained by an employer of a dependent or a child under the age of 27 at the end of the tax year.

Medical and other benefits for retired employees. A child under age 27 at the end of a calendar year is considered a dependent for purposes of the rule which allows a qualified pension or annuity plan to provide benefits for sickness, accident, hospitalization, and medical expenses to retired employees, their spouses, and their dependents if the benefits are subordinate to the retirement benefits and certain other conditions are met. A child for this purpose is also defined by reference to Code Sec. 152(f)(1) (see above) (Code Sec. 401(h), as amended by the 2010 Reconciliation Act).

Voluntary employees' beneficiary association (VEBA). A child under the age of 27 is considered a dependent of a VEBA member for purposes of the rule that treats a VEBA as a tax-exempt entity if it provides sick and accident benefits to its members and their dependents (Code Sec. 501(c)(9), as amended by the 2010 Reconciliation Act). A child for purposes of this law change is defined by reference to Code Sec. 152(f)(1). Thus, it is no longer necessary that the child actually satisfy the rules for claiming a dependency exemption.

¶220

LAW EXPLAINED

Comment: In addition to sickness and accident benefits, a VEBA may also provide life and other benefits to its members and dependents. Only benefits with respect to health care are affected by extension of coverage to children under age 27. Note that unlike the other provisions extending dependent treatment to children under age 27, the VEBA provision does not specifically provide that the child needs to be less than age 27 at the end of the tax year in the case of such benefits.

▶ **Effective date.** No effective is provided. The provision is therefore considered effective on March 30, 2010, the date of enactment of the Health Care and Education Reconciliation Act of 2010 (P.L. 111-152).

Law source: Law at ¶5050, ¶5100, ¶5170, and ¶5180.

— Act Sec.1004(d)(1) of the Health Care and Education Reconciliation Act of 2010 (P.L. 111-152), amending Code Sec. 105(b);

— Act Sec.1004(d)(2), amending Code Sec. 162(l)(1);

— Act Sec.1004(d)(3), amending Code Sec. 162(l)(2)(B);

— Act Sec.1004(d)(4), amending Code Sec. 501(c)(9);

— Act Sec. 1004(d)(5), amending Code Sec. 401(h).

Reporter references: For further information, consult the following reporters.

— Standard Federal Tax Reporter, ¶6702.027; ¶22,628.01; ¶18,105.01; ¶8522.03

— Tax Research Consultant, HEALTH:12,056.05; COMPEN: 54,052.10; RETIRE: 9,412; HEALTH: 9,112.05

— Practical Tax Explanation, § 42,155.20; § 42,215.10; § 42,220; § 42,310.05

¶220

Businesses

¶305 Employer Mandate to Provide Health Insurance

SUMMARY OF NEW LAW

Beginning in 2015, applicable large employers (generally, those averaging 50 or more full-time employees) are subject to the employer mandate. Under these rules, an employer that has any full-time employees that claim a health insurance premium tax credit or receive a cost-sharing reduction may be subject to a shared responsibility assessment by the IRS. If the employer does not offer minimum essential health coverage to at least 95 percent of its full-time employees and their dependents, the employer's assessed payment will be based on the total number of its full-time employees (minus 30). If it does offer such coverage, the assessed payment amount will be based solely on the number of full-time employees who claimed a premium tax credit whether because they were offered no coverage, or because the coverage offered to them was unaffordable or did not meet minimum value standards. Safe harbors are available both for counting full-time employees, and for affordable coverage. Transition rules apply for the 2015 plan year so that employers with fewer than 100 (instead of 50) full-time employees are not applicable large employers, the

SUMMARY

offer of coverage does not have to include dependents, and an employer is considered to have offered coverage if it offers it to 70 (instead of 95) percent of its full-time employees.

BACKGROUND

Most large employers and many small businesses provide health insurance coverage for their employees. The employer's cost in providing health care benefits is generally deductible as an ordinary and necessary business expense for compensation, though special rules may apply if the benefits are provided through a funded welfare benefit plan. Employees are allowed to exclude from gross income the value of the employer-provided health coverage under an accident or health plan as well as the value of any medical care received under such a plan.

Employer group health plans typically involve the purchase of medical insurance coverage by the employer, but some employers self-insure. Historically, self-insured plans have been subject to nondiscrimination rules so they would not unduly favor highly compensated employees.

LAW EXPLAINED

Applicable large employers are subject to the employer mandate.—Beginning in 2015, applicable large employers are subject to the shared responsibility rules, popularly known as the "employer mandate" or "pay or play." Under these rules, an applicable large employer may be subject to assessable shared responsibility payments if one or more of its full-time employees receive a health insurance premium tax credit or cost-sharing reduction when obtaining individual coverage on a health insurance marketplace exchange. The IRS will determine whether an employer is subject to shared responsibility payments based on individual tax returns, and information reported by applicable large employers and insurance providers for the particular period. The IRS will contact an affected employer, and the employer will have an opportunity to respond. For discussion of companion large employer reporting requirements, see ¶ 415, and for discussion of insurer/self-insured plan reporting requirements, see ¶ 410.

> **Comment:** Most states have not established their own exchanges, and the majority are being run by the federal government. This turn of events might have serious consequences for the premium tax credit, which is a trigger for the employer mandate. The premium tax credit is only available for individuals who obtain coverage through an exchange.

An applicable large employer is subject to a shared responsibility payment determined on a monthly basis if at least one of its full-time employees is certified to have received an applicable premium tax credit or cost-sharing reduction during the period, and either:

¶305

LAW EXPLAINED

(1) The employer does not offer the opportunity to enroll in minimum essential coverage to almost all (95 percent) of its full-time employees and their dependents (Code Sec. 4980H(a), as added by the Patient Protection and Affordable Care Act (PPACA) (P.L. 111-148)); or

(2) The employer does offer such coverage, but the offered coverage does not meet affordability or minimum value requirements for certain individual employees or is not offered to them at all (Code Sec. 4980H(b), as added by the Patient Protection and Affordable Care Act (PPACA) (P.L. 111-148)).

Comment: These are two distinct tax regimes and an employer is never liable under both regimes for the same period. Note that the second regime is capped so an employer will never pay more as a result of offering coverage.

Comment: Transition relief for 2015 postpones the requirement to offer dependent coverage until 2016 (Preamble, T.D. 9655, Pt. XV.D.5). As enacted, the employer mandate was scheduled to apply starting in 2014. However, the IRS pushed back the starting date for this mandate and its reporting requirements from January 1, 2014, to January 1, 2015 (Notice 2013-45).

Comment: Effective for plan years beginning in 2014, ACA imposes a wide range of employer health plan access requirements known as "market reforms" to the existing list of group health care portability requirements that are enforceable through a $100 a day per affected participant excise tax under Code Sec. 4980D. One of the side-effects of these reforms is that employers may no longer use simple health insurance premium reimbursment plans under which the employer picks up some or all of the cost of its employees' premiums for individual coverage (Notice 2013-54). Such plans are still permitted if they are stand-alone plans for retirees, plans that have fewer than two participants, after-tax payroll arrangements, or reimbursement plans for "excluded" benefits such as vision or dental care. FSAs used for non-excluded benefits must be integrated into an employer health plan offering minimum essential coverage.

An "applicable premium tax credit and cost-sharing reduction" for an employee that will trigger the mandate for large employers includes:

(1) any premium assistance tax credit allowed to a full-time employee (see ¶210);

(2) any cost-sharing reduction for individuals enrolled in qualified health plans (see ¶520); and

(3) any advance payment of the premium tax credit or cost-sharing reduction (see ¶525) (Code Sec. 4980H(c)(3), as added by PPACA, and redesignated by the 2010 Reconciliation Act).

For purposes of determining whether an applicable large employer offers coverage to its full-time employees, coverage offered to at least 95 percent of them suffices (Reg. § 54.4980H-4(a)). Under transition relief for 2015, 70 percent suffices (Preamble, T.D. 9655, Pt. XV.D.7).

Threshold issue: whether the employer is an "applicable large employer." The employer mandate only affects applicable large employers. An employer is an applicable large employer if it employed an average of at least 50 full-time employees on business days during the *preceding calendar year*.

¶305

LAW EXPLAINED

> **Comment:** Under transition relief, qualifying employers with between 50 and 99 full-time employers are excused from share responsibility payments for 2015. In the case of a noncalendar plan year, the relief extends throughout the 2015 plan year including the portion that falls in 2016 (T.D. 9655, Pt. XV.D.6).

The average number of full-time employees is calculated by taking the sum of the total number of full-time employees (including any seasonal workers) for each calendar month in the preceding calendar year, and the total number of full-time equivalents (FTEs) (including any seasonal workers) for each calendar month in the preceding calendar year, and dividing by 12. The result is rounded to the next lowest whole number. If the result is 50 or more, the employer is an applicable large employer for the current calendar year, unless the seasonal worker exception applies (Code Sec. 4980H(c)(2)(A), as added by PPACA, and redesignated by the 2010 Reconciliation Act; Reg. § 54.4980H-2(b)(1)).

> **Comment:** For 2015, the first year of the mandate, the preceding calendar year is 2014. Under transition relief for 2015, when counting full-time employees in 2014 the employer only needs to look at 6 months rather than the whole calendar year. Full-time means 30 hours per week. Note that converting full time positions to part time equivalents (e.g., making a 40 hour per week position in to two 20 hour per week positions) would not enable an employer to escape applicable large employer status (though it might reduce exposure to liability if the employer is an applicable large employer).

The employer is not an applicable large employer if the seasonal worker exception applies. This exception applies if:

- the employer's workforce exceeds 50 full-time employees for 120 or fewer days during the calendar year; and
- its employees in excess of 50 employed during the 120-day period are seasonal workers (Code Sec. 4980H(c)(2)(B)(i), as added by PPACA, and redesignated by the 2010 Reconciliation Act).

Four calendar months counts as 120 days, and the months or days do not have to be consecutive (Reg. § 54.4980H-2(b)(2)).

A seasonal worker is a worker who performs labor or services on a seasonal basis (as defined by the Department of Labor (DOL)), including workers covered by 29 C.F.R. § 500.20(s)(1), and retail workers employed exclusively during holiday seasons (Code Sec. 4980H(c)(2)(B)(ii), as added by PPACA, and redesignated by the 2010 Reconciliation Act). Under 29 C.F.R. § 500.20(s)(1), labor is performed on a seasonal basis if, ordinarily, the employment pertains to or is of the kind exclusively performed at certain seasons or periods of the year and which, from its nature, may not be continuous or carried on throughout the year. A worker who moves from one seasonal activity to another, while employed in agriculture or performing agricultural labor, is employed on a seasonal basis even though the employee may continue to be employed during a major portion of the year.

> **Caution:** Just because an employer relies on seasonal employees does not necessarily mean the employer can take advantage of the seasonal worker exception. The exception applies only for employers that exceed 50 full-time employees

LAW EXPLAINED

(*including* seasonal workers) for 120 or fewer days during the calendar year. So, for example, an agricultural employer that relies heavily on seasonal employees for longer periods (as many do) would not qualify for the exception if the employer's full-time employee head count (including seasonal workers) exceeds 50 for more than 120 days during the year. Note that these days do not have to be consecutive.

Aggregating employers. In determining the employer's size, all entities treated as a single employer under the aggregation rules of Code Sec. 414(b), (c), (m), or (o) are treated as one employer. These include controlled groups of corporations, partnerships and proprietorships under common control, and affiliated service groups. An employer for these purposes includes the employer's predecessors. If the employer was not in existence throughout the preceding calendar year, applicable large employer status in the current year is determined based on the average number of employees the employer reasonably expects to employ on business days in the current calendar year (Code Sec. 4980H(c)(2)(C), as added by PPACA, and redesignated by the 2010 Reconciliation Act; Reg. § 54.4980H-2(b)(3)).

Compliance Tip: Although related employers are aggregated for purposes of counting full-time employees to determine applicable large employer status, shared responsibility payments are assessed on an individual employer basis. For example, suppose for 2016 shared responsibility payments, Employer A has 40 full-time employees and related Employer B has 40 full-time employees. They both are considered applicable large employers (or in the technical language of the regulations, they comprise *one* applicable large employer of which each is a *member*). Suppose that Employer A offers all of its full-time employees qualifying coverage, and Employer B offers none of its full-time employees qualifying coverage. In that case, only Employer B would be subject to shared responsibility payments for failing to offer coverage to full-time employees and it would be assessed directly.

Transition rule for an employer's first year as an applicable large employer. An employer that become an applicable large employers for the first time has a grace period during which it can "fix" its coverage so that it complies with the shared responsibility requirements. For the first calendar year the employer is an applicable large employer, the employer has until April 1 to make the changes. If it fails to make adequate changes to avoid liability, there is no forgiveness for the first three months. This rule applies only during the first year that an employer is an applicable large employer, and would not apply if for example the employer falls below the 50 full-time employee threshold for a subsequent calendar year and then increases employment and becomes an applicable large employer again (Reg. § 54.4980H-2(b)(5)).

Full-time equivalents (FTEs). Solely for purposes of determining if it is an applicable large employer, an employer must also include, in addition to its full-time employees, the number of full-time equivalent employees determined by dividing the aggregate number of hours of service of employees who are not full-time employees for the month, by 120 (Code Sec. 4980H(c)(2)(E), as added and redesignated by the 2010 Reconciliation Act; Reg. § 54.4980H-2(c)).

LAW EXPLAINED

Example 1: For 2015 and 2016, ParentCo. owns 100 percent of all classes of stock of Sub1 and Sub2, and they are a controlled group of corporations. ParentCo has no employees at any time in 2015. For every calendar month in 2015, Sub1 has 40 full-time employees and Sub2 has 60 full-time employees. Because ParentCo, Sub1 and Sub2 have a combined total of 100 full-time employees during 2015, they are an applicable large employer and each is treated as an applicable large employer member for 2016.

Example 2: During each calendar month of 2015, the employer company has 20 full-time employees (each averages 35 hours of service per week), 40 part time employees (each averages 90 hours of service per month), and no seasonal workers. Each of the 20 employees who average 35 hours of service per week count as one full-time employee for each month. To determine the number of FTEs for each month, the total hours of service of the employees who are not full-time employees (but not more than 120 hours of service per employee) are aggregated and divided by 120. The result is that the employer has 30 FTEs for each month ($40 \times 90 = 3,600$, and $3,600 \div 120 = 30$). Because the company has 50 full-time employees (the sum of 20 full-time employees and 30 FTEs) during each month in 2015, and because the seasonal worker exception is not applicable, the company is an applicable large employer for 2016.

Example 3: During 2015, the employer 40 full-time employees for the entire calendar year, none of whom is a seasonal worker. In addition, the company has 80 seasonal full-time workers who work for the company from September through December, 2015. The company has no FTEs during 2015. Before applying the seasonal worker exception, the company has 40 full-time employees during each of eight calendar months of 2015, and 120 full-time employees during each of four calendar months of 2015, resulting in an average of 66.5 employees for the year (rounded down to 66 full-time employees). However, the company's workforce equaled or exceeded 50 full-time employees (counting seasonal workers) for no more than four calendar months (treated as the equivalent of 120 days) in calendar year 2015, and the number of full-time employees would be less than 50 during those months if seasonal workers were disregarded. Accordingly, because after application of the seasonal worker exception, the company is not considered to employ more than 50 full-time employees and it is not an applicable large employer for 2016.

Example 4: Same facts as in Example 3, except that the employer company has 20 FTEs in August, some of whom are seasonal workers. The seasonal worker exception does not apply if the number of an employer's full-time employees (including seasonal workers) and FTEs equals or exceeds 50 employees for

¶305

LAW EXPLAINED

more than 120 days during the calendar year. Because the employer has at least 50 full-time employees for a period greater than four calendar months (treated as the equivalent of 120 days) during 2015, the exception does not apply. The employer averaged 68 full-time employees in 2015: [(40 × 7) + (60 × 1) + (120 × 4)] ÷ 12 = 68.33, rounded down to 68, and accordingly, the employer is an applicable large employer for calendar year 2016.

Example 5: The employer is incorporated on January 1, 2016. On January 1, 2016, it has three employees. However, prior to incorporation, its owners purchased a factory intended to open within two months of incorporation and to employ approximately 100 employees. By March 15, 2016, the employer has more than 75 full-time employees. Because the employer can reasonably be expected to employ on average at least 50 full-time employees on business days during 2016, and actually employs an average of at least 50 full-time employees on business days during 2016, the employer is an applicable large employer (Reg. §54.4980H-2(d), Examples 1-5).

Comment: The full-time employee count is reduced by 30 when calculating the tax (80 under 2015 transition relief), but no such reduction is used when counting full-time employees for purposes of determining applicable large employer status.

Payments for employers that do not offer coverage to nearly all full-time employees. The shared responsibility payment for an employer that fails to offer qualifying coverage to at least 95 percent (70 percent in 2015) of its full-time employees is equal to the product of the applicable payment amount, which is $\frac{1}{12}$ of $2,000 for any month (i.e., $166.67 per month), and the number of full-time employees for the month (Code Sec. 4980H(c)(1), as added by PPACA, and amended and redesignated by the Health Care and Education Reconciliation Act of 2010 (P.L. 111-152)). After 2014, the $2,000 amount is adjusted for inflation. In computing the payment, the number of the employer's full-time employees for any month is reduced by 30 (Code Sec. 4980H(c)(2)(D)(i)(I), as added and amended by PPACA, and amended and redesignated by the 2010 Reconciliation Act; Reg. §54.4980H-4(a)). For 2015, the reduction is 80 instead of 30 for employers that qualify to use the 100 full-time employee transition threshold (T.D. 9655, Pt. XV.D.7.b).

Partial calendar month. If an employer fails to offer coverage to a full-time employee for any day of a calendar month, that employee is treated as not being offered coverage during that entire month. However, in a calendar month in which the employment of a full-time employee terminates, if the employee would have been offered coverage for the entire month had the employee been employed for the entire month, the employee is treated as having been offered coverage for that entire month (Reg. §54.4980H-4(c)). Under transition relief for January 2015, if an employer offers coverage to a full-time employee no later than the first day of the first payroll period

LAW EXPLAINED

that begins in January 2015, the employee will be treated as having been offered coverage for January 2015 (Preamble, T.D. 9655, Pt. XV.D.4).

Example 6: Assume the inflation adjusted applicable payment amount of $2,000 remains $2,000 for 2016. In 2016, Gama Corp. fails to offer minimum essential coverage and has 90 full-time employees, 10 of whom receive a premium tax credit for the year for enrolling in a state exchange offered plan. For 60 of its full-time employees (90 full-time employees, less 30), Gama owes $2,000 per employee, for a total assessable payment of $120,000 ($2,000 x 60 full-time employees), which is assessed on a monthly basis.

For employers aggregated into a single applicable large employer for purposes of determining applicable large employer status, only one 30-employee reduction is allowed for all members of the applicable large employer. The reduction is allocated among these applicable large employer members ratably based on the number of full-time employees employed by each (Code Sec. 4980H(c)(2)(D)(ii), as added and amended by PPACA, and amended and redesignated by the 2010 Reconciliation Act).

Example 7: Employers A and B are the two members of an applicable large employer. Employer A employs 40 full-time employees in each calendar month of 2017. Employer B employs 35 full-time employees in each calendar month of 2017. Assuming the inflation adjusted applicable payment amount for a calendar month is $2,000 for 2017, the applicable payment amount for a calendar month is $2,000 divided by 12. Employer A does not sponsor an eligible employer-sponsored plan for any calendar month of 2017, and receives a Section 1411 Certification for 2017 with respect to at least one of its full-time employees. Employer B sponsors an eligible employer-sponsored plan under which all of its full-time employees are eligible for minimum essential coverage. Employer A is subject to a shared responsibility payment for 2017 of $48,000, which is equal to 24 × $2,000 (40 full-time employees reduced by 16 (its allocable share of the 30-employee offset ((40/75) × 30 = 16)) and then multiplied by $2,000). Employer B is not subject to a shared responsibility payment for 2017 (Reg. § 54.4980H-4(g)).

For purposes of these rules, an eligible employer-sponsored plan is defined the same as for the individual requirement to maintain minimum essential health coverage. It includes a group health plan or group health insurance coverage offered by an employer that is a governmental plan, or any other plan or coverage offered in the small or large group market within a state. For further discussion of an eligible employer-sponsored plan and minimum essential coverage, see ¶ 205.

Payments for employers that offer coverage to nearly all full-time employees but fail to meet affordability or minimum value standards for some. An assessable payment is imposed on an applicable large employer that:

¶305

LAW EXPLAINED

- does offer 95 percent (70 percent in 2015) of its full-time employees and their dependents the opportunity to enroll in minimum essential coverage under a Code Sec. 5000A(f)(2) eligible employer-sponsored plan for any month, but
- has one or more full-time employees who have been certified for that month in a qualified health plan offered through a government exchange with respect to which an applicable premium tax credit or cost-sharing reduction is allowed or paid for the employee (Code Sec. 4980H(b)(1), as added by PPACA, and amended and redesignated by the 2010 Reconciliation Act).

> **Comment:** A lower or middle income employee may obtain subsidized coverage on a government health insurance exchange only if the employer does not offer coverage to that employee (the employee may be among the 5 percent not offered coverage), or the coverage offered fails to meet affordability or minimum value standards for that particular employee. Affordability is based on household income, information which of course employers lack. To help the situation, IRS regulations provide three affordability safe harbors based on W-2 reporting, rates of pay, and the federal poverty line data. Under any of these safe harbors, the employer is not treated as failing to offer affordable coverage for purposes of calculating the assessable payment even if the employee in fact qualifies for a premium tax credit due to unaffordability (Reg. § 54.4980H-5(e)). What constitutes minimum value has been fleshed out for purposes of the premium tax credit (see ¶210).

The assessable payment in this case is equal to the product of the number of the full-time employees receiving a premium tax credit or cost-sharing subsidy for the purchase of health insurance through a state exchange for the month and an amount equal to $1/12$ of $3,000 for any month (i.e., $250 per month). After 2014, the $3,000 amount will be adjusted for inflation. The number of employees counted for this purpose is reduced by the number of those employees who: (a) are new full-time employees during their first three months of employment; (b) are new variable hour or new seasonal employees during the months of that employee's initial measurement period (and associated administrative period); or (c) were offered the opportunity to enroll in minimum essential coverage under an eligible employer-sponsored plan that satisfied minimum value and met one or more of the affordability safe harbors (Reg. § 54.4980H-5(a)).

An employer does not offer coverage if the employee does not have an effective opportunity to elect to enroll (or decline to enroll) at least once during the plan year (Reg. § § 54.4980H-4(b), 54.4980H-5(b)).

Liability is capped at what the employer would pay under the first tax regime for not offering coverage to at least 95 percent of its full-time employees so that no employer is worse off for offering coverage. Accordingly, the aggregate amount of the assessable payment with respect to all certified employees for any month is limited to the product of the applicable payment amount ($1/12$ of $2,000 per month) and the number of all full-time employees during that month (Code Sec. 4980H(b)(2), as added by PPACA, and redesignated by the 2010 Reconciliation Act). After 2014, the $2,000 amount will be adjusted for inflation. For purposes of this calculation, the number of

¶305

LAW EXPLAINED

full-time employees for any month is reduced by 30 (Code Sec. 4980H(c)(2)(D)(i)(II), as added and amended by PPACA, and amended and redesignated by the 2010 Reconciliation Act).

> **Comment:** The cap is determined in the same way as the assessable payment imposed for a failure to provide health coverage (see above).

Example 8: In 2016, Omega Corp. offers health coverage and has 100 full-time employees, 10 of whom receive a tax credit for the year for enrolling in a state exchange offered plan. For each employee receiving a tax credit, Omega owes $3,000 (assuming no inflation adjustment for 2016) per employee, for a total assessable payment of $30,000 ($3,000 x 10 employees). The maximum amount of the assessable payment for Omega is capped at the amount of the assessable payment that it would have been assessed for a failure to provide coverage, or $140,000 ($2,000 x 70 full-time employees (100 full-time employees, less 30)). Since the calculated assessable payment ($30,000) is less than the overall limitation ($140,000), Omega owes the $30,000 assessable payment, which is assessed on a monthly basis.

In the case in which certain persons under common control are treated as a single employer for purposes of determining if the employer is an applicable large employer, only one 30-employee reduction is allowed for all such persons in calculating the overall limitation on the assessable payment. The reduction is allocated among these persons ratably based on the number of full-time employees employed by each person (Code Sec. 4980H(c)(2)(D)(ii), as added and amended by PPACA, and amended and redesignated by the 2010 Reconciliation Act).

> **Comment:** A Medicaid-eligible individual can always choose to leave the employer's coverage and enroll in Medicaid, and an employer will not be subject to an assessable payment for any employees enrolled in Medicaid (Joint Committee on Taxation, *Technical Explanation of the Revenue Provisions of the "Reconciliation Act of 2010," as amended, in combination with the "Patient Protection and Affordable Care Act"* (JCX-18-10)).

Safe harbors for counting full-time employees. Regulations provide two optional methods for determining full-time employee status: the monthly measurement method, and the look-back measurement method. The monthly measurement method can be used for determining applicable large employer status, as well as for determining and calculating liability. The look-back measurement method applies solely for determining and calculating liability and not for purposes of determining status as an applicable large employer. These methods provide minimum standards for the identification of full-time employees. Employers may always treat additional employees as eligible for coverage, subject to compliance with any nondiscrimination or other applicable requirements.

Monthly measurement method. An applicable large employer can determine each employee's status as a full-time employee by counting the employee's hours of service for each calendar month (Reg. §§54.4980H-1(a)(21), 54.4980H-3(c)(1)). If an

LAW EXPLAINED

employer is using the monthly method, and one of its employees becomes otherwise eligible for coverage for the first time in a calendar month, the employer has up to three calendar months before it has to offer coverage. This rule cannot apply more than once per period of employment of an employee. However, if an employee terminates employment and returns under circumstances that would constitute a rehire, this rule may apply again (Reg. § 54.4980H-3(c)(2)).

Look-back method. The look-back safe harbor is based on the average hours of service during a look-back period (called a "standard measurement period") of three to twelve months as chosen by the employer to determine full-time status. That status is then locked in for a subsequent "stability period" lasting at least six months and is no shorter than the standard measurement period. A 90-day administrative period can be inserted between the standard measurement period and the stability period to give the employer time to re-determine employee status and make changes in coverage (Reg. § 54.4980H-3(d)). For purposes of applying the safe harbor rules, there are three kinds of employees:

- Ongoing employees who have been employed for at least one full standard measurement period, and whose status for a corresponding stability period is determined by the average hours of service per week during the standard measurement period;

- New employees reasonably expected to work full-time (and who is not a seasonal employees), who are treated as full time (and must be offered coverage within 90 days) until they have completed a standard measurement period, at which point they become ongoing employees subject to the ongoing employee rules; and

- New seasonal, variable hour, or part-time employees who can be treated as part-time until they complete an "initial measurement period" of between 3 and 12 months (starting at the hire date), at which point their status is determined for a corresponding stability period. Upon completion of a standard measurement period, the employee transitions to the ongoing employee rules.

The IRS has issued guidance on which employers may rely regarding approaches to handling measurement period changes for an employee because of a transfer to another position within the same employer, or a change of the employer's measurement methods. Under this guidance, an employee who transfers mid-stability or administrative period retains the status from the first position until the end of the period. If the transfer occurs outside of a stability period, the employee's status is determined by the look-back method of the second position (taking into account the hours in the first position). It there is a change in the employer's method, the affected employee is treated as if the employee transferred to a different position (Notice 2014-49).

Disallowance of deduction, administration and procedure. An employer may not deduct the assessable payment imposed under these rules (Code Sec. 4980H(c)(7), as added by PPACA, and redesignated by the 2010 Reconciliation Act; Code Sec. 275(a)(6)).

¶305

LAW EXPLAINED

> **Comment:** Code Sec. 275(a)(6) generally denies a deduction for certain excise taxes imposed under a number of chapters of the Code, including chapter 43 (Qualified Pension, etc., Plans) where the employer mandate IRC section, Code Sec. 4980H, was added.

An employer must pay the assessable payment upon notice and demand by the Secretary of the Treasury. The payment is assessed and collected in the same manner as an assessable penalty under subchapter B of chapter 68 of the Internal Revenue Code (Code Secs. 6671-6725) (Code Sec. 4980H(d)(1), as added by PPACA, and redesignated by the 2010 Reconciliation Act).

> **Comment:** The Joint Committee on Taxation indicates that the restrictions on assessment under Code Sec. 6213 do not apply to the assessable payment imposed under Code Sec. 4980H (Joint Committee on Taxation, *Technical Explanation of the Revenue Provisions of the "Reconciliation Act of 2010," as amended, in combination with the "Patient Protection and Affordable Care Act"* (JCX-18-10)).

Effective date. The provision as written applies to months beginning after December 31, 2013 (Act Secs. 1513(d), 10106(f)(3) and 10108(i)(1)(B) of the Patient Protection and Affordable Care Act (PPACA) (P.L. 111-148)). However, transition relief has postponed the application date for a full year, so it applies to months beginning after December 31, 2014 (Notice 2013-45). No specific effective date is provided by the Health Care and Education Reconciliation Act of 2010 (P.L. 111-152). The amendments made by the 2010 Reconciliation Act are, therefore, considered effective on March 30, 2010, the date of enactment. Employers may rely on the proposed regulations for guidance pending the issuance of final regulations or other guidance. Final regulations will be effective as of a date not earlier than the date they are published in the Federal Register. If and to the extent future guidance is more restrictive than the guidance in the proposed regulations, the future guidance will be applied without retroactive effect and employers will be given sufficient time to come into compliance with the final regulations.

Law source: Law at ¶ 5320.

— Act Secs. 1513(a), 10106(e), (f)(1) and (2), and 10108(i)(1)(A) of the Patient Protection and Affordable Care Act (PPACA) (P.L. 111-148), adding and amending Code Sec. 4980H;

— Act Secs. 1513(d), 10106(f)(3) and 10108(i)(1)(B), providing the effective date;

— Act Sec. 1003 of the Health Care and Education Reconciliation Act of 2010 (P.L. 111-152), amending Code Sec. 4980H.

Reporter references: For further information, consult the following reporters.

— Standard Federal Tax Reporter, ¶ 34,612.01

— Tax Research Consultant, HEALTH: 6,050

— Practical Tax Explanation, § 42,101

¶305

¶310 Small Employer Health Insurance Credit

SUMMARY OF NEW LAW

An eligible small employer may claim a 50-percent tax credit (35 percent in the case of a tax-exempt eligible small employer) for premiums it pays toward health insurance coverage for its employees in tax years beginning after 2013. In tax years beginning in 2010 through 2013 the credit rate was 35 percent (25 percent for tax-exempt employers). An eligible small employer is an employer that has no more than 25 full-time employees and the average annual compensation of these employees is not greater than $50,000. The credit is reduced by 6.667 percent for each full-time employee in excess of 10 employees and by 4 percent for each $1,000 that average annual compensation paid to the employees exceeds $25,000.

BACKGROUND

Employers may generally deduct, as an ordinary and necessary business expense, the cost of providing health coverage for employees (Code Sec. 162). The value of employer-provided health insurance is not subject to employer paid Federal Insurance Contributions Act (FICA) tax. Employees may exclude from gross income the value of employer-provided coverage under an accident or health plan (Code Sec. 106). An exclusion from gross income also applies to the value of medical care provided under an accident or health plan to the employee and the employee's spouse and dependents (Code Sec. 105(b)). Employees who participate in a cafeteria plan are able to pay premiums on a pre-tax basis through salary reduction (Code Sec. 125).

LAW EXPLAINED

Credit for employee health insurance expenses of eligible small employers.—An eligible small employer may claim a tax credit for premiums it pays toward health coverage for its employees. In tax years beginning in 2014 and later, the credit is equal to 50 percent of premiums paid, although the credit is decreased to 35 percent in the case of a tax-exempt employer (Code Sec. 45R, as added by the Patient Protection and Affordable Care Act (PPACA) (P.L. 111-148)). For tax years beginning in 2010 through 2013, the small employer health insurance credit rate is equal to 35 percent (25 percent for tax-exempt employers) (Code Sec. 45R(b), as added by PPACA).

> **Compliance Note:** The credit is computed on Form 8941, Credit for Small Employer Health Insurance Premium.

As explained below, the credit is phased out based on the number of employees the employer has and the wages paid.

Only premiums paid by the employer for health insurance coverage are included in calculating the credit. If an employer pays only a portion of the premiums for the coverage provided to employees (with employees paying the rest), only the portion paid by the employer is taken into account. Any premium paid pursuant to a salary

LAW EXPLAINED

reduction arrangement under a cafeteria plan is not treated as paid by the employer (Section II F of Notice 2010-44). The final and proposed regulations further provide that amounts made available by an employer under or contributed by an employer to HRAs, FSAs and HSAs are not taken into account for purposes of determining premium payments by the employer (Reg. § 1.45R-3(g); Proposed Reg. § 1.45R-3(g), prior to removal by T.D. 9672).).

> **Comment:** The IRS provided guidance regarding the small employer health insurance credit in Notice 2010-44, as amplified by Notice 2010-82. The guidance provided in these notices apply to tax years beginning before 2014. For tax years beginning after 2013 and before 2015, taxpayers may rely on either proposed or final regulations (Notice of Proposed Rulemaking REG-113792-13; T.D. 9672). Thereafter, final regulations will apply. The proposed and final regulations generally follow the guidance contained in the two notices.

Credit amount for tax years beginning after 2013. For a tax year beginning after 2013, the eligible small employer may claim a health insurance credit during the credit period (Code Sec. 45R(a), as added by PPACA). The credit period is the two-consecutive-tax-year period beginning with the first tax year in which the employer or any predecessor offers one or more qualified health plans to its employees through a state-sponsored market exchange (Code Sec. 45R(e)(2), as added by PPACA; Reg. § 1.45R-1(a)(3); Proposed Reg. § 1.45R-1(a)(3), prior to removal by T.D. 9672). No credit period is treated as beginning with a tax year beginning before 2014 (Code Sec. 45R(g)(1), as added by PPACA).

To prevent avoidance of the two-year limit on the credit period, successor entities are treated as the same employer (Reg. § 1.45R-3(f); Proposed Reg. § 1.45R-3(f), prior to removal by T.D. 9672).

> **Comment:** The health insurance credit may only be claimed for two additional tax years in tax years that begin after 2013 (e.g., for 2014 and 2015 in the case of a calendar-year eligible small employer) and only if the eligible small employer offers one or more qualified health plans through an exchange during those years.

> **Comment:** By January 1, 2014, each state (or the federal government if the state fails to act) is required to establish a Small Business Health Options Program (SHOP) exchange to provide qualified individuals and qualified small business employers access to qualified health plans. See ¶ 505. The federally facilitated SHOP exchanges have been delayed for a year, but the Centers for Medicare and Medicaid Services (CMS) have provided a method of direct enrollment that will allow employers to enroll without going through a SHOP and qualify for the credit. See ¶ 512. Note that employers in a state maintaining its own exchange must follow the enrollment rules in that state to qualify for the credit.

> When a plan year does not begin on the first day of the employer's tax year, it may not be practical or possible for the employer to offer insurance to its employees through an exchange at the beginning of its first tax year beginning in 2014. Under a transitional rule, such an employer may begin offering coverage through an exchange as of the first day of its plan year that begins in 2014 (Reg. § 1.45R-3(i); Proposed Reg. § 1.45R-3(i), prior to removal by T.D. 9672).

LAW EXPLAINED

The credit amount for a tax year beginning after 2013 is equal to 50 percent of the lesser of:

(1) the total amount of non-elective contributions the employer makes on behalf of its employees during the tax year under a contribution arrangement for premiums for qualified health plans offered to its employees through an exchange, or

(2) the total amount of non-elective contributions that would have been made during the tax year if each employee taken into account in item (1) had enrolled in a qualified health plan that had a premium equal to the average premium for the small group market in the rating area in which the employee enrolls for coverage (Code Sec. 45R(b), as added by PPACA; Reg. §1.45R-3(a) and (b); Proposed Reg. §1.45R-3(a) and (b), prior to removal by T.D. 9672).

> **Comment:** The calculation of the credit for post-2013 tax years is identical to the calculation for pre-2014 tax years except that the credit rate increases from 35 percent to 50 percent and health insurance coverage of employees must be obtained under a qualified health plan offered by an employer through an exchange. In addition, the average premium limitation is based on the small group market in the rating area in which the employee enrolls for coverage rather than in the State in which the employer is offering the coverage.

The IRS has issued transition relief allowing certain small employers that cannot offer qualified health plans through a SHOP exchange because the employer's principal business address is in a county in which a qualified health plan through a SHOP exchange will not be available for the 2014 year. This relief applies to employers in listed counties in Wisconsin and Washington. Under the relief, employers will qualify for the credit if they would have qualified under the rules in effect in 2013 (Notice 2014-6).

> **Comment:** The average premium for the small group market can be found in the Instructions to Form 8941. If an employer has employees in multiple states, the employer applies the average premium for the small group market in the state (or area within the state) separately for each employee using the average state premium for the state in which the employee works (Section 4 A of Notice 2010-82).

Credit amount for tax years beginning in 2010 through 2013. In tax years beginning in 2010 through 2013, the amount of the credit for employee health insurance expenses of an eligible small employer is equal to 35 percent of the lesser of (Code Sec. 45R(g), as added by PPACA):

(1) the total amount of non-elective contributions the employer makes on behalf of its employees during the tax year under a contribution arrangement for the payment of premiums for qualified health insurance coverage of its employees; or

(2) the total amount of non-elective contributions that would have been made during the tax year if each employee taken into account in item (1) had enrolled in a plan that had a premium equal to the amount that the average premium for

¶310

LAW EXPLAINED

the small group market in the state (or the area within the state) in which the employer is offering health insurance coverage.

Special rules for tax years beginning in 2010 through 2013. An employer's premium payments are only taken into account if used to pay for health insurance coverage under a qualifying arrangement (Section II G of Notice 2010-44). Health insurance coverage is benefits for medical care (provided directly, through insurance or reimbursement, or otherwise) under any hospital or medical service policy or certificate, hospital or medical service plan contract, or health maintenance organization contract offered by a health insurance issuer. Health insurance coverage also includes:

(1) limited scope dental or vision, long-term care, nursing home care, home health care, community-based care, or any combination thereof;

(2) coverage only for a specified disease or illness;

(3) hospital indemnity or other fixed indemnity insurance; and

(4) Medicare supplemental health insurance, and certain other supplemental coverage, and similar supplemental coverage provided to coverage under a group health plan (Section II G of Notice 2010-44).

Health insurance coverage does not include:

(1) coverage only for accident, or disability income insurance, or any combination thereof;

(2) coverage issued as a supplement to liability insurance;

(3) liability insurance, including general liability insurance and automobile liability insurance;

(4) worker's compensation or similar insurance;

(5) automobile medical payment insurance;

(6) credit-only insurance;

(7) coverage for on-site medical clinics; and

(8) other similar insurance coverage, specified in regulations, under which benefits for medical care are secondary or incidental to other insurance benefits (Section II G of Notice 2010-44).

The coverage must be offered through a health insurer; thus, self-insured plans do not qualify. Because health reimbursement arrangements (HRA) and health flexible spending arrangements (FSA) are self-insured, they also do not qualify. Health savings accounts (HSA) are not insurance coverage and do not qualify (Section III D of Notice 2010-82).

A qualifying arrangement is an arrangement under which an employer pays premiums for each employee enrolled in health insurance coverage offered by the employer in an amount equal to a uniform percentage (but not less than 50 percent) of the premium cost of the coverage (the uniformity requirement) (Section II A of Notice 2010-82).

¶310

LAW EXPLAINED

Different types of health insurance plans are not aggregated for the qualifying arrangement requirement. Thus, if an employer offers a major medical insurance plan and a stand-alone vision plan, the employer must separately satisfy the requirements for a qualifying arrangement with respect to each type of coverage (Section II G of Notice 2010-44).

Example 1: In a year before 2014, ABC Co., an eligible small employer, offered a health insurance plan with single and family coverage. ABC has 9 full-time equivalent employees with average annual wages of $23,000. Four employees are enrolled in single coverage and five are enrolled in family coverage. The employer paid 50 percent of the premiums for all employees enrolled in single coverage and 50 percent of the premiums for all employees enrolled in family coverage. In both cases, the employees paid the remaining 50 percent. The premiums are $4,000 a year for single coverage and $10,000 a year for family coverage. The average premium for the small group market in ABC's state is $5,000 for single coverage and $12,000 for family coverage.

ABC's premium payments for each full-time equivalent employee ($2,000 for single coverage and $5,000 for family coverage) do not exceed 50 percent of the average premium for the small group market in ABC's state ($2,500 for single coverage and $6,000 for family coverage). The amount of premiums paid by ABC that can be used to compute the credit is $33,000 ((4 × $2,000) plus (5 × $5,000)).

If the premiums paid by ABC are $6,000 for single coverage and $14,000 for family coverage, ABC's premium payments for each employee ($3,000 for single coverage and $7,000 for family coverage) exceed 50 percent of the average premium for the small group market in ABC's state ($2,500 for single coverage and $6,000 for family coverage), and ABC must use the lesser amount to compute the credit. Thus, the amount of premiums paid by ABC that can be used to compute the credit is $40,000 ((4 × $2,500) plus (5 × $6,000)).

Uniformity requirement after 2013. For tax years beginning after 2013, the employer must make non-elective contributions on behalf of each employee who enrolls in a qualified health plan offered to employees by the employer through an exchange in an amount equal to a uniform percentage (not less than 50 percent) of the premium cost of the qualified health plan (Code Sec. 45R(d), as added by PPACA; Reg. § 1.45R-4; Proposed Reg. § 1.45R-4, prior to removal by T.D. 9672). The rules for meeting the uniformity requirement depend upon whether the employer has one or more than one qualified health plan, has one or more tiers of coverage, and uses list or composite billing (Reg. § 1.45R-4(b) and (c), prior to removal by T.D. 9672).

The final regulations provide that a tobacco surcharge and amounts paid by the employer to cover the surcharge are not included in premiums for purposes of calculating the uniform percentage requirement, nor are payments of the surcharge treated as premium payments for purposes of the credit. The uniform percentage requirement is

¶310

LAW EXPLAINED

also applied without regard to employee payment of the tobacco surcharges in cases in which all or part of the employee tobacco surcharges are not paid by the employer (Reg. § 1.45R-4(d)(i)).

Any additional amount of an employer contribution attributable to an employee's participation in a wellness program over the employer contribution with respect to an employee that does not participate in the wellness program is not taken into account in calculating the uniform percentage requirement, whether the difference is due to a discount for participation or a surcharge for nonparticipation. The employer contributions for employees that do not participate in the wellness program must be at least 50 percent of the premium (including any premium surcharge for nonparticipation). However, for purposes of computing the credit, the employer contributions are taken into account, including those contributions attributable to an employee's participation in a wellness program (Reg. § 1.45R-4(d)(ii)).

Foreign employers. For tax years beginning after 2013, an employer located outside the United States must have income effectively connected with the conduct of a trade or business in the United States, and otherwise meet all requirements to be an eligible small employer, including offering a qualified health plan through an exchange (Reg. § 1.45R-2(a); Proposed Reg. § 1.45R-2(a), prior to removal by T.D. 9672).

For tax years 2010 - 2013, an eligible small employer located outside the United States that has income effectively connected with a U.S. trade or business can claim the small employer health insurance credit, but only if it pays premiums for an employee's health insurance coverage that is issued in and regulated by one of the 50 states or the District of Columbia. Similarly, a tax-exempt eligible small employer located outside the United States is also required to pay premiums for an employee's health insurance coverage that is issued in and regulated by one of the 50 states of the District of Columbia to obtain the refundable credit (Section II C of Notice 2010-82).

Effect of state tax credit or premium subsidy. If an employer is entitled to a state tax credit (refundable or non-refundable) or a premium subsidy that is paid directly to an employer, the premium payment made by an employer is not reduced by the credit or subsidy for purposes of determining whether an employer has satisfied the uniformity requirement. The maximum amount of the credit is not reduced by any state credit (refundable or non-refundable) or by payments made by a state directly to an employer. The amount of the credit may not exceed the amount of an employer's net premium payment. The net premium payment is equal to the employer's actual premium payments minus the state tax credit or subsidy. In the case of a state payment directly to an insurance company (or another entity licensed under state law to engage in the business of insurance), the employer's net premium payments are the employer's actual premium payments. If a state-administered program (such as Medicaid) makes payments that are not contingent on the maintenance of an employer-provided group health plan, those payments are not taken into account in determining the credit (Reg. § 1.45R-3(d); Proposed Reg. § 1.45R-3(d), prior to removal by T.D. 9672; Section III D of Notice 2010-44).

¶310

LAW EXPLAINED

Example 2: ABC Co.'s state provides a health insurance premium subsidy of up to 40 percent of the health insurance premiums for each eligible employee. The state pays the subsidy directly to the employer. ABC has one employee, Sam. Sam's health insurance premiums are $100 per month and are paid as follows: $80 by the employer and $20 by Sam through salary reductions to a cafeteria plan. The state pays ABC $40 per month as a subsidy for Sam's insurance premiums paid by ABC. ABC otherwise meets the requirements for the credit. For purposes of the qualifying arrangement rules and for calculating the amount of the credit, the state subsidy is disregarded, and ABC is treated as paying $80 per month.

Credit phaseout. The amount of the small employer health insurance credit is reduced (but not below zero) by the sum of:

(1) the product of the credit amount and the number of the employer's full-time equivalent employees for the tax year in excess of 10, divided by 15; and

(2) the product of the credit amount and the employer's average annual full-time employee wages in excess of the applicable dollar amount for the tax year ($25,400 for tax years beginning in 2014 and $25,000 for tax years beginning in 2010 - 2013), divided by the applicable dollar amount (Code Sec. 45R(c), as added by PPACA; Reg. § 1.45R-3(c); Proposed Reg. § 1.45R-3(c), prior to removal by T.D. 9672).

The reduction of the credit amount required by item (1), above, for having more than 10 full-time equivalent employees is in effect equal to 6.667 percent for each qualified employee in excess of 10. If an employer has 25 or more full-time employees, the credit is reduced to zero (6.667 percent times 15 employees (the number in excess of 10) equals a 100 percent reduction). The credit may not be claimed even if the average annual wages for the year do not exceed the $25,400 applicable dollar amount.

The credit reduction for having average annual wages in excess of the $25,400 applicable dollar amount for 2014 is equal to 3.937% for each $1,000 of wages in excess of $25,400 and the credit amounts is reduced to zero if average annual wages are $50,800 or greater (3.937% × 25.4 equals a 100 percent reduction).

The reduction of the credit amount required for item (2), above, for having average annual wages in excess of the $25,000 applicable dollar amount is, in effect, equal to 4 percent for each $1,000 of wages in excess of $25,000. Thus, if average annual wages are $50,000 or greater, the credit amount is reduced to zero (4 percent × 25 equals a 100 percent reduction) even if the employer has fewer than 25 full-time employees.

Example 3: In 2014, Small Manufacturing Corp. has 12 full-time equivalent employees and average annual wages of $30,400. The employer paid $96,000 in health insurance premiums for its employees (which does not exceed the average premium for the small group market in the employer's state) and otherwise meets the requirements for the credit. The initial credit, before any reduction, is $48,000 (50 percent of $96,000). The credit is reduced by $6,400 for

LAW EXPLAINED

full-time equivalent employees in excess of 10 ($48,000 × 2/15). The credit is also reduced for average annual wages in excess of $25,400 by $9,449 ($48,000 × $5,000/$25,400). The total reduction is $15,889 ($6,440 plus $9,449). After reductions, the credit amount equals $32,111 ($48,000 minus $15,889).

Example 4: In 2014, a tax-exempt organization had 12 full-time equivalent employees and average annual wages of $30,400. The employer paid $96,000 in health insurance premiums for its employees (which does not exceed the average premium for the small group market in the employer's state) and otherwise meets the requirements for the credit. The total amount of the employer's withholding and Medicare taxes equalled $30,000. The initial credit, before any reduction, is $33,600 (35 percent of $96,000). The credit is reduced by $4,480 for full-time equivalent employees in excess of 10 ($33,600 × 2/15). The credit is also reduced for average annual wages in excess of $25,400 by $4,880 ($24,400 × $5,000/$25,400). The total reduction is $9,360 ($4,880 plus $4,480). After reductions, the credit amount equals $24,240 ($33,600 minus $9,360), which is the lesser of $24,240 and $30,000.

Eligible small employer. An employer determines its status as an eligible small employer each tax year. An employer is an eligible small employer if the following conditions are satisfied during the tax year:

(1) it has 25 or fewer full-time equivalent employees,

(2) the average annual wages of these employees is not greater than twice the applicable dollar amount for the tax year, and

(3) the employer has a qualified health care arrangement in effect (Code Sec. 45R(d)(1), as added by PPACA; Reg. § 1.45R-2(a); Proposed Reg. § 1.45R-2(a), prior to removal by T.D. 9672).

The applicable dollar amount is $25,400 for tax years beginning in 2014 (Rev. Proc. 2013-35) and $25,000 for tax years beginning in 2010, 2011, 2012, and 2013. In each tax year beginning in a calendar year after 2013, the applicable dollar amount is adjusted for inflation (Code Sec. 45R(d)(3)(B), as added by PPACA; Reg. § 1.45R-3(c)(2); Proposed Reg. § 1.45R-3(c)(2), prior to removal by T.D. 9672).

Certain persons treated as single employer. All persons treated as a single employer under Code Sec. 414(b), (c), (m), or (o) are treated as one employer (Code Sec. 45R(e)(5)(A), as added by PPACA). In general, this includes employers who are corporations in a controlled group, employers who are members of an affiliated service group, employers who are partnerships, proprietorships, etc., under common control, and tax-exempt employers under common control (Reg. § 1.45R-2(c); Proposed Reg. § 1.45R-2(c), prior to removal by T.D. 9672; Reg. § 1.414(c)-2, -3, -4, and -5).

Full-time equivalent employees. The number of full-time equivalent employees of an employer during a tax year is equal to the total number of hours of service for which employees were paid wages by the employer divided by 2,080. The result, if not a whole

¶310

LAW EXPLAINED

number, is rounded to the next lowest whole number. In making this computation, only the first 2,080 hours of each employee's wages are taken into account. Hours in excess of this amount are not counted (Code Sec. 45R(d)(2), as added by PPACA; Reg. §1.45R-2(e); Proposed Reg. §1.45R-2(e), prior to removal by T.D. 9672).

An employee's hours of service for a year include:

(1) each hour for which an employee is paid, or entitled to payment, for the performance of duties for the employer during the employer's tax year; and

(2) each hour for which an employee is paid, or entitled to payment, by the employer on account of a period of time during which no duties are performed due to vacation, holiday, illness, incapacity (including disability), layoff, jury duty, military duty or leave of absence (except that no more than 160 hours of service are required to be counted for an employee on account of any single continuous period during which the employee performs no duties) (Reg. §1.45R-2(d)(2); Proposed Reg. §1.45R-2(d)(2), prior to removal by T.D. 9672; Section II C of Notice 2010-44).

An employer may use any of the three following methods to calculate the total number of hours of service which must be taken into account for an employee for the year:

(1) determine actual hours of service from records of hours worked and hours for which payment is made or due (payment is made or due for vacation, holiday, illness, incapacity, etc.);

(2) use a days-worked equivalency whereby the employee is credited with eight hours of service for each day for which the employee would be required to be credited with at least one hour of service (see the hours of service rule above); or

(3) use a weeks-worked equivalency whereby the employee is credited with 40 hours of service for each week for which the employee would be required to be credited with at least one hour of service (see the hours of service rule above) (Reg. §1.45R-2(d)(1); Proposed Reg. §1.45R-2(d)(1), prior to removal by T.D. 9672; Section II C of Notice 2010-44).

Example 5: During the year, ABC Co.'s payroll records indicate that employee Andrea worked 2,000 hours and was paid for an additional 80 hours on account of vacation, holiday and illness. The employer counts hours actually worked. Using the days-actually-worked method, Andrea must be credited with 2,080 hours of service.

ABC Co.'s records also indicate that employee Brian worked 49 weeks, took two weeks vacation with pay, and took one week of leave without pay. Under the weeks-worked equivalency rule, Brian must be credited with 2,040 hours of service (51 weeks multiplied by 40 hours per week).

An employer's number of full-time equivalent employees is determined by dividing the total hours of service (see above) credited during the year to employees taken into account for the credit (see above) (but not more than 2,080 hours for any employee) by 2,080. The result, if not a whole number, is rounded to the next lowest whole number.

¶310

LAW EXPLAINED

In some circumstances, an employer with 25 or more employees may qualify for the credit if some of its employees work part-time. For example, an employer with 46 half-time employees (meaning they are paid wages for 1,040 hours) has 23 full-time equivalent employees and, therefore, may qualify for the credit (Reg. § 1.45R-2(e)(1); Proposed Reg. § 1.45R-2(e)(1), prior to removal by T.D. 9672; Section II D of Notice 2010-44).

Example 6: During the year, ABC Co. paid five employees wages for 2,080 hours each, three employees wages for 1,040 hours each, and one employee wages for 2,300 hours. The employer does not use an equivalency method to determine hours of service for any of these employees. The total number of full-time equivalent employees is equal to 10,400 hours of service for the five employees paid for 2,080 hours each (5 × 2,080); 3,120 hours of service for the three employees paid for 1,040 hours each (3 × 1,040); and 2,080 hours of service for the one employee paid for 2,300 hours (the lesser of 2,300 and 2,080). Full-time equivalent employees equals 7 (15,600 total hours of service divided by 2,080 equals 7.5, but the result is rounded to the next lowest whole number).

Employee defined. Leased employees are considered employees for purposes of the credit (Code Sec. 45R(e)(1)(B); Reg. § 1.45R-1(a)(5)(ii); Proposed Reg. § 1.45R-1(a)(5)(ii), prior to removal by T.D. 9672). However, premiums paid by the leasing organization are not taken into account in computing the credit (Section III B of Notice 2010-82). In contrast, independent contracts (including sole proprietors), part-ners in a partnership, 2-percent shareholders of an eligible small business which is an S corporation, 5-percent owners of other businesses, and family members of these owners and partners, including household members who qualify as a dependent, are not considered employees (Code Sec. 45R(e)(1)(A); Reg. § 1.45R-1(a)(5); Proposed Reg. § 1.45R-1(a)(5), prior to removal by T.D. 9672; Section II B of Notice 2010-44). The employee-spouse of a shareholder owning more than two percent of the stock of an S corporation; the employee-spouse of an owner of more than five percent of a business; the employee-spouse of a partner owning more than a five percent interest in a partnership; and the employee-spouse of a sole proprietor are not taken into account (Reg. § 1.45R-1(a)(5)(iii); Proposed Reg. § 1.45R-1(a)(5)(iii), prior to removal by T.D. 9672; Section III A of Notice 2010-82).

The employees of the employer are not required to be performing services in a trade or business. Thus, an employer that otherwise meets the requirements for the credit, does not fail to be an eligible small employer merely because the employees of the employer are not performing services in a trade or business of the employer. For example, a household employer that otherwise satisfies the requirements is eligible for the credit (Reg. § 1.45R-2(a); Proposed Reg. § 1.45R-2(a), prior to removal by T.D. 9672; Section II B of Notice 2010-82).

Special rule for seasonal employees. For purposes of determining average annual wages and the number of full-time equivalent employees, hours of service worked by, and wages paid to, a seasonal worker are not taken into account unless the worker works for

LAW EXPLAINED

the employer on more than 120 days during the tax year (Code Sec. 45R(d)(5)(A), as added by PPACA; Reg. §1.45R-1(a)(5)(iv); Proposed Reg. §1.45R-1(a)(5)(iv), prior to removal by T.D. 9672). Note that premiums paid on behalf of seasonal employees may be taken in account in determining the credit even if their hours of service and wages are not taken into account because they do not work more than 120 days (Reg. §1.45R-3(g); Proposed Reg. §1.45R-3(g), prior to removal by T.D. 9672).

A seasonal worker is defined as a worker who performs labor or services on a seasonal basis as defined by the Secretary of Labor and includes workers covered by 29 C.F.R. §500.20(s)(1) and retail workers employed exclusively during holiday seasons (Code Sec. 45R(d)(5)(A), as added by PPACA; Reg. §1.45R-1(a)(16); Proposed Reg. §1.45R-1(a)(16), prior to removal by T.D. 9672).

Average annual wages. The amount of the average annual wages is equal to the aggregate amount of wages paid by the employer to employees during the tax year, divided by the number of full-time equivalent employees of the employer during the tax year. If this amount is not a multiple of $1,000, it is rounded to the next lowest multiple of $1,000 ((Code Sec. 45R(d)(5)(A), as added by PPACA; Code Sec. 45R(d)(3), as added by PPACA). Only wages that are paid for hours of service are taken into account (Reg. §1.45R-1(a)(9); Proposed Reg. §1.45R-1(a)(9), prior to removal by T.D. 9672; Section II E of Notice 2010-44). Wages for purposes of the provision are defined by reference to Code Sec. 3121(a), relating to the definition of wages for purposes of the Federal Insurance Contributions Act (FICA) but without regard to the wage base limitation (Code Sec. 45R(e)(4), as added by PPACA; Reg. §1.45R-1(a)(24); Proposed Reg. §1.45R-1(a)(22), prior to removal by T.D. 9672).

Example 7: ABC Co. paid $224,000 in wages and had ten full-time equivalent employees during the year. The employer's average annual wages are $22,000 ($224,000 divided by 10 equals $22,400, rounded down to the nearest $1,000).

Although no more than 2,080 hours of service of a particular employee is taken into account in determining the number of full-time equivalent employees, the total amount of wages paid to an employee who works more than 2,080 hours is taken into account in determining average annual wages.

Credit is component of general business credit. The small employer health insurance credit is a component of the general business credit (Code Sec. 38(b)(36), as added by PPACA; Reg. §1.45R-5(a); Proposed Reg. §1.45R-5(a), prior to removal by T.D. 9672). The general business credit may be carried back one tax year and forward 20 tax years. Any portion of the small employer health insurance credit that is not claimed by the expiration of the 20-year carryforward period may be claimed as a deduction in the first tax year after expiration of the carryforward period (Code Sec. 196(c)(14), as added by PPACA).

Credit allowed against AMT. The small employer health insurance credit is treated as a specified credit (Code Sec. 38(c)(4)(B)(vi), as added by PPACA; Reg. §1.45R-5(b); Proposed Reg. §1.45R-5(b), prior to removal by T.D. 9672). Consequently, it may be

¶310

LAW EXPLAINED

claimed in full against regular and alternative minimum tax liabilities for tax years beginning after December 31, 2010, and for carrybacks of the credit.

Deduction for health insurance reduced by credit amount. Any business deduction for employer-paid premiums for qualified health plans or, in the case of tax years beginning in 2010 through 2013, for health insurance coverage, is reduced by the amount of the small employer health insurance credit determined with respect to those premiums (Code Sec. 280C(h), as added by PPACA; Reg. §1.45R-5(c); Proposed Reg. §1.45R-5(c), prior to removal by T.D. 9672).

Estates and trusts. An estate or trust must apportion the credit between itself and its beneficiaries based on income allocable to each (Code Sec. 45R(e)(5)(B), as added by PPACA; Code Sec. 52(d); Reg. §1.45R-3(h); Proposed Reg. §1.45R-3(h), prior to removal by T.D. 9672).

Tax-exempt eligible small employers. The small employer health insurance credit for a tax-exempt eligible small employer is refundable, and the credit percentage is 35 percent for a tax year that begins in 2014 or later and 25 percent for a tax year that begins in 2010, 2011, 2012, or 2013 (Code Sec. 45R(b) and (g)(2)(A), as added by PPACA). However, because of the reductions in government expenditures under the sequester provisions in effect starting March 1, 2013, the refundable portion of the credit is reduced by 8.7 percent until September 30, 2013 (the end of the government's fiscal year) or until this is changed by Congressional action.

> **Compliance Note:** Like other taxpayers, a tax-exempt organization uses Form 8941, Credit for Small Employer Health Insurance Premiums, to compute the credit. However, tax-exempt organizations claim the credit on a revised Form 990-T.

A tax-exempt eligible small employer is an eligible small employer that is a Code Sec. 501(c) organization that is exempt from tax under Code Sec. 501(a) (Code Sec. 45R(f)(2), as added by PPACA; Reg. §1.45R-1(a)(20); Proposed Reg. §1.45R-1(a)(19), prior to removal by T.D. 9672). Other tax-exempt organizations generally are not eligible to claim the credit. However, a farmers' cooperative is eligible to claim the credit as a taxable employer if it otherwise meets the requirements (Reg. §1.45R-1(a)(4); Proposed Reg. §1.45R-1(a)(4), prior to removal by T.D. 9672; Section II A of Notice 2010-82).

If the credit exceeds the amount of payroll taxes of the organization during the calendar year in which the tax year begins, then the credit amount is limited to the amount of the payroll taxes (Code Sec. 45R(f)(1), as added by PPACA; Reg. §1.45R-3(e); Proposed Reg. §1.45R-3(e), prior to removal by T.D. 9672; Section III B of Notice 2010-44). Payroll taxes are defined as amounts required to be withheld from the tax-exempt organization's employees and any hospital insurance excise taxes (Code Sec. 45R(f)(3)(A), as added by PPACA; Reg. §1.45R-1(a)(13); Proposed Reg. §1.45R-1(a)(13), prior to removal by T.D. 9672). The special rule which treats amounts paid pursuant to an agreement entered into by American employers with respect to foreign affiliates that are the equivalent of social security taxes or railroad retirement taxes applies (Code Sec. 45R(f)(3)(B), as added by PPACA).

¶310

LAW EXPLAINED

▶ **Effective date.** The small employer health insurance credit and related amendments apply to amounts paid or incurred in tax years beginning after December 31, 2009 (Act Sec. 1421(f)(1) of the Patient Protection and Affordable Care Act (PPACA) (P.L. 111-148), as amended by Act Sec. 10105(e)(4) and Act Sec. 10105(e)(5)). The provision treating the credit as a specified credit is effective for credits determined in tax years beginning after December 31, 2009, and to carrybacks of such credits (Act Sec. 1421(f)(2) of PPACA, as amended by Act Sec. 10105(e)(4)). Final Reg. §§1.45R-1, -2, -3, -4, and -5 apply to tax years beginning after December 31, 2013. However, employers may also rely on the proposed regulations (Notice of Proposed Rulemaking REG-113792-13) for guidance for tax years beginning after December 31, 2013, and before January 1, 2015. Notice 2010-44, as amplified by Notice 2010-82, provides guidance on Code Sec. 45R as in effect for tax years beginning before January 1, 2014.

Law source: Law at ¶5020, ¶5030, ¶5120 and ¶5160.

— Act Sec. 1421(a) of the Patient Protection and Affordable Care Act (PPACA) (P.L. 111-148), adding Code Sec. 45R;

— Act Sec. 10105(e)(1), amending Code Sec. 45R(d)(3), as added by Act Sec. 1421(a);

— Act Sec. 10105(e)(2), amending Code Sec. 45R(g), as added by Act Sec. 1421(a);

— Act Sec. 1421(b), adding Code Sec. 38(b)(36);

— Act Sec. 1421(c), adding Code Sec. 38(c)(4)(B)(vi);

— Act Sec. 1421(d)(1), adding Code Sec. 280C(h);

— Act Sec. 10105(e)(3), amending Code Sec. 280C(h), as added by Act Sec. 1421(d)(1);

— Act Sec. 1421(d)(2), adding Code Sec. 196(c)(14);

— Act Sec. 1421(f), as amended by Act Sec. 10105(e)(4), and Act Sec. 10105(e)(5), providing the effective dates.

Reporter references: For further information, consult the following reporters.

— Standard Federal Tax Reporter, ¶4500ZP.01 and following.

— Tax Research Consultant, HEALTH: 9,200

— Practical Tax Explanation, §42,165.05

¶320 Exchange-Participating Qualified Health Plans Offered Through Cafeteria Plans

SUMMARY OF NEW LAW

Beginning in 2014, a cafeteria plan may not provide a health plan that is offered through the American Health Benefit Exchange unless the employer is a qualified employer for purposes of the Exchange.

¶320

BACKGROUND

Generally, all forms of income and compensation, from whatever source derived, are included in the taxable income of the recipient, unless a specific exclusion of the income exists (Code Sec. 61). This includes any benefits that may be received by an employee from an employer as compensation. There are several exceptions to this rule. For example, amounts received by an employee from an employer as part of an accident or health plan and amounts employers contribute to the cost of accident and health plans covering employees are excluded from income under Code Secs. 105 and 106, respectively.

There are many other exclusions provided by the Internal Revenue Code related to employee benefits. One such exception applies to benefits received through a cafeteria plan under Code Sec. 125. A cafeteria plan is an employer-sponsored plan under which employees have the option of selecting benefits or cash. Employees can select the qualified benefits that fit their situations and receive taxable cash payments in lieu of receiving benefits that they do not select.

Generally, only benefits for which an exclusion is already granted by the Internal Revenue Code can be offered as "qualified benefits" as a part of a cafeteria plan. Some of the "qualified benefits" that can be offered as part of a cafeteria plan include:

- Nontaxable group-term life insurance on the life of an employee in an amount that is less than or equal to $50,000;

- Excludable accident and health plan and benefits;

- Dependent care assistance;

- Disability benefits;

- Adoption assistance;

- Premiums for life insurance on the life or lives of a spouse or dependent with a benefit of up to $2,000; and

- Contributions to Health Savings Accounts (HSAs) (Code Sec. 125(f); Proposed Reg. § 1.125-1(a)(3); Notice 89-110, 1989-2 CB 447).

LAW EXPLAINED

"Qualified benefit" generally does not include certain exchange-participating qualified health plans.—Effective for tax years beginning after December 31, 2013, a cafeteria plan cannot offer a qualified health plan offered through an American Health Benefit Exchange (Code Sec. 125(f)(3)(A), as added by the Patient Protection and Affordable Care Act (PPACA) (P.L. 111-148)).

> **Comment:** By January 1, 2014, each state (or the federal government in the absence of state action) must establish an American Health Benefit Exchange and Small Business Health Options Program (SHOP Exchange) to provide qualified individuals and qualified small business employers access to qualified health plans. For a discussion of the establishment and requirements of the Exchanges, see ¶505. The Exchanges will have four levels of essential benefits coverage available to participants at either a "bronze," "silver," "gold," or "platinum"

LAW EXPLAINED

level. The bronze level plans must provide benefits that are actuarially equivalent to 60 percent of the full actuarial value of the benefits provided under the plan. The percentage increases to 70 percent for silver level plans, 80 percent for gold level plans, and 90 percent for platinum level plans.

A "qualified health plan" is one that:

- has in effect a certification that such plan meets the criteria for certification issued or recognized by each Exchange through which such plan is offered;
- provides the essential health benefits package; and
- is offered by a health insurance issuer that (a) is licensed and in good standing to offer health insurance coverage in each state in which the issuer offers health insurance coverage under the Patient Protection Act, (b) agrees to offer at least one qualified health plan in the silver level and at least one plan in the gold level in each exchange, (c) agrees to charge the same premium rate for each qualified health plan of the issuer without regard to whether the plan is offered directly from the issuer or through an agent and (d) complies with regulations developed under Act Sec. 1311(d) of the Patient Protection Act and any other applicable exchange regulations (Act Sec. 1301(a) of PPACA).

There is an exception to this prohibition in the case of Exchange-eligible employers offering employees the opportunity to enroll in a qualified health plan through an Exchange (Code Sec. 125(f)(3)(B), as added by PPACA). An Exchange-eligible employer is, in tax years beginning after December 31, 2013, a small employer electing to make all of its full-time employees eligible for one or more qualified health plans offered in the small group market through an Exchange (Act Sec. 1312(f)(2)(A) of PPACA). The "small group market" is the health insurance market under which employees obtain health insurance coverage through a group health plan maintained by a small employer (Act Sec. 1304(a)(3) of PPACA). This exception allows Exchange-eligible employers in the small group market to offer "qualified health plans" through an exchange as a part of a cafeteria plan in tax years beginning after December 31, 2013.

Beginning in 2017, issuers of health insurance coverage in large group markets may be allowed to offer health insurance under the Exchanges, thereby making it possible for all employers to be Exchange-eligible employers (Act Sec. 1312(f)(2)(B) of PPACA). This expanded exception allows all Exchange-eligible employers to offer "qualified health plans" as a part of cafeteria plans beginning in 2017, but only if large employers are allowed to participate in that Exchange in that state.

▶ **Effective date.** The provision applies to tax years beginning after December 31, 2013 (Act Sec. 1515(c) of the Patient Protection and Affordable Care Act (PPACA) (P.L. 111-148)).

Law source: Law at ¶5070.

— Act Sec. 1515(a) of the Patient Protection and Affordable Care Act (PPACA) (P.L. 111-148), adding Code Sec. 125(f)(3);

— Act Sec. 1515(b), amending Code Sec. 125(f);

— Act Sec. 1515(c), providing the effective date.

¶320

LAW EXPLAINED

Reporter references: For further information, consult the following reporters.

— Standard Federal Tax Reporter, ¶7324.044

— Tax Research Consultant, COMPEN: 51,104.15

— Practical Tax Explanation, § 20,815.05

¶325   Health Flexible Spending Accounts Offered in Cafeteria Plans

SUMMARY OF NEW LAW

For plan years beginning after 2012, health flexible spending arrangements (health FSAs) offered as a part of a cafeteria plan must limit contributions through salary reductions to $2,500.

BACKGROUND

Generally, all forms of income and compensation, from whatever source derived, are included in the taxable income of the recipient, unless a specific exclusion of the income exists (Code Sec. 61). There are several exceptions to this rule that do provide such exclusions. One such exception is a cafeteria plan under Code Sec. 125. A cafeteria plan is an employer-sponsored plan under which employees have the option of selecting benefits or cash. Employees can choose which of the offered benefits fits their situations and receive taxable cash payments in lieu of the un-selected benefits. Benefits provided under a cafeteria plan may be funded through employer contributions, employee salary reductions, or a combination of both.

One such benefit that can be provided under a cafeteria plan is a flexible spending arrangement. A flexible spending arrangement (FSA) is a benefit under which participants are given an account that is credited with employer contributions or pre-tax employee salary reductions. The amounts in the account can then be used for dependent care services or health care service expenses, depending on whether the plan is a dependent care FSA or a health FSA. A health FSA must qualify as a health or accident plan under Code Secs. 105 and 106, and can only be used to pay for expenses that would qualify for a deduction for medical services under Code Sec. 213.

Health FSAs have become a very popular method for employees to lower their income tax by paying for common medical expenses, everything from doctor co-pays to prescription medication, with pre-tax income. Generally speaking, there is no limit on the amount which an employee can elect to contribute to a health FSA through salary reductions, other than those that may be imposed by the employer's plan.

Limitation on FSAs offered as part of cafeteria plans.—Effective for plan years beginning after December 31, 2012, a health flexible spending arrangement (FSA) will not be a qualified benefit under a cafeteria plan unless the plan provides for a $2,500 maximum salary reduction contribution to the FSA (Code Sec. 125(i)(1), as added by Act Secs. 9005 and 10902 of the Patient Protection and Affordable Care Act (PPACA) (P.L. 111-148), as amended by Act Sec. 1403(a) of the Health Care and Education Reconciliation Act of 2010 (P.L. 111-152)). If the plan does allow salary reductions in excess of $2,500, then an employee will be subject to tax on distributions from the health FSA, thereby eliminating any of the tax benefits of health FSA contributions.

> **State Tax Consequences:** The limitation of FSA contributions to $2,500 for tax years after 2012 will not impact states that conform to the federal exclusion by the time the provision takes effect. Because most states start their tax calculations with federal adjustable gross income, there should be no impact on those states. States that do not conform may allow an exclusion from taxation for amounts above the federal limitation as well.

The tax year to be used for purposes of the effective date is the plan year of the cafeteria plan. Thus, for example, if the cafeteria plan year does not begin until April 1, the limit first applies to the plan year beginning April 1, 2013. However, if a cafeteria plan has a short plan year that begins after 2012, the amount of the contribution limit must be prorated for the number of months in the short plan year (Notice 2012-40).

The written cafeteria plan must be amended to include the $2,500 limit, but the amendments need not be reflected before December 31, 2014, provided that the plan operates to limit contributions to $2,500. In the case of plans providing for a grace period, amounts contributed for the 2012 plan year that are carried over to the 2013 plan year do not count against the $2,500 limit. A cafeteria plan will continue to qualify under Code Sec. 125, even if employees are allowed to make contributions in excess of the limit, as long as the excess contributions are due to mistake and not willful neglect, the plan terms apply uniformly to all participants, and the excess contributions are paid and reported to the employees as taxable wages (Notice 2012-40).

The limit only applies to health FSAs, and not non-elective credits, other types of FSAs, health savings accounts or health reimbursement arrangements. Thus, for example, if an employer provides flex credits to each employee's health FSA, the amount of the flex credits do not count against the $2,500 limitation, as long as the employees cannot elect to receive the credit amounts as cash or a taxable benefit (Notice 2012-40).

The limit is applied on an employee-by-employee basis, and applies to each employee regardless of the number of dependents or other persons reimbursable under the FSA. If both spouses in a married couple are employed by the same employer and each is entitled to make salary reduction elections, each is allowed separate $2,500 health FSA limits (Notice 2012-40).

¶325

LAW EXPLAINED

All members of a controlled group or affiliated service group are treated as one employer for purposes of the contribution limit. Thus, if an employee participates in multiple cafeteria plans offered by members of a single controlled group or affiliated service group, then a single $2,500 limit applies. However, if the multiple cafeteria plans are offered by two or more employers that are not members of a controlled group or affiliated service group, then separate $2,500 limitations apply to each plan. (Notice 2012-40).

Effective for tax years beginning after December 31, 2013, the $2,500 limitation is adjusted annually for inflation. Any inflation adjustment that is not a multiple of $50 is rounded down to the next lowest multiple of $50 (Code Sec. 125(i)(2), as added by Act Sec. 10902 of PPACA and amended by Act Sec 1403(b) of the 2010 Reconciliation Act). It remains $2,500 for 2014 (Rev. Proc. 2013-35).

▶ **Effective date.** The amendments apply to tax years beginning after December 31, 2012 (Act Secs. 9005(b) and 10902(b) of the Patient Protection and Affordable Care Act (PPACA) (P.L. 111-148), as amended by Act Sec. 1403(a) of the Health Care and Education Reconciliation Act of 2010 (P.L. 111-152)).

Law source: Law at ¶5070.

— Act Sec. 9005(a)(1) of the Patient Protection and Affordable Care Act (PPACA) (P.L. 111-148), redesignating Code Sec. 125(i) and (j) as Code Sec. 125(j) and (k), respectively;

— Act Sec. 9005(a)(2) of PPACA, adding Code Sec. 125(i);

— Act Sec. 10902(a) of PPACA, as amended by Act Sec. 1403(b) of the Health Care and Education Reconciliation Act of 2010 (P.L. 111-152), amending Code Sec. 125(i), as added by Act Sec. 9005(a)(2) of PPACA;

— Act Secs. 9005(b) and 10902(b) of PPACA, as amended by Act Sec. 1403(a) of the 2010 Reconciliation Act, providing the effective date.

Reporter references: For further information, consult the following reporters.

— Standard Federal Tax Reporter, ¶7324.042

— Tax Research Consultant, COMPEN: 51,202

— Practical Tax Explanation, §42,710.40

¶330 Simple Cafeteria Plans

SUMMARY OF NEW LAW

In years beginning after 2010, certain small employers may choose to provide a simple cafeteria plan for their employees, under which the nondiscrimination rules of a classic cafeteria plan are treated as satisfied.

¶330

BACKGROUND

Generally, all forms of income and compensation, from whatever source derived, are included in the taxable income of the recipient, unless a specific exclusion of the income exists (Code Sec. 61). This includes noncash benefits received from an employer. However, there are many specific exclusions provided by the Internal Revenue Code for various benefits received by employees, such as (among others) employer contributions for accident and health plans (Code Sec. 106), dependent care assistance (Code Sec. 129) or group-term life insurance (Code Sec. 79). Where an employer provides these benefits to employees, the employees are subject to tax on the full amounts of benefits they can elect to receive (subject to the exclusions), regardless of whether the employees actually elect to receive the benefits.

Another avenue of providing excludable benefits to employees is through the implementation of a cafeteria plan under Code Sec. 125. A cafeteria plan is an employer-sponsored plan under which employees have the option of selecting benefits or cash. Employees can choose which of the offered benefits fits their situations and receive taxable cash payments in lieu of the unselected benefits.

A cafeteria plan must be a written plan and may not discriminate in favor of highly compensated participants. A highly compensated participant is: (1) an officer or spouse or dependent of an officer of the employer, (2) a stockholder or spouse or dependent of a stockholder owning more than five percent (determined by voting power or value) of all classes of the stock of the employer, or (3) a highly compensated employee or spouse or dependent of a highly compensated employee (Code Sec. 125(e)). A cafeteria plan discriminates in favor of highly compensated participants if the plan provides greater benefits to those employees in comparison to non-highly compensated employees. This can be determined based upon either the benefits available to be elected by the participants, by the benefits actually elected by the participants or by the amount contributed by the employer for the benefits (Proposed Reg. § 1.125-7(c)).

Additionally, a cafeteria plan may not favor key employees. A cafeteria plan favors key employees if more than 25 percent of the nontaxable qualified benefits provided under the plan are provided to key employees (Code Sec. 125(b)(2)).

A violation of the nondiscrimination rules with regard to either highly compensated participants or key employees does not invalidate the cafeteria plan for all participants. However, it does invalidate the protections of a cafeteria plan for the highly compensated participants or key employees. In such an instance, the highly compensated participants or key employees will be subject to tax on the benefits they receive under the plan (Code Sec. 125(b)(1), (2)). Because of this risk of increased tax for highly compensated participants and key employees, small employers, who may have a higher percentage of these employees compared to larger employers, may not be able to offer cafeteria plans to their employees.

LAW EXPLAINED

Small employers can provide simple cafeteria plans.—In years beginning after December 31, 2010, certain small employers' cafeteria plans can qualify as simple cafeteria plans, under which the applicable nondiscrimination requirements of a classic

LAW EXPLAINED

cafeteria plan are treated as satisfied (Code Sec. 125(j)(1), as added by the Patient Protection and Affordable Care Act (PPACA) (P.L. 111-148)). A simple cafeteria plan is a cafeteria plan established and maintained by an eligible employer that meets certain contribution, eligibility and participation requirements (Code Sec. 125(j)(2), as added by PPACA).

An applicable nondiscrimination requirement that will be deemed as met by an employer establishing a simple cafeteria plan is any nondiscrimination requirement applicable to a classic cafeteria plan under Code Sec. 125(b), group-term life insurance under Code Sec. 79(d), an accident and health plan under Code Sec. 105(h), or a dependent care assistance program under Code Sec. 129(d)(2), (3), (4) or (8) (Code Sec. 125(j)(6), as added by PPACA).

> **Comment:** Small employers may find it difficult to justify providing a classic cafeteria plan to employees if it requires diminishing benefits enjoyed by owner-employees to satisfy the nondiscrimination requirements of a classic cafeteria plan. Through the establishment of a simple cafeteria plan, employers can retain potentially discriminatory benefits for highly compensated and key employees (subject to some restrictions relating to contributions, discussed below) while allowing other employees to enjoy the benefits of a cafeteria plan without worrying about running afoul of the nondiscrimination requirements of a classic cafeteria plan.

An employer eligible to establish a simple cafeteria plan is any employer that, during either of the two preceding years, employed an average of 100 or fewer employees on business days. For purposes of this rule, a year may only be taken into account if the employer was in existence throughout the year (Code Sec. 125(j)(5)(A), as added by PPACA). If an employer was not in existence throughout the preceding year, the employer may nonetheless be considered as an eligible employer if it reasonably expects to average 100 or fewer employees on business days during the current year (Code Sec. 125(j)(5)(B), as added by PPACA).

If an employer has 100 or fewer employees for any year and establishes a simple cafeteria plan for that year, then it can be treated as meeting the requirement for any subsequent year even if the employer employs more than 100 employees in the subsequent year (Code Sec. 125(j)(5)(C)(i), as added by PPACA). However, this exception does not apply if the employer employs an average of 200 or more employees during the subsequent year (Code Sec. 125(j)(5)(C)(ii), as added by PPACA).

> **Comment:** This provision allows small but growing employers to continue to offer simple cafeteria plan benefits to employees without the concern of having to meet the discrimination requirements by having to switch to a classic cafeteria plan. Without this exception, the establishment of simple cafeteria plans could create a disincentive to increased hiring.

A simple cafeteria plan must also meet rigid contribution requirements on the part of the employer. The contribution requirements are met if the employer is required by the plan, regardless of whether a qualified employee makes any salary reduction contribution, to make a contribution to provide qualified benefits on behalf of each qualified employee, in an amount equal to: (1) a uniform percentage (not less than

LAW EXPLAINED

two percent) of the employee's compensation for the year, or (2) an amount not less than the lesser of: (a) six percent of the employee's compensation for the plan year or (b) twice the amount of the salary reduction contributions of each qualified employee (Code Sec. 125(j)(3)(A), as added by PPACA).

If the employer bases the satisfaction of the contribution requirements on the second option, it will not be treated as met if the rate of contributions with respect to any salary reduction contribution of a highly compensated or key employee is greater than that with respect to any other employee (Code Sec. 125(j)(3)(B), as added by PPACA). Beyond this prohibition, the established contribution requirements are not to be treated as prohibiting an employer from making contributions to provide qualified benefits under the plan in addition to the required contributions.

For purposes of the contribution requirements, a salary reduction contribution is any amount contributed to the plan at the election of the employee and not includable in the employee's gross income under the cafeteria plan provisions (Code Sec. 125(j)(3)(D)(i), as added by PPACA). The terms "highly compensated employee" and "key employee" retain their definitions under the classic cafeteria plan provisions. A "qualified employee" is any employee who is not a highly compensated or key employee.

Employee eligibility and participation requirements. A simple cafeteria plan must also satisfy minimum eligibility and participation requirements. The requirements are met if all employees who had at least 1,000 hours of service for the preceding plan year are eligible to participate and if each employee eligible to participate may elect any benefit under the plan, subject to terms and conditions applicable to all participants (Code Sec. 125(j)(4)(A), as added by PPACA).

An employer may elect to exclude from the plan, regardless of the satisfaction of the 1,000 hour requirement, employees who have not attained the age of 21 before the close of the plan year, who have less than one year of service with the employer as of any day during the plan year, who are covered under a collective bargaining agreement if there is evidence that the benefits covered under the plan were the subject of good faith bargaining between employee representatives and the employer, or are nonresident aliens working outside the United States whose income did not come from a U.S. source (Code Sec. 125(j)(4)(B), as added by PPACA).

References to employers with regard to simple cafeteria plans include references to predecessors of such employers (Code Sec. 125(j)(5)(D)(i), as added by PPACA). This means that, among other considerations, for purposes of determining the qualification of a business that has recently changed ownership, the fact that the previous owner had 100 or fewer employees in a preceding year can be used to determine eligibility of the current ownership to establish a simple cafeteria plan. Also, any person treated as a single employer for purposes of the Work Opportunity Credit under Code Sec. 52(a) or (b) or for purposes of deferred compensation rules under Code Sec. 414(n) or (o) shall be treated as one person for purposes of simple cafeteria plans (Code Sec. 125(j)(5)(D)(ii), as added by PPACA).

▶ **Effective date.** The provision applies to years beginning after December 31, 2010 (Act Sec. 9022(b) of the Patient Protection and Affordable Care Act (PPACA) (P.L. 111-148)).

¶330

LAW EXPLAINED

Law source: Law at ¶5070.

— Act Sec. 9022(a) of the Patient Protection and Affordable Care Act (PPACA) (P.L. 111-148), redesignating Code Sec. 125(j) and (k) as Code Sec. 125(k) and (l), respectively, and adding Code Sec. 125(j);

— Act Sec. 9022(b), providing the effective date.

Reporter references: For further information, consult the following reporters.

— Standard Federal Tax Reporter, ¶7324.05

— Tax Research Consultant, COMPEN: 51,250

— Practical Tax Explanation, § 20,840

¶335 Elimination of Deduction for Federal Subsidies for Certain Retiree Prescription Drug Plans

SUMMARY OF NEW LAW

The rule that allowed an employer, as a plan sponsor, to disregard the value of any qualified retiree prescription drug plan subsidy in calculating the employer's business deduction for retiree prescription drug costs is repealed, effective for tax years beginning after December 31, 2012.

BACKGROUND

A business that provides a qualified retiree prescription drug plan to its retired employees is eligible for a special subsidy payment each year from the federal government based on the cost of providing such coverage (Section 1860D-22 of the Social Security Act (SSA) (P.L. 108-173)). The amount of the subsidy is 28 percent of allowable retiree drug costs between $250 and $5,000, indexed annually for inflation. The subsidy payment is excludable from income for both regular tax and alternative minimum tax (including the adjustment for current earnings) purposes (Code Secs. 56(g)(4)(B) and 139A).

A "qualified retiree prescription drug plan" is employment-based retiree health coverage that has an actuarial value at least equal to the Medicare Part D standard plan for the risk pool and that meets certain other disclosure and recordkeeping requirements (Section 1860D-22(a)(2) of SSA). "Employment-based retiree health coverage" is health insurance or other coverage of health care costs, whether provided by voluntary insurance coverage, or pursuant to statutory or contractual obligation, for Medicare Part D eligible individuals (including spouses and dependents of such individuals) under group health plans based on their status as retired participants in such plans (Section 1860D-22(c)(1) of SSA). A "qualified retiree," for these purposes, is an individual who is eligible for Medicare but not enrolled in either a Medicare Part D prescription drug plan or a Medicare Advantage-Prescription Drug plan, but who is covered under a qualified retiree prescription drug plan.

¶335

BACKGROUND

"Allowable retiree drug costs," in general, are, with respect to prescription drug costs under a qualified retiree prescription drug plan, the part of the actual costs paid by the plan sponsor on behalf of a qualifying retiree under the plan.

> **Comment:** According to the Joint Committee on Taxation, *Technical Explanation of the Revenue Provisions of the "Reconciliation Act of 2010," as amended, in combination with the "Patient Protection and Affordable Care Act"* (JCX-18-10), March 21, 2010, "[f]or purposes of calculating allowable retiree costs, actual costs paid are net of discounts, chargebacks, and average percentage rebates, and exclude administrative costs."

Employer's deduction. The gross income of an employer does not include any special subsidy payment received under these rules. Prior to PPACA, the value of any qualified retiree prescription drug plan subsidy received by an employer could be disregarded in calculating the employer's business deduction for prescription drug costs (Code Sec. 139A). Therefore, an employer could claim a deduction for prescription drug expenses incurred even though the employer also received an excludable subsidy related to the same expenses (Joint Committee on Taxation, *Technical Explanation of the Revenue Provisions of the "Reconciliation Act of 2010," as amended, in combination with the "Patient Protection and Affordable Care Act"* (JCX-18-10), March 21, 2010). This is an exception to the general rule disallowing a deduction under any Code provision for any expense or amount that would otherwise be allowable as a deduction if such expense or amount is allocable to a class or classes of exempt income (Code Sec. 265(a); Reg. § 1.265-1(a)).

LAW EXPLAINED

Deduction repealed for expenses allocable to Medicare Part D subsidy. The provision that allows an employer to disregard the value of any qualified retiree prescription drug plan subsidy in calculating the employer's business deduction for retiree prescription drug costs is repealed, effective for tax years beginning after December 31, 2012 (Code Sec. 139A, as amended by the Patient Protection and Affordable Care Act (PPACA) (P.L. 111-148); Act Sec. 9012(b) of PPACA, as amended by Act Sec. 1407 of the Health Care and Education Reconciliation Act of 2010 (P.L. 111-152)). Thus, the amount otherwise allowable as a business deduction for retiree prescription drug expenses is reduced by the amount of the excludable subsidy payments received.

> **State Tax Consequences:** The repeal of the provision that allows an employer to disregard the value of any qualified retiree prescription drug plan subsidy in calculating the employer's business deduction for retiree prescription drug costs, effective for tax years beginning after 2012, impact states that adopt Code Sec. 162, but that have Code conformity dates that would not include this amendment, unless their conformity dates are updated to include the amendment. States that annually update their conformity dates will most likely adopt the amendment by the time it takes effect. Those states that do not conform may allow a subtraction for the amount of subsidy used to reduce the federal deduction.

LAW EXPLAINED

▶ **Effective date.** This provision is effective for tax years beginning after December 31, 2012 (Act Sec. 9012(b) of the Patient Protection and Affordable Care Act (PPACA) (P.L. 111-148), as amended by Act Sec. 1407 of the Health Care and Education Reconciliation Act of 2010 (P.L. 111-152)).

Law source: Law at ¶5080.

— Act Sec. 9012(a) of the Patient Protection and Affordable Care Act (PPACA) (P.L. 111-148), amending Code Sec. 139A;

— Act Sec. 9012(b) of PPACA, as amended by Act Sec. 1407 of the Health Care and Education Reconciliation Act of 2010 (P.L. 111-152), providing the effective date.

Reporter references: For further information, consult the following reporters.

— Standard Federal Tax Reporter, 7649A.01

— Tax Research Consultant, HEALTH: 9,250

— Practical Tax Explanation, § 42,170

¶340   Limit on Health Insurance Provider Deduction for Excessive Employee Remuneration

SUMMARY OF NEW LAW

For compensation earned after 2009 and deductible after 2012, health insurance providers are subject to a $500,000 compensation deduction limitation deduction for remuneration paid to their officers, directors, employees, or other service providers.

BACKGROUND

A publicly held corporation may not deduct applicable employee remuneration in excess of $1 million for covered employees (Code Sec. 162(m)(1)). Generally, "covered employees" include the chief executive officer of the corporation and the four most highly compensated employees of the corporation other than the chief executive officer (CEO), whose compensation is required to be reported to the shareholders by the Securities Exchange Act of 1934 (Code Sec. 162(m)(3)). "Applicable employee remuneration" generally includes the taxable wages paid to the employee, but excludes commissions and other performance-based compensation (Code Sec. 162(m)(4)).

A $500,000 deduction limit applies to compensation paid to "covered executives" by certain employers who participated in the Troubled Asset Relief Program (TARP) (Code Sec. 162(m)(5)(A)). Covered executives include the CEO, the chief financial officer (CFO), and the three most highly compensated employees of the employer, other than the CEO or CFO (Code Sec. 162(m)(5)(D)). Subject to limited exceptions, recipients of assistance under TARP cannot pay or accrue any bonus, retention award, or executive compensation while any obligation arising from such assistance remains outstanding (Act Sec. 7001 of the American Recovery and Reinvestment Act of 2009 (P.L. 111-5)).

LAW EXPLAINED

Limit on deduction for health insurance providers for excessive employee remuneration.—In a disqualified tax year, applicable individual remuneration for services performed is not deductible above the amount of $500,000 (Code Sec. 162(m)(6)(A)(i), as added by the Patient Protection and Affordable Care Act (PPACA) (P.L. 111-148)). A disqualified tax year is any tax year for which the employer is a covered health insurance provider (Code Sec. 162(m)(6)(B), as added by PPACA). An applicable individual is an officer, director, or employee of a covered health insurance provider (Code Sec. 162(m)(6)(F), as added by PPACA). Applicable individual remuneration means the aggregate amount of remuneration for a disqualified tax year that would be deductible except for this new limitation. Applicable individual remuneration does not include deferred deduction remuneration (Code Sec. 162(m)(6)(D), as added by PPACA).

> **State Tax Consequences:** The limitation on the deduction for employee remuneration paid by certain health insurance providers that applies to certain individuals who are paid in excess of $500,000 in tax years beginning after December 31, 2012, will impact states that have not conformed to the limitation by the time it takes effect. In such states, a subtraction may be allowed for amounts exceeding the federal limitation.

For tax years beginning after December 31, 2009, and before January 1, 2013, a covered health insurance provider is an employer that is a health insurance issuer (Code Sec. 9832(b)(2)) and receives premiums from providing health insurance coverage (Code Sec. 9832(b)(1)). For tax years beginning after December 31, 2012, a covered health insurance provider is an employer that is a health insurance issuer that receives gross premiums from providing health insurance coverage such that not less than 25 percent of those gross premiums is from essential health benefits coverage (Code Sec. 5000A(f)(1); Code Sec. 162(m)(6)(C)(i), as added by PPACA). Premiums include amounts received by a health insurance provider from providing health insurance, but do not include amounts received under an indemnity reinsurance contract or direct service payments. Under proposed regulations on which taxpayers can rely, maintaining a self-insured health insurance plan does not cause an entity to be a health insurance provider (Proposed Reg. § 1.162-31(b)(4)). In addition, a *de minimis* exception provides that for a tax year beginning after December 31, 2009, and before January 1, 2013, a health insurance issuer that would otherwise be a covered health insurance provider is not treated as a covered health insurance provider if the premiums received from providing health insurance are less than 2 percent of gross revenue for the year. For a tax year beginning after December 31, 2012, the measure includes the premiums receives for providing minimum essential health insurance coverage. There is a one year grace period for a health insurance provider that qualifies for the *de minimis* exception for one year and fails to qualify for it for the following tax year (Proposed Reg. § 1.162-31(b)(4)).

¶340

LAW EXPLAINED

Two or more persons who are treated as a single employer under the aggregation rules (Code Sec. 414(b), (c), (m), or (o)) are treated as a single employer for the purpose of this limitation except that the brother/sister controlled group and combined group rules (Code Sec. 1563(a)(2) and (3)) are disregarded (Code Sec. 162(m)(6)(C)(ii), as added by PPACA).

In addition to officers, directors, and employees of a covered health insurance provider, applicable individuals include any individual who provides services for or on behalf of the covered health insurance provider. Thus, they can include independent contractors (Code Sec. 162(m)(6)(F), as added by PPACA). However, under proposed regulations on which taxpayers can rely, there is an exception for independent contractors that provide services for multiple unrelated service recipients (Proposed Reg. § 1.162-31(b)(7)).

Deferred deduction remuneration. There is a separate limitation for deferred deduction remuneration for a tax year beginning after December 31, 2012, for services performed by an applicable individual during any disqualified tax year beginning after December 31, 2009. The deduction is limited to the amount that the remuneration exceeds $500,000 reduced, but not below zero, by the sum of two items. The first item is the applicable individual remuneration for the disqualified tax year. The second item is the portion of deferred deduction remuneration taken into account in a preceding tax year (or the portion that would have been taken into account if the limitation were applicable to a tax year beginning after December 31, 2009) (Code Sec. 162(m)(6)(A)(ii), as added by PPACA). Deferred deduction remuneration is remuneration that would be applicable individual remuneration for services performed in a disqualified tax year where the deduction (without regard to this new limitation) is allowable in a subsequent tax year (Code Sec. 162(m)(6)(E), as added by PPACA).

Coordination rules apply that are based on the disallowed golden parachute payment rule (Code Sec. 162(m)(4)(F)) and the rule on stock compensation excise tax (Code Sec. 162(m)(4)(G)) (Code Sec. 162(m)(6)(G), as added by PPACA).

▶ **Effective date.** The amendment made by this section applies to tax years beginning after December 31, 2009, with respect to services performed after that date (Act Sec. 9014(b) of the Patient Protection and Affordable Care Act (PPACA) (P.L. 111-148)). The proposed regulations are proposed to be effective when published as final in the Federal Register, and applicable to tax years that begin after December 31, 2012, and end on or after April 2, 2013. Taxpayers can rely on them until the publication of final regulations. The IRS anticipates that final regulations will be issued before a covered health insurer is required to file a return reflecting the deduction limitation. However, to the extent the final regulations contain rules more restrictive than those in the proposed regulations, a covered health insurer will be able to rely on the proposed regulations for its first tax years beginning after December 31, 2012. Although the regulations will not apply to tax years beginning after December 31, 2012, and ending before April 2, 2013, taxpayers can rely on the proposed regulations with respect to those tax years to the same extent as taxpayers may rely with respect to tax years to which the regulations apply.

¶340

LAW EXPLAINED

Law source: Law at ¶5100.

— Act Sec. 9014(a) of the Patient Protection and Affordable Care Act (PPACA) (P.L. 111-148), adding Code Sec. 162(m)(6);

— Act Sec. 9014(b), providing the effective date.

Reporter references: For further information, consult the following reporters.

— Standard Federal Tax Reporter, ¶8636.0269

— Tax Research Consultant, COMPEN: 12,360

— Practical Tax Explanation, § 9,310.05, § 9,310.30

¶345 Excise Tax on High Cost Employer-Sponsored Health Coverage

SUMMARY OF NEW LAW

A 40-percent excise tax will be imposed on health coverage providers starting in 2018 to the extent that the aggregate value of employer-sponsored health coverage for an employee exceeds a threshold amount. This is the tax on so-called "Cadillac" health plans.

BACKGROUND

Employer-offered group health plans are highly regulated, and the regulations are generally enforced through excise taxes. For example, excise taxes are imposed for failure to comply with continuation of benefits (i.e., COBRA) requirements (Code Sec. 4980B), group health plan portability requirements (Code Sec. 4980D), and comparable health savings account contribution requirements (Code Sec. 4980G). Historically, however, health coverage itself has not been taxed. Indeed, it has been a highly tax-favored employee benefit.

LAW EXPLAINED

Excise tax imposed on high cost employer-sponsored health coverage starting in 2018.—A 40-percent excise tax will be imposed on health coverage providers starting in 2018 to the extent that the aggregate value of employer-sponsored health coverage for an employee exceeds a threshold amount (Code Sec. 4980I, as added by the Patient Protection and Affordable Care Act (PPACA) (P.L. 111-148), and amended by the Health Care and Education Reconciliation Act of 2010 (P.L. 111-152)).

The tax is imposed with respect to coverage for a tax period if: (1) an employee is covered under any applicable employer-sponsored coverage of an employer at any time during the tax period, and (2) there is any "excess benefit" with respect to the coverage.

LAW EXPLAINED

The tax is 40 percent of the excess benefit (Code Sec. 4980I(a), as added by PPACA). A tax period for these purposes is the calendar year, or a shorter period if the Secretary of the Treasury so prescribes (Code Sec. 4980I(f)(8), as added by PPACA). The tax is not deductible for federal income tax purposes (Code Sec. 275(a)(6); Code Sec. 4980I(f)(10), as added by PPACA). "Employee" for these purposes includes former employees, surviving spouses, or other primary insured individuals (Code Sec. 4980I(d)(3), as added by the 2010 Reconciliation Act).

> **Comment:** This provision was among the more controversial parts of health care reform. The purpose is to raise money to pay for the premium tax credit, as well as provide an incentive to reduce the cost of health insurance premiums in order to constrain the rapid rise in medical costs. In general, unions supported health care reform in 2009, but they strongly objected to this tax. If health reform is ever seriously revisited in Congress, or there is ever a corrections bill for PPACA (as is common for most major legislation), this tax might be eliminated. So far, however, Congressional polarization has prevented even the slightest change in the PPACA since it was adopted in 2009.

Taxable excess benefit. The tax is on the excess benefit, which is the sum of the monthly excess amounts during the tax period (Code Sec. 4980I(b)(1), as added by PPACA). A monthly excess amount is the excess of: (a) the aggregate cost of the applicable employer-sponsored coverage of the employee for the month, over (b) an amount equal to 1/12 of the annual limitation for the calendar year in which the month occurs (Code Sec. 4980I(b)(2), as added by PPACA).

Annual limitation for calculating excess benefit. The annual limitation for any calendar year is the statutory dollar limit for that year as adjusted for inflation (Code Sec. 4980I(b)(3)(A), as added by PPACA), and for certain other factors. The annual limitation applicable for any month depends on the type of coverage provided as of the beginning of the month (Code Sec. 4980I(b)(3)(B), as added by PPACA and amended by the 2010 Reconciliation Act). An employee is treated as having self-only coverage for these purposes, unless: (1) the coverage is provided under a multiemployer plan (Code Sec. 4980I(b)(3)(B), as added by PPACA and amended by the 2010 Reconciliation Act); or (2) the employee is enrolled in coverage other than self-only coverage in a group health plan that provides minimum essential coverage to the employee and at least one other beneficiary and these benefits do not vary based on whether the covered individual is the employee or another beneficiary (Code Sec. 4980I(f)(1); Code Sec. 5000A(f), as added by PPACA).

The dollar limits for determining the tax thresholds are:

- $10,200 (for 2018) multiplied by the health cost adjustment percentage for an employee with self-only coverage, and
- $27,500 (for 2018) multiplied by the health cost adjustment percentage for an employee with coverage other than self-only coverage.

> **Comment:** The $10,200 and $27,500 amounts are just starting points for determining the thresholds for taxing excess benefits.

Health cost adjustment percentages. The health cost adjustment percentages, which are applied to the $10,200 and $27,500 amounts, are designed to capture upward

LAW EXPLAINED

deviations in the rise of the cost of good health care coverage between 2010 and 2018 as compared to an expected change (i.e., 55 percent). The percentage equals 100 percent plus:

- the excess (if any) of the percentage by which the per employee cost for providing coverage under the Blue Cross/Blue Shield standard benefit option under the Federal Employees Health Benefits Plan for plan year 2018 (determined by using the benefit package for such coverage in 2010) exceeds such cost for plan year 2010,
- over 55 percent (Code Sec. 4980I(b)(3)(C)(ii), as added by the 2010 Reconciliation Act).

Example 1: Suppose the per employee cost of the Blue Cross/Blue Shield standard benefit option under the Federal Employees Health Benefits Plan for self-only coverage goes up by 80 percent between 2010 and 2018 (controlling for the same 2010 benefits package). The adjustment percentage for coverage under self-only plans is 135 percent (100 + (80 − 55)).

> **Comment:** Note that the adjustment percentage is not reduced below 100 percent if the cost goes up by less than 55 percent.

The health cost adjustment percentage is determined for employees with self-only coverage by taking only self-only coverage into account, and it is determined for employees with coverage other than self-only coverage by taking only coverage other than self-only coverage into account (Code Sec. 4980I(b)(3)(C)(i), as added by PPACA and amended by the 2010 Reconciliation Act).

Employer-specific age and gender adjustment to the threshold amounts. An employer-specific adjustment is made each tax period to the threshold amounts so that an employer with a workforce that is more expensive to insure due to age or gender characteristics will not be put at a disadvantage. The threshold dollar limits for any tax period (i.e., the $10,200 and $27,500 amounts as adjusted by the applicable health cost percentage in 2018, and inflation thereafter) are increased by an amount equal to the excess (if any) of: (a) the premium cost of the Blue Cross/Blue Shield standard benefit option under the Federal Employees Health Benefits Plan for the type of coverage provided such individual in such taxable period if priced for the age and gender characteristics of all employees of the individual's employer, over (b) that premium cost for the provision of such coverage under such option in such taxable period if priced for the age and gender characteristics of the national workforce (Code Sec. 4980I(b)(3)(C)(iii), as added by the 2010 Reconciliation Act).

Example 2: Suppose in 2018, Acme Corporation's workforce is older than the average age of the national workforce. The threshold amounts that would otherwise apply to Acme's employees to calculate the excess benefit will be adjusted upwards. The amount is determined by taking the premium cost of the Blue Cross/Blue Shield standard benefit option for federal employees in 2018 priced for the age and gender characteristics of Acme's workforce in 2018,

---

LAW EXPLAINED

> and subtracting the premium cost if the Blue Cross/Blue Shield plan were priced for the age and gender characteristic of the national workforce. Suppose the premium difference for a self-only plan is $1,000, and $2,500 for plans that are not self-only plans. $1,000 is added to the threshold amounts for employees with self-only coverage, and $2,500 is added for employees with coverage from plans that are not self-only.

Additions to thresholds for coverage of retirees and high risk professions. More generous thresholds apply for coverage of individuals who: (1) have attained age 55, receive retiree coverage, and are not eligible for Medicare, or (2) participate in a plan sponsored by an employer, the majority of whose employees are engaged in high risk professions, which include law enforcement officers, firefighters, members of a rescue squad or ambulance crew, longshore workers, and individuals engaged in the construction, mining, agriculture (not including food processing), forestry, and fishing industries, or are employed to repair or install electrical or telecommunications lines (Code Sec. 4980I(f)(2), (3), as added by PPACA). In either of those cases:

- the $10,200 amount (as adjusted by the health cost adjustment percentage) is increased by $1,650, and

- the $27,500 amount (as adjusted by the health cost adjustment percentage) is increased by $3,450 (Code Sec. 4980I(b)(3)(C)(iv), as added by PPACA and amended by the 2010 Reconciliation Act).

An individual cannot qualify for more than one such increase, even if the individual qualifies both as a retiree and as engaged in a high risk profession.

> **Example 3:** In 2018, Fern Rodriguez is 60 years old, receives retiree benefits, and has self-only coverage. Suppose the adjustment percentage is 110 percent. Suppose also there is no adjustment for the age or gender characteristics of her employer's workforce. The threshold amount for her coverage for 2018 is ($10,200 × 110 percent) plus $1,650, or $12,870.

Inflation adjustments. The threshold amounts, as determined for 2018 (including the adjustments for the health care adjustment percentage, and the adjustments for retirees and individuals in high risk occupations), are indexed to the Consumer Price Index for Urban Consumers (CPI-U) as determined by the Department of Labor beginning in 2019. For 2019 only, an additional one percent is added to the cost of living adjustment (Code Sec. 4980I(b)(3)(C)(v), as added by PPACA, and amended by the 2010 Reconciliation Act).

Paying the tax. A coverage provider must pay the tax on its applicable share of the excess benefit with respect to an employee for any tax period (Code Sec. 4980I(c)(1), as added by PPACA). A coverage provider for these purposes includes:

- The health insurer, if the applicable employer-sponsored coverage consists of coverage under a group health plan which provides health insurance coverage;

LAW EXPLAINED

- The employer, in the case of contributions to an employer-sponsored Health Savings Account (HSA) or Medical Savings Account (MSA); and

- The person that administers plan benefits (including the plan sponsor if the plan sponsor administers benefits under the plan (Code Sec. 4980I(f)(6), as added by PPACA) in the case of any other applicable employer-sponsored coverage (Code Sec. 4980I(c)(2), as added by PPACA).

Accordingly, the plan administrator pays the excise tax in the case of a self-insured group health plan, a Health Flexible Spending Account (Health FSA), or a Health Reimbursement Arrangement (HRA). On the other hand, the employer pays the excise tax where the employer acts as plan administrator to a self-insured group health plan, a Health FSA, or an HRA, and with respect to employer contributions to an HSA. A plan sponsor for these purposes includes the employer or employee organization that established and maintains the plan. In the case of a plan established or maintained by multiple employers or by one or more employers with one or more employee organizations, the committee or board that established or maintains the plan is the plan sponsor (Code Sec. 4980I(f)(7), as added by PPACA; ERISA Sec. 3(16)(B)).

> **Comment:** Placing the tax on coverage providers will provide an incentive for them to cap their rates at the threshold amounts.

Example 4: For 2018, the cost of applicable employer-sponsored coverage provided by the provider is $30,000, and the aggregate cost of all applicable employer-sponsored coverage provided to the employee is $35,000. If the total excess benefit is $7,500, the provider's applicable share is $6,429 (($30,000 / $35,000) × $7,500).

Employer's responsibility to calculate the tax and applicable shares. An employer must: (a) calculate for each tax period the amount of the excess benefit subject to the tax and the applicable share of the excess benefit for each coverage provider, and (b) notify the Treasury Secretary and each coverage provider of the amount determined for the provider (Code Sec. 4980I(c)(4)(A), as added by PPACA). In the case of coverage through a multiemployer plan (as defined in Code Sec. 414(f)), the plan sponsor must make the calculations and provide the required notice (Code Sec. 4980I(c)(4)(B), as added by PPACA).

Example 5: For 2018, employee Jennifer Jackson elects family coverage under a fully-insured health care policy covering major medical and dental with a value of $35,000. Suppose her adjusted threshold amount is $27,500 for 2018. The amount subject to the excise tax is $7,500 ($35,000 less the threshold of $27,500). The employer reports $7,500 as taxable to the insurer, which calculates and remits the excise tax to the IRS.

> **Example 6:** For 2018, employee Randy Segal elects family coverage under a fully-insured major medical policy with a value of $30,000 and a separate fully-insured dental policy with a value of $2,000. Randy also contributes $3,000 to a Health FSA. Randy has an aggregate health insurance coverage value of $33,000 (the dental plan is not counted as coverage subject to tax). Suppose the adjusted threshold amount is $27,500 for 2018. The amount subject to the excise tax is $5,500 ($33,000 less the threshold of $27,500). The employer reports $5,000 ($5,500 × $30,000 / $33,000) as taxable to the major medical insurer which then calculates and remits the excise tax to the IRS. If the employer uses a third-party administrator for the Health FSA, the employer reports $500 ($5,500 × $3,000/$33,000) to the administrator and the administrator calculates and remits the excise tax to the IRS.

Coverage subject to tax. Applicable employer-sponsored coverage subject to the excise tax includes coverage under any group health plan made available to the employee by an employer which is excludable from the employee's gross income, or would be so excludable if it were employer-provided coverage, including coverage in the form of reimbursements under a Health FSA or an HRA, employer contributions to an HSA, and coverage for dental, vision, and other supplementary health insurance coverage (Code Sec. 4980I(d)(1)(A), as added by PPACA; Code Sec. 106). It does not include employer-sponsored coverage for:

- separate dental or vision coverage;
- fixed indemnity health coverage purchased by the employee with after-tax dollars (Code Sec. 4980I(d)(1)(B)(i), as added by PPACA and amended by the 2010 Reconciliation Act; Code Sec. 162(l));
- disability benefits or long term care under an accident or health plan;
- liability insurance (including general liability insurance and auto liability insurance), or coverage issued as a supplement to liability insurance;
- workers' compensation or similar insurance;
- automobile medical payment insurance;
- credit-only insurance; and
- other similar insurance coverage under which benefits for medical care are secondary or incidental to other insurance benefits (Code Sec. 4980I(d)(1)(B)(iii), as added by PPACA and amended by 2010 Reconciliation Act; Code Sec. 9832(c)(1) and (3); Reg. §54.9831-1(c)(3)).

Fixed indemnity coverage pays fixed dollar amounts based on the occurrence of qualifying events, including but not limited to the diagnosis of a specific disease, an accidental injury, or a hospitalization, provided that the coverage is not coordinated with other health coverage.

Coverage paid by employee. Employer-sponsored health insurance coverage is health coverage offered by an employer to an employee without regard to whether the employer pays for the coverage (in which case it is excludable from the employee's

LAW EXPLAINED

gross income), or the employee pays for the coverage with his or her own after-tax dollars (Code Sec. 4980I(d)(1)(C), as added by PPACA).

Coverage for self-employed. For a self-employed individual, coverage under any group health plan providing health insurance coverage is treated as applicable employer-sponsored coverage if a deduction is allowable under Code Sec. 162(l) with respect to all or any portion of the cost of the coverage (Code Sec. 4980I(d)(1)(D), as added by PPACA).

Coverage by government plans. Applicable employer-sponsored coverage includes coverage under any group health plan established and maintained for its civilian employees by the federal, state, and local governments, or by any agency or instrumentality of any such government (Code Sec. 4980I(d)(1)(E), as added by PPACA).

Determining cost of coverage. The aggregate value of all employer-sponsored health insurance coverage, including dental, vision, and other supplementary health insurance coverage, is generally calculated in the same manner as the applicable premiums for the tax year for the employee determined under the rules for COBRA continuation coverage. If the plan provides for the same COBRA continuation coverage premium for both individual coverage and family coverage, the plan would have to calculate separate individual and family premiums for this purpose. In determining the coverage value for retirees, employers can elect to treat retirees who retire before age 65 together with those who retire at or after age 65 (Code Sec. 4980I(d)(2)(A), as added by PPACA; Code Sec. 4980B(f)(4)).

> **Comment:** The applicable premium under COBRA for any period of continuation coverage is the cost to the plan for such period of coverage for similarly situated non-COBRA beneficiaries with respect to whom a qualifying event has not occurred, and is determined without regard to whether the cost is paid by the employer or employee. Special rules apply for determining the applicable premium in the case of self-insured plans (Code Sec. 4980B(f)(4)).

Cost of Health FSAs and HSAs. The cost of the coverage of a Health FSA is the dollar amount of the aggregate salary reduction contributions for the year. To the extent that the FSA provides for reimbursement in excess of this amount, the value of the coverage generally is determined in the same manner as the applicable premium for COBRA continuation coverage. If the plan provides for the same COBRA continuation coverage premium for both individual coverage and family coverage, the plan would be required to calculate separate individual and family premiums for this purpose (Code Sec. 4980I(d)(2)(B), as added by PPACA; Code Sec. 106(c)(2)). For HSAs and MSAs, the cost of the coverage equals the amount of employer contributions under the arrangement (Code Sec. 4980I(d)(2)(C), as added by PPACA).

Cost allocation on a monthly basis. If cost is determined on other than a monthly basis, the cost shall be allocated to months in a tax period on such basis as the Secretary may prescribe (Code Sec. 4980I(d)(2)(D), as added by PPACA).

Penalty for failure to properly calculate excess benefit. If the employer reports to insurers and plan administrators (as well as the IRS) a lower amount of insurance cost subject to the excise tax than required, the employer is subject to a penalty equal

LAW EXPLAINED

to any additional excise tax that each such insurer and administrator would have owed if the employer had reported correctly, increased for interest from the date that the tax was otherwise due to the date paid by the employer (Code Sec. 4980I(e)(1), as added by PPACA). This may occur, for example, if the employer undervalues the aggregate premium and thereby lowers the amount subject to the excise tax for all insurers and plan administrators (including the employer when acting as plan administrator of a self-insured plan).

This penalty may be waived if the employer can show that the failure is due to reasonable cause and not to willful neglect (Code Sec. 4980I(e)(2)(C), as added by PPACA). The penalty is in addition to the amount of excise tax owed, which may not be waived.

The penalty is not to be imposed if the employer or plan sponsor neither knew, nor exercising reasonable diligence would have known, that such failure existed (Code Sec. 4980I(e)(2)(A), as added by PPACA). Nor is it imposed if the failure was due to reasonable cause and not willful neglect, and the failure is corrected during the 30-day period beginning on the first date that the employer knew, or exercising reasonable diligence would have known, that such failure existed (Code Sec. 4980I(e)(2)(B), as added by PPACA).

Aggregation of employers. The employer aggregation rules for controlled groups of corporations, partnerships or proprietorships under common control, affiliated service groups, and leased employees apply to the excise tax on high cost plans (Code Sec. 4980I(f)(9), as added by PPACA; Code Sec. 414(b), (c), (m) and (o)).

Liability for any applicable excise tax may need to be allocated among up to three types of coverage providers—health insurance issuers, employers and plan administrators. Responsibility for the correct computation of taxable excess benefits falls on the employer or plan sponsor. To the extent such computation understates the taxable excess benefit, a penalty plus underpayment interest applies. The Act places responsibility for the penalty only on the employer or the plan sponsor (and not on the insurer, if any).

▶ **Effective date.** The excise tax applies to tax years beginning after December 31, 2017 (Act Secs. 9001(c) and 10901(c) of the Patient Protection and Affordable Care Act (PPACA) (P.L. 111-148)), and Act Sec. 1401(b) of the Health Care and Education Reconciliation Act of 2010 (P.L. 111-152).

Law source: Law at ¶5330.

— Act Sec. 9001(a), as amended by Act Sec. 10901(a), of the Patient Protection and Affordable Care Act P.L. 111-148), as amended by Act Sec. 1401(a) of the Health Care and Education Reconciliation Act of 2010 (P.L. 111-152), adding Code Sec. 4980I;

— Act Secs. 9001(c) and 10901(c), of PPACA, and Act Sec. 1401(b) of the 2010 Reconciliation Act providing the effective date.

Reporter references: For further information, consult the following reporters.

— Standard Federal Tax Reporter, ¶34,619ZH.01

— Tax Research Consultant, HEALTH: 9,302

— Practical Tax Explanation, § 42,175

¶350 Excise Tax on Sales of Medical Devices

SUMMARY OF NEW LAW

A 2.3 percent excise tax is imposed on sales of medical devices. The excise tax applies to sales after December 31, 2012.

BACKGROUND

Prior to the passage of the excise tax on medical devices imposed by Code Sec. 4191, no excise tax was imposed under the Internal Revenue Code on companies that manufacture medical devices for sale in the United States.

LAW EXPLAINED

Excise tax imposed on sales of medical devices.—Starting in 2013, an excise tax is imposed on any manufacturer, producer or importer of certain medical devices. The tax is equal to 2.3 percent of the price for which the medical device is sold (Code Sec. 4191(a), as added by the Health Care and Education Reconciliation Act of 2010 (P.L. 111-152)). The excise tax applies to sales after December 31, 2012 (Act Sec. 1405(c) of the 2010 Reconciliation Act).

For purposes of the medical device excise tax (MDET), a taxable medical device means any "device"—as defined in section 201(h) of the Federal Food Drug and Cosmetic Act (FDC Act or FFDCA)—intended for humans. In turn, under the final regulations, a device defined in FFDCA § 201(h) means a device that is listed as a device with the Food and Drug Administration under section 510(j) of the FDC Act and 21 CFR part 807, unless the device qualifies for an exemption from the tax (Code Sec. 4191(b)(1); Reg. § 48.4191-2(a)(1)). Sales of eyeglasses, contact lenses, and hearing aids are exempt from the MDET. In addition, any other medical device determined to be of a type that is generally purchased by the general public at retail for individual use is not subject to the MDET (Code Sec. 4191(b)(2)). This is referred to as the "retail exemption."

A facts and circumstances approach is used to determine whether a medical device meets the retail exemption, and final regulations provide several non-exclusive factors. No one factor is determinative; whether a given device falls under the retail exemption is based on the overall balance of factors (Reg. § 48.4191-2(b)(2)). The final regulations also provide a safe harbor for certain devices that fall within the retail exemption (Reg. § 48.4191-2(b)(2)(iii)).

The medical device tax is a manufacturers excise tax, and as a result, the manufacturer or importer of a taxable medical device is responsible for filing Form 720, Quarterly Federal Excise Tax Return, and paying the tax. Therefore, consumers generally have no reporting or recordkeeping requirements. Form 720 is filed quarterly. Semi-monthly deposits will generally be required if tax liability exceeds $2,500 for the quarter (Medical Device Excise Tax: FAQs, December 5, 2012).

LAW EXPLAINED

Under certain circumstances, a manufacturer or importer of a taxable medical device may sell the device tax-free for use by the purchaser for further manufacture or for export. To make a tax-free sale for further manufacture or export, both parties to the sale must have registered with the IRS using Form 637, Application for Registration for Certain Excise Tax Activities.

Definition of a "taxable medical device." *Listing requirement.* Code Sec. 4191(b)(1) provides that, in general, a "taxable medical device" is any device, as defined in section 201(h) of the Federal Food, Drug & Cosmetic Act (21 U.S.C. 301 et seq.) that is intended for humans. Thus, Congress linked the definition of a taxable medical device to the definition of a "device" under FFDCA § 201(h).

In general, under FFDCA § 201(h), the term "device" is any article that either (1) is intended for use in the diagnosis, prevention, treatment or cure of disease in man or animals; (2) is intended to affect the structure or any function of the body; or (3) is recognized in the National Formulary or the United States Pharmacopoeia.

To fall within this definition, a medical device cannot achieve any of its primary intended purposes by means of chemical action within or on the body, and it cannot be dependent on being metabolized for the achievement of any principal intended uses.

Under the final regulations, a device defined in FFDCA § 201(h) — the basic criterion under Code Sec. 4191(b)(1) for whether a device is a "taxable medical device" —means a device that is listed as a device with the FDA under FFDCA § 510(j) and 21 CFR part 807, pursuant to FDA requirements (Reg. § 48.4191-2(a)(1)).

How, then, does a device get "listed"? Upon manufacturing or processing a device for the first time, a firm's owner must register with the FDA, and then register annually (FFDCA § 510(b) and (c)). Under FFDCA § 510(j), a list of devices must be submitted at the time of registration and must state the basis for considering an article to be a device rather than a drug, along with other information. Lists are updated by the FDA once each year, and all registered manufacturers must submit new listing information annually.

Biologic devices. The FDA Center for Biologics Evaluation and Research (CBER) regulates and licenses products called "biologics," such as in vitro diagnostic tests for blood donor screening. Biologics are listed with the FDA under 21 CFR part 607. They are not, however, listed with the FDA under FFDCA § 510(j) and 21 CFR part 807. Therefore, biologics are not taxable medical devices.

Devices not used directly on patients. The stipulation in Code Sec. 4191(b)(1) that a taxable medical device must be a device "intended for humans" does not exclude from taxation devices such as sterilization process indicators, software, and containers used to hold or transport medical products and specimens. Although these devices are not used in the direct treatment, diagnosis, or monitoring of a patient, the medical device tax is not limited to devices intended for use directly on patients or in patient care.

Veterinary devices. The definition of a device in section 201(h) of the FFDCA includes devices used in veterinary medicine. However, Code Sec. 4191 limits the definition of a taxable medical device to devices described in section 201(h) of the FFDCA that are

LAW EXPLAINED

intended for humans. But note that a device need not be intended exclusively for humans to be subject to the tax.

"Dual use" devices. A dual use device is a device that has medical and non-medical applications. More technically, it is a device defined in section 201(h) of the FDC Act that is listed as a device with the FDA under 21 CFR part 807, but that is also used for a non-medical purpose. Code Sec. 4191 does not limit the definition of a taxable medical device to a device that is intended exclusively for medical purposes. As a result, there is no tax exemption based on whether an end user intends to use a particular dual use device for a medical purpose or a non-medical purpose.

Humanitarian use devices. A Humanitarian Use Device (HUD) is a device within the meaning of FFDCA § 201(h) that is intended to benefit patients by treating or diagnosing a disease or condition that affects or is manifested in fewer than 4,000 individuals in the United States per year. In order to market an HUD, the manufacturer must obtain a Humanitarian Device Exemption (HDE) from the Food and Drug Administration (FDA). A HUD that is marketed under an HDE exemption, however, is still a taxable medical device unless it falls within one of the statutory exemptions provided in Code Sec. 4191(b)(2).

Software upgrades. Sales of software and software upgrades that are not required to be separately listed with the FDA do not fall within the definition of a taxable medical device, and therefore are not subject to the MDET.

Devices that should have been listed with the FDA. If a device should have been listed with the FDA by the manufacturer, it is considered to have been listed on the date the FDA provides written notice that the listing must be corrected. Further, for purposes of this rule, the notice that establishes the date of listing need not be the final written notice (Reg. § 48.4191-2(a)(2)).

Devices that are not required to be listed with the FDA. If a manufacturer lists a device with the FDA that was not required to be listed, a credit or refund may be available under Code Sec. 6416(a) once the device has been de-listed.

Combination products. Combination products are therapeutic and diagnostic products that comprise some combination of drugs, devices, and biological products. A combination product that is listed as a device with the FDA under FFDCA § 510(j) and 21 CFR part 807, and that does not fall under a statutory exemption, is subject to the medical device excise tax.

Retail exemption. Code Sec. 4191(b)(2) provides that the term "taxable medical device" does not include eyeglasses, contact lenses, hearing aids, and any other medical device determined to be of a type that is generally purchased by the general public at retail for individual use.

A device will be considered to be of a type that is generally purchased by the general public at retail for individual use if—

(1) it is regularly available for purchase and use by individual consumers who are not medical professionals (Reg. § 48.4191-2(b)(2)(i)), and

¶350

LAW EXPLAINED

(2) the design of the device demonstrates that it is not primarily intended for use in a medical institution or office or by a medical professional (Reg. §48.4191-2(b)(2)(ii)).

Whether these two factors result in a retail exemption for a given device is based on an evaluation of all the relevant facts and circumstances. These two factors are not, however, exclusive. There may be additional facts and circumstances relevant to whether the retail exemption applies. And no one factor is determinative. Whether a device qualifies for the retail exemption is based on the overall balance of factors relevant to the particular type of device. For example, the mere fact that an individual device is sold for use in a professional setting does not settle the question. Note, too, that whether a device requires a prescription is not a factor (Reg. §48.4191-2(b)(2)).

Regularly available for purchase and use by individual customers. In determining whether the retail exemption applies, among the relevant factors is whether consumers who are not medical professionals can purchase the device and use it safely and effectively for its intended purpose with minimal or no training from a medical professional. Even if a device does not satisfy this factor, however, it may qualify for the retail exemption. (See Reg. §48.4191-2(b)(2)(i) for a complete list of factors relating to this consideration.)

Primarily for use in a medical institution or office or by a medical professional. Another of the relevant factors is whether the device must be implanted, inserted, or operated by a medical professional, and whether the device is not affordable for the average individual customer. (See Reg. §48.4191-2(b)(2)(ii) for a complete list of factors relating to this consideration.)

Safe harbors: generally. The final regulations provide four safe harbors for the retail exemption—that is, four categories of devices that will be considered to be of a type that is generally purchased by the general public at retail for individual use (Reg. §48.4191-2(b)(2)(iii)).

Safe harbors: durable medical equipment, prosthetics, orthotics and supplies (DMEPOS). The final regulations provide a safe harbor for devices that qualify as durable medical equipment, prosthetics, orthotics and supplies (Reg. §48.4191-2(b)(2)(iii)(D)).

Prosthetic and orthotic devices, as defined in 42 CFR 414.202, that do not require implantation or insertion by a medical professional fall under the retail exemption safe harbor (Reg. §48.4191-2(b)(2)(iii)(D)(1)). Accordingly, such prosthetic and orthotic devices are considered to be of a type that are generally purchased by the general public at retail for individual use, whether or not they require initial or periodic fitting or adjustment.

A prosthetic or orthotic device that is not in the safe harbor may qualify for the retail exemption based on an application of the facts and circumstances test. The final regulations include an example of a prosthetic device that falls within the retail exemption: a single axis endoskeletal knee shin system, which is used in the manufacture of prosthetic legs (Reg. §48.4191-2(b)(2)(iv), Example 8).

Devices that fall within the definition of DMEPOS but that are not included in the retail exemption safe harbor, such as oxygen equipment and other rental durable medical

¶350

LAW EXPLAINED

equipment devices, may still qualify for the retail exemption by applying the facts and circumstances test.

Examples in the final regulations apply the retail exemption to a number of medical devices (see Reg. § 48.4191-2(b)(2)(iv)).

Application of manufacturers excise tax rules. Because Code Sec. 4191 is one of the manufacturers excise taxes under chapter 32, subtitle D of the Internal Revenue Code, the existing manufacturer excise tax rules apply. One consequence of this is that, under Code Sec. 4216(a), with respect to the tax base, the medical device excise tax is excluded from the sale price upon which the tax is imposed, whether or not the tax is stated as a separate charge.

Exemptions and overpayments. The excise tax on sales of medical devices does not apply to the sale by the manufacturer of a medical device (1) for use by the purchaser for further manufacture, or (2) for resale by the purchaser to a second purchaser for use by the second purchaser in further manufacture. The excise tax also does not apply to the sale by the manufacturer of a medical device for export or for resale by the purchaser to a second purchaser for export (Code Sec. 4221(a)).

Overpayments of the MDET may be allowed as a credit or refund in certain circumstances (Code Sec. 6416(b)(2)).

Installment sales, leases, and long-term contracts: Transitional relief. The IRS provided a transitional rule with respect to payments made on or after January 1, 2013, pursuant to a written binding contract for the lease, installment sale, or sale on credit of a taxable medical device that was in effect prior to March 30, 2010. Those payments are not subject to tax under Code Sec. 4191 unless the contract was materially modified on or after March 30, 2010. A material modification is a modification that materially affects the property to be provided, the terms of payment, or the amount payable under the contract. A material modification does not include a modification to the contract required by applicable federal, state, or local law (Reg. § 48.4191-1(f)).

Uses. In general, if the manufacturer of a taxable article uses the article for any purpose other than in the manufacture of another taxable article, then the manufacturer is liable for tax on the article as if the manufacturer had sold it (Reg. § 48.4218-1(b)).

With regard to demonstration products used for health care professionals and product awareness, such as samples used to demonstrate the type of device to be implanted in a patient, the provision or use of a taxable medical device as a demonstration product may constitute a taxable use, depending on the facts and circumstances of the arrangement (see T.D. 9604 preamble).

With regard to "evaluation and testing products" provided to help health care professionals determine whether and when to use, order, purchase, or recommend the device, Rev. Rul. 76-119, 1976-1 CB 345, holds that if a manufacturer uses a taxable article in the testing of another article of its own manufacture, the use of the taxable article is not a taxable use (see T.D. 9604 preamble).

Self-kitters. Hospitals or medical institutions that produce kits for their own use are known as self-kitters. Self-kitters are exempt from the FDA's registration and listing

¶350

LAW EXPLAINED

requirements (see 21 CFR 807.65(f)). Therefore, under the definition of a taxable medical device in Reg. §48.4191-2(a)(1), use of a kit by the hospital or medical institution that produced it would not be a taxable use under the rules of Code Sec. 4218.

Rebates. Under Reg. §48.4216(a)-3(c), a manufacturer may take a rebate into account in determining sale price, but only if the rebate is made before the close of the quarter during which the sale is made. If, afterwards, the manufacturer allows a rebate for a tax-paid medical device, it may make a claim for credit or refund for tax paid on that part of the price that is rebated.

Software sold together with services. If an entire software and service bundle is not a taxable medical device, the excise tax attaches only to the devices within the bundle that are listed with the FDA under section 510(j) of the FFDCA and 21 CFR part 807 (Reg. §48.4216(a)-1(e)).

Refurbished and remanufactured medical devices. Under existing chapter 32 rules, if a remanufacturer or refurbisher produces a new and different taxable article, the tax is imposed upon the sale or use of the remanufactured or refurbished article.

Replacement parts. If a taxable device is returned to the manufacturer under a warranty and the manufacturer provides a replacement free or at a reduced price, the tax on the replacement is computed on the actual amount, if any, paid for the replacement (see Reg. §48.4216(a)-3(b) and Rev. Rul. 75-272 (1975-2 CB 421)).

As to replacements that are not made under warranty, replacement parts that are listed with the FDA under section 510(j) of the FFDCA and 21 CFR part 807 are taxable medical devices, and their sale by the manufacturer is generally subject to tax.

Filing Form 720: Affiliated groups. The MDET is reported on Form 720, which generally must be filed on a quarterly basis. Each business unit that has or is required to have a separate employer identification number (EIN) must file a separate Form 720. As a result, manufacturers and importers of taxable medical devices who are members of an affiliated group for income tax purposes are not permitted to file Form 720 on a consolidated basis.

Filing Form 720: Disregarded entities. A Form 720 reporting the MDET on sales after December 31, 2012, must be filed under the name and employer identification number of the disregarded entity, rather than under the name and EIN of the entity's owner.

Semimonthly deposits. Medical device manufacturers will generally be required to make semimonthly deposits of tax unless the manufacturer's net tax liability does not exceed $2,500 for the quarter (see Code Sec. 6302 and the related regulations).

Interim guidance under Notice 2012-77. In Notice 2012-77, the IRS provided interim guidance, effective January 1, 2013, on certain issues that the final regulations contained in T.D. 9604 do not address, but that the IRS and Treasury are continuing to study.

Constructive sale price. Code Sec. 4216(b) provides rules for constructing a sale price when a manufacturer sells a taxable article to a purchaser other than an independent wholesale distributor. Many medical device manufacturers do not sell to independent

¶350

LAW EXPLAINED

wholesale distributors, and may use more than one distribution chain. The constructive sale price is intended to approximate the price an independent wholesale distributor would pay for the article. Further, current published guidance does not address some distribution chains regularly used in the medical device industry, creating a need for interim guidance.

Under the interim guidance, based on the distribution chain that a taxpayer uses, it calculates its medical device tax liability under the following rules (Notice 2012-77, Section 3). If the manufacturer:

— sells taxable articles directly to unrelated end-users and does not regularly sell to independent wholesale distributors, the constructive sale price is 75 percent of the actual selling price after taking into account Code Sec. 4216(a) adjustments.

— sells taxable articles to unrelated retailers and does not regularly sell to independent wholesale distributors, the constructive sale price is 90 percent of the lowest price for which the articles are sold to unrelated retailers.

— sells taxable articles to a related retailer, and the related retailer sells the articles at retail to unrelated end-users, and the manufacturer and related retailer do not regularly sell the articles to independent wholesale distributors, the constructive sale price is 75 percent of the product of 95 percent and the actual selling price.

— sells taxable articles to a related reseller, the related reseller sells the articles at retail to unrelated end-users, and also leases articles to unrelated end-users, the constructive sale price is 75 percent of the product of 95 percent and the actual selling price.

— sells taxable articles to a related reseller, the related reseller leases the articles to unrelated end-users, but does not sell articles at retail, and the manufacturer and related reseller do not regularly sell the articles to independent wholesale distributors, the price is the actual selling price to the related reseller, if that price reasonably approximates the fair market price of the article.

Sales to a hospital or doctor's office. The interim rules treat the sale of a taxable article to a medical institution or office as a "sale at retail" (Notice 2012-77, Section 4(a)).

Licenses. The interim rules treat a license of a taxable medical device as a lease of that taxable medical device as of the date both parties entered into the license agreement. Note in connection with this that, under Code Sec. 4217, the lease of an article by the manufacturer, producer, or importer is considered a sale of that article (Notice 2012-77, Section 4(b)).

Charitable donations of medical devices. The donation of a taxable medical device by the manufacturer to an eligible donee described in Code Sec. 170(c) will not constitute a taxable use as defined in Code Sec. 4218. But if the manufacturer has reason to believe that the donation is not being made to an eligible donee, or that the article will be resold by the eligible donee, the manufacturer remains liable for the medical device tax (Notice 2012-77, Section 4(c)).

LAW EXPLAINED

Convenience kits. Under the interim guidance (Notice 2012-77, Section 5), a convenience kit is defined as "a set of two or more devices within the meaning of section 201(h) of the FFDCA that is enclosed in a single package, such as a bag, tray, or box, for the convenience of a health care professional or the end user." And, under the interim guidance, no tax will be imposed upon the sale of a domestically produced convenience kit that is a "taxable medical device" under Code Sec. 4191 and Reg. § 48.4191-2(b). Instead, the tax is imposed a step earlier. That is, the sale of the taxable medical device *that goes into* a domestically produced convenience kit will be subject to tax when sold by the manufacturer or importer. The sale of the convenience kit by the kit producer, however, will not be subject to tax.

As to imported convenience kits, tax is imposed upon the sale by an importer of a convenience kit that is a taxable medical device, but only on that portion of the importer's sale price that is properly allocable to the individual taxable medical devices included in the convenience kit.

Deposit penalty relief. During the first three calendar quarters of 2013, the IRS did not impose the Code Sec. 6656 penalty on a taxpayer that failed to make timely semi-monthly deposits of the medical device tax as required by Reg. § § 40.6302(c)-1 and (c)-2 (September deposit rule). This temporary relief applied, however, only if the taxpayer demonstrated a good-faith attempt to comply with the regulatory deposit requirements, and the failure was not due to willful neglect. As of the fourth quarter of 2013, a taxpayer may avoid penalties if it makes an affirmative showing that the failure to deposit is due to reasonable cause and not due to willful neglect (Notice 2012-77, Section 6).

▶ **Effective date.** The excise tax on sales of medical devices applies to sales after December 31, 2012 (Act Sec. 1405(c) of the 2010 Reconciliation Act). The final regulations (T.D. 9604) became effective on December 7, 2012. The interim guidance provided by Notice 2012-77 is effective on and after January 1, 2013.

Law source: Law at ¶5250, ¶5260, and ¶5400.

— Act Sec. 1405(a) of the 2010 Reconciliation Act, adding Code Sec. 4191;

— Act Sec. 1405(b) of the 2010 Reconciliation Act, amending Code Secs. 4221(a) and 6416(b)(2);

— Act Sec. 1405(c) of the 2010 Reconciliation Act providing the effective date.

Reporter references: For further information, consult the following reporters.

— Standard Federal Tax Reporter, ¶14,502.01

— Tax Research Consultant, BUSEXP: 21,350 and EXCISE: 6,162.05

— Practical Tax Explanation, § 9,940.10

— Federal Excise Tax Reporter, ¶14,230.01

¶352 Fee on Manufacturers and Importers of Prescription Drugs

SUMMARY OF NEW LAW

An annual fee is imposed on manufacturers and importers of branded prescription drugs.

BACKGROUND

Prior to the passage of the annual fee on manufacturers and importers of branded prescription drugs, no excise tax or fee was imposed under the Internal Revenue Code on companies that manufacture or import branded prescription drugs for sale in the United States.

LAW EXPLAINED

An annual fee is imposed on manufacturers and importers of branded prescription drugs.—For calendar years beginning after December 31, 2010, a fee is imposed on any manufacturer or importer of certain branded prescription drugs or biological products (also called biologics) offered for sale in the United States (Act Sec. 9008 of the Patient Protection and Affordable Care Act (PPACA) (P.L. 111-148), as amended by Act Sec. 1404 of the Health Care and Education Reconciliation Act (P.L. 111-152)). The fee applies to both domestic and foreign manufacturers and importers of these products with gross receipts of over $5 million from branded prescription drug sales to any specified government program (or pursuant to coverage under such program) (Act Secs. 9008(a) and 9008(d) of PPACA, amended by Act Sec. 1404 of P.L. 111-152).

Definition—Manufacturer or Importer: A manufacturer or importer of a branded prescription drug is defined as the person identified in the Labeler Code of the National Drug Code (NDC) for that drug. The NDC is a unique identifier assigned by the Food and Drug Administration (FDA) to a branded prescription drug (Reg. §51.2(i) and (j)).

The annual fee imposed on each manufacturer or importer of branded prescription drugs or biologics is a portion of the "applicable amount"—an aggregate fee imposed on all covered entities. That applicable amount is $2.5 billion for 2011, $2.8 billion for 2012, $2.8 billion for 2013, $3 billion for 2014, $3 billion for 2015, $3 billion for 2016, $4 billion for 2017, $4.1 billion for 2018, and $2.8 billion for 2019 and the following years (Act Sec. 9008(b)(4) of PPACA, as added by Act Sec. 1404(a)(2)(B) of P.L. 111-152).

The Secretary of the Treasury will annually apportion the fee based on each entity's relative market share of covered domestic sales of branded prescription drugs for the prior year (Act Sec. 9008(b) of PPACA, as amended by Act Sec. 1404(a)(2) of P.L. 111-152). Specifically, the annual fee for each covered entity is calculated by determining the ratio of the covered entity's branded prescription drug sales taken into account during the preceding calendar year to the aggregate branded prescription drug sales

LAW EXPLAINED

taken into account for all covered entities during the same year, and applying this ratio to the applicable amount for that year (Act Sec. 9008(b)(1) of PPACA, as amended by Act Sec. 1404(a)(2)(A) of P.L. 111-152). "Sales taken into account" means sales after the application of the percentage adjustment table in Act Sec. 9008(b)(2) of the Patient Protection and Affordable Care Act. Under the percentage adjustment, increasingly higher percentages of sales are taken into account for progressively higher brackets of the covered entity's aggregate branded prescription drug sales.

As mentioned above, the domestic sales that are included in determining an entity's annual fee are only those that are made to or funded by specified government programs, such as Medicare, Medicaid, the Veterans Administration, the Department of Defense, and TRICARE (Reg. §51.2(h)).

Orphan drugs. Sales of orphan drugs for which a credit under Code Sec. 45C was allowed for any tax year are excluded from the annual fee (Act Sec. 9008(e) of PPACA). An orphan drug does not include any drug for any sales year after the calendar year in which the FDA approved the drug for any indication other than the treatment of a rare disease or condition for which a Code Sec. 45C credit was allowed (Reg. §51.2(k)). See the detailed examples illustrating the treatment of orphan drugs in Reg. §51.2(k)(4).

Each covered entity's fee is due no later than the annual payment date for each calendar year beginning after 2010 (Act Sec. 9008(a)(1) of PPACA, as amended by Act Sec. 1404(a)(1) of P.L. 111-152). The annual payment date is determined by the Secretary of the Treasury, but cannot be later than September 30 of the calendar year. If more than one person is liable for the fee with respect to a single covered entity, all such persons are jointly and severally liable for payment of the fee (Act Sec. 9008(d)(3) of PPACA, as amended by Act Sec. 1404(a)(3) of P.L. 111-152).

The fees collected from manufacturers and importers of branded prescription drugs will be credited to the Medicare Part B trust fund (Joint Committee on Taxation, Technical Explanation of the Revenue Provisions of the "Reconciliation Act of 2010," as amended, in combination with the "Patient Protection and Affordable Care Act" (JCX-18-10), March 21, 2010).

Note that the annual fee may not be deducted for federal income tax purposes.

Annual fee calculation. For every "fee year"—the calendar year in which the fee must be paid for a particular sales year—the IRS will determine a covered entity's total fee (Reg. §§51.2(g) and 51.5). The "sales year"—the calendar year of the branded prescription drug sales that will be used to determine the amount of the fee—is the second calendar year preceding the fee year. For example, for the fee year of 2015, the sales year is 2013 (Reg. §51.2(m)). Each covered entity's branded prescription drug sales will be reduced by its Medicaid state supplemental rebate amounts (Reg. §51.5(b)).

Information provided by drug manufacturers. Each covered entity may submit Form 8947, Report of Branded Prescription Drug Information, to provide information relevant to determining the annual fee. The submission of that form is voluntary (Reg. §51.3(a)).

Adjustment amount. Since use of the second preceding year as the sales year, rather than the immediately preceding year, may affect the amount of the fee paid by any

LAW EXPLAINED

particular entity, the fee due in every year includes an adjustment amount discussed in detail in the regulations (Reg. § § 51.5(a) and (e)).

The IRS does not make interest payments for adjustment amounts that are credited to a covered entity. An adjustment amount itself is neither an overpayment nor an underpayment, but a component of the current year's fee. As a result, any increase in the current year's fee resulting from any adjustment amount, along with the remainder of the fee, is treated as due on the due date for the current year's fee. Conversely, any adjustment amount that decreases the current year's fee is treated as a payment towards the current fee amount made on the due date of the current fee year (Reg. § 51.5(e)).

Annual dispute resolution process. A dispute resolution process gives each covered entity an opportunity to dispute the preliminary fee calculation by submitting an error report to the IRS (Reg. § 51.7).

Annual deadlines. The IRS will send each covered entity its final fee calculation no later than August 31 of each fee year. Each covered entity must then pay its final fee by September 30 of the fee year (Reg. § 51.8). The fee must by paid by electronic funds transfer (Reg. § 51.8(c) and Reg. § 51.6302-1). No tax return is filed for the fee. The IRS must assess the amount of the fee for any fee year within three years of September 30 of that fee year (Reg. § 51.9(c)).

Deadlines for each fee year. Effective on October 1, 2014, the following deadlines relating to the branded prescription drug fee apply for each fee year: (1) a covered entity that chooses to submit Form 8947, Report of Branded Prescription Drug Information, has until November 1 of the year preceding the fee year to do so; (2) a covered entity may request an electronic copy of the National Drug Code (NDC) attachment by February 15 of the fee year; (3) the IRS will mail each covered entity a paper notice of its preliminary fee calculation and, if requested, the NDC attachment by March 1 of the fee year; (4) with the preliminary fee calculation, the IRS will send each covered entity a template to prepare an error report; (5) a covered entity has until May 15 of the fee year to mail an error report regarding its preliminary fee calculation; (6) the IRS will mail a notice to each covered entity of its final fee calculation along with a final NDC attachment by August 31 of the fee year; and (7) each covered entity must pay the fee by September 30 of the fee year (Notice 2014-42, I.R.B. 2014-34, 387).

Tax treatment. The branded prescription drug fee is treated as an excise tax for which only civil action for refund under subtitle F procedures apply. As a result, the deficiency procedures of Code Secs. 6211 to 6216 do not apply (Reg. § 51.9).

Refund claims. Any claim for a refund of the fee must be made on Form 843, Claim for Refund and Request for Abatement, by the person who paid the fee (Reg. § 51.10).

▶ **Effective date.** The annual fee on drug manufacturers and importers applies to calendar years beginning after December 31, 2010 (Act Sec. 9008(j) of the Patient Protection and Affordable Care Act (PPACA) (P.L. 111-148), as amended by Act Sec. 1404(a)(4) of the Health Care and Education Reconciliation Act of 2010 (P.L. 111-152)). The final regulations (T.D. 9684) became effective on July 28, 2014.

¶352

LAW EXPLAINED

Law source: Law at ¶7030, ¶7036 and ¶7106.

— Act Sec. 9008 of the Patient Protection and Affordable Care Act (PPACA) (P.L. 111-148), as amended by Act Sec. 1404 of the Health Care and Education Reconciliation Act of 2010 (P.L. 111-152);

— Act Sec. 9008(j) of PPACA, as amended by Act Sec. 1404(a)(4) of the 2010 Reconciliation Act, providing the effective date.

Reporter references: For further information, consult the following reporters.

— Standard Federal Tax Reporter, ¶14,502.01 and ¶26,135.01

— Tax Research Consultant, BUSEXP: 21,350 and EXCISE: 6,166.05

— Practical Tax Explanation, §9,940.10, §50,210 and §51,405

— Federal Excise Tax Reporter, ¶14,300.01

¶355 Additional Requirements for Charitable Hospitals

SUMMARY OF NEW LAW

Four additional requirements have been imposed on charitable hospitals that must be met for the hospitals to maintain their Code Sec. 501(c)(3) tax-exempt status. Under these new requirements, charitable hospitals must perform community health needs assessments (CHNAs). The requirements also relate to financial assistance policies, limitation on charges, and billing and collection requirements.

BACKGROUND

Charitable organizations, i.e., organizations described in Code Sec. 501(c)(3), generally are exempt from federal income tax, are eligible to receive tax deductible contributions, have access to tax-exempt financing through state and local governments, and generally are exempt from state and local taxes. A charitable organization must operate primarily in pursuit of one or more tax-exempt purposes constituting the basis of its tax exemption. The Internal Revenue Code specifies such purposes as religious, charitable, scientific, educational, literary, testing for public safety, fostering international amateur sports competition, or preventing cruelty to children or animals. In general, an organization is organized and operated for charitable purposes if it provides relief for the poor and distressed or the underprivileged.

The Code does not provide a per se exemption for hospitals. Rather, a hospital qualifies for exemption if it is organized and operated for a charitable purpose and otherwise meets the requirements of Code Sec. 501(c)(3). The promotion of health has been recognized by the IRS as a charitable purpose that is beneficial to the community as a whole. It includes not only the establishment or maintenance of charitable hospitals, but also clinics, homes for the aged, and other providers of health care.

BACKGROUND

Since 1969, the IRS has applied a "community benefit" standard for determining whether a hospital is charitable. According to Rev. Rul. 69-545, community benefit can include, for example: maintaining an emergency room open to all persons regardless of ability to pay; having an independent board of trustees composed of representatives of the community; operating with an open medical staff policy, with privileges available to all qualifying physicians; providing charity care; and utilizing surplus funds to improve the quality of patient care, expand facilities, and advance medical training, education and research.

Beginning in 2009, hospitals generally are required to submit information on community benefit on their annual information returns filed with the IRS. There are no sanctions short of revocation of tax-exempt status for hospitals that fail to satisfy the community benefit standard.

Exempt organizations are required to file an annual information return, stating specifically the items of gross income, receipts, disbursements, and such other information as the IRS may prescribe. Code Sec. 501(c)(3) organizations that are classified as public charities must file Form 990, Return of Organization Exempt From Income Tax, which requests information specific to Code Sec. 501(c)(3) organizations. Additionally, an organization that operates at least one facility that is, or is required to be, licensed, registered, or similarly recognized by a state as a hospital must complete Schedule H (Form 990), which requests information regarding charity care, community benefits, bad debt expense, and certain management company and joint venture arrangements of a hospital.

LAW EXPLAINED

Additional requirements imposed on charitable hospitals.—The Patient Protection and Affordable Care Act establishes four new requirements applicable to Code Sec. 501(c)(3) hospitals (Code Sec. 501(r)(1), as added by the Patient Protection and Affordable Care Act (PPACA) (P.L. 111-148)). The new requirements are in addition to, and not in lieu of, the requirements otherwise applicable to an organization described in Code Sec. 501(c)(3). The requirements generally apply to any Code Sec. 501(c)(3) organization that operates at least one hospital facility (Code Sec. 501(r)(2)(A), as added by PPACA).

For purposes of the provision, a hospital facility generally includes:

(1) any facility that is, or is required to be, licensed, registered, or similarly recognized by a state as a hospital; and

(2) any other facility or organization the Secretary of the Treasury (the "Secretary") determines has the provision of hospital care as its principal purpose.

An organization is required to comply with the following requirements with respect to each hospital facility operated by such organization (Code Sec. 501(r)(2)(B), as added by PPACA).

LAW EXPLAINED

> **Comment:** The requirements appear to reflect concerns that have arisen about whether nonprofit hospitals are providing adequate public benefits to justify their tax-exempt status, according to the Congressional Research Service ("501(c)(3) Hospitals and the Community Benefit Standard" (November 10, 2009)).

> **Comment:** If a charitable hospital fails to meet one or more of the new requirements imposed by Code Sec. 501(r), there is a chance that it will lose its tax-exempt status, said Ruth Madrigal, attorney advisor, Treasury Office of Tax Policy, during a May 15, 2013, panel hosted by the District of Columbia Tax Section in Washington, D.C. However, revocation would not be a knee-jerk reaction, and such instances would be uncommon and reserved generally for willful and egregious violations. "A willful or egregious failure would be a very rare case indeed," she said.

Community health needs assessment. Starting with its first tax year beginning after March 23, 2012, each hospital facility is required to conduct a community health needs assessment (CHNA) at least once every three tax years and adopt an implementation strategy to meet the community needs identified through the assessment (Code Sec. 501(r)(3), as added by PPACA). The assessment process must take into account input from persons who represent the broad interests of the community served by the hospital, including those with special knowledge or expertise of public health issues. Each hospital facility is required to make the assessment widely available.

Under proposed regulations on which taxpayers can rely, a charitable hospital generally must conduct a separate CHNA at least once every three years, for each hospital facility that it operates. An organization that owns a controlling interest in a hospital facility through a partnership must also conduct a CHNA (Proposed Reg. § 1.501(r)-1(c)(2)). A facility may collaborate with other facilities in conducting its CHNA. Each facility generally must issue a separate report, but may duplicate portions of the reports. Facilities that serve all the same communities may issue a joint report (Proposed Reg. § 1.501(r)-3(b)(7)(iv)).

Every three years. The facility must conduct a CHNA in the current year or either of the two preceding years. The hospital must define each community it serves and assess the health needs of that community (Proposed Reg. § 1.501(r)-3(b)(1)). The hospital can identify a community based on geography, target populations, and principal functions. Hospitals must also assess and address the needs of medically underserved, lower-income, and minority populations in the area it serves.

Significant needs. To assess community health needs, the facility must identify significant health needs, prioritize the significant needs, and identify measures and resources to address those needs (Proposed Reg. § 1.501(r)-3(b)(4)).

> **Comment:** The proposed regulations clarify that only significant needs must be identified and assessed, not all needs.

Input. The proposed regulations require that the facility obtain input from:

- a state, regional, or local public health department;
- members of medically underserved populations; and
- others.

LAW EXPLAINED

The names of individuals contacted for input will not be required (Proposed Reg. § 1.501(r)-3(b)(7)(iii)).

Widely available. The CHNA must be made widely available to the public, such as by posting it on the hospital's website and by providing printed copies on request (Proposed Reg. § 1.501(r)-1(c)(4)).

Implementation strategy. By the end of the year in which the CHNA is issued, the hospital must issue an implementation strategy that either describes how the hospital plans to meet the health need, or explains (in a brief manner) why it does not intend to address the need (Proposed Reg. § 1.501(r)-3(c)). The strategy must also explain the anticipated impact of its actions and provide a plan to evaluate the impact.

Relief/penalties. An omission or error in a policy or report would not cause loss of tax-exempt status if it was minor, inadvertent, due to reasonable cause, and corrected promptly after discovery. Further, a more serious failure that is not willful or egregious would be excused if the facility corrects and provides disclosure.

The correction should be reasonable, appropriate, and be made timely. To the extent reasonable feasible, the correction should restore the affected person to the position he or she would have been in if the failure had not occurred (Notice 2014-3). A hospital organization's correction and disclosure of a failure does not create a presumption that the failure was not willful or egregious.

Financial assistance policy. Each hospital facility is required to adopt, implement, and widely publicize a written financial assistance policy (FAP) (Code Sec. 501(r)(4)(A), as added by PPACA). The financial assistance policy must indicate the eligibility criteria for financial assistance and whether such assistance includes free or discounted care. For those eligible for discounted care, the policy must indicate the basis for calculating the amounts that will be billed to such patients. The policy must also indicate how to apply for such assistance. If a hospital does not have a separate billing and collections policy, the financial assistance policy must also indicate what actions the hospital may take in the event of nonpayment, including collections action and reporting to credit agencies.

Each hospital facility is required to adopt and implement a written policy to provide, without discrimination, emergency medical treatment to individuals regardless of their eligibility under the financial assistance policy (Code Sec. 501(r)(4)(B), as added by PPACA). A hospital organization must use reasonable efforts to determine eligibility for assistance under an FAP (Proposed Reg. § 1.501(r)-4(b)(4)(i)).

In addition, the proposed regulations under Code Sec. 501(r)(4) describe the information that a hospital facility must include in its FAP (e.g., eligibility criteria, basis for calculating amounts charged, method for applying) and the methods a hospital facility must use to widely publicize its FAP (Proposed Reg. § 1.501(r)-4(b)). They also describe what a hospital facility must include in its emergency medical care policy (Proposed Reg. § 1.501(r)-4(c)).

Limitation on charges. Each hospital facility is permitted to bill patients who qualify for financial assistance no more than the amount generally billed to insured patients (Code Sec. 501(r)(5), as added by PPACA). A hospital facility may not use gross

LAW EXPLAINED

charges (i.e., "chargemaster" rates) when billing individuals who qualify for financial assistance (Proposed Reg. §1.501(r)-5(c)).

> **Comment:** The limitation on what could be charged by a charitable hospital for emergency or other medically necessary care was originally "the lowest amounts charged." Americans for Tax Reform has said that the change to "the amount generally billed" makes the limitation less onerous on hospitals.

> **Comment:** It is intended that amounts billed to those who qualify for financial assistance may be based on either the best, or an average of the three best, negotiated commercial rates, or Medicare rates.

The proposed regulations describe how a hospital facility determines the maximum amounts it can charge individuals eligible for financial assistance for emergency and other medically necessary care (Proposed Reg. §1.501(r)-4(b)(2)).

In the case of an eligible individual who has not applied for financial assistance at the time charges are made, the proposed regulations provide that a hospital facility will not fail to satisfy Code Sec. 501(r)(5) if it charges the individual more than the insurance rate, provided the hospital facility is complying with all the requirements regarding notifying individuals about the FAP and responding to applications submitted, including correcting the amount charged and seeking to reverse any extraordinary collection action (ECA) previously initiated if an individual is later found to be eligible for assistance.

Billing and collection requirements. Fourth, a hospital facility (or its affiliates) may not undertake certain extraordinary collection actions (even if otherwise permitted by law) against a patient without first making reasonable efforts to inform the patient about the hospital's financial assistance policy and to determine whether the patient is eligible for assistance under the policy (Code Sec. 501(r)(6), as added by PPACA).

> **Comment:** Such extraordinary collection actions include lawsuits, liens on residences, arrests, body attachments, or other similar collection processes (Committee Report for Senate Finance Healthcare Reform, America's Healthy Future Act of 2009 (October 19, 2009)).

> **Comment:** It is intended that, for this purpose, "reasonable attempts" include notification by the hospital of its financial assistance policy upon admission and in written and oral communications with the patient regarding the patient's bill, including invoices and telephone calls, before collection action or reporting to credit rating agencies is initiated (Committee Report for Senate Finance Healthcare Reform, America's Healthy Future Act of 2009 (October 19, 2009)).

The proposed regulations under Code Sec. 501(r)(6) describe the actions that are considered "extraordinary collection actions" and the "reasonable efforts" a hospital facility must make to determine assistance eligibility before engaging in such actions (Proposed Reg. §1.501(r)-6). In general, to have made reasonable efforts under the proposed regulations, a hospital facility must determine whether an individual is assistance-eligible or provide required notices during a period ending 120 days after the date of the first billing statement.

Although a hospital facility may undertake extraordinary collection actions after this 120-day notification period, a hospital facility that has not determined whether an

LAW EXPLAINED

individual is assistance-eligible must still accept and process a financial assistance application from the individual for an additional 120 days. Accordingly, the total period during which a hospital facility must accept and process FAP applications is 240 days from the date of the first billing statement.

> **Comment:** The proposed regulations make it possible for patients to delay payment. For example, regardless of whether he or she has insurance or the ability to pay, a patient may refuse to engage in meaningful discussion with the hospital regarding payment options.

If a hospital facility receives a financial assistance application during the application period, it must suspend any ECAs until it has processed the application and, if it determines the individual is assistance-eligible, must seek to reverse the ECAs and promptly refund any overpaid amounts. While debts may be referred to third parties to assist with collection actions at any time, including during the initial 120-day notification period, they may not be sold to third parties during the notification period unless and until an eligibility determination has been made.

Excise tax for failure to meet hospital exemption requirements. If a hospital organization must meet the additional requirements under Code Sec. 501(r), and fails to meet the community health needs assessments requirements under Code Sec. 501(r)(3), an excise tax is imposed on the hospital (Code Sec. 4959, as added by PPACA). The tax on the organization is $50,000 for any applicable tax year. For example, if a facility does not complete a community health needs assessment in tax years one, two, or three, it is subject to the penalty in year three. If it then fails to complete a community health needs assessment in year four, it is subject to another penalty in year four (for failing to satisfy the requirement during the three-year period beginning with tax year two and ending with tax year four).

The excise tax will apply to a hospital organization that fails to meet the Code Sec. 501(r)(3) requirements during a tax year in which its Code Sec. 501(c)(3) status is revoked (Proposed Reg. § 53.4959-1(a)).

The $50,000 excise tax can be imposed for any three-year period on a facility-by-facility basis. Thus, if a hospital organization that operates two hospitals facilities fails to meet the requirements of Code Sec. 501(r)(3) with respect to both facilities in any tax year, the hospital organization will be subject to a total excise tax of $100,000 ($50,000 for each hospital facility) for that tax year (Proposed Reg. § 53.4959-1(a)).

A hospital organization must report the amount of any excise tax imposed on it under Code Sec. 4959 on its annual Form 990 information return (Proposed Reg. § 1.6033-2(a)(2)(ii)(l)). In addition, a hospital organization liable for the excise tax must file a Form 4720, Return of Certain Excise Taxes Under Chapters 41 and 42 of the Internal Revenue Code, by the 15th day of the fifth month after the end of the organization's tax year during which the liability under Code Sec. 4959 was incurred (Temporary Reg. § 53.6071-1T(h)).

Mandatory review of tax exemption for hospitals. The Secretary of the Treasury will review at least once, every three years, the community benefit activities of each hospital organization to which Code Sec. 501(r) applies (Act Sec. 9007(c) of PPACA).

¶355

LAW EXPLAINED

Additional reporting requirements. A hospital must disclose, in its annual information report to the IRS (Form 990 and related schedules), how it is addressing the needs identified in the community health needs assessment and, if all identified needs are not addressed, the reasons why (e.g., lack of financial or human resources) (Code Sec. 6033(b)(15)(A), as added by PPACA).

The Patient Protection Act also requires each organization to which Code Sec. 501(r)(3) applies to file with its annual information return a copy of its audited financial statements (or, in the case of an organization the financial statements of which are included in a consolidated financial statement with other organizations, such consolidated financial statements) (Code Sec. 6033(b)(15)(B), as added by PPACA).

Reports. The Patient Protection Act requires the Secretary, in consultation with the Secretary of Health and Human Services, to report annually to Congress the levels of charity care, bad debt expenses, unreimbursed costs of means-tested government programs, and unreimbursed costs of non-means tested government programs incurred by private tax-exempt, taxable, and governmental hospitals, as well as the cost of community benefit activities incurred by private tax-exempt hospitals (Act Sec. 9007(e)(1) of PPACA).

In addition, the Secretary, in consultation with the Secretary of Health and Human Services, must conduct a study of the trends in these amounts with the results of the study provided to Congress five years from March 23, 2010 (Act Sec. 9007(e)(2) of PPACA).

▶ **Effective date.** The additional requirements imposed on charitable hospitals generally apply to tax years beginning after March 23, 2010, the date of enactment (Act Secs. 9007(f)(1) and 10903(b) of the Patient Protection and Affordable Care Act (PPACA) (P.L. 111-148)). The requirements of Code Sec. 501(r)(3) apply to tax years beginning after the date which is two years after March 23, 2010, the date of enactment (Act Sec. 9007(f)(2) of PPACA). The excise tax for failure to meet the exemption requirements applies to failures occurring after March 23, 2010, the date of enactment (Act Sec. 9007(f)(3) of PPACA). A hospital facility may rely on Proposed Reg. § 1.501(r)-3 for any CHNA conducted or implementation strategy adopted on or before the date that is six months after the date the proposed regulations are published as final or temporary regulations in the Federal Register (NPRM REG-106499-12). The regulations under Code Sec. 501(r)(4) through 501(r)(6) are proposed to apply for tax years beginning on or after the date these rules are published in the Federal Register as final or temporary regulations (NPRM REG-130266-11). Taxpayers may rely on the proposed regulations until final or temporary regulations are issued. The temporary regulation under Code Sec. 6071 requiring filing of the Form 4720 expires on or before August 12, 2016 (T.D. 9629).

Law source: Law at ¶5180, ¶5310 and ¶5350.

— Act Sec. 9007(a) of the Patient Protection and Affordable Care Act (PPACA) (P.L. 111-148), redesignating Code Sec. 501(r) as Code Sec. 501(s) and adding a new Code Sec. 501(r);

— Act Sec. 9007(b), adding Code Sec. 4959;

— Act Sec. 9007(d), amending Code Sec. 6033(b);

— Act Sec. 10903(a), amending Code Sec. 501(r)(5);

— Act Secs. 9007(f) and 10903(b), providing the effective dates.

¶355

LAW EXPLAINED

Reporter references: For further information, consult the following reporters.
— Standard Federal Tax Reporter, ¶22,609.032
— Tax Research Consultant, EXEMPT: 3,154
— Practical Tax Explanation, § 33,105

Information Reporting Requirements

4

¶405 Inclusion of Cost of Employer-Sponsored Health Coverage on W-2

SUMMARY OF NEW LAW

Employers are required to disclose the aggregate cost of employer-sponsored health insurance coverage provided to their employees on the employee's Form W-2. Contributions to any health savings account (HSA) or Archer medical savings account (MSA) of the employee or the employee's spouse or salary reduction contributions to a flexible spending arrangement under a cafeteria plan will not be included. This requirement is generally effective for 2012 Forms W-2. Until the IRS issues further guidance, smaller employers that are required to file fewer than 250 Forms W-2 for the preceding calendar year are not subject to the reporting requirement.

BACKGROUND

Employers are required to provide each employee with a Form W-2, Wage and Tax Statement, on an annual basis, generally on or before January 31 of the following year. Form W-2 is a written statement that contains information with respect to wages and tax withholdings. This information includes:

- the name of the employer;
- the name of the employee (and his social security account number, if wages have been paid);
- the total amount of wages as defined in Code Sec. 3401(a);
- the total amount deducted and withheld as tax under Code Sec. 3402;
- the total amount of wages as defined in Code Sec. 3121(a);
- the total amount deducted and withheld as tax under Code Sec. 3101;

BACKGROUND

- the total amount paid to the employee under Code Sec. 3507 with respect to advance payment of earned income credit;
- the total amount of elective deferrals under Code Sec. 402(g)(3) and compensation deferred under Code Sec. 457, including any designated Roth contributions under Code Sec 402(A);
- the total amount incurred for dependent care assistance with respect to that employee under a dependent care assistance program;
- in the case of an employee who is a member of the U.S. Armed Forces, the employee's earned income determined for purposes of the Code Sec. 32 earned income credit;
- the amount contributed to any Archer medical savings account of that employee or the employee's spouse;
- the amount contributed to any health savings account of that employee or the employee's spouse; and
- the total amount of deferrals for the year under a nonqualified deferred compensation plan under Code Sec. 409A(d) (Code Sec. 6051(a)).

Special rules also apply with respect to compensation paid to members of the military and uniformed services, Peace Corps volunteers, and employees receiving tips in the course of their employment.

There is no requirement that the employer report the total value of employer-sponsored health insurance coverage on the Form W-2. However, some employers voluntarily report the amount of salary reduction under a cafeteria plan that results in tax-free benefits to the employee in box 14 of Form W-2. The portion of the employer sponsored coverage that is paid for by the employee with after-tax contributions is included on the Form W-2.

LAW EXPLAINED

Employers required to disclose cost of employer-sponsored health coverage on Form W-2.—Employers are required to disclose the aggregate cost of "applicable employer-sponsored coverage" provided to employees annually on the employee's Form W-2 (Code Sec. 6051(a)(14), as added by the Patient Protection and Affordable Care Act (PPACA) (P.L. 111-148)). Regardless of whether the employee or employer pays for the coverage, the aggregate cost of the coverage reported is determined under rules similar to those used in Code Sec. 4980B(f)(4) to determine the applicable premiums for purposes of the COBRA continuation coverage requirements of group health plans (Code Sec. 6051(a)(14), as added by PPACA). They are determined on an annual basis, and may be based on the information available on December 31 of the year (Notice 2012-9).

For purposes of the new reporting requirement, "applicable employer-sponsored coverage" means, with respect to any employee, coverage under any group health plan made available to the employee by the employer which is excludable from the employee's gross income under Code Sec. 106 or would be so excludable if it were considered

LAW EXPLAINED

employer-provided coverage under Code Sec. 106 (Code Sec. 4980I(d)(1)(A), as added by PPACA).

Coverage is treated as applicable employer-sponsored coverage regardless of whether the employer or employee pays for the coverage. Applicable employer-sponsored coverage does not include coverage for long-term care, accidents, or disability income insurance. Nor does it include coverage that applies to only a specified disease or illness, hospital indemnity, or other fixed indemnity insurance, the payment for which is not excludable from gross income and deductible under Code Sec. 162(l) (Code Sec. 4980I(d)(1)(B) and (C), as added by PPACA). On the other hand, if an employer makes a contribution to pay for indemnity insurance or coverage for a specific disease or illness that is excludable or is purchased on a pre-tax basis under a cafeteria plan, the cost must be reported (Notice 2012-9).

Applicable employer-sponsored coverage includes coverage under any group health plan established and maintained by the U.S. government, the government of any state or its political subdivision, by any agency or instrumentality of such government. In the case of qualifying self-employed individuals (i.e., individuals treated as employees under Code Sec. 401(c)(1)), coverage under any group health plan providing health insurance coverage will be treated as applicable employer-sponsored coverage if a deduction is allowable under Code Sec. 162(l) with respect to all or any portion of the cost of such coverage (Code Sec. 4980I(d)(1)(D) and (E), as added by PPACA).

> **Comment:** Code Sec. 4980I, as added by PPACA and amended by the Health Care and Education Reconciliation Act of 2010 P.L. 111-152), imposes an excise tax on high cost employer-sponsored health coverage. For a discussion of this excise tax, see ¶335.

Applicable employer-sponsored coverage does *not* include any salary reduction contributions to a flexible spending arrangement under a cafeteria plan or contributions to an Archer medical savings account or health savings account of the employee or the employee's spouse (Code Sec. 6051(a)(14), as added by PPACA). A health reimbursement account (HRA) of the employee is also not reportable, even if the HRA is the only coverage provided (Notice 2012-9). However, an employer may choose to report the amount of coverage that generally is not reportable, such as coverage under an HRA or wellness program (Notice 2012-9).

> **Comment:** This provision only requires disclosure of the aggregate cost of employer-sponsored health insurance coverage by the employer. It does not require a specific breakdown of the various types of medical coverage. Thus, if an employee enrolls in employer-sponsored health insurance coverage under a medical plan, a dental plan and a vision plan, the employer must report the total cost of all of these health related insurance policies.

The amount is reported in Box 12, Code DD, of Form W-2. If a terminated employee requests a Form W-2 before the end of the year, the employer is not required to report any amount (Notice 2012-9).

The reporting requirement was set to begin on Forms W-2 issued for tax year 2011. However, the IRS deferred the requirement under Code Sec. 6051(a)(14) for employers to report the cost of coverage under an employer-sponsored health plan, making the reporting by employers optional for 2011. Accordingly, an employer will not be

LAW EXPLAINED

subject to any penalties for failure to meet such requirements for 2011 (Notice 2010-69). However, for 2012 Forms W-2 (and Forms W-2 for later years unless and until further guidance is issued), an employer is not subject to the reporting requirement for any calendar year if the employer was required to file fewer than 250 Forms W-2 for the preceding calendar year. Whether an employer is required to file fewer than 250 Forms W-2 for a calendar year is determined based on the Forms W-2 that employer would be required to file if it filed Forms W-2 to report all wages paid by that employer and without regard to the use of an agent under Code Sec. 3504 (Notice 2012-9).

▶ **Effective date.** The provision applies to tax years beginning after December 31, 2010 (Act Sec. 9002(b) of the Patient Protection and Affordable Care Act (PPACA) (P.L. 111-148). However, Notice 2010-69 provides that no penalties apply for failure to meet the requirements for 2011, and Notice 2012-9 provides that unless and until further guidance is issued, reporting is not required by employers who were required to file fewer than 250 Forms W-2 for the preceding year.

Law source: Law at ¶5360.

— Act Sec. 9002(a) of the Patient Protection and Affordable Care Act (PPACA) (P.L. 111-148), amending Code Sec. 6051(a)(12) and (a)(13), and adding Code Sec. 6051(a)(14);

— Act Sec. 9002(b), providing the effective date.

Reporter references: For further information, consult the following reporters.

— Standard Federal Tax Reporter, ¶36,425.04

— Tax Research Consultant, HEALTH: 6,102

— Practical Tax Explanation, § 42,180.05

¶410 Health Care Coverage Reporting

SUMMARY OF NEW LAW

Beginning in 2015, any person or entity (including self-insured employers) who provides minimum essential health care coverage to an individual during a calendar year is required to file a return in the following calendar year reporting such coverage in the form and manner prescribed by the Secretary of the Treasury. Such a person is also required to furnish a written statement to the individual with respect to whom information is reported, detailing the contents of the information return. The first returns will be filed in 2016 for 2015 coverage.

BACKGROUND

The Code imposes a variety of information reporting requirements on participants in certain transactions (Code Secs. 6031 through 6060). For example, every person engaged in a trade or business generally is required to file information returns for each calendar year for payments of $600 or more made in the course of the payor's trade or business (Code Sec. 6041).

BACKGROUND

A penalty applies for failing to timely file an information return or including incorrect or incomplete information on an information return. The amount of the penalty ranges from $15 to $50 for each return with respect to which such a failure occurs, depending on how soon the failure is corrected, up to a maximum total penalty of $250,000 for all failures during a calendar year (Code Sec. 6721). Similarly, failures to furnish correct information statements to recipients of payments for which information reporting is required is subject to a penalty of $50 for each statement, up to a maximum penalty of $100,000 for all failures during a calendar year (Code Sec. 6722). The information returns and payee statements that are subject to these penalties are described in Code Sec. 6724(d)(1) and (2), respectively.

In addition, a failure to comply with various other information reporting requirements results in a penalty of $50 for each failure up to a maximum penalty of $100,000 for all such failures during the calendar year (Code Sec. 6723).

LAW EXPLAINED

Information reporting required for health insurance coverage.—Beginning in 2015, every provider of minimum essential health care coverage to an individual during a calendar year is required to file a return reporting such coverage, at such time as the Secretary of the Treasury may prescribe (Code Sec. 6055(a), as added by the Patient Protection and Affordable Care Act (PPACA) (P.L. 111-148); Notice 2013-45). The first returns will be filed in 2016 for 2015 coverage. A provider required to file a return under these rules is also required to furnish a written statement to the individual with respect to whom information is reported, detailing the contents of the information return (Code Sec. 6055(c)(1), as added by PPACA).

> **Comment:** As of 2014, applicable individuals are required to ensure that they and their dependents have minimum essential health coverage, and a penalty is imposed on applicable individuals who fail to do so. For discussion of the penalty and the definition of minimum essential coverage, see ¶ 205. The information reported under Code Sec. 6055 will enable taxpayers to establish and the IRS to verify that the taxpayers have the required minimum essential coverage during a calendar year. The Secretary of the Treasury, in consultation with the Secretary of Health and Human Services, is required to send a written notification to each individual who files an individual income tax return and who is not enrolled in minimum essential coverage. The notification must be sent no later than June 30 of each year, and must contain information on the services available through the Exchange operating in the state in which the individual resides (Act Sec. 1502(c) of PPACA).

> **Comment:** The reporting requirements under Code Sec. 6055 were originally slated to apply beginning after December 31, 2013 (Act Sec. 1502(e) of PPACA). However, the IRS has provided transition relief delaying this requirement for one year, to periods beginning after December 31, 2014 (Notice 2013-45). The transition relief also applies to the information reporting requirements for applicable large employers under Code Sec. 6056 (see ¶ 415) and the employer shared responsibility provisions of Code Sec. 4980H (the employer mandate) (see ¶ 305).

¶410

LAW EXPLAINED

Who is required to report. The reporting requirements apply to:

- health insurance issuers, or carriers (as defined in 5 U.S.C. 8901), for all insured coverage;
- plan sponsors of self-insured group health plan coverage;
- the executive department or agency of a governmental unit that provides coverage under a government-sponsored program (within the meaning of Code Sec. 5000A(f)(1)(A)), and
- any other person that provides minimum essential coverage to an individual (Reg. § 1.6055-1(c)(1)).

A "plan sponsor" of a single employer plan is the employer. For a self-insured group plan or arrangement maintained by a multiple employer welfare arrangement, each participating employer is the plan sponsor with respect to the participating employer's own employees. For a self-insured multiemployer plan, the association, committee, joint board of trustees, or other similar group of representatives of the parties who establish or maintain the plan is the plan is the plan sponsor. For a self-insured group plan maintained solely by an employee organization, the employee organization is the plan sponsor. In other cases, a person may be designated by plan terms as the plan sponsor or plan administrator, or if no person is designated as the administrator and a plan sponsor cannot be identified, each entity that maintains the plan or arrangement will be considered the plan sponsor (Reg. § 1.6055-1(c)(2)(i)).

If coverage is provided by a governmental unit, an agency or instrumentality of a governmental unit or an agency, the required returns and statements must be made by the officer or employee who enters into the agreement to provide the coverage, or by the person appropriately designated for purposes of this reporting requirement (Code Sec. 6055(d), as added by PPACA). A government employer that maintains a self-insured plan for its employees may chose to report on its own behalf or designate another governmental unit, agency, or instrumentality of the government unit that is part of or related to the same governmental unit as the employer required to file the return. The government employer must make or revoke the designation before the earlier of the deadline for filing the return or furnishing the statement to the covered individual (Reg. § 1.6055-1(c)(2)(ii)).

Special rules apply for certain government-sponsored programs. In the case of Medicaid and Children's Health Insurance (also known as "CHIP"), the state agency that administers those programs would be responsible for the information reporting requirements. The executive department or agency of a governmental unit that provides coverage under a government-sponsored program through a health insurance issuer such as Medicaid, CHIP, or Medicare (including Medicare Advantage) and not the issuer, is responsible for the required reporting (Reg. § 1.6055-1(c)(3)(i)).

Reporting rules. Self-insured applicable large employers that are subject to reporting requirements under Code Sec. 6056, report on Forms 1094-C (transmittal) and 1095-C (employee statement). Other providers file Forms 1094-B (transmittal) and 1095-B (employee statement) (Reg. § 1.6055-1(f)(2)). The required return must contain the name, address and taxpayer identification number (TIN) of the responsible individ-

LAW EXPLAINED

ual insured, and the name and TIN of each other individual obtaining coverage under the policy (Code Sec. 6055(b)(1), as added by PPACA). The return must also include the name, address, and employer identification number (EIN) for the reporting entity (Reg. § 1.6055-1(e)(1)(i)). Reporting entities can report the date of birth of a responsible or covered individual (but not employee) if a TIN is not available (Reg. § 1.6055-1(e)(1)). However, this alternative should not be used unless the reporting entity has made reasonable efforts to obtain the TIN from the individual (Preamble to T.D. 9660).

> **Comment:** The regulations use the term "responsible individual" rather than the term "primary insured" because minimum essential coverage may not be insured coverage (for example, health coverage provided by the Department of Veterans Affairs) (Preamble to NPRM REG-132455-11).

The required return must also include the dates during which the insured was covered under minimum essential coverage during the calendar year (Code Sec. 6055(b)(1), as added by PPACA). Final regulations do not require reporting of the specific dates of coverage, and instead require reporting of the months for which, for at least one day, the individual was enrolled in coverage and entitled to receive benefits (Reg. § 1.6055-1(e)(1)(iv)).

> **Comment:** For purposes of Code Sec. 5000A, an individual who has coverage on any day in a month is treated as having minimum essential coverage for the entire month. Therefore, the specific coverage dates are not necessary for administering and complying with rules relating to minimum essential coverage.

Under regulations, a health insurance issuer is not required to file a return to report coverage in an qualified health plan in the individual market enrolled in through an Exchange (Reg. § 1.6055-1(d)(1)). Note that the IRS adopted this rule despite language in the code requiring the reporting of such information in an effort to streamline reporting as much as possible (Code Sec. 6055(b)(1)(B)(iii), as added by PPACA).

> **Comment:** By January 1, 2014, each state (or the federal government in the absence of state action) must establish an American Health Benefit Exchange and Small Business Health Options Program (SHOP Exchange) to provide qualified individuals and qualified small business employers access to qualified health plans. For a discussion of the establishment and requirements of the Exchanges, see ¶505. Individuals who are eligible for participation in a qualified health plan through an Exchange may also be eligible for a premium assistance tax credit (see ¶210) and cost-sharing subsidy (see ¶520). The Exchange is required to certify to an employer if it has an employee enrolled in a qualified health plan through the Exchange. There have been delays in implementing SHOP exchanges (see ¶512 for discussion of SHOP exchanges).

If the provided minimum essential coverage consists of health insurance coverage of a health insurance issuer provided through a group health plan of an employer, the return must include the name, address and employer identification number of the employer sponsoring the plan, and the portion of the premium, if any, required to be paid by the employer. If the coverage is a qualified health plan in the small group market offered through an Exchange, the return must also include such other infor-

¶410

LAW EXPLAINED

mation as the Secretary of the Treasury may require for administration of the new credit for employee health insurance expenses of small employers under Code Sec. 45R, as added and amended by PPACA (Code Sec. 6055(b)(2), as added by PPACA). For this purpose, the return must report whether the coverage is qualified health plan enrolled in through a SHOP Exchange and the SHOP's unique identifier (Reg. § 1.6055-1(e)(2)). For a discussion of the small employer health insurance credit, see ¶ 210.

No information reporting is required for arrangements that provide benefits in addition or as a supplement to minimum essential coverage, such as a health reimbursement arrangement (Reg. § 1.6055-1(d)(2)). Additionally, no reporting is required for coverage offered to individuals who do not enroll (Reg. § 1.6055-1(d)(3)).

The required return and transmittal form must be filed on or before February 28 (or March 31, if filed electronically) of the year following the calendar year in which the reporting entity provided minimum essential coverage to an individual (Reg. § 1.6055-1(f)(1)). High-volume filers (i.e., those who file at least 250 health coverage provider returns during the calendar year) have to file electronically (Reg. § § 301.6011-2(c)(2)(i), 1.6055-1(f)(1)).

Written statements required. A person required to file a return under these rules is also required to furnish a written statement to each individual whose name is reported on the return, showing the name, address and phone number of the person required to make the return, and the information required to be shown on the return with respect to that individual (Code Sec. 6055(c)(1), as added by PPACA). The statement must be furnished on or before January 31 of the year following the calendar year for which the information return was required to be made (Code Sec. 6055(c)(2), as added by PPACA). A reporting entity may furnish the statement electronically (Reg. § 1.6055-2(a)(1)). However, the recipient must have affirmatively consented to receive the statement in an electronic format (Reg. § 1.6055-2(a)(2)). Further, the furnisher must provide to the recipient a clear and conspicuous disclosure statement that informs the recipient of the availability of a paper statement, the scope and duration of the consent, the conditions under which the furnisher will cease furnishing statements electronically, a description of the hardware and software required to access, print and retain the statement, and procedures for making a post-consent request for a paper statement, withdrawing consent, and updating information (Reg. § 1.6055-2(a)(3)).

Penalties. Failure to file an information return reporting health insurance coverage or failure to include correct or complete information on such a return is subject to the existing penalties for failure to file correct information returns under Code Sec. 6721 (Code Sec. 6724(d)(1)(B)(xxiv), as added by PPACA). Similarly, the present-law penalties for failure to furnish correct payee statements under Code Sec. 6722 apply to failure to furnish statements to individuals with respect to whom information is reported or failure to include correct or complete information on such statements (Code Sec. 6724(d)(2)(GG), as added by PPACA).

¶410

LAW EXPLAINED

▶ **Effective date.** The provision applies to calendar years beginning after 2013 (Act Sec. 1502(e) of the Patient Protection and Affordable Care Act (PPACA) (P.L. 111-148)). However, transition relief has made the reporting requirements optional for 2014 (Notice 2013-45). The final regulations are effective for calendar years beginning after December 31, 2014.

Law source: Law at ¶5370 and ¶5420.

— Act Sec. 1502(a) of the Patient Protection and Affordable Care Act (PPACA) (P.L. 111-148), adding Code Sec. 6055;

— Act Sec. 1502(b), amending Code Sec. 6724(d)(1)(B) and (d)(2);

— Act Sec. 1502(e), providing the effective date.

— Act Sec. 10108(j)(3), amending Code Sec. 6724(d).

Reporter references: For further information, consult the following reporters.

— Standard Federal Tax Reporter, ¶36,466H.01

— Tax Research Consultant, HEALTH: 6,104

— Practical Tax Explanation, § 42,135.15

¶415 Reporting of Employer Health Insurance Coverage

SUMMARY OF NEW LAW

Beginning in 2015, applicable large employers that are subject to the Code Sec. 4980H rules for shared responsibility regarding health care insurance coverage will be required to report to the Secretary of the Treasury whether they offer full-time employees and their dependents the opportunity to enroll in minimum essential coverage under an eligible employer-sponsored plan and provide details regarding the coverage offered and other required information. Such employers will also be required to furnish a written statement to each full-time employee with respect to whom information is reported, detailing the contents of the information return.

BACKGROUND

The Code imposes a variety of information reporting requirements on participants in certain transactions (Code Secs. 6031 through 6060). For example, every person engaged in a trade or business generally is required to file information returns for each calendar year for payments of $600 or more made in the course of the payor's trade or business (Code Sec. 6041).

A penalty applies for failing to timely file an information return or including incorrect or incomplete information on an information return. The amount of the penalty ranges from $15 to $50 for each return with respect to which such a failure occurs, depending on how soon the failure is corrected, up to a maximum total

BACKGROUND

penalty of $250,000 for all failures during a calendar year (Code Sec. 6721). Similarly, failures to furnish correct information statements to recipients of payments for which information reporting is required are subject to a penalty of $50 for each statement, up to a maximum penalty of $100,000 for all failures during a calendar year (Code Sec. 6722). The information returns and payee statements that are subject to these penalties are described in Code Sec. 6724(d)(1) and (2), respectively.

In addition, a failure to comply with various other information reporting requirements results in a penalty of $50 for each failure up to a maximum penalty of $100,000 for all such failures during the calendar year (Code Sec. 6723).

LAW EXPLAINED

Applicable large employers required to report on health insurance coverage.— Beginning in 2015, applicable large employers that are subject to the shared responsibility rules (popularly known as the "employer mandate") are required to file a return reporting on health care coverage offered to full-time employees and their dependents (Code Sec. 6056(a), as added and amended by the Patient Protection and Affordable Care Act (PPACA) (P.L. 111-148), and amended by the Department of Defense and Full-Year Continuing Appropriations Act, 2011 (P.L. 112-10); Notice 2013-45). For a discussion of the employer shared responsibility rules under Code Sec. 4980H, see ¶ 305.

> **Comment:** In addition to assisting with the administration of the employer shared responsibility provisions of Code Sec. 4980H, the information reporting requirements under Code Sec. 6056 will also be used for the administration of the premium tax credit under Code Sec. 36B, which allows a refundable income tax credit to certain individuals who purchase qualified health care coverage through a Health Insurance Exchange. Employees eligible for coverage under an employer-sponsored health plan are not eligible for the credit unless the employer's coverage is unaffordable for the employee or fails to provide a minimum value. For this purpose, an employer-sponsored plan is unaffordable if the employee's cost for the lowest-cost self-only coverage offered exceeds 9.5 percent of the employee's household income. The IRS and individuals will use the information on the cost of the lowest-cost employer-sponsored self-only coverage that provides minimum value to verify an individual's eligibility for the premium tax credit. For further information about the premium tax credit under Code Sec. 36B, see ¶ 210.

> **Comment:** The reporting requirements under Code Sec. 6056, and the employer mandate itself, were originally slated to apply to periods beginning after December 31, 2013 (Act Secs. 1514(d) and 10108(j)(4) of the PPACA; Act Sec. 1858(d) of the 2011 Appropriations Act). However, the IRS has provided transition relief delaying the employer mandate and the associated employer reporting requirements for one year, to periods beginning after December 31, 2014 (Notice 2013-45). The transition relief also applies to information reporting requirements applicable to insurers, self-insuring employers, and certain other providers of minimum essential coverage under Code Sec. 6055. See ¶ 410.

¶415

LAW EXPLAINED

ALE members must report. An applicable large employer for this purpose is, with respect to a calendar year, an employer who employed an average of at least 50 full-time employees on business days during the preceding calendar year (100 full-time employees for qualifying employers in 2015 under transition relief). For purposes of determining applicable large employer status, all persons or entities treated as a single employer under the aggregation rules of Code Sec. 414(b), (c), (m), or (o) are treated as one employer. The person or entities that comprise the applicable large employer are referred to as applicable large employer members, or ALE members. Reporting is done at the ALE member level (Reg. § 301.6056-1(b)(2)). For further discussion of applicable large employer status, see ¶ 305. The Code Sec. 6056 reporting requirements are applied separately to each ALE member (Reg. § 301.6056-1(c)).

Information to be reported. Under final regulations, every applicable large employer member has to report the following:

(1) Name, address, and employer identification number of the applicable large employer member, the name and telephone number of the applicable large employer's contact person, and the calendar year for which the information is reported;

(2) Certification as to whether the applicable large employer member offered to its full-time employees and their dependents the opportunity to enroll in minimum essential coverage (Code Sec. 5000A(f)(2)) under an eligible employer-sponsored plan by calendar month;

(3) Number of full-time employees for each month during the calendar year;

(4) For each full-time employee, the months during the calendar year for which coverage under the plan was available;

(5) For each full-time employee, the employee's share of the lowest cost monthly premium for coverage providing minimum value offered to that full-time employee under an eligible employer-sponsored plan, by calendar month; and

(6) Name, address, and taxpayer identification number of each full-time employee during the calendar year and the months, if any, during which the employee was covered under an eligible employer-sponsored plan (Code Sec. 6056(b)(2); Reg. § 301.6056-1(d)(1)).

Comment: Thankfully, the IRS final regulations do not require the reporting of the following four items stated as required in the legislation: (1) the length of any waiting period; (2) the employer's share of the total allowed costs of benefits provided under the plan; (3) the monthly premium for the lowest-cost option in each of the enrollment categories; and (4) the months, if any, during which any of the employee's dependents were covered under the plan.

An ALE member that provides a "qualifying offer" to any of its full time employees may use a simplified alternative reporting method. A qualifying offer is an offer of minimum value coverage that provides employee-only coverage at a cost to the employee of no more than about $1,100 in 2015 (9.5 percent of the Federal Poverty Level), combined with an offer of coverage for the employee's family. For employees who receive qualifying offers for all 12 months of the year, employers will need to report only the names, addresses, and taxpayer identification numbers (TINs) of

LAW EXPLAINED

those employees and the fact that they received a full-year qualifying offer. Employers will also give the employees a copy of that simplified report or a standard statement indicating that the employee received a full-year qualifying offer (Reg. § 301.6056-1(j)(1)).

An ALE member that otherwise meets its reporting obligation is not required to identify on its ALE return whether a particular employee is a full-time employee for one or more calendar months of the reporting year or report the total number of its full-time employees for the reporting year, if it certifies that it offered minimum essential coverage providing minimum value that was affordable to at least 98 percent of the employees (and their dependents) with respect to whom it reports (regardless of whether the employee is a full-time employee for purposes of employer shared responsibility liability for a calendar month during the year) (Reg. § 301.6056-1(j)(2)).

Time and manner. Every ALE member must file a return with respect to each full-time employee on Form 1095-C or on a substitute form. The ALE member must also submit Form 1094-C, a transmittal form. ALE members that self-insure and therefore have coverage provider reporting duties under Code Sec. 6055 may combine their reporting on Form 1095-C (Reg. § 301.6056-1(c) and -1(d)(2)).

The required return and transmittal form must be filed on or before February 28 (or March 31, if filed electronically) of the year succeeding the calendar year to which it relates (Reg. § 301.6056-1(e)). High-volume filers (i.e., those who file 250 or more ALE member returns during the calendar year) must file electronically (Reg. § § 301.6011-2, 301.6056-1(e)).

For reporting facilitated by third parties, a separate information return must be filed for each ALE member. If more than one return is being filed for an ALE member, there must be one authoritative transmittal (Form 1094-C) reporting aggregate employer-level data for all full-time employees of that member. Additionally, there must be only one ALE employee statement (Form 1095-C) for each full-time employee with respect to that full-time employee's employment with the applicable large employer member, so that all required information for a particular full-time employee of the member is reflected on a single Form 1095-C (Reg. § 301.6056-1(c)(2)).

The Secretary of the Treasury has the authority to review the accuracy of the information provided pursuant to the new reporting requirements, including the applicable large employer's share under of the total allowed costs of benefits provided under the plan (Code Sec. 6056(b), as added and amended by PPACA).

Employee statements. An ALE member required to file a return under these rules is also required to furnish a written statement to each full-time employee whose name is required to be reported on the return, showing the reporting entity's name, address and phone number, and the information required to be shown on the return with respect to such an employee (Code Sec. 6056(c)(1), as added by PPACA). The required statement must be furnished on or before January 31 of the year following the calendar year for which the information return was required to be made (Code Sec. 6056(c)(2), as added by PPACA). However, the IRS may grant an extension of time not exceeding 30 days in which to furnish the statements, for good cause upon

¶415

LAW EXPLAINED

written application of the person required to furnish such statements (Reg. §301.6056-1(g)(2)).

An ALE member may furnish the employee statement electronically (Reg. §301.6056-2(a)(1)). However, the recipient must have affirmatively consented to receive the statement in an electronic format (Reg. §301.6056-2(a)(2)). The furnisher must provide the recipient with a clear and conspicuous disclosure statement that informs the recipient of the availability of a paper statement, the scope and duration of the consent, the conditions under which the furnisher will cease furnishing statements electronically, a description of the hardware and software required to access, print and retain the statement, and procedures for making a post-consent request for a paper statement, withdrawing consent, and updating information (Reg. §301.6056-2(a)(3)). If the required statement is furnished on a website, the furnisher must notify the recipient that the statement is posted on a website and provide instructions on how to access and print the statement (Reg. §301.6056-2(a)(5)).

If the applicable large employer is a governmental unit, an agency or instrumentality of a governmental unit or an agency, the required returns and statements must be made by the person appropriately designated for purposes of this reporting requirement (Code Sec. 6056(e), as added by PPACA and amended by the 2011 Appropriations Act).

Penalties. Failure to file an information return reporting on health insurance coverage or failure to include correct or complete information on the return is subject to the existing penalties for failure to file correct information returns under Code Sec. 6721 (Code Sec. 6724(d)(1)(B)(xxv), as added and amended by PPACA). Similarly, the present-law penalties for failure to furnish correct payee statements under Code Sec. 6722 apply to failure to furnish statements to individuals with respect to whom information is reported or failure to include correct or complete information on such statements (Code Sec. 6724(d)(2)(HH), as added and amended by PPACA).

▶ **Effective date.** The provision applies to periods beginning after December 31, 2013 (Act Secs. 1514(d) and 10108(j)(4) of the Patient Protection and Affordable Care Act (PPACA) (P.L. 111-148)). However, transition relief has made the reporting requirements optional for 2014 (Notice 2013-45). Final regulations are effective for calendar years beginning after December 31, 2014.

Law source: Law at ¶5380 and ¶5420.

— Act Secs. 1514(a), 10106(g) and 10108(j)(1), (2) and (3)(A)-(D) of the Patient Protection and Affordable Care Act (PPACA) (P.L. 111-148), adding and amending Code Sec. 6056;

— Act Secs. 1514(b) and 10108(j)(3)(E), (F), amending Code Sec. 6724(d)(1) and (d)(2);

— Act Sec. 1514(c);

— Act Secs. 1514(d) and 10108(j)(4), providing the effective dates.

Reporter references: For further information, consult the following reporters.

— Standard Federal Tax Reporter, ¶36,473.01

— Tax Research Consultant, HEALTH: 6,106

— Practical Tax Explanation, §42,135.10

¶415

Health Care Exchanges and Other Provisions Governing Health Care Plans

>>> *Caution: The explanation below reflects certain nontax provisions of the Patient Protection and Affordable Care Act (P.L. 111-148) and the Health Care and Education Reconciliation Act of 2010 (P.L. 111-152). While the issues discussed do not have a direct effect on federal taxes, this explanation is helpful in understanding some of the tax-related explanations that appear in this publication.*

¶505 Establishment of Health Insurance Exchanges

SUMMARY OF NEW LAW

The Affordable Care Act requires the establishment of American Health Benefit Exchanges and Small Business Health Options Program (SHOP) Exchanges. Under these Exchanges, individuals and small businesses can purchase qualified coverage, though, eventually, larger businesses may be allowed to purchase coverage in the SHOP Exchange.

BACKGROUND

Historically, only Massachusetts had a health insurance marketplace exchange.

LAW EXPLAINED

Health Insurance Exchanges are to be established by each state or the federal government.—The Patient Protection and Affordable Care Act (PPACA), directs each state to establish an American Health Benefit Exchange for that state to facilitate the purchase of qualified health plans by qualified individuals (Act Sec. 1311(b) of PPACA (P.L. 111-148)). See ¶ 510. Each state is also required to establish a Small Business Health Options Program (SHOP) Exchange designed to assist qualified small employers in the state in enrolling their employees in qualified health plans in the state's small group market (Act Sec. 1311(b)(1)(C) of PPACA). See ¶ 512. A state may elect to provide for only one state Exchange that would provide both American Health Benefit Exchange services and SHOP Exchange services to both qualified individuals and qualified small employers, but this can be done only if the single Exchange has adequate resources to assist individuals and small employers (Act Sec. 1311(b)(2) of PPACA). If a state does not elect to establish an exchange, the U.S. Department of Health and Human Services (HHS) must establish and operate an exchange within the state.

> **Comment:** Most states have not established their own exchanges, and therefore the majority are being run by the federal government. This turn of events might have serious consequences for the premium tax credit (which is a trigger for the employer mandate). The premium tax credit is only available for individuals who obtain coverage through an exchange.

An Exchange may operate in more than one state (i.e., a regional or interstate Exchange) if: (1) each state in which the Exchange operates permits it to do so, and (2) the Secretary of HHS approves the regional or interstate Exchange. Also, a state may establish one or more subsidiary Exchanges if each subsidiary Exchange serves a geographically distinct area. However, the area served by each subsidiary Exchange must be at least as large as a rating area described in Act Sec. 2701(a) of the Public Health Service.

A state may elect to authorize an Exchange established by the state to enter into an agreement with an eligible entity to carry out one or more Exchange responsibilities. An "eligible entity" is defined as either:

- a person that (a) is incorporated, (b) has demonstrated experience on a state or regional basis in the individual and small group health insurance markets and in benefits coverage; and (c) is not a health insurance issuer or that is treated under as a member of the same controlled group of corporations (or under common control with) as a health insurance issuer; or

- the State Medicaid agency (Act Sec. 1311(f) of PPACA).

LAW EXPLAINED

Exchange coverage offerings. An Exchange must make qualified health plans available to qualified individuals and qualified employers. An Exchange is barred from making available any health plans that are not qualified. For a discussion of the essential health benefits that a qualified health plan must offer, see the discussion below and ¶530. However, each Exchange must require plan issuers providing limited scope dental benefits (Code Sec. 9832(c)(2)(A)) to offer the plan through the Exchange. This can be done either separately or in connection with a qualified health plan if the plan provides pediatric dental benefits (Act Sec. 1311(d)(2) of PPACA).

Exchanges may make available a qualified health plan notwithstanding any provision of law that may require benefits other than the essential health benefits specified. Further, a state may require that a qualified health plan offered in the state offer benefits in addition to the essential health benefits. However, in this instance, the state must assume the cost by: (1) making payments to an qualified individual enrolled in a qualified health plan offered in such state, or (2) making payments directly to the qualified health plan in which such individual is enrolled, on behalf of the individual. This is intended to defray the cost of any additional benefits (Act Sec. 1311(d)(3) of PPACA, as amended by 10104(e)(1)).

Exchange's certification of qualified health plans. A qualified health plan is a health plan that is eligible to be offered by an exchange, is offered by a duly licensed health insurer that has agreed to offer plans that meet cost-sharing requirements, and provides a specific package of health benefits at certain coverage levels (minimum essential health benefits package, as discussed in ¶530), coupled with prescribed cost-sharing amounts. The Affordable Care Act allows for Exchanges to certify health plans as qualified health plans. This certification may be done if:

- the health plan meets the rules for certification by the Department of Health and Human Services (HHS); and
- the Exchange determines that making such health plan available through the Exchange is in the interests of qualified individuals and qualified employers in the state or states in which the Exchange operates.

However, an Exchange may not exclude a health plan due to the fact that the health plan is a fee-for-service plan or through the imposition of premium price controls. Nor may a health plan be excluded on the basis that the plan provides treatments necessary to prevent patients' deaths in circumstances the Exchange determines are inappropriate or too costly.

The Exchange must require health plans seeking certification to submit a justification for any premium increase prior to implementation of the increase. These plans must prominently post such information on their web sites. The Exchange is to take this information, and the information and the recommendations provided to the Exchange by the state (relating to patterns or practices of excessive or unjustified premium increases) into consideration when determining whether to make the health plan available through the Exchange. The Exchange must also take into account any excess of premium growth outside the Exchange as compared to the rate of such

¶505

LAW EXPLAINED

growth inside the Exchange, including information reported by the state (Act Sec. 1311(e) of PPACA).

Coverage transparency. The Exchange must require health plans seeking certification as qualified health plans to submit to the Exchange, the HHS Secretary, and the State insurance commissioner (and make available to the public), accurate and timely disclosure of the following information:

- claims payment policies and practices;

- periodic financial disclosures;

- data on enrollment;

- data on disenrollment;

- data on the number of claims that are denied;

- data on rating practices;

- information on cost-sharing and payments with respect to any out-of-network coverage;

- information on enrollee and participant rights; and

- any other information considered to be appropriate by the HHS Secretary.

> **Comment:** The information required to be submitted under the coverage transparency rule must be provided in plain language. The term "plain language" is defined as language that the intended audience, including individuals with limited English proficiency, can readily understand and use because that language is concise, well-organized, and follows other best practices of plain language writing. The Secretaries of HHS and Labor must jointly develop and issue guidance on best practices of plain language writing.

The Affordable Care Act imposes additional rules relating to cost-sharing transparency as well. Specifically, the Exchange must require health plans seeking certification as qualified health plans to permit individuals to learn the amount of cost-sharing (including deductibles, copayments, and coinsurance), under the individual's plan or coverage, that the person would be responsible for paying. This applies with regard to the furnishing of a specific item or service by a participating provider in a timely manner at the request of the individual. At a minimum, this information must be made available to the individual through an internet web site and also via other means, for individuals without Internet access.

HHS certification of qualified health plans. The HHS Secretary must establish criteria, by regulation, for certifying health plans as qualified health plans, for purposes of the Exchange rules. At a minimum, these criteria must:

- meet marketing requirements, and not use marketing practices or benefit designs that discourage plan enrollment by individuals with significant health needs;

LAW EXPLAINED

- ensure a sufficient choice of providers (consistent with network adequacy provisions under Act Sec. 2702(c) of the Public Health Service Act) and provide information both to enrollees and prospective enrollees on the availability of in-network and out-of-network providers;

- include within health insurance plan networks those essential community providers, where available, that serve predominately low-income, medically-underserved individuals (but this is not to be construed as requiring any health plan to provide coverage for any specific medical procedure);

- be accredited with respect to local performance on clinical quality measures, patient experience ratings, as well as consumer access, utilization management, quality assurance, provider credentialing, complaints and appeals, network adequacy and access, and patient information programs by HHS-recognized accreditation entity or receive this performance accreditation within a period established by an Exchange for such accreditation that is applicable to all qualified health plans;

- implement a quality improvement strategy;

- utilize a uniform enrollment form (either electronically or paper-based) that qualified individuals and qualified employers may use in enrolling in qualified health plans offered through an Exchange;

- utilize the standard format established for presenting health benefits plan options; and

- provide information to enrollees and prospective enrollees, and to each Exchange in which the plan is offered, on any Public Health Service Act-endorsed quality measures for health plan performance (Act Sec. 1311(c)(1) of PPACA).

Voluntary nature of Exchanges. The Affordable Care Act makes clear that nothing is to be construed as restricting the choice of a qualified individual to enroll or not to enroll in a qualified health plan or to participate in a Exchange (Act Sec. 1312(d)(3) of PPACA). However, for a catastrophic plan, a qualified individual may enroll only if eligible to enroll in a plan under the Exchange. Similarly, nothing is to be interpreted as prohibiting a qualified employer from selecting for its employees a health plan offered outside of the Exchange (Act Sec. 1312(d)(1) of PPACA). Also, nothing is to be construed as prohibiting a health insurance issuer from offering a health plan to a qualified individual or qualified employer outside of the Exchanges.

▶ **Effective date.** No effective date is provided by the Act. The provision is therefore considered effective on March 23, 2010, the date of enactment.

— Act Sec. 1311 of the Patient Protection and Affordable Care Act (PPACA) (P.L. 111-148), as amended by Act Secs. 10104(e)-(h).

>>>→ *Caution: The explanation below reflects certain nontax provisions of the Patient Protection and Affordable Care Act (P.L. 111-148) and the Health Care and Education Reconciliation Act of 2010 (P.L. 111-152). While the issues discussed do not have a direct effect on federal taxes, this explanation is helpful in understanding some of the tax-related explanations that appear in this publication.*

¶510 Exchange Requirements—American Health Benefit Exchanges

SUMMARY OF NEW LAW

By January 1, 2014, American Health Benefit Exchanges must be established to facilitate the purchase of qualified health plans. These Exchanges must meet the rules for Exchanges.

BACKGROUND

Historically, there was no health exchange provision in federal law.

LAW EXPLAINED

Health Insurance Exchange clarified—By January 1, 2014, each state must establish an American Health Benefit Exchange for that state that would facilitate the purchase of qualified health plans (Act Sec. 1311(b) of the Patient Protection and Affordable Care Act (PPACA) (P.L. 111-148). Each state is also required to establish a Small Business Health Options Program (SHOP Exchange). A SHOP Exchange is designed to assist qualified small employers in the state in enrolling their employees in qualified health plans in the state's small group market. See ¶ 512. These Exchanges must meet the requirements for Exchanges.

> **Comment:** In the event a state does not act to establish its exchanges, the federal government must step in and provide and them. Most states do not have their own exchanges.

State operated American Health Benefit Exchange must be operated by a state-established governmental agency or nonprofit entity. Exchanges also must comply with a number of other rules relating to coverage offerings, required benefits, and other provisions, including issuing certificates of exemption, performing eligibility determinations, establishing an appeals process for eligibility determinations, and performing required functions related to oversight and financial integrity requirements (Act Sec. 1311(d)(1) of PPACA; HHS Final Reg. 155.200).

Requirements for Exchanges. At minimum, an Exchange must:

- implement procedures for the certification, recertification, and decertification of health plans as qualified health plans;

- provide for the operation of a toll-free telephone hotline to respond to assistance requests;

LAW EXPLAINED

- maintain an internet website through which enrollees and prospective enrollees of qualified health plans may obtain standardized comparative information on health plans;

- assign a rating to each qualified health plan offered through the Exchange;

- utilize a standardized format for presenting health benefits plan options in the Exchange, including the use of the uniform outline of coverage;

- inform individuals of eligibility requirements for the Medicaid program, the Children's Health Insurance Program (CHIP), or any applicable state or local public program, and, if through screening of the application by the Exchange, it determines that such individuals are eligible for any such program, enroll such individuals in such program;

- establish and make available by electronic means a calculator to determine the actual cost of coverage after the application of any premium assistance tax credit (see ¶ 210) and any cost-sharing reduction (see ¶ 520);

- subject to the procedures for determining eligibility, grant a certification attesting that, for purposes of the individual responsibility penalty for failure to maintain minimum essential health coverage (see ¶ 205), an individual is exempt from the requirement or from the penalty imposed because (a) there is no affordable qualified health plan available through the Exchange or the individual's employer covering the individual; or (b) the individual meets the requirements for any other exemption from the individual responsibility requirement or penalty;

- transfer to the Secretary of the Treasury:

  — a list of the individuals who are issued a certification of an exemption from the penalty for failing to carry health insurance (see ¶ 205) (including the name and taxpayer identification number of each individual);

  — the name and taxpayer identification number of each individual who was an employee of an employer but who was determined to be eligible for the premium assistance tax credit (see ¶ 210) because the employer did not provide minimum essential coverage or the employer provided the minimum essential coverage but it was determined to either be unaffordable to the employee or did not provide the required minimum actuarial value; and

  — the name and taxpayer identification number of each individual who notifies the Exchange that they have changed employers and of each individual who ceases coverage under a qualified health plan during a plan year (and the effective date of such cessation);

- provide each employer with the name of each of its employees who ceases coverage under a qualified health plan during a plan year (and the effective date of such cessation); and

- establish the Navigator program, under which entities known as Navigators will do such things as distributing fair and impartial information about enrollment in qualified health plans, premium tax credits, and cost-sharing reductions and assisting consumers in selecting qualified health plans (Act Sec. 1311(d)(4) of PPACA; HHS Final Reg. 155.210).

¶510

LAW EXPLAINED

Exchanges must consult with stakeholders in carrying out their activities. These stakeholders include health care consumers who enroll in qualified health plans; individuals and entities experienced in facilitating enrollment in qualified health plans; representatives of small businesses and self-employed individuals; State Medicaid offices; and advocates for enrolling hard-to-reach populations (Act Sec. 1311(d)(6) of PPACA).

Exchanges are required to publish the average costs of licensing, regulatory fees, and any other payments required by the Exchange, as well as the Exchange's administrative costs. This information should be published on an Internet website to help educate consumers on such costs. Such information shall also include information as to monies lost to waste, fraud, and abuse (Act Sec. 1311(d)(6) of PPACA).

Any notice required to be sent by an Exchange to applicants, qualified individuals, qualified employees, qualified employers, and enrollees must be in writing and include contact information for available customer service resources, an explanation of appeal rights, if applicable, and a citation to or identification of the specific regulation supporting the action (HHS Final Reg. 155.230).

Exchange enrollment periods. An Exchange must provide for:

- an open enrollment period, beginning October 1, 2013, and extending through March 31, 2014;

- annual open enrollment periods, as determined by the HHS Secretary for calendar years after the initial enrollment period (for benefit years beginning on or after January 1, 2015, the annual open enrollment period begins October 15 and extends through December 7 of the preceding calendar year);

- special enrollment periods as available for group health plans under Code Sec. 9801; and

- special monthly enrollment periods for Indians (Act Sec. 1331(c)(6) of PPACA).

A qualified individual may enroll in any qualified health plan under the American Health Benefit Exchange that is available to the individual in the state he or she resides and for which the individual is eligible (Act Sec. 1312(a)(1), as amended by Act Sec. 10104(i)(1) of PPACA). A qualified individual is defined as someone who is seeking to enroll in a qualified health plan in the individual market offered through an Exchange, and resides in the state that established the Exchange. Individuals who are incarcerated, other than those whose incarceration is pending the disposition of charges, are not to be treated as qualified individuals (Act Sec. 1312(f)(1), as amended by Act Sec. 10104(i)(3) of PPACA).

A person is not considered a qualified individual if he or she is not (or is not reasonably expected to be) for the entire enrollment period, a U.S. citizen or national, or an alien lawfully present in the United States. A person who does not come within this definition is not a qualified individual and may not be covered under a qualified health plan in the individual market that is offered through an Exchange (Act Sec. 1312(f)(3) of PPACA).

> **Comment:** A qualified individual who is enrolled in a qualified health plan may pay any applicable premium owed by that person to the insurance issuer that has issued the qualified health plan (Act Sec. 1312(b) of PPACA).

LAW EXPLAINED

An Exchange, or a qualified health plan offered under an Exchange, may not impose a penalty or other fee on an individual who cancels enrollment in a plan because he or she becomes eligible for minimum essential coverage (other than under a grandfathered plan) (see ¶205), or such coverage becomes affordable.

Effective coverage dates. For qualified health plan (QHP) selections received by the Exchange from a qualified individual during the initial open enrollment period (HHS Final Reg 155.410):

- on or before December 24, 2013, the Exchange must ensure a coverage effective date of January 1, 2014; and
- between the first and fifteenth day of any subsequent month during the initial open enrollment period, the Exchange must ensure a coverage effective date of the first day of the following month; and
- between the sixteenth and last day of the month for any month between December 2013 and March 31, 2014 (25th and last day for December 2013), the Exchange must ensure a coverage effective date of the first day of the second following month.

The Exchange must ensure coverage is effective as of the first day of the following benefit year for a qualified individual who has made a QHP selection during the annual open enrollment period.

- on the first day of the following month for all QHP selections made between the first and the fifteenth day of any month,
- on the first day of the second following month for all QHP selections made between the 16th and last day of the second following month, or
- in the case of birth, adoption or placement for adoption effective on the date of birth, adoption, or placement for adoption

Once a qualified individual is determined eligible for a special enrollment period, during which qualified individuals may enroll in QHPs and enrollees may change QHPs, the Exchange must ensure that the qualified individual's effective date of coverage is:

Single risk pool. Health insurance issuers are to consider all enrollees in all qualified health plans, other than certain grandfathered plans, offered by the issuer in the individual market to be members of a single risk pool. This includes those enrollees who do not enroll in such plans through the Exchange (Act Sec. 1312(c)(1) of PPACA). For a discussion of grandfathered plans, see ¶535.

> **Comment:** Nothing in this portion of the Affordable Care Act is to be construed as terminating, abridging or otherwise limiting the operation of any state law requirements regarding any health plans or policies that are offered outside of an Exchange, to offer benefits (Act Sec. 1312(d)(2) of PPACA).

Multi-state plans. At least two multi-state qualified health plans must be available as part of the Exchange in each state. The Director of the Office of Personnel Management will enter into contracts with private insurers to offer the multi-state plans. The multi-state plans will provide coverage in the individual and small employer markets (Act Sec. 1334(a)(1), as added by Act Sec. 10104(q) of the PPACA).

▶ **Effective date.** No effective date is provided by the Act. The provision is therefore considered to be effective on March 23, 2010, the date of enactment.

¶510

LAW EXPLAINED

— Act Sec. 1311 of the Patient Protection and Affordable Care Act (PPACA) (P.L. 111-148), as amended by Act Sec. 10104.

— Act Sec. 1312 of the Patient Protection and Affordable Care Act (PPACA) (P.L. 111-148), as amended by Act Sec. 10104.

— Act Sec. 1334 of the Patient Protection and Affordable Care Act (PPACA) (P.L. 111-148), as amended by Act Sec. 10104.

»»→ Caution: The explanation below reflects certain nontax provisions of the Patient Protection and Affordable Care Act (P.L. 111-148) and the Health Care and Education Reconciliation Act of 2010 (P.L. 111-152). While the issues discussed do not have a direct effect on federal taxes, this explanation is helpful in understanding some of the tax-related explanations that appear in this publication.

¶512 Small Business Health Options Program (SHOP Exchange)

SUMMARY OF NEW LAW

By January 1, 2014, each state is to establish a Small Business Health Options Program (SHOP Exchange) to provide qualified small business employers access to qualified health plans.

BACKGROUND

Historically, there had been no insurance exchange provision in federal law.

LAW EXPLAINED

Small Business Health Options Program established.—An Exchange must provide for the establishment of a Small Business Health Options Program (SHOP) that meets certain requirements and is designed to assist qualified employers and facilitate the enrollment of qualified employees into qualified health plans (QHP) (HHS Final Reg. 155.700). States are encouraged to set up and operate their own state-based SHOP marketplace exchanges, or they can let the federal government set up and operate a federally facilitated marketplace SHOP exchange. Some states have partnership marketplace SHOP exchanges under which a state performs many SHOP tasks while using a federally facilitated exchange. Some states have their own SHOP exchange even though they use a federally facilitated marketplace exchange for individual coverage.

Starting in 2014, small businesses have to purchase SHOP coverage to obtain the small employer tax credit (see ¶ 310). Qualified employers may purchase SHOP coverage through brokers, agents and insurers. The online component for the federally facilitated SHOP exchange is postponed until 2015, with applications scheduled to being taken

LAW EXPLAINED

online starting in November 2014. States are permitted but not required to delay their online presence as well.

Qualified employers. A qualified employer is a small employer that either has its principal business address in the Exchange service area and offers coverage to all its employees through that SHOP or offers coverage to each eligible employee through the SHOP serving that employee's primary worksite that elects to make all of its full-time employees eligible for one or more qualified health plans offered in the small group market through an Exchange (Act Sec. 1312(f)(2)(A) of PPACA). Beginning in 2017, each state may allow health insurance coverage issuers to offer qualified health plans in the large group market through an Exchange. A qualified employer may participate in more than one SHOP.

A small employer, in connection with a group health plan, is defined by the HHS as one who, with respect to a calendar year, employed an average of at least one but not more than 100 employees on business days during the preceding calendar year and who employs at least one employee on the first day of the plan year. For plan years beginning before January 1, 2016, HHS allows small employers to be limited to those with not more than 50 employees, and the Exchanges have done this (HHS Final Reg. 155.20). The SHOP must treat a qualified employer which ceases to be a small employer solely by reason of an increase in the number of employees of such employer as a qualified employer until the qualified employer otherwise fails to meet the eligibility criteria of this section or elects to no longer purchase coverage for qualified employees through the SHOP.

Qualified employer participation process. When joining the SHOP, a qualified employer must comply with certain requirements, processes, and timelines and must remain in compliance for the duration of the employer's participation in the SHOP (HHS Final Reg. 157.205). A qualified employer participating in the SHOP must disseminate information to its qualified employees about the process to enroll in a QHP through the SHOP. Qualified employers must provide employees hired outside of the initial or annual open enrollment period with a specified period to seek coverage in a QHP beginning on the first day of employment and information about the enrollment process. Qualified employers participating in the SHOP must provide the SHOP with information about individuals or employees whose eligibility status for coverage purchased through the employer in the SHOP has changed, including: (1) newly eligible individuals and employees; and (2) loss of qualified employee status.

Enrollment of employees. The SHOP must establish a uniform enrollment timeline and process that all QHP issuers and qualified employers comply with for the following activities to occur before the effective date of coverage for qualified employees (HHS Final Reg. 155.720).

- determination of employer eligibility for purchase of coverage in the SHOP;
- qualified employer selection of QHPs offered through the SHOP to qualified employees;
- provision of a specific timeframe during which the qualified employer can select the level of coverage or QHP offering, as appropriate;

LAW EXPLAINED

- provision of a specific timeframe for qualified employees to provide relevant information to complete the application process;
- determination and verification of employee eligibility for enrollment through the SHOP;
- processing enrollment of qualified employees into selected QHPs; and
- establishment of effective dates of employee coverage.

If any employee terminates coverage from a QHP, the SHOP must notify the individual's employer.

If a SHOP authorizes a minimum participation rate, that rate must be based on the rate of employee participation in the SHOP, not on the rate of employee participation in any particular QHP or QHPs or any particular issuer (HHS Final Reg. 155.705(b)(10)).

For plan years beginning on or after January 1, 2014, and before January 1, 2015, a SHOP will not be required to permit qualified employers to offer their qualified employees a choice of QHPs at a single level of coverage, but will have the option of doing so. With regard to QHPs offered through the SHOP for plan years beginning on or after January 1, 2015, the SHOP must allow a qualified employer to select a level of coverage in which all QHPs within that level are made available to the qualified employees of the employer (HHS Final Reg. 155.705(b)).

Enrollment periods. The SHOP must adhere to the start of the initial open enrollment period (October 1, 2013 through March 31, 2014) and ensure that enrollment transactions are sent to QHP issuers and that such issuers adhere to coverage effective dates. The SHOP must permit a qualified employer to purchase coverage for its small group at any point during the year. The employer's plan year must consist of the 12-month period beginning with the qualified employer's effective date of coverage (HHS Final Reg. 155.725(a), (b).

The SHOP must provide qualified employers with a period of no less than 30 days prior to the completion of the employer's plan year and before the annual employee open enrollment period, in which the qualified employer may change its participation in the SHOP for the next plan year, including the method by which qualified employers makes QHPs available to qualified employees, the employer contribution towards the premium cost of coverage, the level of coverage offered to qualified employees, or the QHP or plans offered to qualified employees (HHS Final Reg. 155.725(c)).

Special enrollment periods. The SHOP must provide special enrollment periods during which certain qualified employees or a dependent of a qualified employee may enroll in QHPs and enrollees may change QHPs (HHS Final Reg. 155.725). The SHOP must provide a special enrollment period for a qualified employee or dependent of a qualified employee who:

- experienced a qualifying event including losing minimum essential coverage, gaining a dependent or becoming a dependent through marriage, birth, adoption or placement for adoption, enrollment or non-enrollment in a QHP is unintentional, inadvertent, or erroneous and is the result of the error, misrepresentation, or inaction of an officer, employee, or agent of the Exchange or HHS, gaining access to new QHPs as

LAW EXPLAINED

a result of a permanent move, qualifying as an Indian, as defined by section 4 of the Indian Health Care Improvement Act, who may enroll in a QHP or change from one QHP to another one time per month, or demonstrating to the Exchange, in accordance with guidelines issued by HHS, that the individual meets other exceptional circumstances as the Exchange may provide;

- loses eligibility for Medicaid or CHIP coverage, or
- becomes eligible for state premium assistance under a Medicaid or CHIP program.

A qualified employee or dependent of a qualified employee who has obtained coverage through the SHOP has 30 days from the date of most of the triggering events to select a QHP. Additionally, a qualified employee or dependent of a qualified employee who has lost eligibility for Medicaid or CHIP coverage, or who has become eligible for state premium assistance under a Medicaid or CHIP program, is eligible for a special enrollment period in a SHOP and has 60 days from the date of the triggering event to select a QHP. A dependent of a qualified employee is not eligible for a special election period if the employer does not extend the offer of coverage to dependents (HHS Final Reg. 155.725(j)).

Direct Enrollment Process for 2014. On December 2, 2013, the Administration announced that it is delaying the start of its health insurance marketplace for small businesses until November 2014. Employers in states using the federally facilitated marketplace who want to buy marketplace plans for their workers will need to go through an agent, broker or insurance company to buy coverage for 2014, instead of using a government website. Employers in states running their own marketplaces will go through those marketplaces under the rules prescribed in each state, as described above. In conjunction with this delay, the Centers for Medicare and Medicaid (CMS) has announced a new enrollment process for small business owners in states that are using the federally facilitated SHOP marketplace. Note that employers using the new process can qualify for the small employer tax credit that is only available for insurance purchased through an exchange.

Under the new enrollment process, an employer will go directly to an agent, broker, or insurance company that offers plans through a SHOP Marketplace. The insurer must be one that has agreed to offer direct enrollment in SHOP coverage and that can conduct enrollment according to CMS standards. Working with the agent, broke, or insurance company, the employer selects a Qualified Health Plan. The agent, broker, or insurance company helps the employer fill out a paper application for SHOP eligibility and send it in to the federally facilitated SHOP Marketplace. Alternatively, the employer can submit the application itself, directly to the SHOP. The SHOP will send the employer an eligibility determination, and will send employee enrollment information to the IRS to ensure that, if otherwise eligible, the employer can claim the tax credit for tax year 2014. The employer can wait to enroll employees until it receives the official notice of eligibility, but it is not required to do so. The insurance company can tell the employer exactly how much coverage will cost and can enroll employees directly into the plan. If the SHOP later determines that the business is ineligible to participate in the SHOP Marketplace, the employer would lose eligibility for the credit, but the insurance company is not required to terminate the coverage.

¶512

LAW EXPLAINED

▶ **Effective date.** No specific effective date is provided by the Act. The provision is, therefore, considered effective on March 23, 2010, the date of enactment.

— Act Sec. 1411 of the Patient Protection and Affordable Care Act (PPACA) (P.L. 111-148).

>>>→ *Caution: The explanation below reflects certain nontax provisions of the Patient Protection and Affordable Care Act (P.L. 111-148) and the Health Care and Education Reconciliation Act of 2010 (P.L. 111-152). While the issues discussed do not have a direct effect on federal taxes, this explanation is helpful in understanding some of the tax-related explanations that appear in this publication.*

¶515 Procedures for Determining Eligibility for Exchange Participation, Tax Credits, and Cost-Sharing Reductions

SUMMARY OF NEW LAW

General procedures are established for determining eligibility for Exchange participation, premium tax credits, reduced cost-sharing, and individual responsibility exemptions. An applicant's citizenship/immigration status, income, and family size will be verified against federal records.

BACKGROUND

By January 1, 2014, each state is directed to establish an American Health Benefit Exchange and Small Business Health Options Program (SHOP Exchange) to provide qualified individuals and qualified small business employers access to qualified health plans. For a discussion of the establishment and requirements of the Exchanges (see ¶505). Individuals who are eligible for participation in a qualified health plan through an Exchange, may also be eligible for a premiums assistance tax credit (see ¶210) and cost-sharing subsidy (see ¶520). Historically, there was no federal law regarding insurance exchanges, the premium assistance tax credit, or the cost-sharing subsidies. In addition, there was no federal law to establish procedures for determining if an individual may be exempted from the penalty for failure to maintain minimum essential health care coverage (see ¶205).

LAW EXPLAINED

A qualified employer may support employee coverage under a qualified health plan provided through a Small Business Health Options Program (SHOP) Exchange. An employer selects any level of coverage permissible to be made available to employees under an Exchange. Within the selected level, each employee may choose to enroll in a qualified health plan offering coverage at that level (Act Sec. 1312(a)(2) of the Patient Protection and Affordable Care Act (PPACA)). For a discussion of the establishment of

LAW EXPLAINED

American Health Benefit and SHOP Exchanges, see ¶ 505. For a discussion of the essential health benefits that must be provided by a qualified plan, and the level of coverage, see ¶ 530).

Qualified employers. A "qualified employer" is a small employer that elects to make all of its full-time employees eligible for one or more qualified health plans offered in the small group market through an Exchange (Act Sec. 1312(f)(2)(A) of PPACA). Beginning in 2017, each state may allow health insurance coverage issuers to offer qualified health plans in the large group market through an Exchange. The Patient Protection Act makes it clear that it is not to be construed as requiring an issuer to offer such plans through an Exchange.

If a state chooses to allow issuers to offer qualified health plans in the large group market through an Exchange, the Patient Protection Act clarifies that the term "qualified employer" includes a large employer that elects to make all of its full-time employees eligible for one or more qualified health plans offered in the large group market through an Exchange (Act Sec. 1312(f)(2)(B) of PPACA).

Procedures for eligibility determinations outlined.—As part of the establishment of Health Insurance Exchanges and the requirement that individuals maintain minimum essential health care coverage (Act Sec. 1411(a) of PPACA) (P.L. 111-148)), the Secretary of Health and Human Services (HHS) has established standards for determining eligibility (HHS Final Reg. 155.305), redeterminations of eligibility through the course of a benefit year (HHS Final Reg. 155.330), and annual redeterminations (HHS Final Reg. 155.335). These standards are aimed at implementing PPACA rules that require the following determinations:

- whether an individual to be covered by an Exchange-offered qualified health plan in the individual market, or claiming a premium assistance tax credit (see ¶ 210) or reduced cost-sharing ¶ 520), is a U.S. citizen or national, or an alien lawfully present in the United States;

- whether an individual claiming a premium assistance tax credit or reduced cost-sharing meets income and coverage requirements, and the amount of the credit or reduced cost-sharing;

- whether an individual's employer-sponsored health coverage is "unaffordable"; and

- whether to grant certification of exemption for an individual from the requirement to maintain minimum essential health coverage, or applicable penalty (see ¶ 205).

Applicant information. HHS has issued procedural rules for making the eligibility determination (HHS Final Reg. 155.310). These rules implement the PPACA information requirements, which require information regarding:

- *Applicants for enrollment in Exchange-offered qualified health plans in the individual market:* Name, address, and date of birth of each individual to be covered by the plan (*i.e.,* enrollee) (Act Sec. 1411(b)(1) of PPACA).

- *Enrollees with eligibility based on attestation of citizenship:* Social Security number (Act Sec. 1411(b)(2)(A)) of PPACA).

¶515

LAW EXPLAINED

- *Enrollees with eligibility based on attestation of immigration status:* Social Security number (if applicable) and identifying information regarding immigration status (Act Sec. 1411(b)(2)(B) of PPACA).

- *Enrollees claiming premium tax credits or reduced cost-sharing:* Income and family size information for the tax year ending with (or within) the second calendar year preceding the calendar year in which the plan year begins. This information includes: taxpayer identity information, filing status, number of individuals for which a personal or dependency exemption is claimed, modified adjusted gross income (AGI), the tax year to which the information relates, and other information prescribed by regulation (Act Sec. 1411(b)(3)(A) of PPACA). Information regarding changed circumstances (for individuals with significant reductions in income or changes in marital status or family size, as well as those who were not required to file a tax return for the relevant tax year) may also be required (Act Sec. 1411(b)(3)(B) of PPACA).

- *Enrollees claiming premium tax credits and reduced cost-sharing based on employer-sponsored coverage that lacks minimum essential coverage or affordable minimum essential coverage:* Employer's name, address and employer identification number; whether the enrollee is a full-time employee, and whether the employer provides minimum essential coverage; if minimum essential coverage is provided, the lowest cost option and the required contribution under the employer plan; and, if the employer's minimum essential coverage is unaffordable, information regarding income, family size and changed circumstances. If an enrollee changes (or adds) employment while in a qualified health plan for which the credit or reduction is allowed, he or she must provide such information regarding the new employer (Act Sec. 1411(b)(4) of PPACA).

- *Individuals seeking exemption from the individual responsibility requirement:* Individuals claiming exemption due to lack of affordable coverage or household income less than 100 percent of the poverty line must furnish information regarding income, family size, changed circumstances and employer-sponsored coverage. The HHS Secretary must prescribe required information for those seeking exemption as a member of a religious sect or division, as a member of a health care sharing ministry, as an Indian, or for a hardship (Act Sec. 1411(b)(5) of PPACA).

Verification. Exchanges will transfer applicant-provided information to the HHS Secretary for verification. In turn, the Secretary will (Act Sec. 1411(c) of PPACA):

- submit information regarding citizenship/immigration status (including attestation of the individual) to the Social Security Commissioner and/or Secretary of Homeland Security for comparison with federal records; and

- submit information regarding eligibility for premium tax credits and cost-sharing reductions to the Treasury Secretary for verification of household income and family size.

HHS has issued verification rules related to eligibility for enrollment in a QHP through an exchange (HHS Final Regs. 155.315), and verification rules related to eligibility for insurance affordability programs (HHS Final Regs. 155.320).

LAW EXPLAINED

Verifications and determinations among federal officials will be done via an online system or other approved method (Act Sec. 1411(c)(4) of PPACA). Results must be reported back to the HHS Secretary, who will notify the Exchange (Act Sec. 1411(e) of PPACA). Note that the Secretary may change procedures to reduce administrative costs and burdens on applicants. The HHS Secretary will check the accuracy of information not required to be verified by another federal official, and may delegate this responsibility to the Exchange (Act Sec. 1411(d) of PPACA).

> **Comment:** Critics have alleged that IRS disclosure of taxpayer information for the purpose of verifying eligibility for premium credits and cost-sharing could infringe on individual privacy rights.

If applicant-provided information relating to enrollment, premium tax credits and cost-sharing reductions is positively verified, the HHS Secretary will notify the Treasury Secretary of the amount of any advance payment to be made (see ¶525). Similarly, if applicant-provided information relating to exemption from the individual responsibility requirement is positively verified, the HHS Secretary will issue a certification of exemption (Act Sec. 1411(e)(2) of PPACA).

Inconsistencies. If citizenship/lawful presence is not positively verified with the Social Security Commissioner or Secretary of Homeland Security, the applicant's eligibility will be determined under procedures used for Medicaid (Act Sec. 1411(e)(3) of PPACA; HHS Final Regs. 155.315(f)).

A streamlined verification process is used for individuals declaring they are citizens or nationals of the United States for purposes of establishing eligibility for Medicaid or the Children's Health Insurance Program (CHIP). In lieu of providing documentation, a state may submit, at least monthly, the names and Social Security numbers of newly enrolled individuals to the Social Security Commissioner, for comparison with the agency's records. The state may enter into an agreement with the Social Security Commissioner to electronically submit the information, or to use another method.

The HHS Secretary will notify the Exchange of inconsistencies with other information. In response, the Exchange will first contact the applicant to confirm the accuracy of the information, and take other actions to be identified by the Secretary. If still unresolved, the Exchange must notify the applicant of the inconsistency and provide him or her with the opportunity to present "satisfactory documentary evidence" or resolve the issue with the verifier during a 90-day period beginning when the notice is sent. The Secretary may extend this 90-day period for enrollments occurring in 2014 (Act Sec. 1411(e)(4)(A) of PPACA).

During this 90-day period, the Exchange has several responsibilities (not involving citizenship/immigration status) (Act Sec. 1411(e)(4)(B) of PPACA):

- before the close of the 90-day period, the Exchange must make any determinations based on information contained on the application;
- if, at the close of the 90-day period, an inconsistency is unresolved regarding premium tax credits or cost-sharing reductions, the Exchange must notify the applicant of the credit or reduction amount (if any) based on federal records;
- if the HHS Secretary notifies the Exchange that an enrollee is eligible for a premium tax credit or cost-sharing reduction due to a lack of minimum essential

LAW EXPLAINED

coverage through an employer (or unaffordable coverage), the Exchange must notify the employer of this fact and that the employer may be liable for a tax (for a discussion the employer requirement for providing minimum health care coverage, see ¶305);

- if, at the close of the 90-day period, an inconsistency remains concerning exemption from the individual responsibility requirement, the Exchange must notify the applicant that certification for exemption will not be issued; and

- the Exchange also must notify each individual receiving an inconsistency notice about the appeals process (Act Sec. 1411(e)(4)(C) of PPACA).

Appeals. The HHS Secretary, in consultation with the Treasury Secretary, the Secretary of Homeland Security and the Social Security Commissioner, must establish procedures for hearing and deciding on appeals of verification determinations, and periodically redetermining eligibility in appropriate circumstances (Act Sec. 1411(f)(1) of PPACA).

The HHS Secretary must establish a separate appeals process for employers notified that they may be liable for a tax for not providing minimum essential coverage or affordable coverage. The process must allow the employer to present information, including evidence of the employer-sponsored plan and employer contributions. It also must allow the employer access to the data used for the determination, as permissible by law. An employer generally is not entitled to an employee's tax return information, but may be notified of the employee's name and whether his or her income is above or below the affordability threshold. An employee can provide a waiver, however, allowing the employer to access to his or her tax return information (Act Sec. 1411(f)(2) of PPACA).

Confidentiality. Applicants are required to provide only the information necessary to authenticate identity, determine eligibility, and figure the amount of the premium tax credit or cost-sharing reduction. Individuals receiving such information may not disclose it for unauthorized purposes (Act Sec. 1411(g) of PPACA).

Penalties. Individuals who violate these provisions are subject to civil penalties, in addition to other applicable penalties, as follows (Act Sec. 1411(h) of PPACA):

- up to $25,000, for providing incorrect information on an application due to "negligence or disregard" of the rules and regulations (to be waived if the HHS Secretary determines that there was reasonable cause and that the individual acted in good faith);

- up to $250,000, for knowingly and willfully providing false or fraudulent information; and

- up to $25,000, for knowingly and willfully using or disclosing information, in violation of the confidentiality provisions.

The HHS Secretary (or U.S. Attorney General) may not put a lien or levy on property for failure to pay a penalty (Act Sec. 1411(h)(3) of PPACA).

▶ **Effective date.** No specific effective date is provided by the Act. The provision is, therefore, considered effective on March 23, 2010, the date of enactment.

— Act Sec. 1411 of the Patient Protection and Affordable Care Act (PPACA) (P.L. 111-148).

¶515

>>>→ *Caution: The explanation below reflects certain nontax provisions of the Patient Protection and Affordable Care Act (P.L. 111-148) and the Health Care and Education Reconciliation Act of 2010 (P.L. 111-152). While the issues discussed do not have a direct effect on federal taxes, this explanation is helpful in understanding some of the tax-related explanations that appear in this publication.*

¶520 Cost-Sharing Reductions

SUMMARY OF NEW LAW

Individuals who enroll in a qualified health plan at the silver coverage level in an Health Insurance Exchange may be eligible for cost-sharing reductions (*i.e.,* subsidies) if their household income does not exceed 400 percent of the poverty line. Reductions decrease annual out-of-pocket limits and, for lower-income individuals, further increase a plan's share of total allowed benefits costs. The federal government will pay plan issuers for the value of the reductions they make.

BACKGROUND

Beginning in 2014, a penalty is imposed on applicable individuals for each month they fail to have "minimum essential health coverage" for themselves and their dependents (see ¶205). This penalty is also referred to as a "shared responsibility payment." As is the case with premiums, there is no end in sight to escalating deductibles, coinsurance, and copayments, all elements of cost-sharing contained in most health insurance plans. Even Americans who do have health insurance may be unable to afford the cost-sharing required to actually obtain covered services. A report by the Congressional Research Service points out that premium credits, without cost-sharing assistance, would provide many individuals with health insurance that they could not afford to *use.*

LAW EXPLAINED

Cost-sharing reduced for eligible insureds.—Low-to moderate-income individuals who enroll in an qualified health plan providing silver level coverage through an Health Insurance Exchange may be eligible for cost-sharing reductions. "Cost-sharing" includes deductibles, coinsurance, copayments, and similar charges, as well as qualified medical expenses for essential health benefits covered under the plan. It does not include premiums, balance billing amounts for non-network providers, or spending for noncovered services (Act Sec. 1302(c)(3)(A) of the Patient Protection and Affordable Care Act (P.L. 111-148) (PPACA)).

> **Comment:** The exchanges have four levels of essential benefits coverage available to participants at either a "bronze," "silver," "gold," or "platinum" level. The bronze level plans must provide benefits that are actuarially equivalent to 60 percent of the full actuarial value of the benefits provided under the plan. The percentage increases to 70 percent for silver level plans, 80 percent for gold level

LAW EXPLAINED

plans, and 90 percent for platinum level plans. For a discussion of the required contents of an essential benefits coverage, see ¶530. Individuals who are eligible for participation in a qualified health plan through an Exchange, may be eligible for a premiums assistance tax credit (see ¶210) and the cost-sharing subsidy.

To qualify for the cost-sharing reduction, household income must exceed 100 percent, but may not exceed 400 percent, of the poverty line (for the family size involved). Individuals meeting these criteria are considered "eligible insureds" (Act Sec. 1402(b) of PPACA).

> **Comment:** Limiting cost-sharing reductions to those with household incomes that do not exceed 400 percent of the applicable poverty line targets the financial assistance to low- and moderate- income individuals and families. There is no sort of asset test used to help determine eligibility.

> **Caution:** Be aware that there are two slightly different versions of the federal poverty measure: (1) "poverty thresholds," which are updated annually by the U.S. Census Bureau; and (2) "poverty guidelines," which are issued annually by the U.S. Department of Health and Human Services (HHS). The Act refers to the "poverty line," which most likely means the HHS poverty guidelines, published annually in the *Federal Register*.

> **Example:** Applying the 2014 poverty guidelines, an individual in the contiguous United States with income over $11,670 and up to $46,680 (400 percent of the poverty guideline) would meet the income criterion for the cost-sharing reduction. Similarly, a family of four with household income over $23,850 and up to $95,440 would meet the criterion. The poverty guidelines are typically adjusted annually, so the figures will be higher in 2015.

An alien who is lawfully present in the United States with household income that does not exceed 100 percent of the applicable poverty line, and who is ineligible for Medicaid due to alien status, is treated as having household income equal to 100 percent of the poverty line for purposes of the cost-sharing reduction (Act Sec. 1402(b) of PPACA).

> **Caution:** To be considered an "eligible insured" for the cost-sharing reduction, the law states that household income must "exceed" 100 percent of the applicable poverty line. Treating income for this group of aliens as "equal to" 100 percent would technically exclude them. The language may be corrected in the future, as this most likely was not Congress' intent.

Determining the reduction. Cost-sharing reductions work by lowering the annual out-of-pocket limit for eligible insureds, on a sliding scale, by the following amounts (Act Sec. 1402(c)(1)(A) of PPACA):

- two-thirds, if household income is greater than 100 percent, but not more than 200 percent, of the applicable poverty line;

- one-half, if household income is greater than 200 percent, but not more than 300 percent, of the applicable poverty line; and

- one-third, if household income is greater than 300 percent, but not more than 400 percent, of the applicable poverty line.

LAW EXPLAINED

> **Comment:** Beginning in 2014, the out-of-pocket limit, or "annual limitation on cost-sharing," will be the out-of-pocket limit in effect for health savings accounts (HSAs) for the year. For 2015 and later years, the limit for self-only coverage will be adjusted based on a percentage of average per capita health insurance premium increases, and the limit for family coverage will be twice the amount for self-only coverage (Act Sec. 1302(c)(1) of PPACA). See ¶530 for more information about the cost-sharing limit.

> **Comment:** Financial assistance for cost-sharing becomes more limited as income increases.

Lower-income insureds are eligible for additional reductions. The HHS Secretary will establish procedures for qualified health plan issuers to further reduce cost-sharing so that the plan's share of total allowed costs of benefits under the plan (*i.e.,* actuarial value percentage) is increased to:

- 94 percent, if household income is not less than 100 percent, but is not more than 150 percent, of the applicable poverty line;

- 87 percent, if household income exceeds 150 percent, but is not more than 200 percent, of the applicable poverty line; and

- 73 percent, if household income exceeds 200 percent, but is not more than 250 percent, of the applicable poverty line (Act Sec. 1402(c)(2) of PPACA) as amended by the Health Care and Education Reconciliation Act of 2010 (P.L. 111-152)).

> **Comment:** Liability for these lower-income individuals will range from an average of six percent to 27 percent of the costs for covered benefits under the plan.

The HHS Secretary also will ensure that the initial reductions (lower out-of-pocket limits) do not increase the plan's actuarial value beyond the percentage limits above. For this purpose, the actuarial value limit applicable to eligible insureds with household income that exceeds 250 percent, but is not more than 400 percent, of the applicable poverty line is 70 percent (Act Sec. 1402(c)(1)(B) of PPACA, as amended by the 2010 Reconciliation Act).

Process. The HHS Secretary will notify qualified health plan issuers of enrolled insureds who are eligible for cost-sharing reductions, and issuers will reduce cost-sharing under the plan (Act Sec. 1402(a) of PPACA). Issuers must notify the Secretary of the cost-sharing reductions they make, and the Secretary will make periodic and timely payments to the issuer for the value of the reductions. The Secretary may establish a capitated payment system with appropriate risk adjustments (Act Sec. 1402(c)(3) of PPACA).

Special rules. Unique rules apply to benefits in excess of essential heath benefits, to pediatric dental benefits, and to Indians:

- Cost-sharing reductions do not apply to benefits offered in addition to the essential health benefits required to be provided by the plan, whether offered by a qualified health plan or required by a State (Act Sec. 1402(c)(4) of PPACA).

LAW EXPLAINED

- If an individual enrolls in both a qualified health plan and a stand-alone dental plan that provides pediatric dental benefits for any plan year, the portion of any cost-sharing reduction allocable, per regulations, to pediatric dental benefits included in the health plan's required essential benefits does not apply (Act Sec. 1402(c)(5) of PPACA).

- Plan issuers must eliminate *any* cost-sharing under the plan for Indians who are enrolled in any qualified health plan in the individual market through an Exchange, if their household income does not exceed 300 percent of the poverty line. Also, if an Indian enrolled in a qualified health plan is furnished an item or service directly by an Indian health provider or through referral under contract health services, cost-sharing may not be imposed for the item or service, and a plan issuer may not reduce payment to such entity by the amount of cost-sharing that would otherwise be due from the Indian. The HHS Secretary will pay the issuer an amount that reflects the increased actuarial value of the plan (Act Sec. 1402(d) of PPACA).

  Comment: An "Indian" means a person who is a member of an Indian tribe, that is any band, nation, or other organized group or community, including any Alaska Native village or regional or village corporation, that is recognized as eligible for special programs and services provided by the United States because of their status as Indians (25 U.S.C. § 450b).

Illegal immigrants. Cost-sharing reductions do not apply to eligible insureds who are not lawfully present in the United States. An individual is considered "lawfully present" only if he or she is, and is reasonably expected to be for the entire cost-sharing reduction period, a U.S. citizen or national, or an alien who is lawfully present in the United States (Act Sec. 1402(e) of PPACA).

When figuring reductions for a taxpayer, household income (relative to the poverty line) must be determined under a method that:

- subtracts the unlawfully present individual from the family size; and

- multiplies household income by a fraction where the numerator is the poverty line for the taxpayer's family size after subtracting the unlawfully present individual, and the denominator is the poverty line before the subtraction.

A comparable method that reaches the same result also may be used. The HHS Secretary, in consultation with the Treasury Secretary, will prescribe rules setting forth the methods by which calculations of family size and household income may be made (see ¶515) (Act Sec. 1402(e) of PPACA).

Limitations. Cost-sharing reductions are limited to coverage months for which a premium assistance tax credit is allowed to the insured (or applicable taxpayer on behalf of the insured) (see ¶210). Also, data for determining eligibility for cost-sharing reductions is based on the tax year for which advanced determinations are made (see ¶525), rather than the tax year for which premium credits are allowed (Act Sec. 1402(f) of PPACA).

¶520

LAW EXPLAINED

▶ **Effective date.** No specific effective date is provided for this provision. Therefore, Act Secs. 1402(a) and (b) are considered effective on March 23, 2010, the date of enactment of the Patient Protection and Affordable Care Act (PPACA) (P.L. 111-148). Act Sec. 1402(c) is considered effective on March 30, 2010, the date of enactment of the Health Care and Education Reconciliation Act of 2010 (P.L. 111-152).

— Act Secs. 1402(a) and (b) of the Patient Protection and Affordable Care Act (PPACA) (P.L. 111-148);

— Act Sec. 1402(c), as amended by Act Sec. 1001(b) of the Health Care and Education Reconciliation Act of 2010 (P.L. 111-152);

— Act Secs. 1402(d), (e) and (f).

⟫→ *Caution: The explanation below reflects certain nontax provisions of the Patient Protection and Affordable Care Act (P.L. 111-148) and the Health Care and Education Reconciliation Act of 2010 (P.L. 111-152). While the issues discussed do not have a direct effect on federal taxes, this explanation is helpful in understanding some of the tax-related explanations that appear in this publication.*

¶525 Advance Determinations and Payments

SUMMARY OF NEW LAW

Income eligibility for purposes of premium tax credits and cost-sharing reductions (*i.e.*, subsidies) may be determined in advance, upon request of an Health Benefit Exchange. The Treasury Secretary will make advance payments of the credits and reductions to qualified health plan issuers, providing up-front savings to eligible insured individuals.

BACKGROUND

By January 1, 2014, states or the federal government must establish an American Health Benefit Exchange and Small Business Health Options Program (SHOP Exchange) for each state to provide qualified individuals and qualified small business employers access to qualified health plans. For a discussion of the establishment and requirements of the Exchanges (see ¶505). Individuals who are eligible for participation in a qualified health plan through an Exchange, may also be eligible for a premiums assistance tax credit (see ¶210) and cost-sharing subsidy (see ¶520). Some tax credits, like the Health Coverage Tax Credit (HCTC) and a portion of the Earned Income Credit, are available on an *advance* basis. This allows taxpayers to receive benefits from the credit throughout the year without having to wait and claim it on their income tax returns.

Advance determinations and payments permitted.—A program, allowing advance determinations of income eligibility for purposes of premium assistance tax credit and cost-sharing reductions, must be established by the Secretary of Health and Human Services (HHS) (Act Sec. 1412(a) of the Patient Protection and Affordable Care Act (PPACA) (P.L. 111-148)). For a discussion about the premium assistance tax credit, see ¶ 210. For a discussion of the cost-sharing reductions, see ¶ 520.

Advance determinations will be made during an individual's annual open enrollment period in a qualified health plan, and will be based on an individual's household income for the most recent tax year for which the HHS Secretary determines information is available (Act Sec. 1412(b) of PPACA). When information on an application form demonstrates a significant change in circumstances (such as a 20-percent drop in income or a filing for unemployment benefits) or when a tax return was not required for the relevant tax year, procedures will allow advance determinations to be based on alternative measures of income.

Payments. For premium assistance tax credits, the HHS Secretary will notify the Treasury Secretary and the applicable Exchange of the advance determination. The Treasury Secretary will make the advance payment to the qualified health plan issuer on a monthly or other periodic basis (Act Sec. 1412(c) of PPACA). The issuer will then:

- reduce the insured's premium by the amount of the advance payment;
- notify the Exchange and the HHS Secretary of the reduction;
- include the premium reduction in each billing statement;
- notify the HHS Secretary if an insured fails to pay premiums; and
- allow a three-month grace period for nonpayment, before discontinuing coverage.

For cost-sharing reductions, the HHS Secretary similarly will notify the Treasury Secretary and the applicable Exchange of the advance determination. The Treasury Secretary will make the advance payment of cost-sharing reductions to the qualified health plan issuer at the time and in the amount specified in the notice.

If an Exchange determines that a tax filer is eligible for advance payments of the premium tax credit, an applicant is eligible for cost-sharing reductions, or that such eligibility for such programs has changed, the Exchange must, simultaneously:

- Transmit eligibility and enrollment information to HHS necessary to enable HHS to begin, end, or change advance payments of the premium tax credit or cost-sharing reductions; and
- Notify and transmit information necessary to enable the issuer of the QHP to implement, discontinue the implementation, or modify the level of advance payments of the premium tax credit or cost-sharing reductions, as applicable, including: (i) the

LAW EXPLAINED

dollar amount of the advance payment; and (ii) the cost-sharing reductions eligibility category (HHS Final Reg. 155.340(a)).

The HHS Secretary also must notify the Treasury Secretary of employers that do not provide minimum essential coverage or affordable coverage, enabling one or more employees to qualify for premium tax credits and cost-sharing reductions (Act Sec. 1412(a) of PPACA). For a discussion the assessable penalty imposed on an employer for failing to provide minimum health care coverage, see ¶ 305.

Illegal immigrants. No federal payments, credits or cost-sharing reductions can be made for individuals who are not lawfully present in the United States (Act Sec. 1413(d) of PPACA).

State flexibility. Premium assistance tax credits or cost-sharing reductions do not preclude states from making payments to, or on behalf of, an individual for health coverage offered through an Exchange (Act Sec. 1412(e) of PPACA).

▶ **Effective date.** No specific effective date is provided by the Act. The provision is, therefore, considered effective on March 23, 2010, the date of enactment.

— Act Sec. 1412 of the Patient Protection and Affordable Care Act (PPACA) (P.L. 111-148).

⋙→ *Caution: The explanation below reflects certain nontax provisions of the Patient Protection and Affordable Care Act (P.L. 111-148) and the Health Care and Education Reconciliation Act of 2010 (P.L. 111-152). While the issues discussed do not have a direct effect on federal taxes, this explanation is helpful in understanding some of the tax-related explanations that appear in this publication.*

¶530 Contents of Essential Health Benefits Package

SUMMARY OF NEW LAW

The essential health benefits package offered by qualified health benefit plan through a Health Insurance Exchange must include specific categories of benefits, meet certain cost-sharing standards, and provide certain levels of coverage. The scope of benefits provided must equal benefits provided under a "typical" employer-sponsored plan. Required levels of coverage range from "bronze" (60 percent of the value of plan benefits) to "platinum" (90 percent of the value). Plans offering "catastrophic" coverage may be offered in the individual market (generally only to those under age 30 and those qualifying for hardship exemptions).

BACKGROUND

Beginning in 2014, states (or in the absence of state action, the federal government) must establish American Health Benefit Exchanges and Small Business Health Options Program (SHOP) Exchanges to be administered by a governmental agency or nonprofit organization. Under these Exchanges, individuals and small businesses with 100 or fewer employees can purchase qualified coverage, though, eventually, states may allow businesses with more than 100 employees to purchase coverage in the SHOP Exchange. States may form regional Exchanges or allow more than one Exchange to operate in a state as long as each Exchange serves a distinct geographic area. For a discussion of the establishment of the Exchanges, see ¶505.

Only "qualified health benefit plans" may be sold via an Exchange. A "qualified health plan" is a health plan that is:

- certified as eligible to be offered via an Exchange;

- offered by a duly licensed health insurance issuer that has agreed to offer plans that meet certain cost-sharing requirements; and

- provides a specific package of health benefits at certain coverage levels, coupled with prescribed cost-sharing amounts (this package is referred to as the "essential health benefits package").

LAW EXPLAINED

Certain coverage must be included in the essential health benefits package.— Beginning in 2014, an essential health benefits package provided by a qualified health plan in the individual or small group market (whether or not offered through a Health Insurance Exchange) generally must (1) offer coverage for specific categories of benefits; (2) meet certain cost-sharing standards; and (3) provide certain levels of coverage (Act Sec. 1302(a) of the Patient Protection and Affordable Care Act (PPACA) (P.L. 111-148)).

> **Comment:** Employer plans that are purchased outside of the small group market exchanges as well as self-insured employer plans are not required to offer an Essential Benefit Package (EBP). All employer group health plan coverage is subject to separate accessibility, coverage, and market reform requirements (see ¶540). Large employers that are subject to the employer mandate must offer Minimum Essential Coverage (MEC), which must comply with these separate requirements (see ¶305). Individuals who are offered MEC from an employer that meets affordability and minimum value requirements cannot obtain subsidized coverage through an exchange (see ¶210). An individual who has MEC from an employer is not subject to a penalty under the individual mandate (see ¶205). Although MEC must comply with accessibility, coverage, and market reform requirements that overlap to some extent with EBP requirements, MEC is a lower standard than the EBP in terms of the content of coverage.

Minimum items and services to be covered. In the essential health benefits package, minimum coverage must include the following items and services (Act Sec. 1302(b)(1) of PPACA):

¶530

LAW EXPLAINED

- ambulatory patient services;
- emergency services;
- hospitalization;
- maternity and newborn care;
- mental health and substance use disorder services;
- prescription drugs;
- rehabilitative and habilitative services and devices;
- laboratory services;
- preventive and wellness services (including chronic disease management); and
- pediatric services (including oral and vision care).

Health plans may provide benefits in addition to those included in the essential health benefits package (Act Sec. 1302(b)(5) of PPACA). However, the scope of benefits offered in an essential health benefits package must be equivalent to the scope of benefits provided under the "typical" employer-sponsored plan. The Chief Actuary of the Centers for Medicare and Medicaid Services must certify that this standard is met and this certification must be reported to Congress by the HHS Secretary. Under final regulations issued by HHS, states are to select a benchmark plan from among several options, and all plans that cover essential health benefits must offer benefits substantially equal to benefits offered by the state's chosen benchmark plan. if a benchmark plan does not provide coverage of one of the required categories, it will be supplemented by the state or HHS. Generally, items or services that are missing must be supplemented by adding all benefits in the pertinent category offered under any benchmark plan (HHS Final Reg. 156.110).

Cost-sharing. Limits are placed on the cost-sharing that may be required with respect to the essential health benefits package offered by any qualified health plan. Cost-sharing includes deductibles, copayments, or coinsurance, but does not include premiums or spending for non-covered services (Act Sec. 1302(c)(3) of PPACA). In 2014, total cost-sharing may not exceed the amount applicable out-of-pocket limit for health savings accounts (HSAs) for self-only and family coverage for taxable years beginning in 2014 (Act Sec. 1302(c)(1)(A) of PPACA).

> **Comment:** For 2015 and thereafter, the amount applicable for self-only coverage is increased by the product of the 2014 limit and the premium adjustment percentage. The premium adjustment percentage for a calendar year is the percentage by which the average per capita premium in the United States for the preceding calendar year exceeds the average per capita premium for 2013. For other coverage, the indexed amount for self-only coverage is doubled (Act Sec. 1302(c)(1)(B) and (c)(4) of PPACA). The average per capita premium must be determined by the Secretary no later than October 1 of the preceding year. The indexed amount will be rounded if necessary to the next lowest multiple of $50.

> Generally, deductibles under a plan offered in the small employer group market must not exceed $2,000 for self-only coverage ($4,000 for other coverage). These amounts may be increased by the maximum amount of reimbursement reasonably available to a flexible spending account (FSA) participant. In addition, these

LAW EXPLAINED

amounts will be indexed annually, using the premium adjustment percentage used to adjust cost-sharing limits. These limits may not affect the actuarial value of any health plan (including a plan in the bronze level) (Act Sec. 1302(c)(2)(A)—(C) of PPACA).

Levels of coverage. Qualified health plans must provide coverage of the essential benefits at either the "bronze," "silver," "gold," or "platinum" levels. For bronze level plans, the level of coverage must provide benefits that are actuarially equivalent to 60 percent of the full actuarial value of the benefits provided under the plan. For silver level plans, the percentage increases to 70 percent. For gold and platinum level plans, the percentage increases to 80 percent and 90 percent, respectively (Act Sec. 1302(d)(1) of PPACA).

Exchanges may also offer catastrophic plans to individuals under the age of 30 and individuals who are exempt from the individual mandate. This includes individuals qualifying for hardship exemptions, including those whose plans have been cancelled who are unable to find another plan that is affordable. To fall within the exception, the catastrophic plan must be designed so that it provides the essential health benefits listed above, but provides no benefits for any plan year until the individual's share of the cost has matched the out-of-pocket limits for HSAs (excluding coverage for preventive health services). In addition, coverage must be provided for at least three primary care visits (Act Sec. 1302(e)(1) of PPACA). The catastrophic plans do not qualify for cost-sharing reductions.

If an insurer offers a qualified health plan through an Exchange at a given level of coverage (e.g., bronze, silver, gold, or platinum), it must also offer that plan, with the given level of coverage, as a plan in which all enrollees are individuals under the age of 21 (as of the beginning of the plan year). These child-only plans are treated as qualified health plans (Act Sec. 1302(f) of PPACA).

Prescription coverage. A health plan will generally not be considered to provide essential health benefits unless it covers at minimum the greater of one drug in every U.S. Pharmacopeia category and class or the same number of prescription drugs in each category and class as the benchmark plan. It also must submit its drug list to the Exchange, the state, or the U.S. Office of Personnel Management (OPM). In addition, the health plan must provide enrollees with access to clinically appropriate drugs not covered by the plan.

Treatment of payments to federally-qualified health centers. If an enrollee of a qualified health plan is provided services or items from a federally-qualified health center (FQHC), then the entity providing the plan must pay the FQHC at least the amount it would have received from Medicare or Medicaid for providing the item or service (Act Sec. 1302(g) of PPACA).

> **Comment:** According to CMS, FQHCs include providers such as community health centers, public housing centers, and outpatient health programs funded by the Indian Health Service ("Fact Sheet: Federally Qualified Health Center," http://www.cms.gov).

LAW EXPLAINED

▶ **Effective date.** No specific effective date is provided by the Act. The provision is, therefore, considered effective on March 23, 2010, the date of enactment.

— Act Sec. 1302 of the Patient Protection and Affordable Care Act (PPACA) (P.L. 111-148)

¶535 Grandfathered Plans in the Individual and Group Health Markets

SUMMARY OF NEW LAW

Individuals may keep their individual and group health plans that were in effect upon enactment of the Patient Protection and Affordable Care Act (PPACA) (P.L. 111-148), and these plans are exempt from many of the individual and group market reforms that take effect in 2014.

BACKGROUND

Historically, federal regulation of the private health insurance market has been narrow in scope and applicable mostly to employer-sponsored health insurance. These regulations include a variety of standards under the Internal Revenue Code and the Employee Retirement Income Security Act (ERISA) of 1974. Similar standards for state and local government health care plans exist under the Public Health Service Act. These standards include the following:

- COBRA Continuation of Coverage (Code Sec. 4980B, ERISA Secs. 601 through 608, PHSA Secs. 2201-2207);

- Health Insurance Portability and Accountability Act (HIPAA) Portability, Access, and Renewability Provisions (Code Secs. 9801 through 9803, ERISA Secs. 701 through 706, PHSA Secs. 2701-2702, 2711-2713, 2721-23); and

- Mental Health Parity Act (Code Sec. 9812, ERISA Sec. 712, PHSA Sec. 2705).

Beyond these standards, regulation of the private health insurance market previously has been primarily done at the state level. State regulatory authority is broad in scope and includes requirements related to the issuance and renewal of coverage, benefits, rating, consumer protections, and other issues.

LAW EXPLAINED

Certain individual and group health plans grandfathered.—Individuals who are enrolled in a group health plan or individual health coverage on March 23, 2010, the date of enactment of the Patient Protection and Affordable Care Act (PPACA) (P.L. 111-148) may not be required to terminate that coverage (Act. Sec. 1251(a)(1) of PPACA). Any group health plan or health insurance coverage to which this provision applies is considered a "grandfathered health plan."

LAW EXPLAINED

> **Comment:** Insurers and employers are allowed to continue offering grandfathered plans, but they are not required to do so and many have not.

A "grandfathered health plan" is generally not subject to the provisions of the Patient Protection Act amending the Public Health Service Act (Act Sec. 1251(a) of the PPACA). However, grandfathered plans are subject to the following provisions (Act. Sec 1251(a)(4) of PPACA, as added by Act Sec. 2301 of the Health Care and Education Reconciliation Act of 2010 (P.L. 111-152)):

- PHSA Sec. 2708, relating to excessive waiting periods (effective for plan years beginning on or after January 1, 2014);
- PHSA Sec. 2711, relating to lifetime limits (effective for plan years beginning on or after September 23, 2010, the date that is six months after the date of enactment of PPACA);
- PHSA Sec. 2712, relating to rescissions (effective for plan years beginning on or after September 23, 2010, the date that is six months after the date of enactment of PPACA);
- PHSA Sec. 2714, relating to extension of dependent coverage to older dependents (effective for plan years beginning on or after September 23, 2010, the date that is six months after the date of enactment of PPACA).
- PHSA Sec. 2711, relating to annual limits (effective for plan years beginning on or after September 23, 2010, the date that is six months after the date of enactment of PPACA);
- PHSA Sec. 2704, relating to pre-existing condition exclusions (effective for plan years beginning on or after January 1, 2014);
- PHSA Sec. 2714, relating to extension of dependent coverage in a grandfathered group health plan, but only if the dependent is not eligible to enroll in an eligible employer-sponsored health plan (effective for plan years beginning before January 1, 2014).

Grandfathered plans also must comply with these reform provisions for plan years beginning on or after March 23, 2010 (Act Sec. 1251(a)(3) of PPACA, as amended by Act Sec. 10103(d)):

- requirements to provide uniform explanations of coverage and standardized definitions (Act. Sec. 1001 of PPACA, adding PHSA Sec. 2715); and
- requirements to provide loss-ratio reports and rebate premiums if loss ratios fall below 80 percent (Act. Sec. 1001 of PPACA, adding PHSA Sec. 2718).

See ¶540 for discussion of these provisions.

A grandfathered plan does not cease to be a grandfathered plan merely because one or more (or even all) individuals enrolled on March 23, 2010, cease to be covered, provided that the plan or group health insurance coverage has continuously covered someone since that date (not necessarily the same person, but at all times at least one person). These rules apply separately to each benefit package made available under a group health plan or health insurance coverage (Temporary Reg. §54.9815-1251T-(a)(1)).

¶535

LAW EXPLAINED

Under interim regulations effective March 23, 2010, if an employer or employee organization enters into a new policy, certificate, or contract of insurance after March 23, 2010 (because, for example, any previous policy, certificate, or contract of insurance is not being renewed), then that policy, certificate, or contract of insurance is not a grandfathered health plan with respect to the individuals in the group health plan. However, this regulation was amended effective November 17, 2010, so that such changes do not result in loss of grandfathered status (Temporary Reg. § 54.9815-1251T(a)(1)(ii)). The amendment does not apply retroactively. However, the date the new coverage becomes effective is the operative date rather than the date a contract for a new policy, certificate or contract of insurance is entered into. For example, if a plan enters into an agreement with an issuer on September 28, 2010, for a new policy to be effective on January 1, 2011, then January 1, 2011 is the relevant date for purposes of determining the application of the amendment to the interim final regulations. If, however, the plan entered into an agreement with an issuer on July 1, 2010, for a new policy to be effective on September 1, 2010, then the amendment would not apply and the plan would cease to be a grandfathered health plan.

Disclosure of grandfathered status. To maintain grandfathered health plan status, a plan or health insurance coverage must include a statement that the plan or coverage is a grandfathered health plan (Temporary Reg. § 54.9815-1251T(a)(2)(i)). The IRS has provided model language that can be used for this purpose (Temporary Reg. § 54.9815-1251T(a)(2)(ii)). The plan or coverage must also maintain records documenting the terms of the plan or health insurance coverage in connection with the coverage in effect on March 23, 2010 (including any other documents necessary to verify, explain, or clarify its status as a grandfathered health plan), and it must make such records available for examination upon request (Temporary Reg. § 54.9815-1251T(a)(3)).

Family members, new employees. As long as the terms of the group plan or insurance coverage allow it, family members of an individual may enroll in a grandfathered plan in which that individual is enrolled (Act Sec. 1251(b) of PPACA). This rule applies if the individual was enrolled in the grandfathered plan on the date of enactment and the coverage is later renewed. A grandfathered group health plan may provide for the enrollment of new employees and their families (Act Sec. 1251(c) of PPACA).

> **Comment:** Although the law does not require individuals to terminate their existing coverages, the law also does not prevent a group health plan or insurance coverage from changing those grandfathered plans. Thus, whether an individual can maintain her existing coverage will depend in large part on whether the plan sponsor or insurer continues to provide that type of grandfathered plan.

Collective Bargaining Agreements. Group health coverage that was subject to a collective bargaining agreement ratified before the enactment of the Patient Protection Act is not covered by the Act's market reforms until the collective bargaining agreement terminates (Act Sec. 1251(d) of PPACA). A collective bargaining agree-

LAW EXPLAINED

ment that is modified to conform to any of these provisions will be considered to remain in effect and will not be treated as being terminated.

Mergers and acquisitions. If the principal purpose of a merger, acquisition, or similar business restructuring is to cover new individuals under a grandfathered health plan, the plan ceases to be a grandfathered health plan (Temporary Reg. § 54.9815-1251T(b)(2)(i)).

Changes causing loss of grandfathered status. A group health plan or health insurance coverage (including a benefit package under a group health plan) loses grandfathered status if (a) employees are transferred into the plan or health insurance coverage from a plan or health insurance coverage under which the employees were covered on March 23, 2010, (b) comparing the terms of the transferee plan with those of the transferor plan (as in effect on March 23, 2010) and treating the transferee plan as if it were an amendment of the transferor plan would cause a loss of grandfather status; and (c) there was no bona fide employment-based reason to transfer the employees into the transferee plan. For this purpose, changing the terms or cost of coverage is not a bona fide employment-based reason (Temporary Reg. § 54.9815-1251T(b)(2)(ii)).

Subject to transition rules, the following changes will cause a group health plan or health insurance coverage to lose its grandfathered status.

- Elimination of all or substantially all benefits to diagnose or treat a particular condition, including the elimination of benefits for any necessary element to diagnose or treat a condition (Temporary Reg. § 54.9815-1251T(g)(1)(i)).

- Any increase, measured from March 23, 2010, in a percentage cost-sharing requirement such as an individual's coinsurance requirement (Temporary Reg. § 54.9815-1251T(g)(1)(ii)).

- Any increase in a fixed-amount cost-sharing requirement other than a copayment (for example, deductible or out-of-pocket limit), determined as of the effective date of the increase if the total percentage increase in the cost-sharing requirement measured from March 23, 2010, exceeds the maximum percentage increase (Temporary Reg. § 54.9815-1251T(g)(1)(iii), (3)(ii)).

- Any increase in a fixed-amount copayment, determined as of the effective date of the increase, if the total increase measured from March 23, 2010, exceeds the greater of: (a) 5 times medical inflation plus $5, or (b) the maximum percentage increase determined by expressing the total increase in the copayment as a percentage (Temporary Reg. § 54.9815-1251T(g)(1)(iv), (3)(i), (3)(ii)).

- A decrease in an employer's or employee organization's contribution rate towards the cost of any tier of coverage for any class of similarly situated individuals by more than 5 percentage points below the contribution rate for the coverage period that includes March 23, 2010 (for cost-based reductions); or by more than 5 percent (for rate based reductions) (Temporary Reg. § 54.9815-1251T(g)(1)(v)).

- A group health plan, or group health insurance coverage, that, on March 23, 2010, did not impose an overall annual or lifetime limit on the dollar value of all benefits, but now does; (2) imposed an overall lifetime limit on the dollar value of all benefits but no overall annual limit on the dollar value of all benefits but now

¶535

LAW EXPLAINED

adopts an overall annual limit at a dollar value that is lower than the dollar value of the lifetime limit on March 23, 2010; or (3) imposed an overall annual limit on the dollar value of all benefits, but now decreases the dollar value of the annual limit (regardless of whether the plan or health insurance coverage also imposed an overall lifetime limit on March 23, 2010, on the dollar value of all benefits) (Temporary Reg. § 54.9815-1251T(g)(1)(vi)).

The following changes are considered part of the terms of the plan or health insurance coverage on March 23, 2010, even though they were not effective at that time: (a) changes effective after March 23, 2010, under a legally binding contract entered into on or before March 23, 2010; (b) changes effective after March 23, 2010, under a filing on or before March 23, 2010, with a state insurance department; or (c) changes effective after March 23, 2010, under written amendments to a plan that were adopted on or before March 23, 2010 (Temporary Reg. § 54.9815-1251T(g)(2)(i)).

▶ **Effective date.** This provision is effective for plan years beginning on or after January 1, 2014 (Act Sec. 1253 of Patient Protection and Affordable Care Act (PPACA) (P.L. 111-148)). The final regulations (T.D. 9489) are generally effective June 14, 2010.

— Act Secs. 1251 and 10103(d) of the Patient Protection and Affordable Care Act (PPACA) (P.L. 111-148);

— Act Sec. 2301 of the Health Care and Education Reconciliation Act (P.L. 111-152), amending Act. Sec 1251(a) of PPACA;

— Act Sec. 1253, providing the effective date.

Reporter references: For further information, consult the following reporters.

— Standard Federal Tax Reporter, ¶ 44,089K.04

— Tax Research Consultant, HEALTH: 9,114.05

— Practical Tax Explanation, § 42,155.05

¶540 Market Reforms and Improved Coverage

SUMMARY OF NEW LAW

Group health plans and health insurance issuers offering group or individual health insurance coverage are subject to new requirements, including (among other things) extension of dependent coverage, mandatory coverage of preventive health services, prohibition of lifetime or annual limits on the dollar value of benefits, unreasonable annual limits, and rescission. These new requirements have been incorporated into Chapter 100 of the Internal Revenue Code.

BACKGROUND

Group health care plans and issuers of insurance under such plans are subject to certain portability and coverage requirements that appear in Title XXVII, Part A,

BACKGROUND

Group Market Reforms, of the Public Health Service Act (PHSA). Similar or identical provisions are found in Title 29 of the United States Code (Labor), and the Internal Revenue Code (IRC). These provisions were originally added by the Health Insurance and Portability and Accountability Act of 1996 (HIPAA) (P.L. 104-191). In the PHSA, Part A includes four subparts:

- Subpart 1, Portability, Access, and Renewability Requirements: PHSA Sec. 2701, 42 U.S.C. § 300gg (portability requirements); PHSA Sec. 2702, 42 U.S.C. § 300gg-1 (prohibition of discrimination for health status);

- Subpart 2, Other Requirements: PHSA Sec. 2704, 42 U.S.C. § 300gg-4 (mothers and newborns); PHSA Sec. 2705, 42 U.S.C. § 300gg-5 (mental health benefit parity); PHSA Sec. 2706, 42 U.S.C. § 300gg-6 (reconstructive surgery following mastectomies); PHSA Sec. 2707, 42 U.S.C. § 300gg-7 (coverage of students on medically necessary leave of absence);

- Subpart 3, Provisions Applicable only to Health Insurance Issuers: PHSA Sec. 2711, 42 U.S.C. § 300gg-11 (guaranteed availability of coverage for employers in the group market), PHSA Sec. 2712, 42 U.S.C. § 300gg-12 (guaranteed renewability of coverage for employers in the group market), PHSA Sec. 2713, 42 U.S.C. § 300gg-13 (disclosure of information); and

- Subpart 4, Exclusion of Plans; Enforcement; Preemption: PHSA Sec. 2721, 42 U.S.C. § 300gg-21 (exclusion of certain plans), PHSA Sec. 2722, 42 U.S.C. § 300gg-22 (enforcement), and PHSA Sec. 2723, 42 U.S.C. § 300gg-23 (preemption).

Some of these provisions appear in virtually identical form in Chapter 100, Group Health Plan Requirements, of the IRC (as well as in Title 29 of the United States Code (Labor)). The major difference is that the IRC provisions apply only to group plans while the PHSA provisions apply to both group plans and insurance issuers that provide coverage through such plans. IRC Chapter 100 has three subchapters:

- Subchapter A, Requirements Relating to Portability, Access, and Renewability, which includes Code Secs. 9801 (portability), 9802 (nondiscrimination), and 9803 (guaranteed renewability in multemployer plans);

- Subchapter B, Other Requirements, which includes Code Secs. 9811 (mothers and newborns), 9812 (mental health parity), 9813 (dependent students on leave);

- Subchapter C, General Provisions, Codes Secs. 9831 (exceptions), 9832 (definitions), 9833 (regulations), 9834 (enforcement).

The IRS has enforcement authority over employers and plans for compliance with the provisions of Chapter 100. Failure of a group health plan to comply with these requirements can result in imposition of an excise tax of $100 for each day in the noncompliance period for each individual for whom such failure relates. The tax is generally imposed on the employer, but under certain circumstances it is imposed on the plan. There are exceptions for small employer plans, for noncompliance that was undiscovered despite the exercise of reasonable diligence, and for noncompliance that is corrected within 30 days of becoming known (Code Secs. 9834, 4980D).

The PHSA delegates enforcement authority over health insurance issuers to the states. If a state does not exercise this authority, the Secretary of Health and Human

BACKGROUND

Services is authorized to impose penalties against issuers. The maximum penalty is $100 for each day for each individual with respect to which the noncompliance occurred. Exceptions are made if the noncompliance was not discovered despite the exercise of reasonable diligence, or if it is corrected within 30 days of becoming known (PHSA Sec. 2722, 42 U.S.C. § 300gg-22).

A self-insured medical reimbursement plan cannot discriminate in favor of highly compensated individuals as to eligibility or benefits (Code Sec. 105(h)(2)). Highly compensated individuals for this purpose are: the five highest paid officers of the employer; shareholders who own more than 10 percent (by value) of the employer's stock; and individuals who are among the highest paid 25 percent of all employees, other than those who can be excluded from the plan (Code Sec. 105(h)(5)). A plan is treated as nondiscriminatory as to eligibility if:

- the plan benefits 70 percent or more of all employees, or 80 percent or more of all eligible employees if 70 percent or more of all employees are eligible to benefit, or

- the employees qualify under a classification set up by the employer and found by the IRS not to be discriminatory in favor of highly compensated individuals (Code Sec. 105(h)(3), Reg. § 1.105-11).

All benefits provided to highly compensated individuals must be offered to all other participants (Code Sec. 105(h)(4)). Employers that are members of a controlled group, are under common control, or are part of an affiliated group are treated as a single employer for these purposes (Code Sec. 104(h)(8)).

LAW EXPLAINED

Market and coverage reforms of PHSA incorporated into IRC.—The provisions of Part A, Title XXVII, of the Public Health Service Act (PHSA), as amended by the Patient Protection and Affordable Care Act (PPACA) (P.L. 111-148), apply to group health plans, and health insurance issuers providing health insurance coverage in connection with group health plans, as if those provisions were included in subchapter B of Chapter 100 of the Internal Revenue Code (IRC). The PHSA provisions trump other IRC provisions to the extent there is a conflict (Code Sec. 9815(a), as added by PPACA). As a result, the excise tax on employers and plans for noncompliance with group plan requirements (Code Sec. 4980D) applies for noncompliance with a range of additional requirements designed to improve coverage. Existing plans on March 23, 2010, are grandfathered for these requirements (with certain exceptions) even if insurance contracts are renewed after that date. The new requirements either go into effect for plan years beginning on or after September 23, 2010, or on or after January 1, 2014. For discussion of grandfathered plans, see ¶ 535.

The market reforms do not apply to government plans, plans with fewer than two current employees (e.g., stand-alone retiree plans), or "excepted benefits" under Code Sec. 9831 (such as stand-alone dental or vision plans). The reforms primarily focus on coverage, limits and fees.

LAW EXPLAINED

Compliance Tip: The IRS has amended its regulations to make easier for employers to treat stand-alone dental and vision plans, and employee assistance programs as excepted benefits not subject to the market reforms (Reg. § 54.9831-1).

Comment: An employer uses Form 8928 to report the excise tax under Code Sec. 4980D for failure of a group health plan to meet portability, access, renewability, and market reform requirements under Code Secs. 9801, 9802, 9803, 9811,9812, 9813, and the new Code Sec. 9815 as added by PPACA.

Health insurance market reforms effective in 2014. Amendments to PHSA Title XXVII, Part A, subpart 2, impose new requirements on group health plans and health insurance issuers offering group or individual coverage intended to improve health insurance coverage. The new requirements are effective for plan years beginning on or after January 1, 2014 (Act Sec. 1255 of PPACA). They include the following:

- *Fair premiums.* Limits on the range of health insurance premiums an issuer can charge, with adjustments available only for age, area, tobacco use and family or individual coverage (PHSA Sec. 2701, as added by PPACA);

- *Guaranteed availability of coverage.* An issuer that offers coverage in the individual or group market in a state must accept every employer and individual in that state that applies for such coverage. The issuer can establish special enrollment periods, however (PHSA Sec. 2702, as added by PPACA);

- *Guaranteed renewability of coverage.* If a health insurance issuer offers health insurance coverage in the individual or group market, the issuer must renew or continue in force such coverage at the option of the plan sponsor or the individual, as applicable (PHSA Sec. 2703, as added by PPACA);

- *Portability requirements (applies to group grandfathered plans).* For plan years beginning on or after January 1, 2014, pre-existing condition exclusions are prohibited for group and individual plans. This provision applies to grandfathered health plans that are group health plans with respect to enrollees who are under 19 years of age for plan years beginning on or after September 23, 2010, and generally for plan years beginning on or after January 1, 2014 (PHSA Sec. 2704, as renumbered and amended by PPACA; Temporary Reg. § 54.9815-2704T; Temporary Reg. § 54.9815-1251T(e)).

- *Nondiscrimination for health status.* The PHSA already has health status nondiscrimination requirements for group plans and their insurers. The PHSA provision is amended to extend these requirements to the individual health insurance market (PHSA Sec. 2705, as renumbered and amended by PPACA). Code Sec. 9802 is similar, but applies only to group health plans. As of January 1, 2014, PHSA Sec. 2705 will extend these rules under the IRC to insurers in the individual markets.

- *Nondiscrimination for health care providers.* Discrimination is prohibited against any health care provider who is acting within the scope of that provider's license or certification under applicable state law (PHSA Sec. 2706, as added by PPACA).

- *Cost-sharing.* Group health plans and their insurers must meet certain requirements with respect to limits on cost-sharing; insurers must provide comprehensive coverage in the individual and small group markets, and child-only versions of plans must be offered (PHSA Sec. 2707, as added by PPACA).

LAW EXPLAINED

- *90-day waiting for coverage (applies to grandfathered plans).* Effective for plan years beginning on or after January 1, 2014, plans and issuers cannot impose waiting periods for enrollment in coverage that exceed 90 days after the employee becomes otherwise eligible to enroll. Eligibility to enroll is generally triggered when an employee is hired, transferred, or promoted into an eligible job classification, achieves a job-related licensure requirement, or satisfies an orientation period (not to exceed one month). This requirement applies to grandfathered plans. The IRS has issued final regulations providing detailed rules on the application of the 90-day limit (PHSA Sec. 2708, as added by PPACA; Reg. § 54.9815-2708).

- *Coverage for individuals participating in clinical trials.* An issuer or group plan cannot: (1) deny an individual participation in a clinical trial; (2) deny (or limit or impose additional conditions on) coverage of routine patient costs for items and services furnished in connection with participation in the trial; or (3) discriminate against the individual on the basis of the individual's participation in such trial (PHSA Sec. 2709, as added by PPACA).

  Comment: Transition relief is available for nongrandfathered insurance coverage with respect to market reforms scheduled to go into effect for 2014. Under this relief, coverage in the individual or small group market that is renewed for a policy year starting between January 1, 2014, and October 1, 2014 (and associated group health plans of small businesses), will not be considered to be out of compliance with the 2014 market reforms if the coverage was in effect on October 1, 2013, and certain notice requirements are met. Under the notice requirements, the health insurance issuer must notify affected policy holders of: (1) any changes in the options that are available to them; (2) which market reforms would not be reflected in any coverage that continues; (3) their potential right to enroll in a qualified health plan offered through a Health Insurance Marketplace and possibly qualify for financial assistance; (4) how to access such coverage through a Marketplace; and (5) their right to enroll in health insurance coverage outside of a Marketplace that complies with the specified market reforms. Note that the 2014 market reforms generally do not apply to grandfathered plans (with the exception of the pre-existing condition prohibition), and the transition relief does not apply to them.

  Caution: Except for retiree plans and government plans, stand-alone employer reimbursement plans can only provide excluded benefits (such as vision or dental care) without running afoul of the market reform rules on annual fees and access to preventive care without cost-sharing. That means that starting for plan years beginning in 2014, employers may no longer reimburse their employees for individual health insurance premiums. Noncompliance will subject the employer to a $100 per day per participant excise tax. If an employer has a Health Reimbursement Account plan (HRA), it must be integrated with an employer plans that meet the market reform requirements. It cannot be integrated with individual insurance purchased on an exchange (Notice 2013-54).

Health care coverage improvements effective in 2010. Amendments to PHSA Title XXVII, Part A, subpart 1, subject group health plans and health insurance issuers offering group or individual coverage to several new requirements intended to

¶540

LAW EXPLAINED

improve health care coverage. These requirements are effective for plan years beginning on or after September 23, 2010, the date that is six months after the date of enactment of the Patient Protection Act (Act Sec. 1004 of PPACA):

- *No lifetime or annual limits (applies to grandfathered plans).* Lifetime or annual limits on the dollar value of benefits for any participant or beneficiary are prohibited. A transition rule applies for plan years beginning prior to January 1, 2014, during which a restricted annual limit is permitted on the dollar value of benefits regarding the scope of essential health benefits under Act Sec. 1302(b) of the Patient Protection Act. Per beneficiary lifetime or annual limits are not prohibited on benefits that are not essential health benefits to the extent that such limits are otherwise permitted under federal or state law. This rule applies to grandfathered plans that are group (as opposed to individual) plans (PHSA Sec. 2711 as added by PPACA; Temporary Reg. § 54.9815-1251T(d), (e)). Employer reimbursement health plans need to be integrated with a primary employer health plan that satisfies these requirements (Notice 2013-54).

- *No rescission (applies to grandfathered plans).* Rescission with respect to an enrollee once the enrollee is covered is prohibited, unless the individual has committed fraud or made an intentional misrepresentation of material facts prohibited by the plan or coverage terms. The enrollee must be given prior notice of cancellation. This provision applies to grandfathered plans. (PHSA Sec. 2712 as added by PPACA;Temporary Reg. § 54.9815-2712T; Temporary Reg. § 54.9815-1251T(d)).

- *Preventive health services (including contraceptives).* Plans and issuers must provide coverage (without any cost sharing) for certain preventive health services including, at a minimum, (1) evidence-based items or services that have in effect a rating of A or B in the current recommendations of the United States Preventive Services Task Force (USPSTF); (2) immunizations recommended by the Advisory Committee on Immunization Practices of the Centers for Disease Control and Prevention; (3) for infants, children, and adolescents, evidence-informed preventive care and screenings provided for in the comprehensive guidelines supported by the Health Resources and Services Administration (HRSA); and (4) with respect to women, any additional preventive care and screenings as provided for in comprehensive guidelines supported by the HRSA. Employer reimbursement health plans need to be integrated with a primary employer health plan that satisfies the preventive care requirements (Notice 2013-54). A high deductible health plan that satisfies these requirements can qualify for companion Health Savings Accounts (Notice 2013-57). The availability of contraceptives is mandated under this provision, but there is an accommodation for objecting religious non-profit employers. In response to *Burwell v. Hobby Lobby Stores, Inc.,* SCt, 2014-2 USTC ¶ 50,341, the government has issued proposed regulations extending the accommodation to certain for-profit closed corporation employers. The accommodation requires the employer to notify HHS and the employer may do so using EBSA Form 700, but the employer is not required to use any particular form as long as the employer states its religious objection and the basis for the accommodation, identifies itself and its health insurance provider and administrator, provides all contact information, and states the type of plan it is (PHSA Sec. 2713, as added by PPACA; Temporary Reg.

LAW EXPLAINED

§ 54.9815-2713T; Reg. § 54.9815-2713A; Proposed Reg. § 54.9815-2713A(a); Temporary Reg. § 54.9815-2713AT; *Burwell v. Hobby Lobby Stores, Inc.*, SCt, 2014-2 USTC ¶ 50,341).

- *Extension of coverage for children under 26 (includes grandfathered plans).* Coverage must be extended to children until they reach 26 years of age. This rule does not extend to a child of a child receiving dependent coverage. Under a transition rule for grandfathered plans, for plan years beginning before January 1, 2014, the rule applies only if the adult child is not eligible to enroll in an eligible employer-sponsored health plan other than a grandfathered health plan of a parent. For plan years beginning on or after January 1, 2014, the rule applies without regard to whether an adult child is eligible to enroll in any other coverage (PHSA Sec. 2714, as added by PPACA, and amended by the Health Care and Education Reconciliation Act of 2010 (P.L. 111-152); Temporary Reg. § 54.9815-2714T; Temporary Reg. § 54.9815-1251T(e)). Note that rules extending medical deductions and exclusions for medical care provided to children under age 27 was enacted separately. See ¶ 220.

- *Development and use of uniform explanation of coverage documents (applies to grandfathered plans).* Within 24 months of March 23, 2010, the date of enactment of the Patient Protection Act, health insurance issuers (including a group health plan that is not a self-insured plan) offering health insurance coverage within the United States (or in the case of a self-insured group health plan the plan sponsor or designated administrator) must provide, prior to any enrollment restriction, a summary of benefits and coverage explanation pursuant to the standards developed by the HHS Secretary to (1) an applicant at the time of application; (2) an enrollee prior to the time of enrollment or re-enrollment; and (3) a policyholder or certificate holder at the time of issuance of the policy or delivery of the certificate. An entity that willfully fails to provide the required information will be subject to a fine of up to $1,000 per failure (PHSA Sec. 2715, as added by PPACA; Reg. § 54.9815-2715T; Temporary Reg. § 54.9815-1251T(d)).

- *Transparency in coverage.* Group plans and health insurance issuers must submit to the American Health Benefit Exchange accurate information required for certification as a qualified health plan under Act Sec. 1311(e)(3). Plans and issuers must also submit this information to the HHS Secretary and the state insurance commissioner, and must make it available to the public. Required information includes: (1) claims payment policies and practices; (2) periodic financial disclosures; (3) data on enrollment and disenrollment; (4) data on the number of claims denied; (5) data on rating practices; (6) information on cost-sharing and payments for out-of-network coverage; (7) information on enrollee and participant rights; and (8) other information deemed appropriate by the HHS Secretary. A plan or coverage that is not offered through an Exchange is not required to submit the information to an Exchange (PHSA Sec. 2715A, as added by PPACA).

- *Nondiscrimination in favor of highly compensated individuals.* A group health plan must satisfy the nondiscrimination requirements that already apply to self-insured plans (Code Sec. 105(h)). Compliance with the nondiscrimination requirements will not be required until after regulations or other administrative guidance of

LAW EXPLAINED

general applicability has been issued. Such guidance will not apply until plan years beginning a specified period after issuance. Before the beginning of those plan years, an insured group health plan sponsor will not be required to file IRS Form 8928 with respect to excise taxes arising from the nondiscrimination requirements (PHSA Sec. 2716 and Code Sec. 9815(b), as added by PPACA; Notice 2011-1).

- *Ensuring quality care.* Annual reporting requirements to the HHS Secretary and enrollees are to be developed by the HHS Secretary over the 24 months after March 23, 2010, and imposed on group health plan and a health insurance issuers with respect to benefits and reimbursement structures. The reporting will focus on efforts to improve health outcomes, implement activities to prevent hospital readmissions, implement activities to improve patient safety and reduce medical errors, and implement wellness and prevention programs. Second Amendment gun rights are protected, with limitations on collecting, storing and disclosing information, increasing premiums, denying health insurance coverage, and reducing or withholding discounts, rebates or rewards, based on lawful ownership, use, possession or storage of firearms or ammunition (PHSA Sec. 2717, as added by PPACA);

- *Making sure enrollees get value (applies to grandfathered plans).* Except for self-insured plans, issuers and group plans must provide annual reports concerning the proportion of premiums spent on (1) reimbursement for clinical services, (2) activities that improve health care quality, and (3) all other non-claims costs, including an explanation of the nature of such costs. The report must identify the ratio of the incurred loss (or incurred claims) plus the loss adjustment expense (or change in contract reserves) to earned premiums. Starting no later than January 1, 2011, issuers and plans must provide annual medical loss ratio rebates of excess costs to their enrollees the year following the payment of the premiums. See ¶555 for the tax treatment of recipients of the rebates. These provisions specifically do not apply to self-insured group health plans (PHSA Sec. 2718, Code Sec. 9815(b), as added by PPACA; Temporary Reg. §54.9815-1251T(d));

- *Appeals process.* Issuers and group health plans must have an effective appeals process for coverage determinations and claims. At a minimum, the plan or issuer must (1) have in effect an internal claims appeal process; (2) provide notice to enrollees of available internal and external appeals processes, and the availability of any applicable office of health insurance consumer assistance or ombudsman to assist enrollees with the appeals processes; and (3) allow enrollees to review their files, present evidence and testimony as part of the appeals process, and receive continued coverage pending the outcome of the appeals. Plans and issuers must also provide an external review process that includes consumer protections. The appeals process will be subject to external review by state commissioners (PHSA Sec. 2719, as added by PPACA).

- *Patient protections.* Issuers and group health plans are subject to requirements for providing patients with a choice of doctors within the plan, coverage of emergency services (no prior approval, and the same requirements applying to both participating and nonparticipating health care providers), access to pediatric care, and to

LAW EXPLAINED

obstetrical or gynecological care (PHSA Sec. 2719A, as added by PPACA; Temporary Reg. § 54.9815-2719AT).

Reorganized existing PHSA sections. The remainder of PHSA Part A includes a range of existing sections, some of which are already mirrored in the IRC (though only applicable to group health plans). These are renumbered by the PPACA, and are now treated as applying as if they were in the IRC. These include the following:

- Requirements for mothers and newborns (PHSA Sec. 2725, as renumbered by PPACA). This is already mirrored in Code Sec. 9811.

- Parity in mental health and substance abuse disorder benefits (PHSA Sec. 2726, as renumbered by PPACA). This almost identical to Code Sec. 9812, which applies only to group health plans.

- Reconstructive surgery following mastectomies, PHSA Sec. 2727, as renumbered by PPACA).

- Coverage of students on medically necessary leave of absence (PHSA Sec. 2728, as renumbered by PPACA). This is almost identical to Code Sec. 9813, which applies only to group health plans.

- Guaranteed availability of coverage for employers in the group market (PHSA Sec. 2731, as renumbered by PPACA).

- Guaranteed renewability of coverage for employers in the group market (PHSA Sec. 2732, as renumbered by PPACA).

- Disclosure of information (PHSA Sec. 2733, as renumbered by PPACA).

- Exclusion of certain plans (PHSA Sec. 2735, as renumbered by PPACA). There is some overlap with Code Sec. 9831.

- Enforcement (PHSA Sec. 2736, as renumbered by PPACA).

- Preemption (PHSA Sec. 2737, as renumbered by PPACA).

▶ **Effective date.** No effective date is provided for Code Sec. 9815, the provision is therefore considered effective on March 23, 2010, the date of enactment of Patient Protection and Affordable Care Act (PPACA) (P.L. 111-148). The amendments to Act Secs. 2711-2719A of the Public Health Service Act (PHSA) are effective for plan years beginning on or after September 23, 2010, six months after the date of enactment of the Patient Protection Act. The amendments to PHSA Secs 2701-2709 are effective for plan years beginning on or after January 1, 2014.

Law source: Law at ¶5440.

— Act Sec. 1563(f) of the Patient Protection and Affordable Care Act (PPACA) (P.L. 111-148), as redesignated by Act Sec. 10107, adding Code Sec. 9815;

— Act Sec. 1001, adding and amending Public Health Service Act (PHSA) Secs. 2711-2719A;

— Act Sec. 1201, adding and amending PHSA Secs. 2701-2708;

— Act Sec. 10101, amending PHSA Secs. 2711, 2715, 2716, 2718, 2719, and adding 2715A and 2719A;

— Act Sec. 10103, amending PHSA Secs. 2701, 2708, and adding 2709;

¶540

LAW EXPLAINED

— Act Secs. 1004 and 1255, as redesignated by Act Sec. 10103, providing the effective dates; and

— Act Secs. 1004(d)(3)(B) and 2301(b) of the Health Care and Education Reconciliation Act of 2010 (P.L. 111-152), amending PHSA Sec. 2714.

Reporter references: For further information, consult the following reporters.

— Standard Federal Tax Reporter, ¶44,089K.01

— Tax Research Consultant, HEALTH: 9,112.05 and HEALTH: 9,114

— Practical Tax Explanation, § 42,155.05

¶543 Fee on Health Insurance Providers

SUMMARY OF NEW LAW

An annual fee is imposed on providers of health insurance for U.S. health risks.

BACKGROUND

An excise tax is imposed on premiums paid to foreign insurers and re-insurers covering U.S. risks (Code Secs. 4371-4374). Prior to the passage of the annual fee on health insurance providers, however, no excise tax or fee was imposed under the Internal Revenue Code on providers of health insurance.

LAW EXPLAINED

An annual fee is imposed on providers of health insurance for U.S. health risks.—For calendar years beginning after 2013, a fee is imposed on providers of insurance for any "United States health risk," which means the health risk of any individual who is a U.S. citizen, a resident of the United States (as defined by Code Sec. 7701(b)(1)(A)), or located in the United States (Act Sec. 9010(a), (c) and (d) of the Patient Protection and Affordable Care Act (PPACA) (P.L. 111-148), as amended by Act Sec. 10905 of PPACA and Act Sec. 1406 of the Health Care and Education Reconciliation Act (P.L. 111-152); Reg. §§ 57.2(i) and (n)). The fee is determined with respect to net premiums written after December 31, 2012.

The aggregate fee imposed on all covered entities is $8 billion for 2014, $11.3 billion for 2015 and 2016, $13.9 billion for 2017, and $14.3 billion for 2018. For 2019 and following years, the aggregate fee is indexed to the rate of premium growth (Act Sec. 9010(b) and (e) of PPACA, as amended by Act Sec. 10905(a) and (b) of PPACA and Act Sec. 1406(a)(4) of the 2010 Reconciliation Act).

The Secretary of the Treasury will annually apportion the fee based on each entity's relative market share of net premiums written for the prior year.

LAW EXPLAINED

Covered entities. The Act Sec. 9010 fee is imposed on "covered entities" engaged in the business of providing health insurance (Act Sec. 9010(a) of the Patient Protection and Affordable Care Act (PPACA) (P.L. 111-148), as amended by Act Sec. 10905 of PPACA and Act Sec. 1406 of the Health Care and Education Reconciliation Act (P.L. 111-152)). A "covered entity" is defined as any entity with net premiums written for health insurance for United States health risks in the fee year if the entity is one of the following:

(1) a health insurance issuer under Code Sec. 9832(b)(2);

(2) a health maintenance organization (HMO) under Code Sec. 9832(b)(3);

(3) an insurance company subject to tax under Part I or II of Chapter 1 subchapter L of the Tax Code (Insurance Companies);

(4) an entity that provides health insurance under Medicare Advantage, Medicare Part D, or Medicaid; or

(5) a multiple employer welfare arrangement (MEWA) under section 3(40) of ERISA, to the extent not fully insured (but see Reg. § 57.2(b)(2) for exclusions) (Reg. § 57.2(b)(1)).

Health insurance issuers. Regarding the first category of covered entity, a health insurance issuer under Code Sec. 9832(b)(2) means an insurance company, insurance service, or insurance organization that is required to be licensed to engage in the business of insurance in a state, and that is subject to state law that regulates insurance. Under the final regulations, a health insurance issuer must be licensed to engage in the business of insurance in a state and not merely required to be licensed (T.D. 9643 Preamble).

HMOs. Regarding the second category of covered entity, health maintenance organizations, even HMOs that are tax-exempt Code Sec. 501(c)(3) organizations are covered entities (see T.D. 9643 Preamble for discussion).

Exclusions: Self-insured employers. The term *covered entity* does not include any entity (including a voluntary employees' beneficiary association under Code Sec. 501(c)(9) (VEBA)) that is part of a self-insured employer plan to the extent that the entity self-insures its employees' health risks. The term "self-insured employer" means an employer that sponsors a self-insured medical reimbursement plan within the meaning of Reg. § 1.105-11(b)(1)(i).

Scope of VEBA exclusion. The term *covered entity* does not include any Code Sec. 501(c)(9) entity that is established by an entity (other than by an employer or employers) for purposes of providing health care benefits. The final regulations clarify that a VEBA established by a union qualifies for the exclusion. In addition, the exclusion applies to any VEBA established by a joint board of trustees in the case of a multi-employer plan within the meaning of section 3(37) of ERISA. The preamble to the final regulations explains that the VEBA exclusion covers these entities because the union or joint board of trustees is an entity other than the employer or employers. Thus, in the case of a multi-employer plan that maintains a VEBA, neither the plan nor the VEBA is a covered entity (T.D. 9643 Preamble).

¶543

LAW EXPLAINED

MEWAs, generally. The term "self-insured employer" does not include a multiple employer welfare arrangement (MEWA) (Reg. § 57.2(b)(2)(i)). However, a fully-insured MEWA is not a covered entity because, even though the MEWA receives premiums, it applies those premiums to pay an insurance company to provide the coverage it purchases. But if the MEWA is not fully insured, it is a covered entity to the extent that it uses the premiums it receives to provide health coverage rather than pay an insurance company to provide the coverage. And this is so regardless of whether the MEWA is subject to regulation under state insurance law (T.D. 9643 Preamble).

MEWAs excepted from DOL reporting requirements. An entity that would not be a MEWA but for the fact that it provides coverage to two or more trades or businesses that share a common control interest of at least 25 percent at any time during the plan year is not considered a covered entity. Also, under certain conditions, an entity that would not be a MEWA but for the fact that it provides coverage to persons who are not employees or former employees of the plan sponsor is not considered a covered entity.

These two filing exemptions are intended to address situations in which the status as a MEWA derives not from the design of the arrangement but instead from the limited participation by individuals who are not the employees of a single employer, or from a desire to have a single plan for entities sharing substantial common ownership (T.D. 9643 Preamble).

Non-fully insured MEWA that is also a VEBA. The final regulations explain that the Act Sec. 9010(c)(2)(D) exclusion for VEBAs does not apply to an entity that is both a non-fully insured MEWA and a VEBA. This is because the entity has been established by the employers whose employees participate in the MEWA, and the VEBA exclusion does not apply to an employer-established VEBA. Further, the entity does not qualify as a self-insured arrangement that is eligible for the exclusion for self-insured employers (see Act Sec. 9010(c)(2)(A)) because a non-fully insured MEWA is not a self-insured employer. Therefore, a MEWA that is also a VEBA is a covered entity (T.D. 9643 Preamble).

Exclusions: Government entities. The term "government entity" includes the federal government, state governments and their subdivisions, Indian tribal governments and their subdivisions, or any agency of these governmental entities (Reg. § 57.2(b)(2)(ii)). The term "state" includes the District of Columbia, and any of the possessions of the United States, including American Samoa, Guam, the Northern Mariana Islands, Puerto Rico, and the Virgin Islands (Reg. § 57.2(b)(3)). In addition, the final regulations define governmental entity to include any instrumentality of the United States, a state, a political subdivision of a state, an Indian tribal government, or a subdivision of an Indian tribal government. An entity may jeopardize its status as an agency or instrumentality, however, if it engages in the business of providing insurance on the commercial market on a continuing and regular basis (T.D. 9643 Preamble).

Exclusions: Educational institutions. While the final regulations contain no exclusion for educational institutions, other exceptions may apply (T.D. 9643 Preamble).

¶543

LAW EXPLAINED

> **Example 1:** If an educational institution uses the premiums it receives from students to purchase insurance from a separate, unrelated issuer, the issuer, and not the educational institution, will be the covered entity.

> **Example 2:** The exclusion for governmental entities applies if an educational institution is a wholly-owned instrumentality of a state.

> **Example 3:** Although an educational institution that is a covered entity must report to the IRS its net premiums written, it will not be subject to the fee unless the institution (or its controlled group that is treated as a single covered entity) has net premiums written for United States health risks of more than $25 million.

> **Example 4:** If an educational institution provides students with health coverage through a self-insured arrangement, the exclusion for self-insuring employers does not apply because the institution is not providing health coverage as an employer.

Controlled groups. A controlled group is treated as a single covered entity for purposes of the fee. The term "controlled group" means a group of two or more persons, including at least one person that is a covered entity, that is treated as a single employer under Code Sec. 52(a), 52(b), 414(m), or 414(o). Note that a foreign entity subject to tax under Code Sec. 881 is included within a controlled group under Code Sec. 52(a) or (b). A person is treated as being a member of the controlled group if it is a member of the group at the end of the day on December 31 of the data year (Reg. § 57.2(c)).

Whether to include nonprofit organizations in controlled groups. The IRS is considering whether further guidance is needed regarding when a nonprofit organization is included in a controlled group. Until the IRS issues further guidance, two types of organizations may either rely on a reasonable, good-faith application of Code Sec. 52(a) (controlled group), or apply the rules in Reg. § 1.414(c)-5(a) through (d) (certain tax exempt organizations) (but substituting "more than 50 percent" in place of "at least 80 percent" each place it appears in Reg. § 1.414(c)-5). The two types of organizations to which this rule applies are:

(1) organizations exempt from tax under Code Sec. 501(a), and

(2) nonprofit organizations that, although not exempt from tax under Code Sec. 501(a), do not have members or shareholders that are entitled to receive distributions of the organization's income or assets (including upon dissolution) or that otherwise retain equity interests similar to those generally held by owners of for-profit entities (T.D. 9643 Preamble).

LAW EXPLAINED

Designated entity. The designated entity (DE) is the person within a controlled group that acts on behalf of the controlled group regarding the fee. The DE files Form 8963, Report of Health Insurance Provider Information; receives IRS communications for the group; if needed, files a corrected Form 8963 for the group; and pays the fee for the group. The final regulations contain rules for selecting the DE, and provide that the IRS will select a DE if a controlled group fails to do so (Reg. §57.2(e)).

Designated entity for a consolidated group. The final regulations provide that the designated entity of a controlled group that is a consolidated group is the agent for the group. In the case of a controlled group that is not a part of an affiliated group that files a consolidated return, the final regulations require the controlled group to select its designated entity (see T.D. 9643 Preamble).

Health insurance. For purposes of the Act Sec. 9010 fee, "health insurance" does not include insurance coverage for long-term care, disability, accidents, specified illnesses, hospital indemnity or other fixed indemnity insurance, or Medicare supplemental health insurance (as defined in Sec. 1882(g)(1) of the Social Security Act) (Act Sec. 9010(h)(3) of PPACA, as amended by Act Sec. 10905(d) of PPACA (P.L. 111-148)).

In general, the term "health insurance" has the same meaning as the term "health insurance coverage" in Code Sec. 9832(b)(1)(A). In turn, Code Sec. 9832(b)(1)(A) defines health insurance as benefits consisting of medical care under any hospital or medical service policy or certificate, hospital or medical service plan contract, or health maintenance organization contract, when these benefits are offered by an entity meeting the definition of a covered entity under Reg. §57(b)(1). The term "health insurance" includes limited scope dental and vision benefits under Code Sec. 9832(c)(2)(A) and retiree-only health insurance (Reg. §57.2(h)(1)). The final regulations clarify that the benefits listed above constitute health insurance when offered by any type of entity, even if that entity is not a health insurance issuer within the meaning of Code Sec. 9832(b)(2) (T.D. 9643 Preamble).

Health insurance: Exclusions. The term health insurance does not include he following types of coverage as defined in Code Sec. 9832 and its associated regulations:

  (i) Coverage only for accident or disability income insurance, or any combination of them;

 (ii) Coverage issued as a supplement to liability insurance;

(iii) Liability insurance, including general liability insurance and automobile liability insurance;

 (iv) Workers' compensation or similar insurance;

  (v) Automobile medical payment insurance;

 (vi) Credit-only insurance;

(vii) Coverage for on-site medical clinics;

(viii) Other insurance coverage that is similar to the insurance coverage listed above under which benefits for medical care are secondary or incidental to other insurance benefits;

¶543

LAW EXPLAINED

(ix) Benefits for long-term care, nursing home care, home health care, community-based care, or any combination of these;

(x) Coverage only for a specified disease or illness;

(xi) Hospital indemnity or other fixed indemnity insurance;

(xii) Medicare supplemental health insurance (as defined under section 1882(g)(1) of the Social Security Act), coverage supplemental to the coverage provided under chapter 55 of title 10, United States Code, and similar supplemental coverage provided to coverage under a group health plan;

(xiii) Coverage under an employee assistance plan, a disease management plan, or a wellness plan, if the benefits provided under the plan constitute excepted benefits under Code Sec. 9832(c)(2) (or do not otherwise provide benefits consisting of health insurance under Reg. § 57.2(h)(1));

(xiv) Student administrative health fee arrangements, as defined in Reg. § 57.2(h)(3);

(xv) Travel insurance, as defined in Reg. § 57.2(h)(4); or

(xvi) Indemnity reinsurance, as defined in paragraph Reg. § 57.2(h)(5)(i) (Reg. § 57.2(h)(2)).

Indemnity reinsurance. Indemnity reinsurance is an agreement under which the reinsuring company indemnifies the issuing insurance company for the risk of loss under specified policies and the issuing company retains its liability to, and its contractual relationship with, the insured individuals. Under the final regulations, the definition of "indemnity reinsurance" extends to reinsurance obtained by HMOs. The final regulations also clarify that the issuer of the policies specified in the indemnity reinsurance agreement may be any covered entity. Carve-out arrangements—where one insurer accepts responsibility for all or part of the health risk within a defined category of medical benefits that another insurer is obligated to provide—may, based on the circumstances, meet the definition of indemnity reinsurance (T.D. 9643 Preamble).

Subcapitation. Under a typical subcapitation arrangement, a Medicaid plan provider contracts with a separate service provider to provide certain services to the Medicaid plan participants and share some of the provider's risk. Amounts paid to a service provider under this arrangement are not treated as premiums for state regulatory and reporting purposes; therefore, they are not included in net premiums written for health insurance (T.D. 9643 Preamble).

Employee assistance programs. The final regulations do not expressly define "health insurance" to include benefits under an employee assistance program (EAP), and the government is considering guidance that would treat an EAP as an excepted benefit under Code Sec. 9832(c). The final regulations state that if an EAP provides significant medical care or treatment benefits, those benefits would meet the definition of health insurance. Otherwise, benefits under an EAP will not be treated as health insurance.

Further, according to the preamble to the final regulations, a stand-alone wellness plan or disease management program do not exhibit the risk shifting and risk distribution characteristics of insurance. If these programs provide significant medical care or

LAW EXPLAINED

treatment benefits, however, the benefits would meet the definition of health insurance. Otherwise, coverage under these programs will not be treated as health insurance unless the relevant agencies determine that the benefits do not qualify as an excepted benefit (T.D. 9643 Preamble).

Medicare managed long-term care premiums. To the extent Medicaid plan providers can separately identify premiums received for long-term care, these amounts are not for health insurance and are not included in net premiums written (T.D. 9643 Preamble).

Medicare Advantage and Medicare Part D Plans. Some employers or unions provide Medicare Advantage or Medicare Part D benefits in connection with an Employer Group Waiver Plan (EGWP) for employees and retirees who are Medicare beneficiaries. The benefits provided by these arrangements may constitute health insurance under Act Sec. 9010. But if the arrangement is eligible for the self-insuring employer exception (Act Sec. 9010(c)(2)(A)), an employer or union that provides benefits under an EGWP or similar arrangement is not a covered entity (T.D. 9643 Preamble).

Reporting requirements and penalties. Annually, each covered entity, including each controlled group that is treated as a single covered entity, must report its *net premiums written for health insurance of United States health risks* during the data year to the IRS by April 15 of the fee year. Reporting is done on Form 8963, Report of Health Insurance Provider Information. The term "data year" means the calendar year immediately before the fee year. For example, 2014 is the data year for fee year 2015 (Reg. §57.2(d)). The term "fee year" means the calendar year in which the fee must be paid (Reg. §57.2(g)). This reporting requirement also applies to each controlled group that is treated as a single covered entity. Even if a covered entity's net premiums written are not taken into account because they fall below the $25 million threshold in Reg. §57.4(a)(4), the reporting requirement still applies (Reg. §57.3(a)(1); Notice 2013-76).

Guidance on covered entities for 2014 fee year only. For the 2014 fee year only, the IRS will not treat any entity as a "covered entity" if it is excluded, during either of two periods, from the definition of a covered entity. Specifically, for the 2014 fee year, an entity is not a covered entity if it qualifies for one of the exclusions under Act Sec. 9010(c)(2) either (1) for the entire 2013 *data year*, or (2) for the entire 2014 *fee year*. An entity thereby excluded from the definition of a covered entity should not report its net premiums written for the 2013 data year, which is the calendar year immediately before the fee year (Notice 2014-47, I.R.B. 2014-36, 522).

Guidance on controlled groups for 2014 fee year only. For the 2014 fee year only, a controlled group must report net premiums written only for those persons (1) who are controlled group members at the end of the day on December 31 of the 2013 data year, and (2) who would qualify as a covered entity in the fee year if it were a single-person covered entity. In connection with this, an entity that needed to correct a previously submitted Form 8963, "Report of Health Insurance Provider Information," had until August 18, 2014, to submit a corrected form. Entities that reasonably projected that they would qualify for an exclusion under Act Sec. 9010(c)(2) for the entire 2014 fee year could submit a corrected Form 8963 on or before August 18, 2014, even though the 2014 fee year was not yet over (Notice 2014-47, I.R.B. 2014-36, 522).

¶543

LAW EXPLAINED

Act Sec. 9010(g)(4) provides that Code Sec. 6103, which relates to the confidentiality and disclosure of returns and return information, does not apply to any information reported by covered entities under Act. Sec. 9010(g). Also, the final regulations provide that the information reported on each Form 8963 will be open for public inspection or available upon request. The IRS expects that certain information will be made available on www.irs.gov, including the identity of each reporting entity and the amount of its reported net premiums written (T.D. 9643 Preamble; Reg. §57.3(a)(3); Notice 2013-76).

Failure to report penalty. A covered entity that fails to timely submit a Form 8963 report is liable for a failure to report penalty unless the failure was due to reasonable cause (see Reg. §57.3(b)(1)(iii) for a definition or "reasonable cause"). The amount of the penalty is (A) $10,000, plus (B) the lesser of (1) An amount equal to $1,000 multiplied by the number of days during which such failure continues; or (2) the amount of the covered entity's fee for which the report was required (Reg. §57.3(b)(1)). The penalty will be treated as a penalty for purposes of Subtitle F of the tax code and must be paid on notice and demand and in the same manner as a tax. Only civil actions for refund of the penalty under the procedures of Subtitle F apply (Act Sec. 9010(g)(2) of PPACA).

Accuracy-related penalty. A covered entity that understates its net premiums written for health insurance of United States health risks in the Form 8963 report is liable for an accuracy-related penalty. The amount of the accuracy-related penalty for the fee year is the excess of (A) the amount of the fee that the covered entity should have paid absent any understatement, over (B) the amount of the covered entity's fee that the IRS determined based on the understatement (Act Sec. 9010(g)(3) of PPACA; Reg. §57.3(b)(2)). This penalty is subject to the provisions of Subtitle F of the tax code that apply to assessable penalties.

The failure to report penalty and the accuracy-related penalty apply in addition to the fee. Note also that a covered entity may be liable for both penalties (T.D. 9643 Preamble).

Each member of a controlled group that is required to provide information to the controlled group's designated entity for purposes of the Form 8963 report is jointly and severally liable for any penalties imposed for reporting failures by the designated entity (Reg. §57.3(b)(3)).

Fee calculation and payment process. Each covered entity's Act Sec. 9010 fee for any fee year is a portion of the "applicable amount"—$8 billion in 2014, for example. The covered entity's portion of the applicable amount for any fee year—referred to as the covered entity's "allocated fee"—is determined by a ratio. This ratio, which represents the covered entity's market share, is the ratio of—

(a) the covered entity's net premiums written for health insurance of United States health risks during the data year taken into account, to

(b) the aggregate net premiums written for health insurance of United States health risks of all covered entities during the data year taken into account (Reg. §57.4(a)(2)).

LAW EXPLAINED

The "applicable amount"—that is, the aggregate fee imposed on all covered entities—is $8 billion for 2014, $11.3 billion for 2015 and 2016, $13.9 billion for 2017, and $14.3 billion for 2018. For 2019 and following years, the applicable amount is indexed to the rate of premium growth (Act Sec. 9010(b) and (e) of PPACA, as amended by Act Sec. 10905(a) and (b) of PPACA and Act Sec. 1406(a)(4) of the 2010 Reconciliation Act; Reg. §57.4(a)(3)).

> **Example:** Eagle Insurance Company (Eagle) is a covered entity. It's net premiums written for health insurance of United States health risks taken into account during 2013, the data year, amount to $2.1 billion. Suppose the aggregate premiums written for health insurance of United States health risks taken into account for all covered entities during 2013 amount to $300 billion. These figures make up the fraction $2.1 billion / $300 billion. For the 2014 fee year, to determine Eagle's allocated fee, the IRS will multiply the applicable amount for 2014—$8 billion—by that fraction: $8 billion x $2.1 billion / $300 billion = $56 million. Thus, Eagle's allocated fee for 2014 is $56 million (see Reg. §§57.4(a)(2) and (d)).

The regulations define "net premiums written" as premiums (including reinsurance premiums) written, reduced by reinsurance ceded, and reduced by ceding commissions and medical loss ratio (MLR) rebates for the data year. The term *net premiums written* does not include premiums written for indemnity reinsurance (as defined in Reg. §57.2(h)(5)(i)) and is not reduced by indemnity reinsurance ceded. However, the term *net premiums written* does include assumption reinsurance (as defined in Reg. §57.2(h)(5)(ii)) and is reduced by assumption reinsurance premiums ceded (Reg. §57.2(k)).

Computing MLR rebates. The final regulations clarify that medical loss ratio (MLR) rebates are computed on an accrual basis. Instructions to Form 8963 will provide the specific SHCE (Supplemental Health Care Exhibit) line numbers to use as the source of data for computing MLR rebates (T.D. 9643 Preamble).

Dollar thresholds. The amount of net premiums written that are taken into account for purposes of determining a covered entity's market share is subject to dollar thresholds. Net premiums written during the calendar year that are not more than $25 million are not taken into account. For net premiums written during the calendar year that are more than $25 million but not more than $50 million, 50 percent are taken into account. And 100 percent of net premiums written in excess of $50 million are taken into account (Reg. §57.4(a)(4)(i)).

Thresholds for controlled groups. The dollar thresholds discussed above apply to all net premiums written for health insurance of United States health risks during the data year, in the aggregate, of the entire controlled group. Any net premiums written by any member of the controlled group that is a nonprofit corporation (see Reg. §57.2(b)(2)(iii)) or a voluntary employees' beneficiary association (see Reg. §57.2(b)(2)(iv)) are not taken into account (Reg. §57.4(a)(4)(ii)).

¶543

LAW EXPLAINED

Partial exclusion for certain exempt activities. Net premiums written that are attributable to exempt activities of a tax-exempt health organization may be partially excluded (Act Sec. 9010(b) of PPACA, as amended by Act Sec. 10905(a) of PPACA and Act Sec. 1406(a)(2) of the 2010 Reconciliation Act).

Specifically, if a covered entity's net premiums written exceed the dollar thresholds (see Reg. § 57.4(a)(4)(i)), and the covered entity is tax-exempt under Code Sec. 501(c)(3), (4), (26) or (29) as of December 31 of the data year, it qualifies for a partial exclusion of its net premiums. Only 50 percent of its remaining net premiums written for health insurance of United States health risks that are attributable to its exempt activities during the data year are taken into account. This exemption does not apply to activities of an unrelated trade or business as defined in Code Sec. 513.

If an entity to which this partial exclusion applies is a member of a controlled group, then the partial exclusion applies to that entity after first applying the Reg. § 57.4(a)(4)(i) thresholds on a pro rata basis to all members of the controlled group (Reg. § 57.4(a)(4)(iii)). Then, the Act Sec. 9010(b)(2)(B) partial exclusion for certain exempt activities applies only to eligible members of the group (T.D. 9643 Preamble).

> **Example:** If a controlled group consists of one member with $100 million in net premiums written and a second member with $50 million in net premiums written, two-thirds of the group's total $37.5 million reduction under Act Sec. 9010(b)(2)(A), or $25 million, applies to the first member, and the remaining one-third, or $12.5 million, applies to the second member. Therefore, after this initial reduction, the first member has $75 million of net premiums written ($100 million minus $25 million), and the second member has $37.5 million of net premiums written ($50 million minus $12.5 million). If the second member is eligible for the 50 percent exclusion under Act Sec. 9010(b)(2)(B), the 50 percent exclusion applies to this member's remaining net premiums written, resulting in $18.75 million (50 percent of $37.5 million) being taken into account. Thus, total net premiums written taken into account for this controlled group are $93.75 million ($150 million minus $37.5 million minus $18.75 million) (T.D. 9643 Preamble).

Determination of net premiums written. The IRS will determine net premiums written for each covered entity based on Form 8963, Report of Health Insurance Provider Information, submitted by each covered entity. In addition, the IRS may use the Supplemental Health Care Exhibit (SHCE), which supplements the annual statement filed with National Association of Insurance Commissioners (NAIC) pursuant to state law (Reg. § 57.4(b)(1)). The IRS may use other sources of information as well (see Act. Sec. 9010(b)(3) of PPACA, Reg. § 57.4(b)(1) and Notice 2013-76).

For any covered entity that files the SHCE with the NAIC, the amount reported on the SHCE establishes a presumption. Thus, unless the covered entity can demonstrate otherwise, the entire amount reported on the SHCE as direct premiums written will generally be considered to be for health insurance of United States health risks as

LAW EXPLAINED

described in Reg. §57.2(n) (but subject to any applicable exclusions provided in Reg. §57.2(h)(2)) (see Reg. §57.4(b)(2)). The regulations do not, however, provide specific rules for expatriate policies.

Safe harbor for expatriate plans. The IRS has provided a temporary safe harbor for covered entities that report direct premiums written for expatriate plans on an SHCE (Notice 2014-24, I.R.B. 2014-16, 942). Expatriate policies are defined by the Department of Health and Human Services (HHS) as group health insurance policies that provide coverage to employees, substantially all of whom are: (1) working outside their country of citizenship; (2) working outside their country of citizenship and outside the employer's country of domicile; or (3) non-U.S. citizens working in their home country (45 CFR 158.120(d)(4)). The IRS says that while information reporting under Code Sec. 6055 and related regulations ultimately could provide insurers with information they need to determine more precisely the health risks covered by their expatriate plans, the reporting required under Code Sec. 6055 is delayed until 2016 for coverage in 2015. In the interim, the Notice 2014-24 provides a temporary safe harbor only for fee years 2014 and 2015. The safe harbor applies to a covered entity that reports direct premiums written for expatriate plans on its SHCE that include coverage of at least one non-United States health risk. Under the safe harbor, a covered entity can treat 50 percent of certain premiums written for expatriate plans as being attributable to non-United States health risks. A covered entity that satisfies the requirements of the Notice will be considered to have rebutted the presumption in Reg. §57.4(b)(2) that the entire amount of direct premiums is for United States health risks. In turn, the excluded amount allowed by the safe harbor is excluded in reporting direct premiums written on Form 8963.

Notice of preliminary fee calculation. Each fee year, the IRS will notify each covered entity of its preliminary fee calculation by June 15 (Notice 2013-76). This notification will include—

(1) The covered entity's allocated fee;

(2) The covered entity's net premiums written for health insurance of United States health risks;

(3) The covered entity's net premiums written for health insurance of United States health risks taken into account after the application of the dollar thresholds in Reg. §57.4(a)(4);

(4) The aggregate net premiums written for health insurance of United States health risks taken into account for all covered entities; and

(5) Instructions for how to submit a corrected Form 8963, Report of Health Insurance Provider Information, to correct any errors through the error correction process (Reg. §57.5).

Error correction process. Each covered entity has the chance to review the IRS's preliminary fee calculation. If the covered entity identifies errors in its preliminary fee calculation, it submits to the IRS a corrected report by July 15 of each fee year. The covered entity makes the error correction report by completing *in full* a new Form 8963, Report of Health Insurance Provider Information. Therefore, the correct form must

¶543

LAW EXPLAINED

include all of the information required by the form's instructions. The corrected form will replace the original Form 8963. The IRS will not accept a corrected Form 8963 after the end of the error correction period, and it will not change the final fee calculations based on information provided after the end of that period. The IRS will provide its final determination regarding the covered entity's submission no later than the time the IRS provides a covered entity with a final fee calculation (Reg. § 57.6; Notice 2013-76).

As with the original Form 8963, the corrected Form 8963 is not confidential (Reg. § 57.3(a)(3); Notice 2013-76).

Notification and fee payment. Each fee year, the IRS will send a final calculation of the fee for each covered entity by August 31 of the fee year (Reg. § 57.7(b); Notice 2013-76). The notification to a covered entity of its final fee calculation will include—

(1) The covered entity's allocated fee;

(2) The covered entity's net premiums written for health insurance of United States health risks;

(3) The covered entity's net premiums written for health insurance of United States health risks taken into account after the application of the dollar thresholds in Reg. § 57.4(a)(4);

(4) The aggregate net premiums written for health insurance of United States health risks taken into account for all covered entities; and

(5) The final determination on the covered entity's corrected Form 8963, Report of Health Insurance Provider Information, if a corrected form was submitted (Reg. § 57.7(a)).

Each covered entity must pay its final fee by September 30 of the fee year (Reg. § 57.7(b); Notice 2013-76). For a controlled group, the payment must be made using the designated entity's Employer Identification Number as reported on Form 8963. The fee must be paid by electronic funds transfer as if the fee were a depository tax (Reg. § 57.6302-1). There is no tax return filed with the payment of the fee.

For a controlled group, all members of the controlled group are jointly and severally liable for the fee (Reg. § 57.8).

Limitation on assessment. The IRS must assess the amount of the fee for any fee year within three years of September 30 of that fee year (Reg. § 57.8).

Refund claims. Any claim for a refund of the fee must be made by the entity that paid the fee to the government. All refund claims are made on Form 843, Claim for Refund and Request for Abatement (Reg. § 57.9).

Charges to policyholders to offset fee. The IRS has ruled that amounts a health insurance company collects from policyholders to offset the cost of the annual fee are included in gross income under Code Sec. 61 (Rev. Rul. 2013-27).

▶ **Effective date.** The annual fee on health insurance providers applies to calendar years beginning after December 31, 2013 (Act Sec. 9010(j) of PPACA, as amended by Act Sec. 1406(a)(6) of the 2010 Reconciliation Act). The final regulations apply to any fee that is due on or after September 30, 2014 (Reg. § 57.10).

LAW EXPLAINED

Law source: Law at ¶7036, ¶7051 and ¶7112.

— Act Sec. 9010 of PPACA, as amended by Act Sec. 10905 of PPACA and Act Sec. 1406 of the 2010 Reconciliation Act;

— Act Sec. 9010(j) of PPACA, as amended by Act Sec. 1406(a)(6) of the 2010 Reconciliation Act, and Act Sec. 1405(c) of the 2010 Reconciliation Act, providing the effective date.

Reporter references: For further information, consult the following reporters.

— Standard Federal Tax Reporter, ¶14,502.01 and ¶26,135.01

— Tax Research Consultant, BUSEXP: 21,350 and EXCISE: 13,100

— Practical Tax Explanation, §51,480

— Federal Excise Tax Reporter, ¶24,300.01, ¶24,300.012, ¶24,300.014, ¶24,300.016 and ¶24,300.018.

¶545 Fee Imposed on Health Insurance Policies

SUMMARY OF NEW LAW

The Patient Protection and Affordable Care Act (PPACA) of 2010 imposes a fee on each "specified health insurance policy." The fee applies for policy years ending on or after October 1, 2012, and before October 1, 2019. The issuer of the policy pays the fee. For each policy year ending after September 30, 2012, the fee is equal to the product of $2 ($1 for policy years ending in fiscal 2013) multiplied by the average number of lives covered under the policy. For policy years ending in any fiscal year beginning after September 30, 2014, the $2 amount is adjusted for increases in projected per capita health care spending.

BACKGROUND

From time to time, Congress establishes trust funds for special purposes. For example, there is the Black Lung Disability Trust Fund (Code Sec. 9501), the Airport and Airway Trust Fund (Code Sec. 9502), and the Highway Trust Fund (Code Sec. 9503). In general, these trust funds are funded by fees, excise taxes, penalties, or appropriations.

Employer-offered group health plans are highly regulated, and these regulations are generally enforced through excise taxes. For example, taxes are imposed for failure to comply with continuation of benefits (i.e., COBRA) requirements (Code Sec. 4980B), group health plan portability requirements (Code Sec. 4980D), and comparable health savings account contribution requirements (Code Sec. 4980G). These excise taxes on health insurers and plans are compliance-driven rather than imposed with an eye toward raising revenue for a specific purpose.

LAW EXPLAINED

PCORI fee imposed by Code Sec. 4375 on health insurance policies.—Under Sec. 1181 of the Social Security Act, which was added by the Patient Protection and Affordable Care Act (PPACA) (P.L. 111-148), the Secretary of Health and Human Services must establish a Patient-Centered Outcomes Research Institute (PCORI) to conduct, support, and synthesize research about the outcomes, effectiveness, and appropriateness of health care services and procedures. The purpose of the research is to identify how diseases, disorders, and other health conditions can best be prevented, diagnosed, treated, and managed clinically. The PCORI research institute is funded by the "Patient-Centered Outcomes Research Trust Fund" (PCORTF) (Code Sec. 9511(a)). In turn, the research trust fund is supplied in part by fees imposed by Code Sec. 4375 on health insurance policies.

Appropriations to PCORTF. The following amounts are appropriated to the PCORTF: $10,000,000 for fiscal year 2010; $50,000,000 for fiscal year 2011; and $150,000,000 for fiscal year 2012. For each fiscal year beginning with fiscal year 2013 and ending with 2019, the amount appropriated to the PCORTF is:

- an amount equal to the "net revenues" received in the Treasury from the fees imposed on health insurance and self-insured plans under new Code Secs. 4375, 4376 and 4377 (as added by PPACA) for such fiscal year, and

- $150 million (Code Sec. 9511(b), as added by PPACA).

"Net revenues" for purposes of the first item above means the amount, as estimated by the Treasury Secretary, equaling the excess of the fees received in the Treasury on account of the new fees on insured and self-insured health plans, over the decrease in income tax revenue resulting from taxpayers deducting the fees as ordinary and necessary business expenses against income (Code Sec. 9511(e), as added by PPACA).

The fixed dollar amounts (e.g., $150 million in 2013) are to be funded out of general revenue, and additional amounts are to be transferred from the Federal Hospital Insurance Trust Fund, the Federal Supplementary Medical Insurance Trust Fund, and the Medicare Prescription Drug Account. No amount may be appropriated or transferred to the PCORTF on and after the date of any expenditure that is not expressly permitted (Code Sec. 9511(b), as added by PPACA).

Amounts in the PCORTF are available to the Patient-Centered Outcomes Research Institute without the need for further appropriations (Code Sec. 9511(d)(1) as added by PPACA). The Secretary of the Treasury, as the PCORTF trustee, must transfer 20 percent of the amounts appropriated or credited to the PCORTF for each of fiscal years 2011 through 2019 to the Secretary of Health and Human Services (HHS) to carry out the purposes of the Institute, and these amounts remain available until spent. Of these amounts, the HHS Secretary will distribute 80 percent to the Office of Communication and Knowledge Transfer of the Agency for Healthcare Research and Quality, and 20 percent to the HHS Secretary to disseminate information generated by the Institute (Code Sec. 9511(d)(2), as added by PPACA; Sec. 937 of the Public Health Services Act).

¶545

LAW EXPLAINED

No amounts are to be transferred to the PCORTF after September 30, 2019, and any amounts in the fund after that date are to be transferred to the general fund of the Treasury (Code Sec. 9511(f), as added by PPACA).

Code Sec. 4375, enacted under the Patient Protection and Affordable Care Act (ACA) (P.L. 111-148), imposes a fee on each "specified health insurance policy." The fee, referred to as the "PCORI fee" in connection with the trust fund that it supports, applies for policy years ending on or after October 1, 2012, and before October 1, 2019 (Code Sec. 4375(e)). The issuer of the policy pays the fee (Code Sec. 4375(b)).

For each policy year ending after September 30, 2012, the fee is equal to the product of $2 ($1 for policy years ending in fiscal 2013) multiplied by the average number of lives covered under the policy (Code Sec. 4375(a)). For policy years ending in any fiscal year beginning after September 30, 2014, the $2 amount is adjusted for increases in projected per capita health care spending (Code Sec. 4375(d)).

Residing in the United States. Generally, the PCORI fee applies to each *specified health insurance policy*, which is defined as any accident or health insurance policy issued with respect to individuals "residing in the United States" (including possessions) (Code Secs. 4375(c)(1) and 4377(a)(3)).

For purposes of the PCORI fee, "an individual residing in the United States" means an individual who has a place of abode in the United States. Therefore, someone on a temporary U.S. visa who has a place of abode in the United States is residing in the United States (Reg. § 46.4377-1(a)(2)).

If the address on file with the issuer or plan sponsor for the primary insured is outside of the United States, the issuer or plan sponsor may treat the primary insured and his or her spouse, dependents, or other beneficiaries covered under the policy as having the same place of abode and not residing in the United States (Reg. § 46.4377-1(a)(2)(ii)).

Policies subject to the PCORI fee. The PCORI fee is imposed on "specified health insurance policies" (Code Sec. 4375(a)). In general, a *specified health insurance policy* is any accident or health insurance policy (including a policy under a group health plan) issued with respect to individuals residing in the United States (including possessions) (Code Secs. 4375(c)(1) and 4377(a)(3)).

Prepaid health coverage arrangements. The term *specified health insurance policy* includes "prepaid health coverage arrangements," and the person agreeing to provide coverage is treated as the issuer (Code Sec. 4375(c)(3); Reg. § 46.4375-1(b)(1)(i)). Under a *prepaid health coverage arrangement*, a person agrees to provide accident and health coverage to individuals residing in the United States in exchange for fixed payments or premiums. Any hospital or medical service policy or certificate, hospital or medical service plan contract, or health maintenance organization contract is a *specified health insurance policy* (Reg. § 46.4375-1(b)(2)).

Retiree coverage and retiree-only plans. The PCORI fee applies to *specified health insurance policies* that provide accident and health coverage to retirees, including retiree-only policies and plans (Reg. § 46.4375-1(b)(1)(i)).

LAW EXPLAINED

COBRA coverage. Final regulations state explicitly that continuation coverage under the Consolidated Omnibus Budget Reconciliation Act of 1985 (COBRA), or similar continuation coverage under other federal law or under state law, must be taken into account in determining the PCORI fee, unless the arrangement is otherwise excluded (Reg. § 46.4375-1(b)(1)(i)).

FSAs. The PCORI fee applies to an employee's flexible spending arrangement (FSA) if the employee is covered by a major medical plan, unless the FSA meets the requirements for being an excepted benefit.

Policies exempt from the PCORI fee. Several categories of health insurance policies are not subject to the PCORI fee imposed by Code Sec. 4375. These are discussed below.

Excepted benefits. Certain kinds of insurance policies are exempt from the PCORI fee because, under Code Sec. 4375(c)(2), they are not deemed *specified health insurance policies*. Specifically, policies are exempt if substantially all of their coverage is of excepted benefits described in Code Sec. 9832(c).

Excepted benefits under Code Sec. 9832(c) include the following:

- coverage for only accident or disability
- liability insurance (including general liability and auto liability insurance)
- workers' compensation or similar insurance
- auto medical payment insurance
- coverage for on-site medical clinics
- limited scope dental or vision benefits
- benefits for long-term care, nursing home care, or community-based care
- coverage for only a specified disease or illness
- hospital indemnity or other fixed indemnity insurance
- Medicare supplemental coverage

EAPs and wellness programs. The definition of a *specified health insurance policy* does not include any insurance policy to the extent that the policy provides for an employee assistance program (EAP), disease management program, or wellness program, if the program does not provide significant medical care or treatment benefits (Reg. § 46.4375-1(b)(1)(ii)(D)).

Stop loss policies. The term *specified health insurance policy* does not include "stop loss policies" (Reg. § 46.4375-1(b)(ii)(C)). A stop loss policy is a policy issued to a person establishing or maintaining a self-insured health plan. Under a stop loss policy, the issuer becomes liable for losses in excess of a set amount that the person establishing or maintaining the plan incurs in covering the applicable lives. The person establishing or maintaining the self-insured health plan, however, retains its contractual relationship with the applicable lives covered and remains liable to them (Reg. § 46.4375-1(b)(iii)).

Indemnity reinsurance policies. Similar to stop loss policies, the term *specified health insurance policy* does not include "indemnity reinsurance policies" (Reg.

LAW EXPLAINED

§ 46.4375-1 (b) (ii) (C)). An indemnity reinsurance policy is an agreement between insurance companies under which a reinsuring company indemnifies an issuing company for risk of loss under specified policies. The issuing company, however, retains its contractual relationship with the applicable lives covered and remains liable to them (Reg. § 46.4375-1 (b) (iv)).

Expatriate policies. The term *specified health insurance policy* does not include any group policy issued to an employer if the facts and circumstances show that the group policy was designed and issued specifically to cover primarily employees who are working and residing outside of the United States (Reg. § 46.4375-1 (b) (1) (ii) (B)).

Calculating the fee. *Generally.* The PCORI fee for a policy year is the average number of lives covered under the policy for the policy year multiplied by the applicable dollar amount (Reg. § 46.4375-1 (c) (1)).

Average number of lives, generally. To determine the average number of lives covered under a *specified health insurance policy* during a policy year, an issuer must use one of four methods: the actual count method, the snapshot method, the member months method, or the state form method (Reg. § 46.4375-1 (c) (2) (i)).

Applicable dollar amount. For policy years ending on or after October 1, 2012, and before October 1, 2013, the applicable dollar amount is $1. For policy years ending on or after October 1, 2013, and before October 1, 2014, the applicable dollar amount is $2 (Reg. § 46.4375-1 (c) (4)).

For any policy year ending in any federal fiscal year beginning on or after October 1, 2014, the applicable dollar amount is the sum of (1) the applicable dollar amount for the policy year ending in the previous federal fiscal year; plus (2) that amount multiplied by the percentage increase in the projected per capita amount of the National Health Expenditures most recently released by the Department of Health and Human Services before the beginning of the federal fiscal year (Reg. § 46.4375-1 (c) (4)). For policy years that end on or after October 1, 2014, and before October 1, 2015, the applicable dollar amount is $2.08 (Notice 2014-56, I.R.B. 2014-41).

Lives taken into account. The PCORI fee may apply multiple times if accident and health coverage is provided to one individual through more than one policy or self-insured arrangement. This can happen, for example, where an individual is covered by a fully-insured major medical insurance policy and a self-insured prescription arrangement. Another example is where an employee is covered by both a group insurance policy and a health reimbursement arrangement (HRA). In that case, the group insurance policy falls within the definition of a *specified health insurance policy* to which the Code Sec. 4375 fee applies, and the HRA falls within the definition of an *applicable self-insured health plan* to which the Code Sec. 4376 fee applies.

On the other hand, an *applicable self-insured health plan* that provides accident and health coverage through fully-insured options and self-insured options is permitted to determine the fee imposed by Code Sec. 4376 by disregarding the lives that are covered solely under the fully-insured options. Barring this exception, an issuer or plan sponsor

¶545

LAW EXPLAINED

generally may not disregard a covered life merely because that individual is also covered under another *specified health insurance policy* or *applicable self-insured plan*.

HRAs. A plan sponsor may not treat a fully-insured plan and a health reimbursement arrangement (HRA) as a single plan or arrangement for purposes of the PCORI fee. This is because the Code Sec. 4375 fee, which applies to fully-insured plans, is separate from the Code Sec. 4376 fee, which applies to HRAs.

Average number of lives: consistency requirements. For the duration of the policy year, an issuer has to use the same method of calculating the average number of lives covered under a policy. Also, if the PCORI fee for multiple policies is reported on Form 720, the same method must be used for all of them.

An issuer that determines the average number of lives covered by using the *actual count method* or the *snapshot method* may switch between those two methods year to year, so long as the issuer uses the same method for all policies reporting a liability on Form 720 for a given year. On the other hand, an issuer that determines the average number of lives covered by using the *member months* or the *state form* method has to use the same method for all policy years for which the fee applies (Reg. § 46.4375-1(c)(2)(ii)).

Average number of lives: actual count method. Under the actual count method, an issuer determines the average number of lives covered under a policy for a policy year by adding the total number of lives covered for each day of the policy year and dividing that total by the number of days in the policy year (Reg. § 46.4375-1(c)(2)(iii)(A)).

Average number of lives: snapshot method. Under this method, the issuer determines the average number of lives covered under a policy for a policy year by adding the totals of lives covered on a date during the first, second, or third month of each quarter. (More than one date in each quarter may instead be used, so long as an equal number of dates is used for each quarter.) That total is then divided by the number of dates on which a count is made.

Each date used for the second, third and fourth quarters must be within three days of the date in that quarter that corresponds to the date used for the first quarter, and all dates used must be within the same policy year.

If an issuer uses multiple dates for the first quarter, the issuer must use dates in the second, third, and fourth quarters that correspond to each of the dates used for the first quarter or are within three days of those first quarter dates. In addition, all dates used must be within the same policy year (Reg. § 46.4375-1(c)(2)(iv)(A)).

Average number of lives: member months method. Under this method, an issuer determines the average number of lives covered under all policies in effect for a calendar year based on the "member months." *Member months* is an amount that equals the sum of the totals of lives covered on pre-specified days in each month of the reporting period reported on the National Association of Insurance Commissioners (NAIC) Supplemental Health Care Exhibit filed for that calendar year. Under this method, the average number of lives covered under the policies in effect for the calendar year equals the member months divided by 12 (Reg. § 46.4375-1(c)(2)(v)(A)).

LAW EXPLAINED

Average number of lives: state form method. Under this method, an issuer that is not required to file NAIC annual financial statements may determine the number of lives covered under all policies in effect for the calendar year using a form that is filed with the issuer's state of domicile and a method similar to the member months method. But the *state form method* may be used only if the state form reports the number of lives covered in the same manner as member months are reported on the NAIC Supplemental Health Care Exhibit (Reg. § 46.4375-1(c)(2)(vi)(A)).

Special rules for the last year: member months and state form method. For 2019, the last year the PCORI fee is in effect, there are special rules that issuers apply to determine the average number of lives covered. These special rules are needed because the fee does not apply for all of 2019, but only for policy years ending before October 1, 2019.

For issuers that determine the average number of lives covered using data reported on the 2019 NAIC Supplemental Health Care Exhibit or a permitted state form that covers the 2019 calendar year, the average number of lives covered for all policies in effect during the 2019 calendar year equals the average number of lives covered for that year under the *member months method* or the *state form method* multiplied by ¾. The resulting number is deemed to be the average number of lives covered for policies with policy years ending on or after January 1, 2019, and before October 1, 2019 (Reg. § 46.4375-1(c)(3)(ii)).

Reporting and payment deadlines. An issuer of a *specified health insurance policy* must report and pay the PCORI fee for a policy year or plan year no later than July 31 of the year following the last day of the policy or plan year (Reg. §§ 40.6071(a)-1(c)(1) and (2)).

Reporting on Form 720. The PCORI fee is reported and paid on Form 720, Quarterly Federal Excise Tax Return. The penalties for late filing or late payment of the fee may be waived or abated if the issuer or plan sponsor has reasonable cause and the failure was not due to willful neglect. Issuers and plan sponsors use Form 720X, Amended Quarterly Federal Excise Tax Return, to make adjustments to liabilities reported on a previously filed Form 720.

Fees on government plans. Governmental entities are not exempt from the PCORI fees except in the case of certain exempt governmental programs. Exempt governmental programs include Medicare, Medicaid, the State Children's Health Insurance Program (SCHIP), and any program established by federal law for providing medical care (other than through insurance policies) to members of the Armed Forces, veterans, or members of Indian tribes (Code Sec. 4377(b); Reg. § 46.4377-1(b)(2)).

Procedure. For purposes of the procedure and administration rules, the Code Sec. 4375 PCORI fee is treated as a tax (Code Sec. 4377(c)). An issuer of a *specified health insurance policy* must report and pay the PCORI fee for a policy year or plan year no later than July 31 of the year following the last day of the policy or plan year (Reg. §§ 40.6071(a)-1(c)(1) and (2)).

No need to pay collected fees over to U.S. possessions. No amount collected from the fee on health insurance policies and self-insured health plans needs to be "covered

LAW EXPLAINED

over" (i.e., paid by the Treasury) to any possession of the United States (Code Sec. 4377(d)). Thus, these fees are not treated in a manner similar to fees on certain shipments to the United States from Puerto Rico or the Virgin Islands that are required to be covered over to the treasuries of these possessions (Code Sec. 7652).

▶ **Effective date.** No effective date is provided by the Act. The provisions, therefore, are considered effective on March 23, 2010. The PCORI fee applies to specified health insurance policies with policy years ending after September 30, 2012, and before October 1, 2019. The final regulations (T.D. 9602) are effective December 6, 2012, and apply to policy years ending on or after October 1, 2012, and before October 1, 2019.

Law source: Law at ¶5180, ¶5270, ¶5280, ¶5290 and ¶5430.

— Act Sec. 6301(a) of the Patient Protection and Affordable Care Act (PPACA) (P.L. 111-148), adding Sec. 1181 of the Social Security Act;

— Act Sec. 6301(e)(1), adding Code Sec. 9511;

— Act Sec. 6301(e)(2), adding Code Secs. 4375, 4376 and 4377;

— Act Sec. 6301(f), adding Code Sec. 501(l)(4).

Reporter references: For further information, consult the following reporters.

— Standard Federal Tax Reporter, ¶34,612.01

— Tax Research Consultant, COMPEN: 45,200 and EXCISE: 13,054

— Practical Tax Explanation, §51,215

— Federal Excise Tax Reporter, ¶23,740.01

¶550 Fee Imposed on Self-Insured Health Plans

SUMMARY OF NEW LAW

The Patient Protection and Affordable Care Act (PPACA) of 2010 imposes a fee on any "applicable self-insured health plan" for each plan year ending on or after October 1, 2012, and before October 1, 2019. The plan sponsor pays the fee. The fee equals the product of $2 ($1 for policy years ending in fiscal 2013) multiplied by the average number of lives covered under the plan. For plan years ending on or after October 1, 2014, the $2 amount is adjusted for increases in health care spending.

BACKGROUND

From time to time, Congress establishes trust funds for special purposes. For example, there is the Black Lung Disability Trust Fund (Code Sec. 9501), the Airport and Airway Trust Fund (Code Sec. 9502), and the Highway Trust Fund (Code Sec. 9503). In general, these trust funds are funded by fees, excise taxes, penalties, or appropriations.

BACKGROUND

Employer-offered group health plans are highly regulated, and these regulations are generally enforced through excise taxes. For example, taxes are imposed for failure to comply with continuation of benefits (i.e., COBRA) requirements (Code Sec. 4980B), group health plan portability requirements (Code Sec. 4980D), and comparable health savings account contribution requirements (Code Sec. 4980G). These excise taxes on health insurers and plans are compliance-driven rather than imposed with an eye toward raising revenue for a specific purpose.

LAW EXPLAINED

PCORI fee imposed by Code Sec. 4376 on self-insured health plans.—Under Sec. 1181 of the Social Security Act, which was added by the Patient Protection and Affordable Care Act (PPACA) (P.L. 111-148), the Secretary of Health and Human Services must establish a Patient-Centered Outcomes Research Institute (PCORI) to conduct, support, and synthesize research about the outcomes, effectiveness, and appropriateness of health care services and procedures. The purpose of the research is to identify how diseases, disorders, and other health conditions can best be prevented, diagnosed, treated, and managed clinically. The PCORI research institute is funded by the "Patient-Centered Outcomes Research Trust Fund" (PCORTF) (Code Sec. 9511(a)). In turn, the research trust fund is supplied in part by fees imposed by Code Sec. 4376 on self-insured health plans. See ¶ 545 for discussion of the PCORTF.

The PCORTF is also supported by fees on health insurance policies (see ¶ 545) and self-insured health plans. Code Sec. 4376, enacted under the Patient Protection and Affordable Care Act (P.L. 111-148), imposes a fee on any "applicable self-insured health plan." The fee, referred to as the "PCORI fee" in connection with the trust fund that it supports, applies for plan years ending on or after October 1, 2012, and before October 1, 2019 (Code Sec. 4376(e)). The plan sponsor pays the fee (Code Sec. 4376(b)(1)).

The fee equals the product of $2 ($1 for policy years ending in fiscal 2013) multiplied by the *average number of lives* covered under the plan (Code Sec. 4376(a)). For plan years ending on or after October 1, 2014, the $2 amount is adjusted for increases in health care spending (Code Sec. 4376(d)).

A "plan sponsor" is the employer for a plan established or maintained by a single employer, and the employee organization for a plan established or maintained by an employee organization.

For the following, the plan sponsor is the association, committee, joint board of trustees, or other similar group of representatives of the parties who establish or maintain the plan:

- a plan established or maintained by two or more employers or jointly by one or more employers and one or more employee organizations,

- a multiple employer welfare arrangement, or

- a Code Sec. 501(c)(9) voluntary employees' beneficiary association (VEBA).

LAW EXPLAINED

In the case of a rural electric cooperative or a rural telephone cooperative, the plan sponsor is the cooperative or association (Code Sec. 4376(b)(2)).

Final regulations provide a more detailed breakdown of how to identify the plan sponsor for various plans (see Reg. § 46.4376-1(b)(2)(i)).

"Accident and health coverage" (the provision of which defines, in part, an *applicable self-insured health plan*) means any coverage which, if provided by an insurance policy, would cause the policy to be a Code Sec. 4375(c) *specified health insurance policy* (Code Sec. 4377(a)(1)).

Residing in the United States. Generally, the PCORI fee applies to any *applicable self-insured health plan*, which is defined as any plan for providing accident or health coverage with respect to individuals "residing in the United States" (including possessions) (Code Sec. 4377(a)(1), which relies on Code Sec. 4375(c); Code Sec. 4377(a)(3) and Reg. § 46.4377-1(a)(3), regarding possessions).

For purposes of the PCORI fee, an individual residing in the United States means an individual who has a place of abode in the United States. Therefore, someone on a temporary U.S. visa who has a place of abode in the United States is residing in the United States (Reg. § 46.4377-1(a)(2)(i)).

If the address on file with the plan sponsor for the primary insured is outside of the United States, the plan sponsor may treat the primary insured and his or her spouse, dependents, or other beneficiaries covered under the policy as having the same place of abode and not residing in the United States (Reg. § 46.4377-1(a)(2)(ii)).

Health plans subject to the PCORI fee. The PCORI fee is imposed on any "applicable self-insured health plan" (Code Sec. 4376(c)). In general, an *applicable self-insured health plan* is any plan for providing accident or health coverage if any portion of the plan's coverage is provided other than through an insurance policy, and the plan is established or maintained:

- by one or more employers for the benefit of their employees or former employees;
- by one or more employee organizations for the benefit of their members or former members;
- jointly by one or more employers and one or more employee organizations for the benefit of employees or former employees;
- by a Code Sec. 501(c)(9) voluntary employees' beneficiary association (VEBA);
- by any Code Sec. 501(c)(6) organization; or
- in the case of a plan not described in any of the other categories, by a multiple employer welfare arrangement (as defined in ERISA Sec. 3(40)), a rural electric cooperative (as defined in ERISA Sec. 3(40)(B)(iv)), or a rural telephone cooperative association (as defined in ERISA Sec. 3(40)(B)(v)) (Code Sec. 4376(c); Reg. § 46.4376-1(b)(1)).

Retiree coverage and retiree-only plans. The PCORI fee applies to *applicable self-insured health plans* that provide accident and health coverage to retirees, including retiree-only policies and plans (Code Sec. 4376(c)(2)(A)).

LAW EXPLAINED

COBRA coverage. The final regulations state explicitly that accident and health coverage (the provision of which defines, in part, an *applicable self-insured health plan*) includes continuation coverage under the Consolidated Omnibus Budget Reconciliation Act of 1985 (COBRA), or similar continuation coverage under other federal law or under state law. Thus, COBRA coverage must be taken into account in determining the Code Sec. 4376 PCORI fee, unless the arrangement is otherwise excluded (Reg. § 46.4377-1(a)(1)).

FSAs and HRAs, generally. A health flexible spending arrangement (health FSA) (as described in Code Sec. 106(c)(2)) is generally within the definition of an *applicable self-insured health plan*, unless the FSA meets the requirements for being an *excepted benefit*. According to the preamble to the final regulations (T.D. 9602, preamble section IV), the same rule applies to health reimbursement arrangements (HRAs) (as described in Notice 2002-45, 2002-2 CB 93).

Health plans exempt from the PCORI fee. Several categories of health plans are not subject to the PCORI fee imposed by Code Sec. 4376. These are discussed below.

Excepted benefits. Certain kinds of health plans are exempt from the fee because they are not deemed *applicable self-insured health plans* (Reg. § 46.4376-1(b)(1)(ii)(A)). Specifically, plans are exempt if substantially all the benefits they provide are "excepted benefits" described in Code Sec. 9832(c).

Excepted benefits under Code Sec. 9832(c) include the following:

- coverage for only accident or disability
- liability insurance (including general liability and auto liability insurance)
- workers' compensation or similar insurance
- auto medical payment insurance
- coverage for on-site medical clinics
- limited scope dental or vision benefits
- benefits for long-term care, nursing home care, or community-based care
- coverage for only a specified disease or illness
- hospital indemnity or other fixed indemnity insurance
- Medicare supplemental coverage

Exception for certain FSAs and HRAs. A health flexible spending arrangement (health FSA) (as described in Code Sec. 106(c)(2)) that qualifies as an excepted benefit under Code Sec. 9832(c) and Reg. § 54.9831-1(c)(3)(v) is not an *applicable self-insured health plan*. According to the preamble to the final regulations, the same rule applies to health reimbursement arrangements (HRAs) (as described in Notice 2002-45, 2002-2 CB 93).

EAPs and wellness programs. The definition of an *applicable self-insured health plan* does not include an employee assistance program (EAP), disease management program, or wellness program if the program does not provide significant medical care or treatment benefits (Reg. § 46.4376-1(b)(1)(ii)(B)).

LAW EXPLAINED

Expatriate plans. The term *applicable self-insured health plan* does not include plans designed to cover primarily employees who are working and residing outside of the United States (Reg. § 46.4376-1(b)(1)(ii)(C)).

Calculating the fee. *Generally.* The Code Sec. 4376 PCORI fee for a plan year is the *average number of lives* covered under the plan for the plan year multiplied by the *applicable dollar amount* (Code Sec. 4376(a); Reg. § 46.4376-1).

Average number of lives, generally. To determine the *average number of lives* covered under an *applicable self-insured health plan* during a plan year, an plan sponsor must use one of three methods: the actual count method, the snapshot method, or the Form 5500 method (Reg. § 46.4376-1(c)(2)(i)).

Applicable dollar amount. For plan years ending on or after October 1, 2012, and before October 1, 2013, the applicable dollar amount is $1. For plan years ending on or after October 1, 2013, and before October 1, 2014, the applicable dollar amount is $2 (Reg. § 46.4376-1(c)(3)).

For any plan year ending in any federal fiscal year beginning on or after October 1, 2014, the applicable dollar amount is the sum of (1) the applicable dollar amount for the plan year ending in the previous federal fiscal year; plus (2) that amount multiplied by the percentage increase in the projected per capita amount of the National Health Expenditures most recently released by the Department of Health and Human Services before the beginning of the federal fiscal year (Reg. § 46.4376-1(c)(3)). For plan years that end on or after October 1, 2014, and before October 1, 2015, the applicable dollar amount is $2.08 (Notice 2014-56, I.R.B. 2014-41).

Lives taken into account. The PCORI fee may apply multiple times if accident and health coverage is provided to one individual through more than one policy or self-insured arrangement. This can happen, for example, where an individual is covered by a fully-insured major medical insurance policy and a self-insured prescription arrangement.

Similarly, a plan sponsor may not treat a fully-insured plan and a health reimbursement arrangement (HRA) as a single plan or arrangement for purposes of the PCORI fee. This is because the Code Sec. 4375 fee, which applies to fully-insured plans, is separate from the Code Sec. 4376 fee, which applies to HRAs. Thus, where an employee is covered by both a group insurance policy and an HRA, the group insurance policy falls within the definition of a *specified health insurance policy* to which the Code Sec. 4375 fee applies, and the HRA falls within the definition of an *applicable self-insured health plan* to which the Code Sec. 4376 fee applies.

Lives taken into account when an FSA or HRA is the only plan. If the only *applicable self-insured health plan* that a plan sponsor establishes and maintains is a health flexible spending arrangement (health FSA) or a health reimbursement arrangement (HRA), the plan sponsor may treat each participant's health FSA or HRA as covering a single life. As a result, the plan sponsor does not have to include as lives covered any spouse, dependent, or other beneficiary of the individual (Reg. § 46.4376-1(c)(2)(vi)).

Lives covered under multiple plans. If two or more arrangements (1) are established or maintained by the same plan sponsor, (2) provide for accident and health coverage

LAW EXPLAINED

other than through an insurance policy, and (3) have the same plan year, they may be treated as a single *applicable self-insured health plan* for purposes of calculating the PCORI fee under Code Sec. 4376 (Reg. § 46.4376-1(b)(1)(iii)).

Thus, for example, if a plan sponsor establishes and maintains a self-insured arrangement providing major medical benefits and a separate self-insured arrangement with the same plan year providing prescription drug benefits, the two arrangements may be treated as one *applicable self-insured health plan*. If treated as one plan, the same life covered under each arrangement would count as only one covered life under the plan for purposes of calculating the fee.

Lives covered under multiple plans: FSAs or HRAs along with other plans. If a single plan sponsor establishes and maintains a health FSA or an HRA along with a different type of self-insured health plan and the plans have the same plan year, the two arrangements may be treated as a single plan under Reg. § 46.4376-1(b)(1)(iii), discussed above. But the special counting rule that allows plan sponsors with nothing but a health FSA or HRA to treat each participant's arrangement as covering a single life applies only to the participants in the health FSA or HRA that do not participate in the other *applicable self-insured health plan*. The participants in the health FSA or HRA that do participate in the other *applicable self-insured health plan* will be counted in accordance with the method applied for counting lives covered under that other plan (Reg. § 46.4376-1(c)(2)(vi)).

Average number of lives: consistency requirements. For the duration of the plan year, a plan sponsor has to use the same method of calculating the *average number of lives* covered under a plan. However, a plan sponsor may use a different method from one plan year to the next (Reg. § 46.4376-1(c)(2)(ii)).

Average number of lives: actual count method. Under the *actual count method*, a plan sponsor determines the *average number of lives* covered under a plan for a plan year by adding the totals of lives covered for each day of the plan year and dividing that total by the number of days in the plan year (Reg. § 46.4376-1(c)(2)(iii)(A)).

Average number of lives: snapshot method. Under this method, the issuer determines the *average number of lives* covered under an *applicable self-insured health plan* for a plan year by adding the totals of lives covered on a date during the first, second, or third month of each quarter. (More than one date in each quarter may instead be used, so long as an equal number of dates is used for each quarter.) That total is then divided by the number of dates on which a count is made.

Each date used for the second, third, and fourth quarters must be within three days of the date in that quarter that corresponds to the date used for the first quarter, and all dates used must fall within the same plan year.

If a plan sponsor uses multiple dates for the first quarter, it must use dates in the second, third, and fourth quarters that correspond to each of the dates used for the first quarter or are within three days of those first quarter dates. In addition, all dates used must be within the same plan year (Reg. § 46.4376-1(c)(2)(iv)(A)).

Snapshot method: two ways to determine number of lives covered. Under the *snapshot method*, the number of lives covered on a designated date may be determined using one

¶550

LAW EXPLAINED

of two methods – either the *snapshot count method* or the *snapshot factor method* (Reg. § 46.4376-1 (c) (2) (iv) (A)).

Snapshot count method. Under the *snapshot count method*, the number of lives covered on a date equals the actual number of lives covered on the designated date (Reg. § 46.4376-1 (c) (2) (iv) (C)).

Snapshot factor method. Under the *snapshot factor method*, the number of lives covered on a date is equal to the sum of: (1) the number of participants with self-only coverage on that date, plus (2) the number of participants with coverage other than self-only coverage on that date multiplied by 2.35 (Reg. § 46.4376-1 (c) (2) (iv) (B)).

Average number of lives: Form 5500 method. Under the *Form 5500 method*, a plan sponsor determines the *average number of lives* covered under a plan for a plan year based on the number of participants reported on Form 5500 (Annual Return/Report of Employee Benefit Plan), or Form 5500-SF (Short Form Annual Return/Report of Small Employee Benefit Plan) that is filed for the plan for that plan year. To use this method, however, the Form 5500 or Form 5500-SF must be filed no later than the due date for the Code Sec. 4376 fee for that plan year (Reg. § 46.4376-1 (c) (2) (v)).

Form 5500 method: self-only coverage. For a plan offering nothing but self-only coverage, the *average number of lives* covered under the plan equals the sum of the total participants covered at the beginning and the end of the plan year, as reported on Form 5500 or Form 5500-SF, divided by 2 (Reg. § 46.4376-1 (c) (2) (v) (A)).

Form 5500 method: self-only and other coverage. For a plan offering self-only coverage and other coverage, the *average number of lives* covered under the plan equals the sum of total participants covered at the beginning and the end of the plan year, as reported on Form 5500 or Form 5500-SF (Reg. § 46.4376-1 (c) (2) (v) (A)).

Special rule for lives covered solely by the fully-insured options under an applicable self-insured health plan. In determining the Code Sec. 4376 fee, a special rule applies to an *applicable self-insured health plan* that provides accident and health coverage through fully-insured options and self-insured options. Under that rule, in determining the lives covered under the *actual count method*, the *snapshot method*, or the *Form 5500 method*, discussed above, the plan sponsor may disregard the lives that are covered solely under the fully-insured options (Reg. § 46.4376-1 (c) (2) (vii) (A)).

Barring this exception, an issuer or plan sponsor generally may not disregard a covered life merely because that individual is also covered under another *specified health insurance policy* or *applicable self-insured health plan*.

Reporting and payment deadlines. A plan sponsor of an *applicable self-insured health plan* must report and pay the PCORI fee for a plan year no later than July 31 of the year following the last day of the plan year (Reg. § 40.6071 (a)-1 (c) (2)).

Reporting on Form 720. The PCORI fee is reported and paid on Form 720, Quarterly Federal Excise Tax Return. The penalties for late filing or late payment of the fee may be waived or abated if the plan sponsor has reasonable cause and the failure was not due to willful neglect. Plan sponsors use Form 720X, Amended Quarterly Federal

LAW EXPLAINED

Excise Tax Return, to make adjustments to liabilities reported on a previously filed Form 720.

Fees on government plans. Governmental entities are not exempt from the PCORI fees except in the case of certain exempt governmental programs. Exempt governmental programs include Medicare, Medicaid, the State Children's Health Insurance Program (SCHIP), and any program established by federal law for providing medical care (other than through insurance policies) to members of the Armed Forces, veterans, or members of Indian tribes (Code Sec. 4377(b); Reg. § 46.4377-1(b)(2)).

Procedure. For purposes of the procedure and administration rules, the Code Sec. 4376 PCORI fee is treated as a tax (Code Sec. 4377(c)). A plan sponsor of an *applicable self-insured health plan* must report and pay the PCORI fee for a plan year no later than July 31 of the year following the last day of the plan year (Reg. § 40.6071(a)-1(c)(2)).

No need to pay collected fees over to U.S. possessions. No amount collected from the fee on health insurance policies and self-insured health plans needs to be "covered over" (i.e., paid by the Treasury) to any possession of the United States (Code Sec. 4377(d)). Thus, these fees are not treated in a manner similar to fees on certain shipments to the United States from Puerto Rico or the Virgin Islands that are required to be covered over to the treasuries of these possessions (Code Sec. 7652).

▶ **Effective date.** No effective date is provided by the Act. The provisions, therefore, are considered effective on March 23, 2010. The PCORI fee applies to applicable self-insured health plans with plan years ending after September 30, 2012, and before October 1, 2019. The final regulations (T.D. 9602) are effective December 6, 2012, and apply to policy years ending on or after October 1, 2012, and before October 1, 2019.

Law source: Law at ¶5180, ¶5270, ¶5280, ¶5290 and ¶5430.

— Act Sec. 6301(a) of the Patient Protection and Affordable Care Act (PPACA) (P.L. 111-148), adding Sec. 1181 of the Social Security Act;

— Act Sec. 6301(e)(1), adding Code Sec. 9511;

— Act Sec. 6301(e)(2), adding Code Secs. 4375, 4376 and 4377;

— Act Sec. 6301(f), adding Code Sec. 501(l)(4).

Reporter references: For further information, consult the following reporters.

— Standard Federal Tax Reporter, ¶34,612.01

— Tax Research Consultant, COMPEN: 45,200 and EXCISE: 13,056

— Practical Tax Explanation, § 51,215

— Federal Excise Tax Reporter, ¶23,840.01

¶555 Medical Loss Ratio Rebates

SUMMARY OF NEW LAW

Health insurers are required to provide medical loss ratio rebates to health insurance policy holders under certain circumstances. These rebates are paid in the year following the year in which the premiums are paid. In general, these rebates are not taxable to the recipient unless the recipient deducted the premium, or used pre-tax dollars to pay the premium. The insurer treats the rebates as return premiums for income purposes.

BACKGROUND

Individuals may deduct health insurance premiums as medical expenses, subject to certain limits (Code Sec. 213). Self-employed individuals may deduct 100 percent of amounts they contribute to a health plan on behalf of themselves, their spouses and their dependents (Code Sec. 162(l)(1)). Employees whose employer has a cafeteria plans may be able to use pre-tax dollars or after-tax dollars to pay for health insurance premiums (Code Sec. 125). Employer contributions to a health plan are deductible (Code Sec. 105(h)), and if the benefits qualify their value is excludable from the employee's income (Code Secs. 106 and 107).

Insurance companies are taxed on the premiums earned during the tax year. Return premiums are deducted from this amount (Code Sec. 832(b)(4)(A); Reg. § 1.832-4(a)(3)). Return premiums include amounts: (a) that are previously paid which have become refundable due to policy cancellations or decreases in risk exposure during the effective period of an insurance contract; (b) that reflect the unearned portion of unpaid premiums for an insurance contract that is canceled or for which there is a decrease in risk exposure during its effective period; or (c) that are either previously paid and refundable or which reflect the unearned portion of unpaid premiums for an insurance contract, arising from the redetermination of a premium due to correction of posting or other similar errors (Reg. § 1.832-4(a)(6)). An insurance company reports the liability for a return premium resulting from the cancellation of an insurance contract for the tax year in which the contract is canceled. An insurance company reports the liability for a return premium attributable to a reduction in risk exposure under an insurance contract for the tax year in which the reduction in risk exposure occurs (Reg. § 1.832-4(a)(7)).

LAW EXPLAINED

Medical loss ratio rebates may be taxable to the recipient.—Starting in 2012, health insurance issuers and plans must provide annual medical loss ratio (MLR) rebates of excess costs to their enrollees (Public Health Safety Act, Sec. 2718, Code Sec. 9815(b), as added by Patient Protection and Affordable Care Act (PPACA)). The MLR rules require insurers to provide rebates to enrollees if less than 85% of premium dollars (80% in the small group and individual markets) are spent on clinical services and health care

LAW EXPLAINED

quality improvement. These rules apply beginning in 2011, and the first rebates are due August 1, 2012. These rules apply to grandfathered plans as well as nongrandfathered plans (Temporary Reg. § 54.9815-1251T(d)).

> **Comment:** Insurers and plans may pay cash to the recipient, or use the rebate against current premiums to reduce this years premium cost.

Individual policy holders. An MLR rebate, whether in the form of cash or a reduction in the current premium, is taxable to the extent the individual received a tax benefit from the premiums paid, and nontaxable if the individual did not receive a tax benefit.

Example 1: In 2013, Andy paid premiums for a health insurance policy for himself. Andy does not deduct the premium payments on his 2013 Form 1040, and he does not receive any reimbursement or subsidy for the premiums. Based on his enrollment during 2013, Andy receives an MLR rebate on July 1, 2014, which is a rebate of part of his 2013 insurance premiums and a purchase price adjustment. Because Andy did not deduct the premium payments on his 2013 Form 1040, the rebate is not taxable whether received as a cash payment or applied as a reduction in the amount of premiums due for 2014.

Example 2: Same facts as Example 1, except Andy deducts the premium payments on Schedule A of his 2013 Form 1040. The MLR rebate is taxable to the extent that he received a tax benefit from the deduction, whether the rebate is received as a cash payment or applied as a reduction in the amount of premiums due for 2014.

Example 3: Same facts as Example 1, except Andy is self-employed so that he deducts the premium payments on line 29 of his 2013 Form 1040. Because Andy deducted the premium payments on line 29 (self-employed health insurance deduction) of his 2013 Form 1040, the MLR rebate is taxable to the extent that he received a tax benefit from the deduction, whether the rebate is received as a cash payment or as a reduction in the amount of premiums due for 2014 (IRS, Medical Loss Ratio FAQs, Q&A 2 - 4 (rev. March 6, 2014).

Group plans: after-tax premium payments. An MLR rebate received by an employee, either through a reduction in the following year premium or in cash, is not subject to income tax if the employee used after-tax dollars to pay premiums. If the employee deducted the premium amount, the rebate amount is subject to income tax, though it is not subject to employment tax. This rule holds whether the plan distributes the benefit only to employees who participated in the plan the previous year and are currently enrolled, or to all employees who are currently enrolled.

¶555

LAW EXPLAINED

Example 4: In 2013, Daisy participated in her employer's group health plan and received health coverage under the group health insurance policy. Under the plan, the employer pays for 60% of the premium for each employee, the employee pays 40% on an after-tax basis, and MLR rebates are allocated to employees who participated both in the year in which the premium was paid and the year in which the MLR is received. Daisy did not deduct the premiums on her 2013 Form 1040. On July 1, 2014, the employer received an MLR rebate of part of the 2013 group health insurance policy premiums in the form of a reduction in the 2014 premium. Under the plan, 60% of the rebate reduces the employer portion of the 2014 premiums, and 40% reduces the employee portion. Because Daisy participated in the plan during 2013 and 2014, she is entitled to a rebate which reduces her premiums for 2014 coverage. The MLR rebate is a rebate of part of Daisy's 2013 insurance premiums which Daisy bought with compensation that was fully taxable and subject to employment tax in 2013. She did not deduct the premiums in 2013, and therefore the rebate is not taxable for 2014 including federal employment taxes.

Example 5: Same facts as Example 4, except the insurer paid the MLR rebate in cash and then the employer distributed cash to Daisy rather than reducing the premiums due for 2014. Daisy is not subject to income or employment taxes on the cash payment.

Example 6: Same facts as Example 4, except Daisy deducted her premium payment on her 2013 Form 1040. The rebate, whether a cash payment or reduction in the current premium, is taxable to the extent that Daisy received a tax benefit from the deduction but is not subject to federal employment taxes.

Example 7: In 2013, Doris participated in her employer's group health plan. The plan provides that the employer pays for 60% of the premium for each employee, the employee pays 40% on an after-tax basis, and MLR rebates are allocated to all current plan participants regardless of whether they participated in the year for which the rebate is made. On July 1, 2014, the employer receives an MLR rebate of part of the 2013 group health insurance policy premiums which the employer allocates to participants as a reduction in the cost of current premiums. Under the plan rules, Doris receives the MLR rebate solely due to her participation in the plan during 2014, regardless of whether she participated in the plan during 2013. The MLR rebate is a purchase price adjustment and is not taxable regardless of whether Doris deducted the 2013 premium payments on her 2013 Form 1040. If Doris deducts the premiums she pays for health care coverage on her 2014 Form 1040, the amount of the MLR rebate reduces the amount of her deduction because she is paying less for premiums. If Doris had

LAW EXPLAINED

received the MLR rebate in cash instead of as a premium reduction, Doris's rebate also would not be subject to federal income tax and would reduce the amount of any 2014 deduction for premiums paid by Doris on her Form 1040. In either case, Doris's rebate would not be wages subject to employment taxes.

Example 8: Same facts as Example 7, except Doris started working for the employer in 2014 and starts participating in the plan on the first day of employment. The MLR rebate is not taxable. If Doris deducts the premiums she pays for health care coverage in 2014 on her Form 1040, the amount of the rebate reduces the amount of the deduction because the premium cost is reduced. If she had received the rebate in cash, the rebate still would not be subject to federal income tax, but would reduce the amount of any 2014 deduction for premiums paid on Form 1040. In either case, the rebate would not be wages subject to employment taxes (IRS, Medical Loss Ratio FAQs, Q&A 5 - 9 (rev. March 6, 2014)).

Caution: MLR rebates in the hands of employers may be plan assets subject to ERISA fiduciary duties. The DOL has issued guidance that all employer's with health plans will need to review for purposes of plan rules regarding the handling of MLR rebates (DOL Technical Release No. 2011-04).

Group plans: pre-tax premium payments. A MLR rebate received by an employee, either through a reduction in the following year premium or in cash, is subject to income tax and employment tax if the employee uses pre-tax dollars to pay the premiums for which the insurer issued the rebate. This rule holds whether the plan distributes the benefit only to employees who participated in the plan the previous year and are currently enrolled, or to all employees currently enrolled.

Example 9: Frank participates in his employer's group health plan in 2013 and 2014. He pays his portion of premiums on a pre-tax basis under the employer's cafeteria plan. The plan provides that the employer pays for 60% of the health insurance premium for each employee, the employee pays for 40% of the premium, and MLRs are allocated to employees who were participants both in the year for which the premium was paid and in the year the rebate was received. On July 1, 2014, the employer receives a MLR rebate relating to 2013 premiums in the form of a reduction in the current year's premium. Because Frank participates in the plan during 2013 and 2014, he is entitled to a rebate of $X. As a result, Frank's salary reduction contribution for 2014 is reduced by $X. Frank's MLR rebate is subject to federal income tax. Because the MLR rebate is distributed as a premium reduction, the amount Frank pays for premiums through a salary reduction contribution in 2014 is decreased by $X. Consequently, in 2014 there is a corresponding increase of $X in his taxable salary that is also wages subject to employment taxes.

LAW EXPLAINED

Example 10: Same facts as Example 9, except the MLR rebate is provided in the form of a cash payment and the employer distributes the rebate in cash instead of reducing premiums for 2014 coverage. Frank will have $X more taxable income in 2014. The amount that Frank paid for premiums was subtracted from his salary on a pre-tax basis under the cafeteria plan. The MLR rebate is a return to Frank of part of that untaxed compensation that is no longer being used to pay for health insurance. Therefore, the MLR rebate that Frank receives in 2014 is an increase in taxable income that is also wages subject to employment taxes (IRS, Medical Loss Ratio FAQs, Q&A 10 - 11 (rev. March 6, 2014)).

Example 11: Emily participates during 2013 and 2014 in her employer's group health plan. She pays her portion of the premiums on a pre-tax basis under the employer's cafeteria plan. The plan provides that the employer pays for 60% of the health insurance premium for each employee, the employee pays for 40% of the premium on a pre-tax basis, and MLR rebates are allocated to employees who are plan participants in the year the rebate is paid. On July 1, 2014, the employer receives a MLR rebate relating to 2013 premiums in the form of a reduction in the current year's premium. Because Emily participates in the plan during 2014, she is entitled to a rebate of $X regardless of whether she was a plan participant in 2013. Because the MLR rebate is distributed as a premium reduction, the amount Emily pays for premiums through a salary reduction contribution in 2014 is decreased by $X and consequently there is a corresponding increase of $X in her 2014 taxable salary that is also wages subject to employment taxes.

Example 12: Same facts as Example 11, except the MLR rebate is made in the form of a cash payment and the plan distributes the rebate to Emily in cash instead of reducing her premiums for 2014 coverage. The MLR rebate results in an increase in 2014 of taxable income of $X that is also wages subject to employment taxes.

Example 13: Same facts as Example 11, except that Emily begins working for the employer in 2014 (and thus did not participate in the plan during 2013). She participates in the plan during 2014. As a result of the rebate and corresponding premium reduction, the amount Emily pays for premiums through a salary reduction contribution is decreased by $X. Consequently, there is a corresponding increase of $X in her salary and the additional salary is taxable income that is also wages subject to employment taxes. If instead Emily received an $X cash payment, she would have an increase in taxable income of $X that is also wages subject to employment taxes (IRS, Medical Loss Ratio FAQs, Q&A 12 - 14 (rev. March 6, 2014)).

LAW EXPLAINED

Insurance companies. MLR rebates paid by insurance companies are treated as return premiums whether paid as cash payments or as premium reductions, which reduces their taxable income. For a cash rebate paid to an individual policyholder, the insurer has to file a Form 1099-MISC only if: (1) the total rebate payments made to that policyholder during the year total $600 or more; and (2) the company knows these payments are taxable income to the individual policyholder or can determine how much of the payments constitute taxable income. If the company is required to file a Form 1099-MISC, it must also furnish a copy to the individual policyholder (IRS, Medical Loss Ratio FAQs, Q&A 1 (revised March 6, 2014)).

For a rebate paid to a group policyholder as a premium reduction, an insurer is required to file a Form 1099-MISC only if: (1) the group policyholder is not an exempt recipient for Form 1099 purposes, (2) the total rebate payments to that group policyholder during the year total $600 or more, and (3) the insurer knows that the rebate payments are taxable income to the group policyholder or can determine how much of the payments constitutes taxable income. Exempt recipients for which Forms 1099 generally are not required to be provided include corporations, tax exempt organizations, and federal and state governments. The insurer can rely on a recipient's claim of exempt recipient status on a Form W-9 (IRS, Medical Loss Ratio FAQs, Q&A 1 (revised March 6, 2014)).

▶ **Effective date.** No effective date is provided for Code Sec. 9815, the provision is therefore considered effective on March 23, 2010, the date of enactment of Patient Protection and Affordable Care Act (PPACA) (P.L. 111-148).

Law source: Law at ¶5440.

— Act Sec. 1562(f) of the Patient Protection and Affordable Care Act (PPACA) (P.L. 111-148), as redesignated by Act Sec. 10107, adding Code Sec. 9815;

— Act Sec. 1001, adding and amending Public Health Service Act (PHSA) Secs. 2718;

— Act Sec. 10101, amending PHSA Sec. 2718;

— Act Secs. 1004 and 1255, as redesignated by Act Sec. 10103, providing the effective dates.

Reporter references: For further information, consult the following reporters.

— Standard Federal Tax Reporter, ¶5504.043

— Tax Research Consultant, HEALTH: 12,106

— Practical Tax Explanation, § 42,230

Net Investment Income Tax and Additional Medicare Tax

¶605 Net Investment Income Tax for Individuals

SUMMARY OF NEW LAW

Effective for tax years beginning after 2012, most individuals are subject to a 3.8-percent tax on the lesser of (i) net investment income, or (ii) modified AGI that exceeds $200,000 ($250,000 for joint filers and surviving spouses, and $125,000 for married taxpayers filing separately).

BACKGROUND

The Federal Insurance Contributions Act (FICA) imposes two taxes on employers and employees. The first finances the federal old-age, survivors and disability insurance (OASDI) program, more commonly known as Social Security. The second finances hospital and hospital service insurance (HI) for those 65 years of age or older, more commonly known as Medicare.

The Medicare tax on an employee wages consists of an employee's portion and an employer's portion, each of which is equal to 1.45 percent of the employee's wages (Code Secs. 3101(b) and 3111(b)). Thus, the equivalent of 2.9 percent of the employee's wages is contributed to Medicare. The Medicare tax also applies to net earnings from self-employment income, but a self-employed worker pays the full 2.9-percent tax (Code Sec. 1401(b). In addition to these traditional Medicare taxes, the Patient Protection and Affordable Care Act (PPACA) (P.L. 111-148) imposes an additional 0.9-percent Medicare tax on wages and self-employment income that exceeds $200,000 ($250,000 for joint filers and surviving spouses, and $125,000 for married taxpayers filing separate returns) (see ¶620).

BACKGROUND

The Medicare tax has been imposed only on wages and net earnings from self-employment. It has not been imposed on investment income.

LAW EXPLAINED

Net investment income tax on unearned income.—For tax years beginning after 2012, individuals are subject to a 3.8-percent tax on the lesser of:

- net investment income for the tax year, or
- modified adjusted gross income for the tax year over a threshold based on filing status (Code Sec. 1411, as added by the Health Care and Education Reconciliation Act of 2010 (P.L. 111-152).

> **Comment:** Although the tax is not limited to net investment income and is not dedicated to the Medicare trust fund, it is often referred to as the "net investment income tax" (NIIT) or the "Medicare surtax." The net investment income tax also applies to estates and trusts, as discussed at ¶610.

> **Comment:** The IRS issued final regulations covering the net investment income tax that generally apply for tax years beginning after December 31, 2013, and can also can be relied on for 2013 (T.D. 9644, December 2, 2013). Proposed reliance regulations issued in 2012 (NPRM REG-130507-11), since withdrawn, can also be relied on until December 31, 2013 (though adjustments may be required if the use of such regulations affects net investment income tax in years after 2013). The final regulations clarify the treatment of dual resident and dual status taxpayers, and provide an additional election opportunity for couples electing resident status for both spouses for the tax year in which a nonresident spouse becomes a resident.

Net investment income includes most types of investment income (dividends, interest, royalties, rents, annuities, etc.); income from a trade or business that is passive with respect to the taxpayer; income from a trade or business of trading in commodities or financial instruments; and net gain on the disposition of most non-business property (Code Sec. 1411(c)). See ¶615 for discussion of net investment income.

> **Key Rates and Figures:** The applicable MAGI threshold amounts are:
>
> - $250,000 for joint returns and surviving spouses,
> - $125,000 for married taxpayers who file separate returns, and
> - $200,000 for other taxpayers (single filers and heads of households) (Code Sec. 1411(b); Reg. §1.1411-2(d)(1)).

These amounts are not adjusted for inflation.

> **Comment:** Since the tax applies to the *lesser* of MAGI over the threshold or net investment income, a taxpayer must have both to be liable for the tax. A taxpayer with no net investment income is not subject to the tax, regardless of MAGI; and a taxpayer whose MAGI does not exceed the threshold is not subject to the tax, regardless of net investment income.

¶605

LAW EXPLAINED

> **Example 1:** Alison is a single filer with MAGI of $190,000, which includes $50,000 of net investment income. Alison is not liable for the net investment income tax because the MAGI threshold for a single individual is $200,000. For the following year, if Alison has MAGI of $220,000 that includes $50,000 of net investment income, her net investment income tax is $760 (3.8% × the lesser of $20,000 (her MAGI over the threshold) or $50,000 (her net investment income) (Reg. § 1.1411-2(b)(2)).

Affected taxpayers. The net investment income tax applies to most individual taxpayers (Code Sec. 1411(a)(1)), other than non-resident aliens (Code Sec. 1411(e)(1); Reg. § 1.1411-2(a)(1)). The following rules apply to nonresident aliens and bona fide residents of U.S. territories:

- A dual resident taxpayer (an individual who is a U.S. resident and also a resident of a treaty country under Reg. § 301.7701(b)-7(a)(1)) is treated as a nonresident for net investment income tax purposes (Reg. § 1.1411-2(a)(2)(i));

- A dual-status individual (an individual who resides in the U.S. for only part of the year) is subject to the net investment income tax only during the portion of the year the individual resides in the U.S. (Reg. § 1.1411-2(a)(2)(ii));

- When a nonresident alien is married to a U.S. citizen or resident, the default rule treats the spouses as married filing separately for purposes of the net investment income tax. Thus, the U.S. spouse separately calculates his or her own net investment income and MAGI and determines liability for the net investment income tax using the MAGI threshold for married taxpayers who file separate returns ($125,000). The non-resident spouse is not subject to the tax. However, married taxpayers who make a Code Sec. 6013(g) election to treat a nonresident alien spouse as a resident alien and file a joint return, or who make a Code Sec. 6013(h) election to treat a nonresident alien spouse as a resident for the year in which he or she becomes a U.S. resident, are eligible to make an election under the net investment income tax rules to apply their Code Sec. 6013(g) or (h) election for net investment income tax purposes. Electing spouses combine their net investment income and MAGI, and use the MAGI threshold for joint returns ($250,000) to determine their joint liability for the net investment income tax. Taxpayers must make the election for the first tax year in which the U.S. taxpayer would be subject to the net investment income tax without regard to the election (that is, based on the U.S. taxpayer's own net investment income or MAGI and the $125,000 MAGI tax threshold) (Reg. § 1.1411-2(a)(2)(iii), (iv)).

- Bona fide residents of U.S. territories with mirror tax systems (Guam, the Northern Mariana Islands, and the United States Virgin Islands) generally are not required to file U.S. returns or pay U.S. tax if they properly report income and pay income tax to the tax administration of the territory in which they reside. Thus, the net investment income tax generally does not apply to these residents who fully comply with the tax laws of their respective territories. Bona fide residents of non-mirror code jurisdictions (American Samoa and Puerto Rico) generally file U.S. returns only to report

¶605

LAW EXPLAINED

income that (i) is not sourced to the territory in which they reside, or (ii) is compensation for services performed as employees of the United States or its agencies. The net investment income tax applies to bona fide residents of non-mirror jurisdictions only if their U.S.-reportable income gives rise to MAGI that exceeds the applicable threshold and is also net investment income (Reg. § 1.1411-2(a)(2)(vi)).

Modified adjusted gross income. For purposes of the net investment income tax, an individual's modified adjusted gross income (MAGI) is:

(1) AGI as calculated for federal income tax purposes, plus

(2) the excess of foreign earned income excluded from gross income under Code Sec. 911, over the amount of deductions or exclusions that are disallowed because of the exclusion (Code Sec. 1411(d); Reg. §§ 1.1411-1(b) and 1.1411-2(c)).

Comment: Thus, MAGI for net investment income tax purposes is modified only for certain U.S. citizens or residents who live abroad. For most taxpayers, MAGI s simply AGI as calculated for other federal tax purposes (that is, gross income less above-the-line deductions).

The MAGI threshold amount is generally not prorated or reduced for a short tax year. However, if the short year is the result of a change of annual accounting period, the applicable threshold amount is reduced by the ratio that the number of months in the short period bears to twelve (Reg. § 1.1411-2(d)(2)).

MAGI is modified for individuals who own shares in controlled foreign corporations or interests in passive foreign investment companies (Reg. § 1.1411-10). See ¶ 615 for discussion of these rules.

Operation. The tax is calculated on Form 8960, Net Investment Income Tax—Individuals, Estates, and Trusts, which is attached to the taxpayer's Form 1040 or 1041. The tax is paid as part of the taxpayer's federal income tax (IRS Net Investment Income Tax FAQs, Q/A 15.

Planning Note: Since the net investment income tax is not imposed on wages, it is not withheld by employers. However, a wage-earner can ask the employer to withhold extra federal income tax to cover the expected liability for the net investment income tax, by updating his or her Form W-4, Employee's Withholding Allowance Certificate.

Caution: The net investment income tax is subject to the estimated tax provisions (Code Sec. 6654(a) and (f)). Thus, taxpayers who expect to be subject to the net investment income tax should adjust their income tax withholding or estimated tax payments to account for the tax increase in order to avoid underpayment penalties.

▶ **Effective date.** The provision applies to tax years beginning after December 31, 2012 (Act Sec. 1402(a)(4) of the Health Care and Education Reconciliation Act of 2010 (P.L. 111-152). The final regulations are generally effective after December 31, 2013, and can be relied on before that date. Proposed reliance regulations issued in 2012, and now withdrawn, can be relied on prior to the effective date of the final regulations. However, to the extent that taxpayers take a position in a tax year beginning before January 1, 2014, that is inconsistent with the final regulations, and such position affects the treatment of one or

LAW EXPLAINED

more items in a tax year beginning after December 31, 2013, such taxpayer must make reasonable adjustments to ensure that their net investment income tax liability in the tax years beginning after December 31, 2013, is not inappropriately distorted. The 2013 proposed regulations are generally proposed to go into effect for tax years after December 31, 2013, and they can be relied on until they are issued as final regulations.

Law source: Law at ¶5220 and ¶5410.

— Act Sec. 1402(a)(1) of the Health Care and Education Reconciliation Act of 2010 (P.L. 111-152), adding Code Sec. 1411;

— Act Sec. 1402(a)(2), amending Code Sec. 6654(a) and (f);

— Act Sec. 1402(a)(4), providing the effective date.

Reporter references: For further information, consult the following reporters.

— Standard Federal Tax Reporter, ¶32,606.0201

— Tax Research Consultant, INDIV: 69,150

— Practical Tax Expert, § 1,022.10

¶610 Net Investment Income Tax on Estates and Trusts

SUMMARY OF NEW LAW

Effective for tax years beginning after 2012, most estates and trusts are subject to a 3.8-percent tax on the lesser of (i) undistributed net investment income, or (ii) AGI that exceeds the threshold for the highest income tax bracket.

BACKGROUND

Estates and trusts are subject to many of the same taxes that apply to individuals. Depending on their circumstances, estates and trusts can be liable for income taxes, property taxes, estate and gift taxes, and generation-skipping transfer taxes. An estate or trust that employs workers may also be liable for the employer share of employment taxes (social security and Medicare taxes). However, estates and trusts do not have to pay self-employment taxes or the employee share of employment taxes. An estate or trust may be liable for income tax on its unearned income but, as with individuals, unearned income is generally taxed at much lower rates than those that apply to earned income.

LAW EXPLAINED

Net investment income tax for estates and trusts.—For tax years beginning after 2012, an estate or trust is subject to a 3.8-percent tax on the lesser of its:

LAW EXPLAINED

- undistributed net investment income, or

- adjusted gross income (AGI) that exceeds the threshold for the highest income tax bracket for estates and trusts (Code Sec. 1411, as added by the Health Care and Education Reconciliation Act of 2010 (P.L. 111-152).

> **Key Rates and Figures:** The highest tax bracket (39.6 percent) for estates and trusts begins in 2013 when AGI reaches $11,950 (Rev. Proc. 2013-15), and in 2014 when AGI reaches $12,150 (Rev. Proc. 2013-35, 2013-47 I.R.B. 537). Wolters Kluwer, projects that for 2015, the highest tax bracket for estates and trusts will begin when AGI reaches $12,300.

> **Comment:** Although the tax is not limited to net investment income and is not dedicated to the Medicare trust fund, it is often referred to as the "net investment income tax" (NIIT) or the "Medicare surtax." The net investment income tax also applies to most individuals (see ¶605). See ¶615 for discussion of net investment income.

> **Comment:** Since the tax applies to the *lesser* of AGI over the threshold or undistributed net investment income, an estate or trust must have both to be liable for the tax. An estate or trust that has no net investment income or that distributes all of its net investment income is not subject to the tax, regardless of AGI; and an estate or trust with AGI below the threshold is not subject to the tax, regardless of its undistributed net investment income

> **Comment:** The IRS issued final regulations covering the net investment income tax that generally apply for tax years beginning after December 31, 2013, but can be relied on for 2013 (T.D. 9644, December 2, 2013). Proposed reliance regulations issued in 2012 (NPRM REG-130507-11), since withdrawn, can also be relied on until December 31, 2013 (though adjustments may be required if the use of the proposed regulations affects net investment income in years after 2013). The final regulations make one change that is effective for 2013, and it is relevant to trusts. For charitable remainder trusts (CRTs), the final regulations adopt rules for categorizing net investment income based on the existing Code Sec. 664 category and class system, discarding the independent classification system that was provided in the 2012 proposed regulations. The IRS also issued new proposed reliance regulations on December 2, 2013 (NPRM REG-130843-13), which include guidance for CRTs with income from certain controlled foreign corporation or passive foreign investment companies (Proposed Reg. §1.1411-3(d)(2)(ii)); and propose an election to allow a CRT to use the generally criticized "simplified method" found in the 2012 proposed regulations, rather than the Code Sec. 664 method, to determine the amount of net investment income in a beneficiary's distribution (Proposed Reg. §1.1411-3(d)(3)).

Affected taxpayers. The net investment income tax applies to all estates and trusts that are subject to the provisions of part I of subchapter J of chapter 1 of subtitle A of the Code (that is, Code Secs. 641 through 685) (Code Sec. 1411(a)(2); Reg. §1.1411-3(a)(1)(i)). Thus, pooled income funds under Code Sec. 642(c)(5), and qualified funeral trusts under Code Sec. 685, are subject to the tax included despite having special computational rules.

¶610

LAW EXPLAINED

Certain trusts and estates are excepted from the net investment income tax, including: (1) a trust or decedent's estate devoted to religious, charitable, scientific, literary, or educational purposes, or to foster national or international amateur sports competition, or for the prevention of cruelty to children or animals as described in Code Sec. 170(c)(2)(B); (2) charitable trusts exempt from tax under Code Sec. 501; (3) charitable remainder trusts exempt from tax under Code Sec. 664, (4) any other trust statutorily exempt from taxes as described in (such as HSAs, Coverdell accounts, and 529 tuition programs); (5) grantor trusts (but not beneficiaries); (6) Electing Alaska Native Settlement Trusts under Code Sec. 646; (7) Cemetery Perpetual Care Funds under Code Sec. 642(i); (8) foreign trusts (distributions to U.S. beneficiaries are not excluded); and (9) foreign estates (distributions to U.S. beneficiaries are not excluded) (Reg. § 1.1411-3(b)). The net investment income tax is applied to a qualified funeral trust by treating each beneficiary's interest as a separate trust (Reg. § 1.1411-3(b)(2)(i)).

> **Comment:** The 2012 proposed regulations did not exclude Electing Alaska Native Settlement Trusts or Cemetery Perpetual Care Funds, nor did they exclude a decedent's estate (as opposed to a trust) devoted to religious, charitable, etc. purposes. The final regulations are effective for 2014, but can be relied upon for 2013.

> **Caution:** Although foreign estate and trusts are not subject to the net investment income tax, the tax does apply to their distributions of current-year income to U.S. beneficiaries (Reg. § 1.1411-3(e)(3)(ii)). The final regulations reserve rules for applying the net investment income tax to a foreign nongrantor trust's accumulation distributions to U.S. beneficiaries (Reg. § 1.1411-4(e)(1)(ii)), and pending the issuance of such guidance, the net investment income tax does not apply to distributions of accumulated income from a foreign trust to U. S. beneficiary.

An individual debtor's bankruptcy estate is treated like a married taxpayer filing a separate return. Thus, the net investment income tax for an individual's bankruptcy estate is equal to 3.8 percent of the lesser of the estate's (i) net investment income, or (ii) modified adjusted gross income that exceeds $125,000 (Reg. § 1.1411-2(a)(2)(v); see Code Sec. 1411(a)(1)). See ¶605 for discussion of the net investment tax on individuals.

Adjusted gross income. Adjusted gross income (AGI) for purposes of the net investment income tax is defined as it is for general income tax purposes (Code Sec. 1411(a)(2)(B)). AGI is computed for a trust or estate generally as it is for an individual, except that a trust or estate can claim three additional above-the-line deductions: (i) administration expenses that are incurred only because property is held in a trust or estate, (ii) distributions to beneficiaries, up to the amount of distributable net income (DNI), and (iii) the entity's personal exemption (Code Sec. 67(e)).

The AGI threshold for the net investment income tax generally is not reduced or prorated for short tax years of less than twelve months. However, if the short tax year results from a change in annual accounting period and not from an individual's death, the AGI threshold is reduced by the ratio that the number of months in the short tax year bears to twelve (Reg. § 1.1411-3(a)(2)).

¶610

LAW EXPLAINED

Special rules may apply to the calculation of AGI if the estate or trust owns, directly or indirectly, an interest in a controlled foreign corporation (CFC), passive foreign investment company (PFIC) or qualified electing fund (QEF). See ¶615 for discussion of these rules.

Undistributed net investment income. Net investment income is generally defined for estates and trusts as it is for individuals (see ¶615). However, *undistributed* net investment income is a concept that applies only to estates and trusts. Undistributed net investment income is the estate's or trust's net investment income, reduced by (a) its distributions of net investment income to beneficiaries, up to the lesser of the estate's or trust's deduction for the distributions or its net investment income); and (b) deductible amounts used or permanently set aside for charitable purposes (Reg. §1.1411-3(e)(2); see Code Secs. 642(c), 651 and 661). This gives effect to the general income tax rules that treat an estate or trust as a conduit by reducing its taxable income to take into account distributions to beneficiaries and the charitable deduction. However, when distributions and donations include both net investment income and non-net investment income, the reduction in net investment income is determined according to the class system of income categorization that is generally embodied in Code Secs. 651 through 663 and Reg. §1.661(c)-1 (Reg. §1.1411-3(e)(3) and (4)). Under these rules, the estate or trust basically reduces its undistributed net investment income by the proportion of its deductible distributions and charitable contributions that are made up of net investment income.

Beneficiaries. The portion of a deductible distribution that consists of the estate's or trust's net investment income is also net investment income in the hands of the beneficiary. Thus, any given item of net investment income is included in the net investment income of either the trust/estate or its beneficiaries. While an estate or trust can avoid the tax by distributing all of its net investment income, doing so may subject its higher-income beneficiaries to the tax (Reg. §1.1411-3(e)(3)(ii)).

CRTs. Charitable remainder trusts (CRTs) are exempt entities and, therefore, are not subject to the net investment income tax. However, their annuity and unitrust distributions may be net investment income to the non-charitable recipient beneficiary. The net investment income tax applies to a CRT's accumulated net investment income (ANII), which is the total amount of net investment income received by the CRT for all tax years that begin after December 31, 2012, less the total amount of net investment income distributed for all prior tax years of the trust that begin after December 31, 2012 (Reg. §1.1411-3(d)(1)(iii)). A CRT with multiple non-charitable beneficiaries must apportion its net investment income among the beneficiaries based on their respective shares of the total annuity or unitrust amount paid by the trust for the tax year (Reg. §1.1411-3(d)(1)(ii)).

The final regulations categorize and distribute a CRT's accumulated net investment income based on the existing Code Sec. 664 category and class system under which the ordering rules for characterizing CRT distributions is generally made first from ordinary income, second from capital gains, third from other income (including tax-exempt income) and last from trust corpus (Reg. §1.1411-3(d)(2)). In contrast, the 2012 proposed regulations provided an independent set of ordering rules for determining whether CRT distributions were net investment income to noncharitable beneficiaries. Although the final regulations generally apply after 2013, this CRT rule

¶610

LAW EXPLAINED

applies to tax years beginning after December 31, 2012 (Reg. § 1.1411-3(f)). However, if a CRT relied on the 2012 proposed regulations for a return filed before December 2, 2013 (the publication date of the final regulations), the CRT and its beneficiaries do not have to amend their returns to comply with the final regulations (Preamble to T.D. 9644). Regulations proposed in 2013 would allow a CRT to elect to use the separate characterization method provided in the withdrawn 2012 proposed regulations (Proposed Reg. § 1.1411-3(d)(3)). The 2013 proposed regulations also provide guidance for CRTs with income from certain CFCs or PFICs (Proposed Reg. § 1.1411-3(d)(2)(ii)).

ESBTs. The portion of an electing small business trust (ESBT) consisting of S corporation stock must be treated as a separate trust for purposes of computing the net investment income tax, but the portions are consolidated into a single trust for purposes of determining the trust's AGI. This process requires three steps:

(1) The ESBT separately calculates the undistributed net investment income of its S-corporation and non-S-corporation portions in accordance with the general net investment income tax rules for trusts, and then combines these amounts to determine its total undistributed net investment income.

(2) The ESBT determines AGI solely for purposes of the net investment income tax by taking the non-S portion's AGI, and then increasing or decreasing that amount by the net income or net loss of the S portion as a single item of ordinary income or ordinary loss, after taking into account all deductions, carryovers, and loss limitations applicable to the S portion.

(3) These amounts—undistributed net investment income calculated in step (1) and AGI calculated in step (2)—are used to determine whether the ESBT is subject to net investment income tax and, if so, the tax base for applying the tax (Reg. § 1.1411-3(c)(1)(ii)).

Effective date. The provision applies to tax years beginning after December 31, 2012 (Act Sec. 1402(a)(4) of the Health Care and Education Reconciliation Act of 2010 (P.L. 111-152). The final regulations are generally effective after December 31, 2013, and can be relied on before that date. Proposed reliance regulations issued in 2012, and now withdrawn, can be relied on prior to the effective date of the final regulations. However, to the extent that taxpayers take a position in a tax year beginning before January 1, 2014, that is inconsistent with the final regulations, and such position affects the treatment of one or more items in a tax year beginning after December 31, 2013, such taxpayer must make reasonable adjustments to ensure that their net investment income tax liability in the tax years beginning after December 31, 2013, is not inappropriately distorted. The 2013 proposed regulations are generally proposed to go into effect for tax years after December 31, 2013, and they can be relied on until they are issued as final regulations.

Law source: Law at ¶ 5220 and ¶ 5410.

— Act Sec. 1402(a)(1) of the Health Care and Education Reconciliation Act of 2010 (P.L. 111-152), adding Code Sec. 1411;

— Act Sec. 1402(a)(2), amending Code Sec. 6654(a) and (f);

— Act Sec. 1402(a)(4), providing the effective date.

LAW EXPLAINED

Reporter references: For further information, consult the following reporters.

— Standard Federal Tax Reporter, ¶ 32,606.025

— Tax Research Consultant, ESTTRST: 12,256

— Practical Tax Expert, § 32,022

¶615 Net Investment Income Tax: Net Investment Income Defined

SUMMARY OF NEW LAW

For purposes of the 3.8-percent net investment income tax that applies in tax years beginning after 2012, net investment income includes unearned income, income from passive activities, income from commodities and financial activities trading businesses, and net gain on the disposition of property that is not held in an active non-trading business.

BACKGROUND

Unearned income is often taxed more favorably than earned income. The highest income tax rate for many types of unearned income, such as long-term capital gains and most dividends, is generally 20 percent—just over half the highest income tax rate for earned income. Some types of unearned income, such as interest on exempt bonds and gains in Roth IRA accounts, are entirely exempt from federal income tax. Unearned income also is not subject to the payroll and self-employment taxes that apply to most earned income at rates as high as 15.3 percent. In addition, payors of many types of unearned income do not withhold taxes or file information returns to report the payments to the IRS.

LAW EXPLAINED

Net investment income subject to tax.—For tax years beginning after 2012, a 3.8-percent net investment income tax is imposed on:

- the lesser of an individual's (a) net investment income or (b) modified adjusted gross income (MAGI) for the tax year over a threshold based on filing status; and

- the lesser of (a) the undistributed net investment income of an estate or trust or (b) its AGI over the threshold for the highest income tax bracket (Code Sec. 1411(a), as added by the Health Care and Education Reconciliation Act of 2010 (P.L. 111-152).

See ¶ 605 for discussion of the tax for individuals and ¶ 610 for discussion of the tax for estates and trusts.

LAW EXPLAINED

Compliance Tip: The net investment income tax is computed and reported on Form 8960, Net Investment Income Tax—Individuals, Estates, and Trusts, which is attached to the taxpayer's Form 1040 or 1041; and is paid as part of the taxpayer's federal income tax (IRS Net Investment Income Tax FAQs, Q/A 15).

Comment: Final regulations covering the net investment income tax generally apply for tax years beginning after December 31, 2013, but can be relied on for 2013 (T.D. 9644, December 2, 2013). Proposed reliance regulations issued in 2012 (NPRM REG-130507-11), since withdrawn, can also be relied on until December 31, 2013 (though adjustments may be required if the use of such regulations affects net investment income in years after 2013). The final regulations are far more taxpayer friendly. They include relief for real estate professionals, self-charged rent, self-charged interest, net operating loss carryovers, and suspended passive losses. They make it easier to effectively allocate losses and other deductions against investment income in calculating net investment income. The IRS also issued new proposed reliance regulations on December 2, 2013 (NPRM REG-130843-13), which include (i) revised rules for calculating net gain from the disposition of an active interest a partnership or S corporation (Proposed Reg. § 1.1411-7); as well as guidance on the treatment of Code Sec. 707(c) guaranteed payments for capital (Proposed Reg. § 1.1411-4(g)(10)), Code Sec. 736 payments to retiring or deceased partners (Proposed Reg. § 1.1411-4(g)(11)), and certain capital loss carryovers (Proposed Reg. § 1.1411-4(d)(4)(iii)).

Net investment income is the excess of the sum of the amounts in the following three categories less any otherwise allowable deductions properly allocable to such income or gain:

(i) Gross income from interest, dividends, annuities, royalties and rents, *unless* the income is derived (a) in the ordinary course of a trade or business that is nonpassive with respect to the taxpayer, or (ii) from a trade or business of trading financial instruments or commodities;

(ii) Other gross income from either: (a) a trade or business that is a passive activity with respect to the taxpayer, or (b) a trade or business of trading in financial investments or commodities; and

(iii) Net gain included in computing taxable income that is attributable to the disposition of property other than property held in an active trade or business (Code Sec. 1411(c)(1); Reg. § 1.1411-4(a)).

Comment: These categories are sometimes referred to as the "little i's." Category (i) is traditional investment income that is normally associated with personal investing, such as dividends, interest, royalties, rent, and annuity income. Category (ii) is income derived in the ordinary course of a financial trading business, or the ordinary course of a trade or business in which the taxpayer has a passive interest. Category (iii) income is gain or loss on the disposition of assets that are not used in an active trade or business. This is a rough description of the three categories, and there are nuances and exceptions. Several other types of income are simply excluded from net investment income, such as income subject to self-employment tax, retirement plan distributions, social security benefits, alimony,

LAW EXPLAINED

tax-exempt interest and Alaska Fund Permanent Dividends (Reg. § 1.1411-1(d)(4)). However, if these items are included in the taxpayer's AGI, they are also taken into account in determining whether the taxpayer exceeds the AGI or MAGI threshold to be subject to the tax.

Category (i) investment income. Category (i) income includes interest, dividends, royalties, rents and annuities. Gross income from annuities includes the amount includible in gross income as a result of the application of Code Sec. 72(a) and (b), and an amount not received as an annuity under an annuity contract that is includible in gross income under 72(e) (Reg. § 1.1411-1(d)(1)).

Active trade or business exclusion. Active trade or business income is generally excluded from category (i) if it meets these three requirements:

(1) The income must be derived form an activity that rises to the level of a trade or business under Code Sec. 162 (for instance, renting out a single property generally does not amount to a trade or business);

(2) The income must be derived from *that* trade or business (for instance, income from renting a parking space owned by a medical business would not qualify for the exception); and

(3) The taxpayer must materially participate in the trade or business under the Code Sec. 469 rules for nonpassive treatment of income (Code Sec. 1411(c)(2); Reg. § 1.1411-4(b)).

"Trade or business" is defined for this purposes as it is for purposes of Code Sec. 162, including all case law and administrative guidance (Reg. § 1.1411-1(d)(12)).

Example 1: Frank's S corporation owns and operates a bank that is not a financial instruments or commodities trading business. Frank is an active participant in the bank. The bank earns $100,000 of interest in the ordinary course of its trade or business, and Frank's pro rata share is $5,000. This $5,000 qualifies for the ordinary course of a trade or business exception and, therefore, is not included in Frank's net investment income. However, the exception would not apply if (a) Frank was not active with respect to the bank, or (b) the bank was a commodities or financial instruments trading business, regardless of Frank's participation.

Ownership levels at which trade or business income is determined. To determine whether gross income from interest, dividends, annuities, royalties, rents, substitute interest payments, and substitute dividend payments is derived in a trade or business, the following rules apply:

- For individuals, estates, or trusts that own or engage in a trade or business directly (or indirectly through ownership of an interest in an entity that is disregarded as an entity separate from its owner), the determination of whether category (i) gross income is derived in a trade or business is made at the individual, estate or trust level (Reg. § 1.1411-4(b)(1)).

¶615

LAW EXPLAINED

- For individuals, estates, or trusts that own an interest in a trade or business through one or more passthrough entities (such as a partnership or S corporation), the determination of whether category (i) gross income is derived from a trade or business that is a passive activity is made at the owner level (Reg. § 1.1411-4(b)(2)(i)).

- For individuals, estates, or trusts that own an interest in a trade or business through one or more passthrough entities (such as a partnership or S corporation), the determination of whether category (i) gross income is derived from a trade or business of a trader trading in financial instruments or commodities is made at the entity level and if the entity is involved in the business, the income retains its character when passing through to the taxpayer (Reg. § 1.1411-4(b)(2)(ii)).

Rental activity as a trade or business. Rental activity does not necessarily rise to the level of a trade or business (Reg. § 1.1411-5(b)(3), Ex. 1), and hence does not necessarily qualify for the active trade or business exception for category (i) income. Whether it does depends on a number of factors, including the type of property, the number of properties rented, the day-to-day involvement of the owner or agent, and the type of rental (see Preamble, T.D. 9644).

Self-charged interest and rent. Self-charged interest and self-charged rent do not readily qualify as income derived in the course of the trade or business, unless the trade or business is in the business of lending money or renting property. However, the net investment income tax incorporates the Reg. § 1.469-7 passive activity self-charged interest rules. Thus, a taxpayer who receives self-charged interest from a nonpassive entity may exclude from net investment income an amount equal to the taxpayer's allocable share of the flow-through entity's interest deduction (Reg. § 1.469-2(f)(5)). Similarly, self-charged rental income is deemed to be derived in the ordinary course of a trade or business and, thus, excluded from net investment income, to the extent that gross rental income is recharacterized as nonpassive under Reg. § 1.469-2(f)(6), or as a consequence of a taxpayer grouping a rental activity with a trade or business activity under Reg. § 1.469-4(d)(1) (Reg. § 1.1411-4(g)(6)).

Income from working capital. Net investment income includes any income, gain, or loss that is attributable to an investment of working capital that is treated as not derived in the ordinary course of a trade or business under Code Sec. 469(e)(1)(B). Income from working capital is generally category (i) income, and gain or loss from the disposition of working capital assets is generally category (iii) income (Code Sec. 1411(c)(3); Reg. § 1.1411-6). In determining whether any item is gross income from or net gain attributable to an investment of working capital, principles similar to those described in Reg. § 1.469-2T(c)(3)(ii) apply (Reg. § 1.1411-6). See Reg. § 1.1411-4(f) for rules regarding properly allocable deductions with respect to an investment of working capital, and 2013 Proposed Reg. § 1.1411-7 upon which taxpayers may rely for rules relating to the adjustment to net gain on the disposition of interests in a partnership or S corporation.

Category (ii) trade or business income. Category (ii) income is income from a trade or business that is a passive activity with respect to the taxpayer, or a trade or business of financial trading (collective known as Category (ii) or Reg. § 1.1411-5 trades or

LAW EXPLAINED

businesses). Generally, category (ii) income is income from the normal operations of a Reg. §1.1411-5 trade or business (for instance, patient billings for a medical practice), as distinguished from side income that falls under category (i) (for instance, rental income for a medical practice from renting a parking space), or category (iii) gain (for instance, disposition of working capital assets) (Reg. §1.1411-4(c)(1)). All trading gains or losses are assigned to category (iii) (Reg. §1.1411-4(c)). This is a change from the 2012 proposed regulations, under which category (ii) included all gross income from a trade or business trading in financial instruments or commodities that is not category (i) income.

For purposes of a category (ii) trading business, "commodities" is defined by reference to the Code Sec. 475(e)(2) rules governing mark to market accounting for securities dealers (Code Sec. 1411(c)(2)(B)). Financial instruments include stocks and other equity interests, evidences of indebtedness, options, forward or futures contracts, notional principal contracts, any other derivatives, and any evidence of an interest in any of these items, such as short positions or partial units (Reg. §1.1411-5(c)).

Nonpassive v. passive activities. The net investment income tax rules generally characterize activities as passive or nonpassive based on the Code Sec. 469 rules for passive activities losses (Code Sec. 1411(c)(2)(A)). These rules generally provide four ways for an activity to be nonpassive: grouping, activity recharacterization, income recharacterization, and material participation.

Recharacterized passive income. A trade or business is not a passive activity with respect to (a) income or gain that is recharacterized as "not from a passive activity" by reason of Temporary Reg. §1.469-2T(f)(2), (f)(5), or (f)(6), or gain that is recharacterized as "not from a passive activity" by reason of Reg. §1.469-2(c)(2)(iii) and does not constitute portfolio income under Reg. §1.469-2(c)(2)(iii)(F). However, when recharacterized income or gain qualifies as portfolio income under Temporary Reg. §1.469-2T(f)(10) or Reg. §1.469-2(c)(2)(iii)(F), the trade or business constitutes a passive activity for net investment income purposes solely with respect to that income or gain (Reg. §1.1411-5(b)).

> **Planning Tip:** The net investment income tax also incorporates the Reg. §1.469-4 rules for grouping different activities together for purposes of determining whether the group, rather than the individual activities, is active or passive. A taxpayer may do a one-time regrouping in the first year the taxpayer is subject to the net investment income tax. The regrouping may be done on an amended return if the taxpayer was not subject to net investment income tax on the original return (Reg. §1.469-11(b)(3)(iv)).

Rental activity as a nonpassive activity. Under the passive activity rules, renting real estate or equipment is generally deemed to be a passive activity (Code Sec. 469(c)(2), (j)(8)), but there are a number of regulatory exceptions (Temporary Reg. §1.469-1T(e)(3)(ii)). For example, a rental of equipment for seven days or less is not a passive activity (Temporary Reg. §1.469-1T(e)(3)(ii)(A)). These exceptions also apply in determining whether the activity is a passive activity for purposes of the net investment income tax. Thus, an activity that is not per se passive for purposes of the

¶615

LAW EXPLAINED

passive activity rules is also not per se passive for purposes of the net investment income tax (Reg. § 1.1411-5(b)(3), Ex. 3).

> **Caution:** A taxpayer who qualifies for one of the exceptions to the per se passive activity rules is not necessarily engaged in Code Sec. 162 a trade or business. Thus, even when a per-se exception applies, if the activity does not qualify as a trade or business, the rental income is included in Category (i) income.

Rental activities by real estate professionals. The rental activity of a real estate professional is not treated as a passive activity under the passive activity rules (Code Sec. 469(c)(7)). This exception applies if more than one-half of the taxpayer's personal services in a trade or business are performed in real property businesses in which the taxpayer materially participates; and the taxpayer performs more than 750 hours of services during the tax year in real property businesses in which the taxpayer materially participates. Under a safe harbor, net investment income does not include rental income and gain or loss on the disposition of rental properties if a real estate professional either (a) participates in rental real estate activities for more than 500 hours per year, or (b) participated in rental real estate activities for more than 500 hours per year in five of the last ten tax years. Failure to qualify for the safe harbor does not preclude the taxpayer from showing that the rental income and gain or loss on the disposition of the rental property is excludable from net investment income under some other provision (Reg. § 1.1411-4(g)(7)).

Category (iii) gain. Category (iii) net investment income comprises gain or loss on dispositions of property that (a) is not held in an active trade or business, or (b) is held in a trade or business that is a commodities or financial instruments trading business (Reg. § 1.1411-4(d)(4)). Common types of Category (iii) income include gains on the sale of stocks, bonds, and mutual funds; capital gain distributions from mutual funds; gain from the sale of investment real estate (including gain from the sale of a second home that is not a primary residence); and gains from the sale of interests in partnerships and S corporations held by a passive owner (IRS Net Investment Income Tax FAQs, Q/A 9).

Net gain is equal to:

- recognized gain from the disposition of property (that is, gain that is recognized in gross income under Code Sec. 61(a)(3)),

- plus gain or loss attributable to the disposition of property from the investment of working capital or a life insurance contract, and gain attributable to the disposition of an annuity contract to the extent the sales price of the annuity exceeds the annuity's surrender value,

- reduced (but not below zero) by Code Sec. 165 deductible losses that are attributable to property that (a) is not held in a trade or business or (b) is held in a category (ii) trade or business (Reg. § 1.1411-4(d)(3)(i)).

A disposition includes a sale, exchange, transfer, conversion, cash settlement, cancellation, termination, lapse, expiration, or other disposition (including a deemed disposition such as under Code Sec. 877A) (Reg. § 1.1411-4(d)(1)). The general federal income tax rules, such as those governing partnership and S corporation distribu-

LAW EXPLAINED

tions, largely determine whether there has been a disposition of property for purposes of the net investment income tax (Reg. § 1.1411-4(d)(3)(i)).

> **Comment:** The limitation of category (iii) income to recognized gain means that deferred gain and gain on nontaxable transfers is not included in category (iii) income. For instance, gain on the sale of a principal residence that is excluded from gross income under Code Sec. 121 is also excluded from category (iii) income.

Example 2: Betty and Carl are married and file a joint return. They sell the home they have owned and occupied for 25 years, realizing a $600,000 gain. Since they file a joint return, they can exclude $500,000 of the gain, and they must include the remaining $100,000 in their gross income. Only this $100,000 in taxable gain is included in their category (iii) net investment income (IRS Net Investment Income Tax FAQs, Q/A 11 , Ex 2).

Interests in partnerships and S corporations. In general, the disposition of a partnership interest or S corporation stock generates category (iii) gain or loss. However, gain on the disposition of an active interest in a partnership or an S corporation is included in category (iii) income only to the extent of the net gain or loss that would be taken into account by the partner or shareholder if all property of the partnership or S corporation were sold at fair market value immediately before the disposition of the interest (Code Sec. 1411(c)(4) as added by P.L. 111-152). Under the 2013 proposed reliance regulations, the gain is the lesser of:

- the seller's overall gain or loss on the sale of the partnership interest or S corporation stock determined under normal income tax rules; or

- the seller's share of a hypothetical asset sale gain that would be included in net investment income because the assets were passive with respect to the seller or not used in a trade or business (2013 Proposed Reg. § 1.1411-7(b)(1)).

The 2013 proposed reliance regulations also provide an optional simplified method when the amount of gain associated with passive assets owned by the entity is likely to be relatively small (Proposed Reg. § 1.1411-7(c)).

Losses. Category (iii) net gain cannot be less than zero (Reg. § 1.1411-4(d)(2)). However, an individual taxpayer can use up to $3,000 in capital losses to offset gain from the disposition of assets other than capital assets that are subject to the net investment income tax (Reg. § 1.1411-4(d)(2)). The 2013 proposed reliance regulations also provide special rules for capital loss carryforwards (Proposed Reg. § 1.1411-4(d)(4)(iii)).

Suspended losses from a former passive activity may be taken against net investment income to the extent they are used for purposes of computing Chapter 1 taxable income, but only to the extent that nonpassive income from the former passive activity is included in net investment income in that year (Reg. § 1.1411-4(g)(8)). Losses under Code Sec. 469(g)(1) are taken into account in calculating net gain or as an allocable

¶615

LAW EXPLAINED

deduction, as applicable, in the same way they are taken into account in computing Chapter 1 taxable income (Reg. § 1.1411-4(g)(9)).

Excess losses may be allocable against investment income to the extent they are actually used to lower the taxpayer's income tax. Losses deductible under Code Sec. 165, whether described in Code Sec. 62 or Code Sec. 63(d), are allowed as a properly allocable deduction to the extent they exceed the amount of gain described in Code Sec. 63(a)(3) and are not taken into account in computing net gain by reason of Reg. § 1.1411-4(d)(2) (Reg. § 1.1411-4(f)(4)). Thus, losses are first applied to calculating net gains, and then the excess losses are applied as properly allocable deductions against investment income (T.D. 9644, Preamble).

Exclusions. Net investment income does not include:

- gross income from interest, dividends, annuities, royalties, rents, substitute interest payments, and substitute dividend payments if derived in the ordinary course of a trade or business that is not a passive activity or a trade or business of a trader trading in financial instruments or commodities (ordinary course of trade or business exception) (Reg. § 1.1411-4(b));

- any distribution (including deemed distributions) from qualified employee benefit plans or arrangements as described in Code Secs. 401(a), 403(a) or (b), 408, 408A or 457(b) (qualified pension, stock bonus, and profit-sharing plans; qualified annuity plans; tax-sheltered annuities; individual retirement accounts (IRAs); Roth IRAs; and deferred compensation plans of governments and exempt organizations) (Code Sec. 1411(c)(5); Reg. § 1.1411-8);

- taxable distributions from an exempt trust, such as a qualified tuition program (QTP), a Coverdell education savings account (ESA), an Archer medical savings account (Archer MSA), or a health savings account (HSA) (Reg. § 1.1411-3(b)).

- any item of income or deduction taken into account in determining self-employment income for the tax year on which an individual pays hospital insurance (Medicare) tax under Code Sec. 1401(b) (Code Sec. 1411(c)(6); Reg. § 1.1411-9);

- income from gains on the sale of an active interest in a partnership or S corporation (2013 Proposed Reg. § 1.1411-7).

- guaranteed Code Sec. 707(c) payment for services to a partnership (but guaranteed payments for use of capital are net investment income) (2013 Proposed Reg. § 1.1411-4(d)(10)).

Items that are taken into account in determining self-employment income are income items included and deductions allowed in determining net earnings from self-employment (Reg. § 1.1411-9(a)). Deductions that are properly allocable by a financial instruments or commodities trading business to category (ii) or category (iii) income are taken into account in determining self-employment income only to the extent they reduce net earnings from self-employment (after aggregating the net earnings from self-employment from any trade or business carried on by the taxpayer as an individual or as a member of a partnership). Any such deductions that exceed the amount of

LAW EXPLAINED

aggregated net earnings from self-employment are allowed in determining the taxpayer's net investment income (Reg. § 1.1411-9(b)).

Example 3: Dan operates a commodities trading business and marks his securities to market at the end of each year. He derives $400,000 of gross income from the business, and has $15,000 in allowable deductions. Under the mark-to-market and self-employment tax rules, none of this gross income is taken into account in determining Dan's net earnings from self-employment and self-employment income and, therefore, the $15,000 in deductions also is not taken into account in determining his self-employment income. Because Dan has $0 net earnings from self-employment, the $15,000 of deductions does not reduce his net earnings from self-employment. Accordingly, those deductions can be taken against $400,000 in category (ii) income, reducing it to $250,000 (Reg. § 1.1411-9(b), Ex 3).

Payments to retiring partners. Under the 2013 proposed reliance regulations, payments to retiring partners under Code Sec. 736 are net investment income. Payments under Code Sec. 736(b) are category (iii) income. If the retiring partner materially participates in a partnership trade or business, Proposed Reg. § 1.1411-7(c) is applied. Gain or loss relating to Code Sec. 736(b) payments is category (iii) income regardless of whether the payments are classified as capital gain or ordinary income. For Code Sec. 736(b) payments that are paid over multiple years, the characterization of gain or loss as passive or nonpassive is determined for all payments as though all payments were made when the liquidation of the exiting partner's interest commenced and is not retested annually (Proposed Reg. § 1.1411-4(g)(11)(iv)). For distributive share payments of partnership income under Code Sec. 736(a)(1), the items of income, gain, loss, and deduction attributable to the share are taken into account in computing net investment income in a manner consistent with the item's character and treatment for chapter 1 purposes (Proposed Reg. § 1.1411-4(g)(11)(ii), see Reg. § 1.469-2(e)(2)(iii) for rules concerning the item's character and treatment for chapter 1). The portion (if any) of a Code Sec. 736(a)(2) payment that is allocable to the unrealized receivables and goodwill of the partnership is category (iii) income as gain from the disposition of a partnership interest. Payments not for unrealized receivables or goodwill is characterized as a payment for services or as the payment of interest in a manner consistent with the payment's characterization under Reg. § 1.469-2(e)(2)(iii) (Proposed Reg. § 1.1411-4(g)(11)(iii).

Properly allocable deductions. Properly allocable deductions that can be taken against investment income include rent or royalty expenses (Code Sec. 62(a)(4)), trade or business expenses (to the extent they are not taken into account in determining self-employment income), the penalty on early savings withdrawals (Code Sec. 62(a)(9)), and net operating losses (see Reg. § 1.1411-4(h) for calculating NOLs) (Reg. § 1.1411-4(f)(2)).

¶615

LAW EXPLAINED

The following itemized deductions can also be properly allocable deductions:

- investment interest expenses under Code Sec. 163(d)(1)),
- investment expenses under Code Sec. 163(d)(4)(C)),
- taxes described in Code Sec. 164(a)(3)),
- items described in Code Sec. 72(b)(3) with respect to the last year of an annuity,
- estate and generation skipping taxes under Code Sec. 691(c),
- expenses paid or incurred in connection with the determination, collection, or refund of any tax under Code Sec. 212(3),
- amortizable bond premium under Code Sec. 171(a)(1), and
- fiduciary expenses for an estate or trust described in Reg. §1.212-1(i) (Reg. §1.1411-4(f)(3)).

Itemized deductions that are properly allocable to net investment income must be reduced to account for any reduction that applies for general income tax purposes due to the two-percent of AGI floor on miscellaneous itemized deductions (the Code Sec. 67 limit) and the overall limit on itemized deductions for higher-income individuals (the Code Sec. 68 limit) (Reg. §1.1411-4(f)(7)). Losses under Code Sec. 165 are taken into account to the extent they do not exceed gains and were not used in calculating net gain (Reg. §1.1411-4(f)(4)).

CFCs, PFICs and QEFs. Special rules apply for an individual, estate, or trust that:

- is a U.S. shareholder of a controlled foreign corporation (CFC),
- is a U.S. person that directly or indirectly owns an interest in a passive foreign investment company (PFIC), or
- owns an interest in a domestic partnership or an S corporation that is (a) a U.S. shareholder of a CFC or (b) has elected to treat a PFIC as a qualified electing fund (QEF) (Reg. §1.1411-10(a)).

Under these rules, category (ii) income includes income derived from a Reg. §1.1411-5 trade or business that is included in income under Code Sec. 951(a) as a dividend to a U.S. shareholder from a CFC, or Code Sec. 1293(a) as income included from a QEF at the same time the income is recognized for normal Chapter 1 income tax purposes (Reg. §1.1411-10(b)).

Under the general federal tax rules, a CFC or QEF is deemed to distribute its subpart F income to U.S. shareholders. These deemed distributions are (a) included in the shareholder's gross income, (b) increase the shareholder's basis in the entity, and (c) are not treated as dividends. Conversely, when the entity makes actual distributions of its earnings and profits (E&P), amounts that were previously taxed to the shareholder as deemed distributions are (a) excludable from the shareholder's gross income, (b) reduce the shareholder's basis in the entity, (c) reduce the entity's E&P, and (d) are not treated as dividends. Since these deemed and actual distributions are not treated as dividends, it is possible that they would never be included in net investment income and, thus, would never be subject to the net investment income tax. The final regula-

LAW EXPLAINED

tions avoid this result by providing that, for purposes of the net investment income tax, actual distributions of previously taxed CFC and QEF E&P are dividends that are included in net investment income as category (i) income (Reg. § 1.1411-10(c)(1)). However, a taxpayer can elect to treat the Code Sec. 951 and Code Sec. 1293 inclusions themselves (rather than the distributions of previously taxed earnings and profits) as dividends that are included in category (i) income (Reg. § 1.1411-10(g)).

Adjustments must be made for purposes of basis adjustments that normally apply under Code Sec. 961 and Code Sec. 1293 (Reg. § 1.1411-10(d)(1)), with special rules for partners and S corporation shareholders that own interests in entities that own directly or indirectly stock of a CFC or QEF (Reg. § 1.1411-10(d)(2), (3)). Similar basis adjustment rules apply for participants in common trust funds (Reg. § 1.1411-10(d)(4)). In addition, conforming adjustments must be made to MAGI for individuals (Reg. § 1.1411-10(e)(1)) and to AGI for estates and trusts (Reg. § 1.1411-10(e)(2)). An estate or trust, or its beneficiaries, must take these adjustments into account in a manner that is reasonably consistent with the general net investment income tax rules for estates and trusts, as well as the federal income tax rules for estates and trusts (Reg. § 1.1411-10(f)).

If the taxpayer disposes of a CFC interest, the Code Sec. 1248 rules governing CFC dispositions are modified in two respects for net investment income tax purposes. First, the basis adjustments discussed above apply for purposes of determining the gain recognized on the disposition. Second, the exclusion for certain E&P applies only with respect to E&P that are attributable to (1) amounts that were taken into account as net investment income under Reg. § 1.1411-10(b), and (b) amounts that were previously included in gross income for general federal income tax purposes in a tax year beginning before December 31, 2012, and have not yet been distributed (Reg. § 1.1411-10(c)(4)).

▶ **Effective date.** The provision applies to tax years beginning after December 31, 2012 (Act Sec. 1402(a)(4) of the Health Care and Education Reconciliation Act of 2010 (P.L. 111-152). The final regulations are generally effective after December 31, 2013, and can be relied on before that date. Proposed reliance regulations issued in 2012, and now withdrawn, can be relied on prior to the effective date of the final regulations. However, to the extent that taxpayers take a position in a tax year beginning before January 1, 2014, that is inconsistent with the final regulations, and such position affects the treatment of one or more items in a tax year beginning after December 31, 2013, such taxpayer must make reasonable adjustments to ensure that their net investment income tax liability in the tax years beginning after December 31, 2013, is not inappropriately distorted. The 2013 proposed regulations are generally proposed to go into effect for tax years after December 31, 2013, and they can be relied on until they are issued as final regulations.

Law source: Law at ¶5220 and ¶5410.

— Act Sec. 1402(a)(1) of the Health Care and Education Reconciliation Act of 2010 (P.L. 111-152), adding Code Sec. 1411;

— Act Sec. 1402(a)(2), amending Code Sec. 6654(a) and (f);

— Act Sec. 1402(a)(4), providing the effective date.

LAW EXPLAINED

Reporter references: For further information, consult the following reporters.

— Standard Federal Tax Reporter, ¶32,606.021

— Tax Research Consultant, INDIV: 69,160

— Practical Tax Expert, § 1,022.15

¶620 Additional Medicare Tax on Wages and Self-Employment Income

SUMMARY OF NEW LAW

An additional 0.9 percent Medicare tax is imposed on the wages and self-employment income of certain high-income taxpayers received with respect to employment for tax years beginning after December 31, 2012.

BACKGROUND

The Federal Insurance Contributions Act (FICA), imposes two taxes on employers and employees. The first finances the federal old-age, survivors and disability insurance (OASDI) program, more commonly known as Social Security. The second is to finance hospital and hospital service insurance (HI) for those 65 years of age or older, more familiarly known as Medicare.

The employee's portion of the Social Security tax is 6.2 percent of the employee's wages, up to the Social Security wage base (Code Sec. 3101(a)). The employer's portion also equals 6.2 percent of the employee's wages, up to the Social Security wage base (Code Sec. 3111(a)). Thus, the equivalent of 12.4 percent of the employee's wages is contributed to the Social Security fund. The wage base for the Social Security portion of the FICA tax is $117,000 for 2014. The Medicare tax on an employee's wages also consists of an employee's portion and an employer's portion. The employee's portion is 1.45 percent of the employee's wages (Code Sec. 3101(b)). The employer's portion of the Medicare tax also equals 1.45 percent of the employee's wages (Code Sec. 3111(b)). Thus, the equivalent of 2.9 percent of the employee's wages is contributed to Medicare.

Individuals engaged in trade or business as sole proprietors or partners must pay self-employment tax on net earnings from self-employment. Self-employment tax has two components. The Social Security component is a 12.4 percent tax imposed on net earnings from self-employment, up to the Social Security wage base (Code Sec. 1401(a)). The wage base is $117,000 for 2014. The Medicare component is a 2.9 percent tax imposed on net earnings from self-employment, without limitation (Code Sec. 1401(b)). Thus, the combined self-employment tax rate is 15.3 percent (12.4 plus 2.9). A self-employed individual is permitted to deduct one-half of the self-employment tax liability for the year as a business expense in arriving at adjusted gross income (AGI) (Code Sec. 164(f)). Alternately, such individual is allowed to reduce self-

BACKGROUND

employment income by an amount equal to one half of the combined self-employment tax rate, or 7.65 percent (1/2 of 15.3 percent) multiplied by the taxpayer's self-employment income (Code Sec. 1402(a)(12)).

LAW EXPLAINED

Additional Medicare tax imposed on high-income taxpayers.—In addition to the 1.45 percent employee portion of the Medicare tax imposed on wages and the 2.9 percent Medicare tax on self-employment income, a 0.9 percent Medicare tax is imposed on every taxpayer (other than a corporation, estate or trust) who receives wages with respect to employment or self-employment income during any tax year beginning after December 31, 2012, in excess of $200,000 ($250,000 in the case of a joint return, $125,000 in the case of a married taxpayer filing separately) (Code Secs. 3101(b)(2) and 1401(b)(2)(A), as added and amended by the Patient Protection and Affordable Care Act (PPACA) (P.L. 111-148), and amended by the Health Care and Education Reconciliation Act of 2010 (P.L. 111-152)).

> **Comment:** For this purpose, the term "employment" is as defined under Code Sec. 3121(b) and generally includes any service, of whatever nature, performed by an employee for the person employing him, irrespective of the citizenship or residence of either.

> **Comment:** The additional Medicare tax means that wages received in connection with employment in excess of the applicable threshold amount are subject to a 2.35 percent employee portion of the Medicare tax. The Medicare tax rate for self-employment income above the applicable threshold amount is 3.8 percent.

Employer information. There is no employer portion of the additional Medicare tax, but employers may be required to withhold the employee portion. An employer is not obligated to withhold the 0.9-percent additional Medicare tax unless an employee receives wages from the employer in excess of $200,000. For this purpose, the employer is permitted to disregard the amount of wages received by the taxpayer's spouse (Code Sec. 3102(f)(1), as added by PPACA). The employer is required to begin withholding the additional tax in the pay period in which it pays wages in excess of $200,000 to an employee. Withholding does not begin at the beginning of the year even if an employee's annual Medicare wages are expected to exceed $200,000. The employer is not required to notify the employee when it begins to withhold the additional tax (IRS Frequently Asked Questions, *Questions and Answers for the Additional Medicare Tax*).

Corrections. If an employer deducts less than the correct amount of the additional tax from the wages of an employee, the employer is required to collect the correct amount from the employee's wages or other remuneration before the end of the calendar year (Reg. § 31.6205-1(d)(1)). The employer is liable for the correct amount of tax that it was required to withhold. If the employee subsequently pays the tax that the employer failed to deduct, the tax will not be collected from the employer. The employer will not be relieved of its liability for payment of the tax required to be withheld unless it can show that the tax has been paid. The employer will remain

¶620

LAW EXPLAINED

subject to any applicable penalties or additions to tax resulting from the failure to withhold as required, however (Code Sec. 3102(f)(3), as added by PPACA; Reg. §31.3102-4(c)).

> **Compliance Note:** Employers may use Form 4669 and Form 4670 to request relief from paying additional Medicare tax that has already been paid by an employee.

If an employer deducts more than the correct amount of the additional tax from the wages of an employee, the employer must repay or reimburse the employee prior to the end of the calendar year in which the overcollection was made by applying the overcollected amount against the employee's FICA taxes during the year, so long as the employer can locate the employee (Reg. §31.6413(a)-1(a)(2)(ii) and (iv)). If an employer repays or reimburses an employee for overcollected additional Medicare tax, the employer may make an interest-free adjustment on a corrected employment tax return only if the repayment or reimbursement occurred in the year in which the overcollection was made (Reg. §31.6413(a)-2(b)(2)). If the overcollected amount is not discovered by the employer in the same year in which the wages were paid, the employer should report the amount of withheld additional Medicare tax on the employee's Form W-2 so that the employee may obtain credit for tax withheld (Reg. §31.6402(a)-2(b); IRS Frequently Asked Questions, *Questions and Answers for the Additional Medicare Tax*).

If an employer reports to the IRS less than the correct amount of additional Medicare tax required to be withheld, and the employer ascertains the error after filing its employment tax return, the employer must correct the error through an interest-free adjustment in the same calendar year in which the relevant wages or compensation were paid to the employee, unless: (1) the underpayment is attributable to an administrative error, (2) Code Sec. 3509 applies to determine the amount of the underpayment (due to the employer's failure to treat the individual as an employee), or (3) the adjustment is the result of an IRS examination (Reg. §31.6205-1(b)(4)).

If an employer overpays the additional Medicare tax to the IRS, the employer cannot claim a credit or refund for the overpayment if the employer deducted or withheld the overpaid additional tax from the employee's wages or compensation (Reg. §31.6402(a)-2(a)(1)(iii)). An employer should only claim a refund of overpaid additional Medicare tax if the employer did not deduct or withhold the overpaid amount from the employee's wages, in which case the employer should correct the error by making an interest-free adjustment on the appropriate corrected return (IRS Frequently Asked Questions, *Questions and Answers for the Additional Medicare Tax*).

Fringe benefits. If an employee receives wages from an employer in excess of $200,000 and the wages include taxable non-cash fringe benefits, the employer calculates wages for purposes of withholding additional Medicare tax in the same way that it calculates wages for withholding the regular Medicare tax.

The employer is required to withhold the additional Medicare tax on total wages, including taxable non-cash fringe benefits, in excess of $200,000. The value of taxable non-cash fringe benefits must be included in wages and the employer must withhold the applicable additional Medicare tax and deposit the tax under the rules for

LAW EXPLAINED

employment tax withholding and deposits that apply to taxable non-cash fringe benefits.

Tips. To the extent that tips and other wages exceed $200,000, an employer applies the same withholding rules for the additional Medicare tax as it does for the regular Medicare tax.

An employer withholds the additional tax on the employee's reported tips from wages it pays to the employee. If the employee does not receive enough wages for the employer to withhold all the taxes that the employee owes, including the additional Medicare tax, the employee may give the employer money to pay the rest of the taxes. If the employee does not give the employer money to pay the taxes, then the employer makes a current period adjustment on its employment tax return to reflect any uncollected employee social security, Medicare, or additional Medicare tax on reported tips. However, unlike the uncollected portion of the regular Medicare tax, the uncollected additional Medicare tax is not reported in box 12 of Form W-2 with code B.

Group-term life insurance. The imputed cost of coverage in excess of $50,000 is subject to social security and Medicare taxes, and to the extent that, in combination with other wages, it exceeds $200,000, it is also subject to additional Medicare tax withholding.

However, when group-term life insurance over $50,000 is provided to an employee (including retirees) after his or her termination, the employee share of social security and Medicare taxes and the additional Medicare tax on that period of coverage is paid by the former employee with his or her tax return and is not collected by the employer. In this case, an employer should report this income as wages on its employment tax return, and make a current period adjustment to reflect any uncollected employee social security, Medicare, or additional Medicare tax on group-term life insurance. However, unlike the uncollected portion of the regular Medicare tax, an employer may not report the uncollected additional Medicare tax in box 12 of Form W-2 with code N.

Third-party sick pay. Wages paid by an employer and a third-party payor of sick pay need to be aggregated to determine whether the $200,000 withholding threshold has been met. The same rules that assign responsibility for sick pay reporting and payment of regular Medicare tax based on which party is treated as the employer (that is, the employer, the employer's agent, or a third party that is not the employer's agent) apply also to the additional Medicare tax.

Non-qualified deferred compensation. An employer calculates wages for purposes of withholding additional Medicare tax from non-qualified deferred compensation in the same way that it calculates wages for withholding the regular Medicare tax.

Thus, if an employee has amounts deferred under a non-qualified deferred compensation plan and the compensation is taken into account as wages for FICA tax purposes, the compensation would likewise be taken into account under a special timing rule for purposes of determining an employer's obligation to withhold the additional Medicare tax.

¶620

LAW EXPLAINED

Mergers and acquisitions. When corporate acquisitions meet certain requirements, wages paid by the predecessor are treated as if paid by the successor for purposes of applying the social security wage base and for applying the additional Medicare tax withholding threshold (that is, $200,000 in a calendar year).

Subsidiaries. When an employee is performing services for multiple subsidiaries of a company, and each subsidiary is an employer of the employee with regard to the services the employee performs for that subsidiary, the wages paid by the payor on behalf of each subsidiary should be combined only if the payor is a common paymaster.

Common paymasters. Liability to withhold the additional Medicare tax with respect to wages disbursed by a common paymaster is computed as if there was a single employer, just as it is for application of the social security wage base.

Agents. Wages paid by an agent with an approved Form 2678, Employer/Payer Appointment of Agent, on behalf of an employer should not be combined with wages paid to the same employee by any of the above other parties in determining whether to withhold additional Medicare tax.

Employee leasing companies. Generally, if an employer provides wages in excess of the $200,000 withholding threshold to an employee leasing company to pay to an employee, the additional Medicare tax should be withheld from the wages in excess of $200,000. The employer is ultimately responsible for the deposit and payment of federal tax liabilities. Even though the employer forwards tax payments to a third party to make the tax deposits, the employer may be responsible for the tax liability.

Employee information. In the case of a joint return, the additional tax 0.9 percent Medicare tax on wages is imposed on the combined wages of the employee and the employee's spouse, unlike with the general 1.45 percent Medicare tax (Reg. § 31.3101-2).

The amount withheld by the employer does not always match the employee's liability. For married taxpayers filing jointly, an employer may withhold on wages exceeding $200,000 even though the couple's joint wages do not exceed the $250,000 threshold that triggers liability for the tax. The employer must withhold the tax; the employee can claim a credit for the withheld tax. Alternatively, an employee with wages above $200,000 may be subject to the additional tax without the tax being withheld from the employee's wages. This outcome may occur if the employee receives wages from more than one employer or if the employee's spouse receives wages (IRS Frequently Asked Questions, *Questions and Answers for the Additional Medicare Tax*). The employee is responsible for any portion of the additional 0.9-percent tax that is not withheld, unlike the 1.45-percent tax for which the employee has no personal liability (Code Sec. 3102(f)(2), as added by PPACA). The employee calculates and reports the tax on his or her Form 1040 income tax return for the year (Reg. § 31.6011(a)-1(g)).

LAW EXPLAINED

> **Example 1:** Cathy, who is married and files a joint return, receives $190,000 in compensation from her employer in 2015. Derek, Cathy's spouse, receives $150,000 in compensation from his employer in 2015. Neither Cathy's nor Derek's compensation is in excess of $200,000, so neither of their employers is required to withhold the additional Medicare tax. Cathy and Derek are liable to pay the additional Medicare tax on $90,000 ($340,000 minus the $250,000 threshold for a joint return). They therefore must include an additional tax of $810 on their 2015 income tax return ($90,000 × 0.9%).

If an employer withholds more than the correct amount of the additional Medicare tax, and the overcollection is not corrected and the employee does not receive a repayment or reimbursement from the employer, then the employee may file a claim for refund or credit on Form 1040 or Form 1040X (Reg. § 31.6402(a)-2(b)(3)).

> **Compliance Note:** Employees must use Form 8959, Additional Medicare Tax, to calculate the individual's tax liability resulting from the additional Medicare tax.

> **Comment:** If an employee repays wages to the employer (such as sign on bonuses paid to employees that are subject to repayment if certain conditions are not satisfied), the employer cannot make an adjustment or file a claim for refund for additional Medicare tax withholding because the employee determines liability for additional Medicare tax on his or her income tax return for the prior year; however, the employee may be able to file an amended return claiming a refund of the additional Medicare tax.

Self-employment. The 0.9 percent additional Medicare tax applies to both employees and self-employed individuals. If an individual earns both wages and self-employment income, then the threshold amounts at which the additional Medicare tax applies to self-employment income are reduced by the amount of wages earned by the individual, but not below zero (Code Sec. 1401(b)(2), as added by PPACA, and amended by the 2010 Reconciliation Act; Reg. § 1.1401-1(d)).

> **Caution:** The text of Code Sec. 1401(b)(2) refers to Code Sec. 3121(b)(2), but it appears that this reference is intended to be to Code Sec. 3101(b)(2).

An individual with both FICA wages and self-employment income calculates his or her liability for the additional Medicare tax in three steps:

(1) Calculate the additional Medicare tax on any wages in excess of the applicable threshold for the filing status, without regard to whether any tax was withheld.

(2) Reduce the applicable threshold for the filing status by the total amount of Medicare wages received, but not below zero.

(3) Calculate the additional Medicare tax on any self-employment income in excess of the reduced threshold.

> **Example 2:** Steve, a single filer, has $145,000 in self-employment income and $130,000 in wages in 2015. Steve's wages are not in excess of the $200,000 threshold for single filers, so Steve is not liable for any additional Medicare tax

LAW EXPLAINED

on these wages. However, the $130,000 of wages reduces the self-employment income threshold to $70,000 ($200,000 threshold minus the $130,000 of wages). Steve is liable to pay the additional Medicare tax on $75,000 of self-employment income ($145,000 in self-employment income minus the reduced threshold of $70,000).

Example 3: Mary, who is married filing separate, has $175,000 in wages and $50,000 in self-employment income in 2015. She is liable to pay additional Medicare tax on $50,000 of her wages ($175,000 minus the $125,000 threshold for married persons who file separate). Before calculating the additional Medicare tax on Mary's self-employment income, the $125,000 threshold for married persons who file separate is reduced by her $175,000 in wages, to $0 (reduced, but not below zero). Mary is therefore liable to pay additional Medicare tax on $50,000 of self-employment income ($50,000 in self-employment income minus the reduced threshold of $0). In total, she is liable to pay additional Medicare tax on $100,000 ($50,000 of her wages and $50,000 of her self-employment income).

Compliance Note: Self-employed individuals must use Form 8959, Additional Medicare Tax, to calculate the individual's tax liability resulting from the additional Medicare tax.

Generally, one-half of self-employment taxes are deductible, but this deduction does not include any of the 0.9-percent additional Medicare tax (Code Sec. 164(f), as amended by PPACA). Similarly, taxpayers who elect to reduce self-employment income by an amount equal to one half of the combined self-employment tax rate do not include the additional Medicare tax in the rate used to make such computation (Code Sec. 1402(a)(12)(B), as amended by PPACA).

Underpayment of estimated tax penalty. An individual subject to the 0.9-percent additional Medicare tax may be required to make estimated tax payments throughout the year (Code Sec. 6654(m), as added by the 2010 Reconciliation Act). The individual cannot designate any estimated payments specifically for the additional Medicare tax; any estimated tax payments will apply to any and all tax liabilities on the individual's Form 1040, including any additional Medicare tax liability (IRS Frequently Asked Questions, *Questions and Answers for the Additional Medicare Tax*).

Comment: As an alternative to making estimated payments, an employee may request on Form W-4 that the employer withhold additional amounts from the employee's wages.

▶ **Effective date.** The provision applies with respect to remuneration received, and tax years beginning, after December 31, 2012 (Act Secs. 9015(c) and 10906(c) of the Patient Protection and Affordable Care Act (PPACA) (P.L. 111-148) and Act Sec. 1402(b)(3) of the Health Care and Education Reconciliation Act of 2010 (P.L. 111-152)). The regulations under Code Secs. 1401, 3101, and 3102 apply to quarters beginning after November 29, 2013. Taxpayers may rely on the rules contained in the proposed regulations under Code

LAW EXPLAINED

Sec. 3101 for quarters beginning before that date. The regulations under Code Sec. 6011 apply to tax years beginning after November 29, 2013. The regulations under Code Secs. 6205, 6402, and 6413 apply to adjustments made and claims for refund filed after November 29, 2013. Taxpayers may rely on the rules contained in the proposed regulations under Code Sec. 6413 for adjusted returns filed before that date.

Law source: Law at ¶5110, ¶5200, ¶5210, ¶5230, ¶5240, and ¶5410.

— Act Secs. 9015(a)(1) and 10906(a) of the Patient Protection and Affordable Care Act (PPACA) (P.L. 111-148), amending and redesignating Code Sec. 3101(b) as Code Sec. 3101(b)(1), deleting Code Sec. 3101(b)(1)-(6), and adding and amending Code Sec. 3101(b)(2);

— Act Sec. 1402(b)(1)(A) of the Health Care and Education Reconciliation Act of 2010 (P.L. 111-152), amending Code Sec. 3101(b)(2), as added and amended by PPACA;

— Act Sec. 9015(a)(2) of PPACA, adding Code Sec. 3102(f);

— Act Secs. 9015(b)(1) and 10906(b) of PPACA, amending and redesignating Code Sec. 1401(b) as Code Sec. 1401(b)(1), and adding and amending Code Sec. 1401(b)(2);

— Act Sec. 1402(b)(1)(B) of the 2010 Reconciliation Act, amending Code Sec. 1401(b)(2), as added by PPACA;

— Act Secs. 9015(b)(2)(A) of PPACA, amending Code Sec. 164(f);

— Act Secs. 9015(b)(2)(B) of PPACA, amending Code Sec. 1402(a)(12)(B);

— Act Sec. 1402(b)(2) of the 2010 Reconciliation Act, redesignating Code Sec. 6654(m) as Code Sec. 6654(n) and adding new Code Sec. 6654(m);

— Act Secs. 9015(c) and 10906(c) of PPACA and Act Sec. 1402(b)(3) of the 2010 Reconciliation Act, providing the effective date.

Reporter references: For further information, consult the following reporters.

— Standard Federal Tax Reporter, ¶37,523.01 and ¶32,543.01

— Tax Research Consultant, INDIV: 69,100

— Practical Tax Expert, §22,205.15 and §23,105

Code Sections Added, Amended Or Repealed

[¶ 5001]

INTRODUCTION.

The Internal Revenue Code provisions amended by the Patient Protection and Affordable Care Act (P.L. 111-148), the Health Care and Education Reconciliation Act of 2010 (P.L. 111-152), the TRICARE Affirmation Act (P.L. 111-159), an act to clarify the health care provided by the Secretary of Veterans Affairs that constitutes minimum essential coverage (P.L. 111-173), the Creating Small Business Jobs Act of 2010 (P.L. 111-240), the Medicare and Medicaid Extenders Act of 2010 (P.L. 111-309), the Comprehensive 1099 Taxpayer Protection and Repayment of Exchange Subsidy Overpayments Act of 2011 (P.L. 112-9), the Department of Defense and Full-Year Continuing Appropriations Act, 2011 (P.L. 112-10), the Surface and Air Transportation Programs Extension Act of 2011 (P.L. 112-30), the VOW to Hire Heroes Act of 2011 (P.L. 112-56), the Surface Transportation Extension Act of 2012 (P.L. 112-102), the Temporary Surface Transportation Extension Act of 2012 (P.L. 112-140), the Highway Investment, Job Creation, and Economic Growth Act of 2012 (P.L. 112-141), are shown in the following paragraphs. Deleted Code material or the text of the Code Section prior to amendment appears in the amendment notes following each amended Code provision. *Any changed or added material is set out in italics.*

[¶ 5010] *CODE SEC. 36B. REFUNDABLE CREDIT FOR COVERAGE UNDER A QUALIFIED HEALTH PLAN.*

(a) IN GENERAL.—In the case of an applicable taxpayer, there shall be allowed as a credit against the tax imposed by this subtitle for any taxable year an amount equal to the premium assistance credit amount of the taxpayer for the taxable year.

(b) PREMIUM ASSISTANCE CREDIT AMOUNT.—For purposes of this section—

(1) IN GENERAL.—The term "premium assistance credit amount" means, with respect to any taxable year, the sum of the premium assistance amounts determined under paragraph (2) with respect to all coverage months of the taxpayer occurring during the taxable year.

(2) PREMIUM ASSISTANCE AMOUNT.—The premium assistance amount determined under this subsection with respect to any coverage month is the amount equal to the lesser of—

(A) the monthly premiums for such month for 1 or more qualified health plans offered in the individual market within a State which cover the taxpayer, the taxpayer's spouse, or any dependent (as defined in section 152) of the taxpayer and which were enrolled in through an Exchange established by the State under 1311 of the Patient Protection and Affordable Care Act, or

(B) the excess (if any) of—

(i) the adjusted monthly premium for such month for the applicable second lowest cost silver plan with respect to the taxpayer, over

(ii) an amount equal to 1/12 of the product of the applicable percentage and the taxpayer's household income for the taxable year.

(3) OTHER TERMS AND RULES RELATING TO PREMIUM ASSISTANCE AMOUNTS.—For purposes of paragraph (2)—

(A) APPLICABLE PERCENTAGE.—

(i) IN GENERAL.—Except as provided in clause (ii), the applicable percentage for any taxable year shall be the percentage such that the applicable percentage for any taxpayer whose household income is within an income tier specified in the following table shall increase, on a sliding scale in a linear manner, from the initial premium percentage to the final premium percentage specified in such table for such income tier:

In the case of household income (expressed as a percent of poverty line) within the following income tier:	The initial premium percentage is—	The final premium percentage is—
Up to 133%	2.0%	2.0%
133% up to 150%	3.0%	4.0%
150% up to 200%	4.0%	6.3%
200% up to 250%	6.3%	8.05%
250% up to 300%	8.05%	9.5%
300% up to 400%	9.5%	9.5%

(ii) INDEXING.—

(I) IN GENERAL.—Subject to subclause (II), in the case of taxable years beginning in any calendar year after 2014, the initial and final applicable percentages under clause (i) (as in effect for the preceding calendar year after application of this clause) shall be adjusted to reflect the excess of the rate of premium growth for the preceding calendar year over the rate of income growth for the preceding calendar year.

(II) ADDITIONAL ADJUSTMENT.—Except as provided in subclause (III), in the case of any calendar year after 2018, the percentages described in subclause (I) shall, in addition to the adjustment under subclause (I), be adjusted to reflect the excess (if any) of the rate of premium growth estimated under subclause (I) for the preceding calendar year over the rate of growth in the consumer price index for the preceding calendar year.

(III) FAILSAFE.—Subclause (II) shall apply for any calendar year only if the aggregate amount of premium tax credits under this section and cost-sharing reductions under section 1402 of the Patient Protection and Affordable Care Act for the preceding calendar year exceeds an amount equal to 0.504 percent of the gross domestic product for the preceding calendar year.

(B) APPLICABLE SECOND LOWEST COST SILVER PLAN.—The applicable second lowest cost silver plan with respect to any applicable taxpayer is the second lowest cost silver plan of the individual market in the rating area in which the taxpayer resides which—

(i) is offered through the same Exchange through which the qualified health plans taken into account under paragraph (2)(A) were offered, and

(ii) provides—

(I) self-only coverage in the case of an applicable taxpayer—

(aa) whose tax for the taxable year is determined under section 1(c) (relating to unmarried individuals other than surviving spouses and heads of households) and who is not allowed a deduction under section 151 for the taxable year with respect to a dependent, or

(bb) who is not described in item (aa) but who purchases only self-only coverage, and

(II) family coverage in the case of any other applicable taxpayer.

If a taxpayer files a joint return and no credit is allowed under this section with respect to 1 of the spouses by reason of subsection (e), the taxpayer shall be treated as described in clause (ii)(I) unless a deduction is allowed under section 151 for the taxable year with respect to a dependent other than either spouse and subsection (e) does not apply to the dependent.

(C) ADJUSTED MONTHLY PREMIUM.—The adjusted monthly premium for an applicable second lowest cost silver plan is the monthly premium which would have been charged (for the rating area with respect to which the premiums under paragraph (2)(A) were determined) for the plan if each

individual covered under a qualified health plan taken into account under paragraph (2)(A) were covered by such silver plan and the premium was adjusted only for the age of each such individual in the manner allowed under section 2701 of the Public Health Service Act. In the case of a State participating in the wellness discount demonstration project under section 2705(d) of the Public Health Service Act, the adjusted monthly premium shall be determined without regard to any premium discount or rebate under such project.

(D) *ADDITIONAL BENEFITS.—If—*

(i) *a qualified health plan under section 1302(b)(5) of the Patient Protection and Affordable Care Act offers benefits in addition to the essential health benefits required to be provided by the plan, or*

(ii) *a State requires a qualified health plan under section 1311(d)(3)(B) of such Act to cover benefits in addition to the essential health benefits required to be provided by the plan,*

the portion of the premium for the plan properly allocable (under rules prescribed by the Secretary of Health and Human Services) to such additional benefits shall not be taken into account in determining either the monthly premium or the adjusted monthly premium under paragraph (2).

(E) *SPECIAL RULE FOR PEDIATRIC DENTAL COVERAGE.—For purposes of determining the amount of any monthly premium, if an individual enrolls in both a qualified health plan and a plan described in section 1311(d)(2)(B)(ii)(I) of the Patient Protection and Affordable Care Act for any plan year, the portion of the premium for the plan described in such section that (under regulations prescribed by the Secretary) is properly allocable to pediatric dental benefits which are included in the essential health benefits required to be provided by a qualified health plan under section 1302(b)(1)(J) of such Act shall be treated as a premium payable for a qualified health plan.*

[CCH Explanation at ¶ 210.]

Amendments

• **2010, Health Care and Education Reconciliation Act of 2010 (P.L. 111-152)**

P.L. 111-152, § 1001(a)(1)(A)-(B):

Amended Code Sec. 36B, as added by section 1401 of the Patient Protection and Affordable Care Act (P.L. 111-148) and amended by section 10105, in clause (i) of subsection (b)(3)(A), by striking "with respect to any taxpayer" and all that follows up to the end period and inserting "for any taxable year shall be the percentage such that the applicable percentage for any taxpayer whose household income is within an income tier specified in the following table shall increase, on a sliding scale in a linear manner, from the initial premium percentage to the final premium percentage specified in such table for such income tier:" and a new table; and by striking clauses (ii) and (iii) of subsection (b)(3)(A) and inserting a new clause (ii). **Effective** 3-30-2010. Prior to amendment, Code Sec. 36B(b)(3)(A) read as follows:

(A) APPLICABLE PERCENTAGE.—

(i) IN GENERAL.—Except as provided in clause (ii), the applicable percentage with respect to any taxpayer for any taxable year is equal to 2.8 percent, increased by the number of percentage points (not greater than 7) which bears the same ratio to 7 percentage points as—

(I) the taxpayer's household income for the taxable year in excess of 100 percent of the poverty line for a family of the size involved, bears to

(II) an amount equal to 200 percent of the poverty line for a family of the size involved.

(ii) SPECIAL RULE FOR TAXPAYERS UNDER 133 PERCENT OF POVERTY LINE.—If a taxpayer's household income for the taxable year equals or exceeds 100 percent, but not more than 133 percent, of the poverty line for a family of the size involved, the taxpayer's applicable percentage shall be 2 percent.

(iii) INDEXING.—In the case of taxable years beginning in any calendar year after 2014, the Secretary shall adjust the initial and final applicable percentages under clause (i), and the 2 percent under clause (ii), for the calendar year to reflect the excess of the rate of premium growth between the preceding calendar year and 2013 over the rate of income growth for such period.

• **2010, Patient Protection and Affordable Care Act (P.L. 111-148)**

P.L. 111-148, § 10105(a):

Amended Code Sec. 36B(b)(3)(A)(ii), as added by Act Sec. 1401(a), by striking "is in excess of" and inserting "equals or exceeds". **Effective** 3-23-2010.

(c) *DEFINITION AND RULES RELATING TO APPLICABLE TAXPAYERS, COVERAGE MONTHS, AND QUALIFIED HEALTH PLAN.—For purposes of this section—*

(1) *APPLICABLE TAXPAYER.—*

(A) *IN GENERAL.—The term "applicable taxpayer" means, with respect to any taxable year, a taxpayer whose household income for the taxable year equals or exceeds 100 percent but does not exceed 400 percent of an amount equal to the poverty line for a family of the size involved.*

(B) *SPECIAL RULE FOR CERTAIN INDIVIDUALS LAWFULLY PRESENT IN THE UNITED STATES.—If—*

(i) *a taxpayer has a household income which is not greater than 100 percent of an amount equal to the poverty line for a family of the size involved, and*

(ii) the taxpayer is an alien lawfully present in the United States, but is not eligible for the medicaid program under title XIX of the Social Security Act by reason of such alien status,

the taxpayer shall, for purposes of the credit under this section, be treated as an applicable taxpayer with a household income which is equal to 100 percent of the poverty line for a family of the size involved.

(C) MARRIED COUPLES MUST FILE JOINT RETURN.—If the taxpayer is married (within the meaning of section 7703) at the close of the taxable year, the taxpayer shall be treated as an applicable taxpayer only if the taxpayer and the taxpayer's spouse file a joint return for the taxable year.

(D) DENIAL OF CREDIT TO DEPENDENTS.—No credit shall be allowed under this section to any individual with respect to whom a deduction under section 151 is allowable to another taxpayer for a taxable year beginning in the calendar year in which such individual's taxable year begins.

(2) COVERAGE MONTH.—For purposes of this subsection—

(A) IN GENERAL.—The term "coverage month" means, with respect to an applicable taxpayer, any month if—

(i) as of the first day of such month the taxpayer, the taxpayer's spouse, or any dependent of the taxpayer is covered by a qualified health plan described in subsection (b)(2)(A) that was enrolled in through an Exchange established by the State under section 1311 of the Patient Protection and Affordable Care Act, and

(ii) the premium for coverage under such plan for such month is paid by the taxpayer (or through advance payment of the credit under subsection (a) under section 1412 of the Patient Protection and Affordable Care Act).

(B) EXCEPTION FOR MINIMUM ESSENTIAL COVERAGE.—

(i) IN GENERAL.—The term "coverage month" shall not include any month with respect to an individual if for such month the individual is eligible for minimum essential coverage other than eligibility for coverage described in section 5000A(f)(1)(C) (relating to coverage in the individual market).

(ii) MINIMUM ESSENTIAL COVERAGE.—The term "minimum essential coverage" has the meaning given such term by section 5000A(f).

(C) SPECIAL RULE FOR EMPLOYER-SPONSORED MINIMUM ESSENTIAL COVERAGE.—For purposes of subparagraph (B)—

(i) COVERAGE MUST BE AFFORDABLE.—Except as provided in clause (iii), an employee shall not be treated as eligible for minimum essential coverage if such coverage—

(I) consists of an eligible employer-sponsored plan (as defined in section 5000A(f)(2)), and

(II) the employee's required contribution (within the meaning of section 5000A(e)(1)(B)) with respect to the plan exceeds 9.5 percent of the applicable taxpayer's household income.

This clause shall also apply to an individual who is eligible to enroll in the plan by reason of a relationship the individual bears to the employee.

(ii) COVERAGE MUST PROVIDE MINIMUM VALUE.—Except as provided in clause (iii), an employee shall not be treated as eligible for minimum essential coverage if such coverage consists of an eligible employer-sponsored plan (as defined in section 5000A(f)(2)) and the plan's share of the total allowed costs of benefits provided under the plan is less than 60 percent of such costs.

(iii) EMPLOYEE OR FAMILY MUST NOT BE COVERED UNDER EMPLOYER PLAN.—Clauses (i) and (ii) shall not apply if the employee (or any individual described in the last sentence of clause (i)) is covered under the eligible employer-sponsored plan or the grandfathered health plan.

(iv) INDEXING.—In the case of plan years beginning in any calendar year after 2014, the Secretary shall adjust the 9.5 percent under clause (i)(II) in the same manner as the percentages are adjusted under subsection (b)(3)(A)(ii).

(3) DEFINITIONS AND OTHER RULES.—

(A) QUALIFIED HEALTH PLAN.—The term "qualified health plan" has the meaning given such term by section 1301(a) of the Patient Protection and Affordable Care Act, except that such term shall not include a qualified health plan which is a catastrophic plan described in section 1302(e) of such Act.

(B) GRANDFATHERED HEALTH PLAN.—The term "grandfathered health plan" has the meaning given such term by section 1251 of the Patient Protection and Affordable Care Act.

[CCH Explanation at ¶ 210.]

Amendments

• **2011, Department of Defense and Full-Year Continuing Appropriations Act, 2011 (P.L. 112-10)**

P.L. 112-10, § 1858(b)(1):

Amended Code Sec. 36B(c)(2) by striking subparagraph (D). **Effective** as if included in the provision of, and the amendments made by, the provision of the Patient Protection and Affordable Care Act (P.L. 111-148) to which it relates [**effective** for tax years beginning after 12-31-2013.—CCH]. Prior to being stricken, Code Sec. 36B(c)(2)(D) read as follows:

(D) EXCEPTION FOR INDIVIDUAL RECEIVING FREE CHOICE VOUCHERS.—The term "coverage month" shall not include any month in which such individual has a free choice voucher provided under section 10108 of the Patient Protection and Affordable Care Act.

• **2010, Health Care and Education Reconciliation Act of 2010 (P.L. 111-152)**

P.L. 111-152, § 1001(a)(2)(A)-(B):

Amended Code Sec. 36B, as added by section 1401 and amended by section 10105 of the Patient Protection and Affordable Care Act (P.L. 111-148), by striking "9.8 percent" in clauses (i)(II) and (iv) of subsection (c)(2)(C) and inserting "9.5 percent", and by striking "(b)(3)(A)(iii)" in clause (iv) of subsection (c)(2)(C) and inserting "(b)(3)(A)(ii)". **Effective** 3-30-2010.

• **2010, Patient Protection and Affordable Care Act (P.L. 111-148)**

P.L. 111-148, § 10105(b):

Amended Code Sec. 36B(c)(1)(A), as added by Act Sec. 1401(a), by inserting "equals or" before "exceeds". **Effective** 3-23-2010.

P.L. 111-148, § 10105(c):

Amended Code Sec. 36B(c)(2)(C)(iv), as added by Act Sec. 1401(a), by striking "subsection (b)(3)(A)(ii)" and inserting "subsection (b)(3)(A)(iii)". **Effective** 3-23-2010.

P.L. 111-148, § 10108(h)(1):

Amended Code Sec. 36B(c)(2), as added by Act Sec. 1401, by adding at the end a new subparagraph (D). **Effective** for tax years beginning after 12-31-2013.

(d) TERMS RELATING TO INCOME AND FAMILIES.—For purposes of this section—

(1) FAMILY SIZE.—The family size involved with respect to any taxpayer shall be equal to the number of individuals for whom the taxpayer is allowed a deduction under section 151 (relating to allowance of deduction for personal exemptions) for the taxable year.

(2) HOUSEHOLD INCOME.—

(A) HOUSEHOLD INCOME.—The term "household income" means, with respect to any taxpayer, an amount equal to the sum of—

(i) the modified adjusted gross income of the taxpayer, plus

(ii) the aggregate modified adjusted gross incomes of all other individuals who—

(I) were taken into account in determining the taxpayer's family size under paragraph (1), and

(II) were required to file a return of tax imposed by section 1 for the taxable year.

(B) MODIFIED ADJUSTED GROSS INCOME.—The term "modified adjusted gross income" means adjusted gross income increased by—

(i) any amount excluded from gross income under section 911,

(ii) any amount of interest received or accrued by the taxpayer during the taxable year which is exempt from tax, and

(iii) an amount equal to the portion of the taxpayer's social security benefits (as defined in section 86(d)) which is not included in gross income under section 86 for the taxable year.

(3) POVERTY LINE.—

(A) IN GENERAL.—The term "poverty line" has the meaning given that term in section 2110(c)(5) of the Social Security Act (42 U.S.C. 1397jj(c)(5)).

(B) POVERTY LINE USED.—In the case of any qualified health plan offered through an Exchange for coverage during a taxable year beginning in a calendar year, the poverty line used shall be the most recently published poverty line as of the 1st day of the regular enrollment period for coverage during such calendar year.

[CCH Explanation at ¶ 210.]

Amendments

• **2011, (P.L. 112-56)**

P.L. 112-56, § 401(a):

Amended Code Sec. 36B(d)(2)(B) by striking "and" at the end of clause (i), by striking the period at the end of clause (ii) and inserting ", and", and by adding at the end a new clause (iii). **Effective** 11-21-2011.

• **2010, Health Care and Education Reconciliation Act of 2010 (P.L. 111-152)**

P.L. 111-152, § 1004(a)(1)(A):

Amended Code Sec. 36B(d)(2)(A)(i)-(ii), as added by section 1401 of the Patient Protection and Affordable Care Act (P.L. 111-148), by striking "modified gross" each place it appears and inserting "modified adjusted gross". **Effective** 3-30-2010.

P.L. 111-152, § 1004(a)(2)(A):

Amended Code Sec. 36B(d)(2)(B), as added by section 1401 of the Patient Protection and Affordable Care Act (P.L. 111-148). **Effective** 3-30-2010. Prior to amendment, Code Sec. 36B(d)(2)(B) read as follows:

(B) MODIFIED GROSS INCOME.—The term "modified gross income" means gross income—

(i) decreased by the amount of any deduction allowable under paragraph (1), (3), (4), or (10) of section 62(a),

(ii) increased by the amount of interest received or accrued during the taxable year which is exempt from tax imposed by this chapter, and

(iii) determined without regard to sections 911, 931, and 933.

(e) RULES FOR INDIVIDUALS NOT LAWFULLY PRESENT.—

(1) IN GENERAL.—If 1 or more individuals for whom a taxpayer is allowed a deduction under section 151 (relating to allowance of deduction for personal exemptions) for the taxable year (including the taxpayer or his spouse) are individuals who are not lawfully present—

(A) the aggregate amount of premiums otherwise taken into account under clauses (i) and (ii) of subsection (b)(2)(A) shall be reduced by the portion (if any) of such premiums which is attributable to such individuals, and

(B) for purposes of applying this section, the determination as to what percentage a taxpayer's household income bears to the poverty level for a family of the size involved shall be made under one of the following methods:

(i) A method under which—

(I) the taxpayer's family size is determined by not taking such individuals into account, and

(II) the taxpayer's household income is equal to the product of the taxpayer's household income (determined without regard to this subsection) and a fraction—

(aa) the numerator of which is the poverty line for the taxpayer's family size determined after application of subclause (I), and

(bb) the denominator of which is the poverty line for the taxpayer's family size determined without regard to subclause (I).

(ii) A comparable method reaching the same result as the method under clause (i).

(2) LAWFULLY PRESENT.—For purposes of this section, an individual shall be treated as lawfully present only if the individual is, and is reasonably expected to be for the entire period of enrollment for which the credit under this section is being claimed, a citizen or national of the United States or an alien lawfully present in the United States.

(3) SECRETARIAL AUTHORITY.—The Secretary of Health and Human Services, in consultation with the Secretary, shall prescribe rules setting forth the methods by which calculations of family size and household income are made for purposes of this subsection. Such rules shall be designed to ensure that the least burden is placed on individuals enrolling in qualified health plans through an Exchange and taxpayers eligible for the credit allowable under this section.

(f) RECONCILIATION OF CREDIT AND ADVANCE CREDIT.—

(1) IN GENERAL.—*The amount of the credit allowed under this section for any taxable year shall be reduced (but not below zero) by the amount of any advance payment of such credit under section 1412 of the Patient Protection and Affordable Care Act.*

(2) EXCESS ADVANCE PAYMENTS.—

(A) IN GENERAL.—*If the advance payments to a taxpayer under section 1412 of the Patient Protection and Affordable Care Act for a taxable year exceed the credit allowed by this section (determined without regard to paragraph (1)), the tax imposed by this chapter for the taxable year shall be increased by the amount of such excess.*

(B) LIMITATION ON INCREASE.—

(i) IN GENERAL.—*In the case of a taxpayer whose household income is less than 400 percent of the poverty line for the size of the family involved for the taxable year, the amount of the increase under subparagraph (A) shall in no event exceed the applicable dollar amount determined in accordance with the following table (one-half of such amount in the case of a taxpayer whose tax is determined under section 1(c) for the taxable year):*

If the household income (expressed as a percent of poverty line) is:	The applicable dollar amount is:
Less than 200%	$600
At least 200% but less than 300%	$1,500
At least 300% but less than 400%	$2,500.

(ii) INDEXING OF AMOUNT.—*In the case of any calendar year beginning after 2014, each of the dollar amounts in the table contained under clause (i) shall be increased by an amount equal to—*

(I) such dollar amount, multiplied by

(II) the cost-of-living adjustment determined under section 1(f)(3) for the calendar year, determined by substituting "calendar year 2013" for "calendar year 1992" in subparagraph (B) thereof.

If the amount of any increase under clause (i) is not a multiple of $50, such increase shall be rounded to the next lowest multiple of $50.

(3) INFORMATION REQUIREMENT.—*Each Exchange (or any person carrying out 1 or more responsibilities of an Exchange under section 1311(f)(3) or 1321(c) of the Patient Protection and Affordable Care Act) shall provide the following information to the Secretary and to the taxpayer with respect to any health plan provided through the Exchange:*

(A) The level of coverage described in section 1302(d) of the Patient Protection and Affordable Care Act and the period such coverage was in effect.

(B) The total premium for the coverage without regard to the credit under this section or cost-sharing reductions under section 1402 of such Act.

(C) The aggregate amount of any advance payment of such credit or reductions under section 1412 of such Act.

(D) The name, address, and TIN of the primary insured and the name and TIN of each other individual obtaining coverage under the policy.

(E) Any information provided to the Exchange, including any change of circumstances, necessary to determine eligibility for, and the amount of, such credit.

(F) Information necessary to determine whether a taxpayer has received excess advance payments.

[CCH Explanation at ¶210.]
Amendments
• **2011, Comprehensive 1099 Taxpayer Protection and Repayment of Exchange Subsidy Overpayments Act of 2011 (P.L. 112-9)**

P.L. 112-9, §4(a):

Amended Code Sec. 36B(f)(2)(B)(i). **Effective** for tax years ending after 12-31-2013. Prior to amendment, Code Sec. 36B(f)(2)(B)(i) read as follows:

(i) IN GENERAL.—In the case of a taxpayer whose household income is less than 500 percent of the poverty line for the size of the family involved for the taxable year, the amount of the increase under subparagraph (A) shall in no event exceed the applicable dollar amount determined in accordance with the following table (one-half of such amount in the case of a taxpayer whose tax is determined under section 1(c) for the taxable year):

If the household income (expressed as a percentage of poverty line) is:	The applicable dollar amount is:
Less than 200%	$600
At least 200% but less than 250%	$1,000
At least 250% but less than 300%	$1,500
At least 300% but less than 350%	$2,000
At least 350% but less than 400%	$2,500
At least 400% but less than 450%	$3,000
At least 450% but less than 500%	$3,500

• **2010, Medicare and Medicaid Extenders Act of 2010 (P.L. 111-309)**

P.L. 111-309, §208(a):

Amended Code Sec. 36B(f)(2)(B). **Effective** for tax years beginning after 12-31-2013. Prior to amendment by P.L. 111-309, Code Sec. 36B(f)(2)(B) read as follows:

(B) LIMITATION ON INCREASE WHERE INCOME LESS THAN 400 PERCENT OF POVERTY LINE.—

(i) IN GENERAL.—In the case of an applicable taxpayer whose household income is less than 400 percent of the poverty line for the size of the family involved for the taxable year, the amount of the increase under subparagraph (A) shall in no event exceed $400 ($250 in the case of a taxpayer whose tax is determined under section 1(c) for the taxable year).

(ii) INDEXING OF AMOUNT.—In the case of any calendar year beginning after 2014, each of the dollar amounts under clause (i) shall be increased by an amount equal to—

(I) such dollar amount, multiplied by

(II) the cost-of-living adjustment determined under section 1(f)(3) for the calendar year, determined by substituting "calendar year 2013" for "calendar year 1992" in subparagraph (B) thereof.

If the amount of any increase under clause (i) is not a multiple of $50, such increase shall be rounded to the next lowest multiple of $50.

P.L. 111-309, §208(b):

Amended Code Sec. 36B(f)(2)(B)(ii) by inserting "in the table contained" after "each of the dollar amounts". **Effective** for tax years beginning after 12-31-2013.

• **2010, Health Care and Education Reconciliation Act of 2010 (P.L. 111-152)**

P.L. 111-152, §1004(c):

Amended Code Sec. 36B(f), as added by section 1401(a) of the Patient Protection and Affordable Care Act (P.L. 111-148), by adding at the end a new paragraph (3). **Effective** 3-30-2010.

(g) REGULATIONS.—*The Secretary shall prescribe such regulations as may be necessary to carry out the provisions of this section, including regulations which provide for—*

(1) the coordination of the credit allowed under this section with the program for advance payment of the credit under section 1412 of the Patient Protection and Affordable Care Act, and

(2) the application of subsection (f) where the filing status of the taxpayer for a taxable year is different from such status used for determining the advance payment of the credit.

[CCH Explanation at ¶210.]
Amendments
• **2010, Patient Protection and Affordable Care Act (P.L. 111-148)**

P.L. 111-148, §1401(a):

Amended subpart C of part IV of subchapter A of chapter 1 by inserting after Code Sec. 36A a new Code Sec. 36B. **Effective** for tax years ending after 12-31-2013.

[¶5020] CODE SEC. 38. GENERAL BUSINESS CREDIT.

* * *

(b) CURRENT YEAR BUSINESS CREDIT.—For purposes of this subpart, the amount of the current year business credit is the sum of the following credits determined for the taxable year:

* * *

(34) the carbon dioxide sequestration credit determined under section 45Q(a)[,]

(35) the portion of the new qualified plug-in electric drive motor vehicle credit to which section 30D(c)(1) applies, *plus*

(36) the small employer health insurance credit determined under section 45R.

[CCH Explanation at ¶310.]

Amendments

• **2010, Patient Protection and Affordable Care Act (P.L. 111-148)**

P.L. 111-148, §1421(b):

Amended Code Sec. 38(b) by striking "plus" at the end of paragraph (34), by striking the period at the end of para-

graph (35) and inserting ", plus", and by inserting after paragraph (35) a new paragraph (36). **Effective** for amounts paid or incurred in tax years beginning after 12-31-2009 [**effective** date changed by Act Sec. 10105(e)(4).—CCH].

(c) LIMITATION BASED ON AMOUNT OF TAX.—

* * *

(4) SPECIAL RULES FOR SPECIFIED CREDITS.—

* * *

(B) SPECIFIED CREDITS.—For purposes of this subsection, the term "specified credits" means—

* * *

(vi) the credit determined under section 45R,

(vii) the credit determined under section 46 to the extent that such credit is attributable to the energy credit determined under section 48,

(viii) the credit determined under section 46 to the extent that such credit is attributable to the rehabilitation credit under section 47, but only with respect to qualified rehabilitation expenditures properly taken into account for periods after December 31, 2007, and

(ix) the credit determined under section 51.

* * *

[CCH Explanation at ¶310.]

Amendments

• **2010, Patient Protection and Affordable Care Act (P.L. 111-148)**

P.L. 111-148, §1421(c):

Amended Code Sec. 38(c)(4)(B) by redesignating clauses (vi), (vii), and (viii) as clauses (vii), (viii), and (ix), respec-

tively, and by inserting after clause (v) a new clause (vi). **Effective** for amounts paid or incurred in tax years beginning after 12-31-2009 [**effective** date changed by Act Sec. 10105(e)(4).—CCH].

[¶5030] *CODE SEC. 45R. EMPLOYEE HEALTH INSURANCE EXPENSES OF SMALL EMPLOYERS.*

(a) GENERAL RULE.—For purposes of section 38, in the case of an eligible small employer, the small employer health insurance credit determined under this section for any taxable year in the credit period is the amount determined under subsection (b).

(b) HEALTH INSURANCE CREDIT AMOUNT.—Subject to subsection (c), the amount determined under this subsection with respect to any eligible small employer is equal to 50 percent (35 percent in the case of a tax-exempt eligible small employer) of the lesser of—

(1) the aggregate amount of nonelective contributions the employer made on behalf of its employees during the taxable year under the arrangement described in subsection (d)(4) for premiums for qualified health plans offered by the employer to its employees through an Exchange, or

(2) the aggregate amount of nonelective contributions which the employer would have made during the taxable year under the arrangement if each employee taken into account under paragraph (1) had enrolled in a qualified health plan which had a premium equal to the average premium (as determined by

the Secretary of Health and Human Services) for the small group market in the rating area in which the employee enrolls for coverage.

(c) PHASEOUT OF CREDIT AMOUNT BASED ON NUMBER OF EMPLOYEES AND AVERAGE WAGES.—The amount of the credit determined under subsection (b) without regard to this subsection shall be reduced (but not below zero) by the sum of the following amounts:

(1) Such amount multiplied by a fraction the numerator of which is the total number of full-time equivalent employees of the employer in excess of 10 and the denominator of which is 15.

(2) Such amount multiplied by a fraction the numerator of which is the average annual wages of the employer in excess of the dollar amount in effect under subsection (d)(3)(B) and the denominator of which is such dollar amount.

(d) ELIGIBLE SMALL EMPLOYER.—For purposes of this section—

(1) IN GENERAL.—The term "eligible small employer" means, with respect to any taxable year, an employer—

(A) which has no more than 25 full-time equivalent employees for the taxable year,

(B) the average annual wages of which do not exceed an amount equal to twice the dollar amount in effect under paragraph (3)(B) for the taxable year, and

(C) which has in effect an arrangement described in paragraph (4).

(2) FULL-TIME EQUIVALENT EMPLOYEES.—

(A) IN GENERAL.—The term "full-time equivalent employees" means a number of employees equal to the number determined by dividing—

(i) the total number of hours of service for which wages were paid by the employer to employees during the taxable year, by

(ii) 2,080.

Such number shall be rounded to the next lowest whole number if not otherwise a whole number.

(B) EXCESS HOURS NOT COUNTED.—If an employee works in excess of 2,080 hours of service during any taxable year, such excess shall not be taken into account under subparagraph (A).

(C) HOURS OF SERVICE.—The Secretary, in consultation with the Secretary of Labor, shall prescribe such regulations, rules, and guidance as may be necessary to determine the hours of service of an employee, including rules for the application of this paragraph to employees who are not compensated on an hourly basis.

(3) AVERAGE ANNUAL WAGES.—

(A) IN GENERAL.—The average annual wages of an eligible small employer for any taxable year is the amount determined by dividing—

(i) the aggregate amount of wages which were paid by the employer to employees during the taxable year, by

(ii) the number of full-time equivalent employees of the employee determined under paragraph (2) for the taxable year.

Such amount shall be rounded to the next lowest multiple of $1,000 if not otherwise such a multiple.

(B) DOLLAR AMOUNT.—For purposes of paragraph (1)(B) and subsection (c)(2)—

(i) 2010, 2011, 2012, AND 2013.—The dollar amount in effect under this paragraph for taxable years beginning in 2010, 2011, 2012, or 2013 is $25,000.

(ii) SUBSEQUENT YEARS.—In the case of a taxable year beginning in a calendar year after 2013, the dollar amount in effect under this paragraph shall be equal to $25,000, multiplied by the cost-of-living adjustment under section 1(f)(3) for the calendar year, determined by substituting "calendar year 2012" for "calendar year 1992" in subparagraph (B) thereof.

(4) CONTRIBUTION ARRANGEMENT.—An arrangement is described in this paragraph if it requires an eligible small employer to make a nonelective contribution on behalf of each employee who enrolls in a

qualified health plan offered to employees by the employer through an exchange in an amount equal to a uniform percentage (not less than 50 percent) of the premium cost of the qualified health plan.

(5) SEASONAL WORKER HOURS AND WAGES NOT COUNTED.—For purposes of this subsection—

(A) IN GENERAL.—The number of hours of service worked by, and wages paid to, a seasonal worker of an employer shall not be taken into account in determining the full-time equivalent employees and average annual wages of the employer unless the worker works for the employer on more than 120 days during the taxable year.

(B) DEFINITION OF SEASONAL WORKER.—The term "seasonal worker" means a worker who performs labor or services on a seasonal basis as defined by the Secretary of Labor, including workers covered by section 500.20(s)(1) of title 29, Code of Federal Regulations and retail workers employed exclusively during holiday seasons.

[CCH Explanation at ¶ 310.]

Amendments

• **2010, Patient Protection and Affordable Care Act (P.L. 111-148)**

P.L. 111-148, § 10105(e)(1):

Amended Code Sec. 45R(d)(3)(B), as added by Act Sec. 1421(a). **Effective** as if included in the enactment of Act Sec. 1421 [**effective** for amounts paid or incurred in tax years beginning after 12-31-2009 [**effective** date changed by Act Sec. 10105(e)(4).—CCH]]. Prior to amendment, Code Sec, 45R(d)(3)(B) read as follows:

(B) DOLLAR AMOUNT.—For purposes of paragraph (1)(B)—

(i) 2011, 2012, AND 2013.—The dollar amount in effect under this paragraph for taxable years beginning in 2011, 2012, or 2013 is $20,000.

(ii) SUBSEQUENT YEARS.—In the case of a taxable year beginning in a calendar year after 2013, the dollar amount in effect under this paragraph shall be equal to $20,000, multiplied by the cost-of-living adjustment determined under section 1(f)(3) for the calendar year, determined by substituting "calendar year 2012" for "calendar year 1992" in subparagraph (B) thereof.

(e) OTHER RULES AND DEFINITIONS.—For purposes of this section—

(1) EMPLOYEE.—

(A) CERTAIN EMPLOYEES EXCLUDED.—The term "employee" shall not include—

(i) an employee within the meaning of section 401(c)(1),

(ii) any 2-percent shareholder (as defined in section 1372(b)) of an eligible small business which is an S corporation,

(iii) any 5-percent owner (as defined in section 416(i)(1)(B)(i)) of an eligible small business, or

(iv) any individual who bears any of the relationships described in subparagraphs (A) through (G) of section 152(d)(2) to, or is a dependent described in section 152(d)(2)(H) of, an individual described in clause (i), (ii), or (iii).

(B) LEASED EMPLOYEES.—The term "employee" shall include a leased employee within the meaning of section 414(n).

(2) CREDIT PERIOD.—The term "credit period" means, with respect to any eligible small employer, the 2-consecutive-taxable year period beginning with the 1st taxable year in which the employer (or any predecessor) offers 1 or more qualified health plans to its employees through an Exchange.

(3) NONELECTIVE CONTRIBUTION.—The term "nonelective contribution" means an employer contribution other than an employer contribution pursuant to a salary reduction arrangement.

(4) WAGES.—The term "wages" has the meaning given such term by section 3121(a) (determined without regard to any dollar limitation contained in such section).

(5) AGGREGATION AND OTHER RULES MADE APPLICABLE.—

(A) AGGREGATION RULES.—All employers treated as a single employer under subsection (b), (c), (m), or (o) of section 414 shall be treated as a single employer for purposes of this section.

(B) OTHER RULES.—Rules similar to the rules of subsections (c), (d), and (e) of section 52 shall apply.

(f) CREDIT MADE AVAILABLE TO TAX-EXEMPT ELIGIBLE SMALL EMPLOYERS.—

(1) IN GENERAL.—In the case of a tax-exempt eligible small employer, there shall be treated as a credit allowable under subpart C (and not allowable under this subpart) the lesser of—

(A) the amount of the credit determined under this section with respect to such employer, or

(B) the amount of the payroll taxes of the employer during the calendar year in which the taxable year begins.

(2) TAX-EXEMPT ELIGIBLE SMALL EMPLOYER.—For purposes of this section, the term "tax-exempt eligible small employer" means an eligible small employer which is any organization described in section 501(c) which is exempt from taxation under section 501(a).

(3) PAYROLL TAXES.—For purposes of this subsection—

(A) IN GENERAL.—The term "payroll taxes" means—

(i) amounts required to be withheld from the employees of the tax-exempt eligible small employer under section 3401(a),

(ii) amounts required to be withheld from such employees under section 3101(b), and

(iii) amounts of the taxes imposed on the tax-exempt eligible small employer under section 3111(b).

(B) SPECIAL RULE.—A rule similar to the rule of section 24(d)(2)(C) shall apply for purposes of subparagraph (A).

(g) APPLICATION OF SECTION FOR CALENDAR YEARS 2010, 2011, 2012, AND 2013.—In the case of any taxable year beginning in 2010, 2011, 2012, or 2013, the following modifications to this section shall apply in determining the amount of the credit under subsection (a):

(1) NO CREDIT PERIOD REQUIRED.—The credit shall be determined without regard to whether the taxable year is in a credit period and for purposes of applying this section to taxable years beginning after 2013, no credit period shall be treated as beginning with a taxable year beginning before 2014.

(2) AMOUNT OF CREDIT.—The amount of the credit determined under subsection (b) shall be determined—

(A) by substituting "35 percent (25 percent in the case of a tax-exempt eligible small employer)" for "50 percent (35 percent in the case of a tax-exempt eligible small employer)",

(B) by reference to an eligible small employer's nonelective contributions for premiums paid for health insurance coverage (within the meaning of section 9832(b)(1)) of an employee, and

(C) by substituting for the average premium determined under subsection (b)(2) the amount the Secretary of Health and Human Services determines is the average premium for the small group market in the State in which the employer is offering health insurance coverage (or for such area within the State as is specified by the Secretary).

(3) CONTRIBUTION ARRANGEMENT.—An arrangement shall not fail to meet the requirements of subsection (d)(4) solely because it provides for the offering of insurance outside of an Exchange.

[CCH Explanation at ¶ 310.]

Amendments

• **2010, Patient Protection and Affordable Care Act (P.L. 111-148)**

P.L. 111-148, § 10105(e)(2):

Amended Code Sec. 45R(g), as added by Act Sec. 1421(a), by striking "2011" both places it appears and inserting

"2010, 2011". **Effective** as if included in the enactment of Act Sec. 1421 [**effective** for amounts paid or incurred in tax years beginning after 12-31-2009 [**effective** date changed by Act Sec. 10105(e)(4).—CCH]].

(h) INSURANCE DEFINITIONS.—Any term used in this section which is also used in the Public Health Service Act or subtitle A of title I of the Patient Protection and Affordable Care Act shall have the meaning given such term by such Act or subtitle.

(i) REGULATIONS.—The Secretary shall prescribe such regulations as may be necessary to carry out the provisions of this section, including regulations to prevent the avoidance of the 2-year limit on the credit period

through the use of successor entities and the avoidance of the limitations under subsection (c) through the use of multiple entities.

[CCH Explanation at ¶ 310.]

Amendments

• **2010, Patient Protection and Affordable Care Act (P.L. 111-148)**

P.L. 111-148, § 1421(a):

Amended subpart D of part IV of subchapter A of chapter 1 by inserting after Code Sec. 45Q a new Code Sec. 45R.

Effective for amounts paid or incurred in tax years beginning after 12-31-2009 [effective date changed by Act Sec. 10105(e)(4).—CCH].

[¶ 5040] CODE SEC. 56. ADJUSTMENTS IN COMPUTING ALTERNATIVE MINIMUM TAXABLE INCOME.

* * *

(b) ADJUSTMENTS APPLICABLE TO INDIVIDUALS.—In determining the amount of the alternative minimum taxable income of any taxpayer (other than a corporation), the following treatment shall apply (in lieu of the treatment applicable for purposes of computing the regular tax):

(1) LIMITATION ON DEDUCTIONS.—

* * *

(B) MEDICAL EXPENSES.—In determining the amount allowable as a deduction under section 213, subsection (a) of section 213 shall be applied *without regard to subsection (f) of such section.*

* * *

[CCH Explanation at ¶ 215.]

Amendments

• **2010, Patient Protection and Affordable Care Act (P.L. 111-148)**

P.L. 111-148, § 9013(c):

Amended Code Sec. 56(b)(1)(B) by striking "by substituting '10 percent' for '7.5 percent'" and inserting "without

regard to subsection (f) of such section". **Effective** for tax years beginning after 12-31-2012.

[¶ 5050] CODE SEC. 105. AMOUNTS RECEIVED UNDER ACCIDENT AND HEALTH PLANS.

* * *

(b) AMOUNTS EXPENDED FOR MEDICAL CARE.—Except in the case of amounts attributable to (and not in excess of) deductions allowed under section 213 (relating to medical, etc., expenses) for any prior taxable year, gross income does not include amounts referred to in subsection (a) if such amounts are paid, directly or indirectly, to the taxpayer to reimburse the taxpayer for expenses incurred by him for the medical care (as defined in section 213(d)) of the taxpayer, his spouse, *his dependents* (as defined in section 152, determined without regard to subsections (b)(1), (b)(2), and (d)(1)(B) thereof), *and any child (as defined in section 152(f)(1)) of the taxpayer who as of the end of the taxable year has not attained age 27.* Any child to whom section 152(e) applies shall be treated as a dependent of both parents for purposes of this subsection.

* * *

[CCH Explanation at ¶ 220.]

Amendments

• **2010, Health Care and Education Reconciliation Act of 2010 (P.L. 111-152)**

P.L. 111-152, § 1004(d)(1)(A)-(B):

Amended the first sentence of Code Sec. 105(b) by striking "and his dependents" and inserting "his dependents";

and by inserting before the period ", and any child (as defined in section 152(f)(1)) of the taxpayer who as of the end of the taxable year has not attained age 27". **Effective** 3-30-2010.

[¶ 5070] CODE SEC. 125. CAFETERIA PLANS.

* * *

(f) QUALIFIED BENEFITS DEFINED.—*For purposes of this section*—

(1) IN GENERAL.—The term "qualified benefit"means any benefit which, with the application of subsection (a), is not includible in the gross income of the employee by reason of an express provision of this chapter (other than section 106(b), 117, 127, or 132). Such term includes any group term life insurance which is includible in gross income only because it exceeds the dollar limitation of section 79 and such term includes any other benefit permitted under regulations.

(2) LONG-TERM CARE INSURANCE NOT QUALIFIED.—The term "qualified benefit" shall not include any product which is advertised, marketed, or offered as long-term care insurance.

(3) CERTAIN EXCHANGE-PARTICIPATING QUALIFIED HEALTH PLANS NOT QUALIFIED.—

(A) IN GENERAL.—The term "qualified benefit" shall not include any qualified health plan (as defined in section 1301(a) of the Patient Protection and Affordable Care Act) offered through an Exchange established under section 1311 of such Act.

(B) EXCEPTION FOR EXCHANGE-ELIGIBLE EMPLOYERS.—Subparagraph (A) shall not apply with respect to any employee if such employee's employer is a qualified employer (as defined in section 1312(f)(2) of the Patient Protection and Affordable Care Act) offering the employee the opportunity to enroll through such an Exchange in a qualified health plan in a group market.

* * *

[CCH Explanation at ¶ 320.]

Amendments

• **2010, Patient Protection and Affordable Care Act (P.L. 111-148)**

P.L. 111-148, § 1515(a):

Amended Code Sec. 125(f) by adding at the end a new paragraph (3). **Effective** for tax years beginning after 12-31-2013.

P.L. 111-148, § 1515(b)(1)-(2):

Amended Code Sec. 125(f) by striking "For purposes of this section, the term" and inserting "For purposes of this section—"

"(1) IN GENERAL.—The term",

and by striking "Such term shall not include" and inserting:

"(2) LONG-TERM CARE INSURANCE NOT QUALIFIED.—The term 'qualified benefit' shall not include".

Effective for tax years beginning after 12-31-2013.

(i) LIMITATION ON HEALTH FLEXIBLE SPENDING ARRANGEMENTS.—

(1) IN GENERAL.—For purposes of this section, if a benefit is provided under a cafeteria plan through employer contributions to a health flexible spending arrangement, such benefit shall not be treated as a qualified benefit unless the cafeteria plan provides that an employee may not elect for any taxable year to have salary reduction contributions in excess of $2,500 made to such arrangement.

(2) ADJUSTMENT FOR INFLATION.—In the case of any taxable year beginning after December 31, 2013, the dollar amount in paragraph (1) shall be increased by an amount equal to—

(A) such amount, multiplied by

(B) the cost-of-living adjustment determined under section 1(f)(3) for the calendar year in which such taxable year begins by substituting "calendar year 2012" for "calendar year 1992" in subparagraph (B) thereof.

If any increase determined under this paragraph is not a multiple of $50, such increase shall be rounded to the next lowest multiple of $50.

[CCH Explanation at ¶325.]

Amendments

• 2010, Health Care and Education Reconciliation Act of 2010 (P.L. 111-152)

P.L. 111-152, § 1403(b)(1)-(2):

Amended Code Sec. 125(i)(2), as added by section 9005 of the Patient Protection and Affordable Care Act (P.L. 111-148) and amended by section 10902 of such Act, by striking "December 31, 2011" and inserting "December 31, 2013" in the matter preceding subparagraph (A); and by striking "2010" and inserting "2012" in subparagraph (B). **Effective** 3-30-2010.

• 2010, Patient Protection and Affordable Care Act (P.L. 111-148)

P.L. 111-148, § 9005(a)(1)-(2):

Amended Code Sec. 125 by redesignating subsections (i) and (j) as subsections (j) and (k), respectively, and by inserting after subsection (h) a new subsection (i). **Effective** for tax years beginning after 12-31-2010.

P.L. 111-148, § 10902(a):

Amended Code Sec. 125(i), as added by Act Sec. 9005. **Effective** for tax years beginning after 12-31-2012 [**effective** date changed by P.L. 111-152, § 1403(a).—CCH]. Prior to amendment, Code Sec. 125(i) read as follows:

(i) LIMITATION ON HEALTH FLEXIBLE SPENDING ARRANGE-MENTS.—For purposes of this section, if a benefit is provided under a cafeteria plan through employer contributions to a health flexible spending arrangement, such benefit shall not be treated as a qualified benefit unless the cafeteria plan provides that an employee may not elect for any taxable year to have salary reduction contributions in excess of $2,500 made to such arrangement.

(j) SIMPLE CAFETERIA PLANS FOR SMALL BUSINESSES.—

(1) IN GENERAL.—An eligible employer maintaining a simple cafeteria plan with respect to which the requirements of this subsection are met for any year shall be treated as meeting any applicable nondiscrimination requirement during such year.

(2) SIMPLE CAFETERIA PLAN.—For purposes of this subsection, the term "simple cafeteria plan" means a cafeteria plan—

(A) which is established and maintained by an eligible employer, and

(B) with respect to which the contribution requirements of paragraph (3), and the eligibility and participation requirements of paragraph (4), are met.

(3) CONTRIBUTION REQUIREMENTS.—

(A) IN GENERAL.—The requirements of this paragraph are met if, under the plan the employer is required, without regard to whether a qualified employee makes any salary reduction contribution, to make a contribution to provide qualified benefits under the plan on behalf of each qualified employee in an amount equal to—

(i) a uniform percentage (not less than 2 percent) of the employee's compensation for the plan year, or

(ii) an amount which is not less than the lesser of—

(I) 6 percent of the employee's compensation for the plan year, or

(II) twice the amount of the salary reduction contributions of each qualified employee.

(B) MATCHING CONTRIBUTIONS ON BEHALF OF HIGHLY COMPENSATED AND KEY EMPLOYEES.—The requirements of subparagraph (A)(ii) shall not be treated as met if, under the plan, the rate of contributions with respect to any salary reduction contribution of a highly compensated or key employee at any rate of contribution is greater than that with respect to an employee who is not a highly compensated or key employee.

(C) ADDITIONAL CONTRIBUTIONS.—Subject to subparagraph (B), nothing in this paragraph shall be treated as prohibiting an employer from making contributions to provide qualified benefits under the plan in addition to contributions required under subparagraph (A).

(D) DEFINITIONS.—For purposes of this paragraph—

(i) SALARY REDUCTION CONTRIBUTION.—The term "salary reduction contribution" means, with respect to a cafeteria plan, any amount which is contributed to the plan at the election of the employee and which is not includible in gross income by reason of this section.

(ii) QUALIFIED EMPLOYEE.—The term "qualified employee" means, with respect to a cafeteria plan, any employee who is not a highly compensated or key employee and who is eligible to participate in the plan.

(iii) HIGHLY COMPENSATED EMPLOYEE.—The term "highly compensated employee" has the meaning given such term by section 414(q).

(iv) KEY EMPLOYEE.—The term "key employee" has the meaning given such term by section 416(i).

(4) MINIMUM ELIGIBILITY AND PARTICIPATION REQUIREMENTS.—

(A) IN GENERAL.—The requirements of this paragraph shall be treated as met with respect to any year if, under the plan—

(i) all employees who had at least 1,000 hours of service for the preceding plan year are eligible to participate, and

(ii) each employee eligible to participate in the plan may, subject to terms and conditions applicable to all participants, elect any benefit available under the plan.

(B) CERTAIN EMPLOYEES MAY BE EXCLUDED.—For purposes of subparagraph (A)(i), an employer may elect to exclude under the plan employees—

(i) who have not attained the age of 21 before the close of a plan year,

(ii) who have less than 1 year of service with the employer as of any day during the plan year,

(iii) who are covered under an agreement which the Secretary of Labor finds to be a collective bargaining agreement if there is evidence that the benefits covered under the cafeteria plan were the subject of good faith bargaining between employee representatives and the employer, or

(iv) who are described in section 410(b)(3)(C) (relating to nonresident aliens working outside the United States).

A plan may provide a shorter period of service or younger age for purposes of clause (i) or (ii).

(5) ELIGIBLE EMPLOYER.—For purposes of this subsection—

(A) IN GENERAL.—The term "eligible employer" means, with respect to any year, any employer if such employer employed an average of 100 or fewer employees on business days during either of the 2 preceding years. For purposes of this subparagraph, a year may only be taken into account if the employer was in existence throughout the year.

(B) EMPLOYERS NOT IN EXISTENCE DURING PRECEDING YEAR.—If an employer was not in existence throughout the preceding year, the determination under subparagraph (A) shall be based on the average number of employees that it is reasonably expected such employer will employ on business days in the current year.

(C) GROWING EMPLOYERS RETAIN TREATMENT AS SMALL EMPLOYER.—

(i) IN GENERAL.—If—

(I) an employer was an eligible employer for any year (a "qualified year"), and

(II) such employer establishes a simple cafeteria plan for its employees for such year,

then, notwithstanding the fact the employer fails to meet the requirements of subparagraph (A) for any subsequent year, such employer shall be treated as an eligible employer for such subsequent year with respect to employees (whether or not employees during a qualified year) of any trade or business which was covered by the plan during any qualified year.

(ii) EXCEPTION.—This subparagraph shall cease to apply if the employer employs an average of 200 or more employees on business days during any year preceding any such subsequent year.

(D) SPECIAL RULES.—

(i) PREDECESSORS.—Any reference in this paragraph to an employer shall include a reference to any predecessor of such employer.

(ii) AGGREGATION RULES.—All persons treated as a single employer under subsection (a) or (b) of section 52, or subsection (n) or (o) of section 414, shall be treated as one person.

(6) APPLICABLE NONDISCRIMINATION REQUIREMENT.—For purposes of this subsection, the term "applicable nondiscrimination requirement" means any requirement under subsection (b) of this section, section 79(d), section 105(h), or paragraph (2), (3), (4), or (8) of section 129(d).

(7) COMPENSATION.—The term "compensation" has the meaning given such term by section 414(s).

[CCH Explanation at ¶ 330.]

Amendments

• 2010, Patient Protection and Affordable Care Act (P.L. 111-148)

P.L. 111-148, § 9022(a):

Amended Code Sec. 125, as amended by this Act, by redesignating subsections (j) and (k) as subsections (k) and (l), respectively, and by inserting after subsection (i) a new subsection (j). **Effective** for years beginning after 12-31-2010.

(k) CROSS REFERENCE.—

For reporting and recordkeeping requirements, see section 6039D.

Amendments

• 2010, Patient Protection and Affordable Care Act (P.L. 111-148)

P.L. 111-148, § 9005(a)(1):

Amended Code Sec. 125 by redesignating subsection (i) as (j). **Effective** for tax years beginning after 12-31-2010.

P.L. 111-148, § 9022(a):

Amended Code Sec. 125, as amended by this Act, by redesignating subsection (j) as subsection (k). **Effective** for years beginning after 12-31-2010.

(l) REGULATIONS.—The Secretary shall prescribe such regulations as may be necessary to carry out the provisions of this section.

Amendments

• 2010, Patient Protection and Affordable Care Act (P.L. 111-148)

P.L. 111-148, § 9005(a)(1):

Amended Code Sec. 125 by redesignating subsection (j) as (k). **Effective** for tax years beginning after 12-31-2010.

P.L. 111-148, § 9022(a):

Amended Code Sec. 125, as amended by this Act, by redesignating subsection (k) as subsection (l). **Effective** for years beginning after 12-31-2010.

[¶ 5080] CODE SEC. 139A. FEDERAL SUBSIDIES FOR PRESCRIPTION DRUG PLANS.

Gross income shall not include any special subsidy payment received under section 1860D-22 of the Social Security Act.

[CCH Explanation at ¶ 335.]

Amendments

• 2010, Patient Protection and Affordable Care Act (P.L. 111-148)

P.L. 111-148, § 9012(a):

Amended Code Sec. 139A by striking the second sentence. **Effective** for tax years beginning after 12-31-2012.

[**effective** date changed by P.L. 111-152, § 1407.—CCH]. Prior to being stricken, the second sentence of Code Sec. 139A read as follows:

This section shall not be taken into account for purposes of determining whether any deduction is allowable with respect to any cost taken into account in determining such payment.

[¶ 5100] CODE SEC. 162. TRADE OR BUSINESS EXPENSES.

* * *

(l) SPECIAL RULES FOR HEALTH INSURANCE COSTS OF SELF-EMPLOYED INDIVIDUALS.—

(1) ALLOWANCE OF DEDUCTION.—In the case of a taxpayer who is an employee within the meaning of section 401(c)(1), there shall be allowed as a deduction under this section an amount equal to the amount paid during the taxable year for insurance which constitutes medical care for—

(A) the taxpayer,

(B) the taxpayer's spouse,

(C) the taxpayer's dependents, and

(D) any child (as defined in section 152(f)(1)) of the taxpayer who as of the end of the taxable year has not attained age 27.

(2) LIMITATIONS.—

* * *

(B) OTHER COVERAGE.—Paragraph (1) shall not apply to any taxpayer for any calendar month for which the taxpayer is eligible to participate in any subsidized health plan maintained by any employer of the taxpayer or of the spouse of, *or any dependent, or individual described in subparagraph (D) of paragraph (1) with respect to,* the taxpayer. The preceding sentence shall be applied separately with respect to—

(i) plans which include coverage for qualified long-term care services (as defined in section 7702B(c)) or are qualified long-term care insurance contracts (as defined in section 7702B(b)), and

(ii) plans which do not include such coverage and are not such contracts.

* * *

(4) DEDUCTION NOT ALLOWED FOR SELF-EMPLOYMENT TAX PURPOSES.—The deduction allowable by reason of this subsection shall not be taken into account in determining an individual's net earnings from self-employment (within the meaning of section 1402(a)) for purposes of chapter 2 *for taxable years beginning before January 1, 2010, or after December 31, 2010.*

* * *

[CCH Explanation at ¶ 220.]

Amendments

• **2010, Creating Small Business Jobs Act of 2010 (P.L. 111-240)**

P.L. 111-240, § 2042(a):

Amended Code Sec. 162(l)(4) by inserting "for taxable years beginning before January 1, 2010, or after December 31, 2010" before the period. **Effective** for tax years beginning after 12-31-2009.

• **2010, Health Care and Education Reconciliation Act of 2010 (P.L. 111-152)**

P.L. 111-152, § 1004(d)(2):

Amended Code Sec. 162(l)(1). **Effective** 3-30-2010. Prior to amendment, Code Sec. 162(l)(1) read as follows:

(1) ALLOWANCE OF DEDUCTION.—

(A) IN GENERAL.—In the case of an individual who is an employee within the meaning of section 401(c)(1), there shall be allowed as a deduction under this section an amount equal to the applicable percentage of the amount paid during the taxable year for insurance which constitutes medical care for the taxpayer, his spouse, and dependents.

(B) APPLICABLE PERCENTAGE.—For purposes of subparagraph (A), the applicable percentage shall be determined under the following table:

For taxable years beginning in calendar year—	The applicable percentage is—
1999 through 2001	60
2002	70
2003 and thereafter	100

P.L. 111-152, § 1004(d)(3):

Amended Code Sec. 162(l)(2)(B) by inserting ", or any dependent, or individual described in subparagraph (D) of paragraph (1) with respect to," after "spouse of". **Effective** 3-30-2010.

(m) CERTAIN EXCESSIVE EMPLOYEE REMUNERATION.—

* * *

(6) SPECIAL RULE FOR APPLICATION TO CERTAIN HEALTH INSURANCE PROVIDERS.—

(A) IN GENERAL.—No deduction shall be allowed under this chapter—

(i) in the case of applicable individual remuneration which is for any disqualified taxable year beginning after December 31, 2012, and which is attributable to services performed by an applicable individual during such taxable year, to the extent that the amount of such remuneration exceeds $500,000, or

(ii) in the case of deferred deduction remuneration for any taxable year beginning after December 31, 2012, which is attributable to services performed by an applicable individual during any disqualified taxable year beginning after December 31, 2009, to the extent that the amount of such remuneration exceeds $500,000 reduced (but not below zero) by the sum of—

(I) the applicable individual remuneration for such disqualified taxable year, plus

(II) the portion of the deferred deduction remuneration for such services which was taken into account under this clause in a preceding taxable year (or which would have been taken into account under this clause in a preceding taxable year if this clause were applied by substituting "December 31, 2009" for "December 31, 2012" in the matter preceding subclause (I)).

(B) DISQUALIFIED TAXABLE YEAR.—For purposes of this paragraph, the term "disqualified taxable year" means, with respect to any employer, any taxable year for which such employer is a covered health insurance provider.

(C) COVERED HEALTH INSURANCE PROVIDER.—For purposes of this paragraph—

(i) IN GENERAL.—The term "covered health insurance provider" means—

(I) with respect to taxable years beginning after December 31, 2009, and before January 1, 2013, any employer which is a health insurance issuer (as defined in section 9832(b)(2)) and which receives premiums from providing health insurance coverage (as defined in section 9832(b)(1)), and

(II) with respect to taxable years beginning after December 31, 2012, any employer which is a health insurance issuer (as defined in section 9832(b)(2)) and with respect to which not less than 25 percent of the gross premiums received from providing health insurance coverage (as defined in section 9832(b)(1)) is from minimum essential coverage (as defined in section 5000A(f)).

(ii) AGGREGATION RULES.—Two or more persons who are treated as a single employer under subsection (b), (c), (m), or (o) of section 414 shall be treated as a single employer, except that in applying section 1563(a) for purposes of any such subsection, paragraphs (2) and (3) thereof shall be disregarded.

(D) APPLICABLE INDIVIDUAL REMUNERATION.—For purposes of this paragraph, the term "applicable individual remuneration" means, with respect to any applicable individual for any disqualified taxable year, the aggregate amount allowable as a deduction under this chapter for such taxable year (determined without regard to this subsection) for remuneration (as defined in paragraph (4) without regard to subparagraphs (B), (C), and (D) thereof) for services performed by such individual (whether or not during the taxable year). Such term shall not include any deferred deduction remuneration with respect to services performed during the disqualified taxable year.

(E) DEFERRED DEDUCTION REMUNERATION.—For purposes of this paragraph, the term "deferred deduction remuneration" means remuneration which would be applicable individual remuneration for services performed in a disqualified taxable year but for the fact that the deduction under this chapter (determined without regard to this paragraph) for such remuneration is allowable in a subsequent taxable year.

(F) APPLICABLE INDIVIDUAL.—For purposes of this paragraph, the term "applicable individual" means, with respect to any covered health insurance provider for any disqualified taxable year, any individual—

(i) who is an officer, director, or employee in such taxable year, or

(ii) who provides services for or on behalf of such covered health insurance provider during such taxable year.

(G) COORDINATION.—Rules similar to the rules of subparagraphs (F) and (G) of paragraph (4) shall apply for purposes of this paragraph.

(H) REGULATORY AUTHORITY.—The Secretary may prescribe such guidance, rules, or regulations as are necessary to carry out the purposes of this paragraph.

* * *

[CCH Explanation at ¶340.]

Amendments

• 2010, Patient Protection and Affordable Care Act (P.L. 111-148)

P.L. 111-148, § 9014(a):

Amended Code Sec. 162(m) by adding at the end a new subparagraph (6). **Effective** for tax years beginning after

12-31-2009, with respect to services performed after such date.

[¶5110] CODE SEC. 164. TAXES.

* * *

(f) DEDUCTION FOR ONE-HALF OF SELF-EMPLOYMENT TAXES.—

(1) IN GENERAL.—In the case of an individual, in addition to the taxes described in subsection (a), there shall be allowed as a deduction for the taxable year an amount equal to one-half of the taxes imposed by section 1401 *(other than the taxes imposed by section 1401(b)(2))* for such taxable year.

* * *

[CCH Explanation at ¶620.]

Amendments

• 2010, Patient Protection and Affordable Care Act (P.L. 111-148)

P.L. 111-148, § 9015(b)(2)(A):

Amended Code Sec. 164(f)[(1)] by inserting "(other than the taxes imposed by section 1401(b)(2))" after "section

1401) [sic]". **Effective** with respect to remuneration received, and tax years beginning, after 12-31-2012.

[¶5120] CODE SEC. 196. DEDUCTION FOR CERTAIN UNUSED BUSINESS CREDITS.

* * *

(c) QUALIFIED BUSINESS CREDITS.—For purposes of this section, the term "qualified business credits" means—

* * *

(12) the low sulfur diesel fuel production credit determined under section 45H(a),

(13) the new energy efficient home credit determined under section 45L(a), *and*

(14) the small employer health insurance credit determined under section 45R(a).

* * *

[CCH Explanation at ¶310.]

Amendments

• 2010, Patient Protection and Affordable Care Act (P.L. 111-148)

P.L. 111-148, § 1421(d)(2):

Amended Code Sec. 196(c) by striking "and" at the end of paragraph (12), by striking the period at the end of para-

graph (13) and inserting ", and", and by adding at the end a new paragraph (14). **Effective** for amounts paid or incurred in tax years beginning after 12-31-2009 **[effective date changed by Act Sec. 10105(e)(4).—CCH]**.

[¶5130] CODE SEC. 213. MEDICAL, DENTAL, ETC., EXPENSES.

(a) ALLOWANCE OF DEDUCTION.—There shall be allowed as a deduction the expenses paid during the taxable year, not compensated for by insurance or otherwise, for medical care of the taxpayer, his spouse, or a dependent (as defined in section 152, determined without regard to subsections (b)(1), (b)(2), and (d)(1)(B) thereof), to the extent that such expenses exceed *10 percent* of adjusted gross income.

* * *

[CCH Explanation at ¶ 215.]

Amendments

• **2010, Patient Protection and Affordable Care Act (P.L. 111-148)**

P.L. 111-148, § 9013(a):

Amended Code Sec. 213(a) by striking "7.5 percent" and inserting "10 percent". **Effective** for tax years beginning after 12-31-2012.

(f) SPECIAL RULE FOR 2013, 2014, 2015, AND 2016.—In the case of any taxable year beginning after December 31, 2012, and ending before January 1, 2017, subsection (a) shall be applied with respect to a taxpayer by substituting "7.5 percent" for "10 percent" if such taxpayer or such taxpayer's spouse has attained age 65 before the close of such taxable year.

[CCH Explanation at ¶ 215.]

Amendments

• **2010, Patient Protection and Affordable Care Act (P.L. 111-148)**

P.L. 111-148, § 9013(b):

Amended Code Sec. 213 by adding at the end a new subsection (f). **Effective** for tax years beginning after 12-31-2012.

[¶ 5160] CODE SEC. 280C. CERTAIN EXPENSES FOR WHICH CREDITS ARE ALLOWABLE.

* * *

(g) CREDIT FOR HEALTH INSURANCE PREMIUMS.—No deduction shall be allowed for the portion of the premiums paid by the taxpayer for coverage of 1 or more individuals under a qualified health plan which is equal to the amount of the credit determined for the taxable year under section 36B(a) with respect to such premiums.

[CCH Explanation at ¶ 210.]

Amendments

• **2010, Patient Protection and Affordable Care Act (P.L. 111-148)**

P.L. 111-148, § 1401(b):

Amended Code Sec. 280C by adding at the end a new subsection (g). **Effective** for tax years ending after 12-31-2013.

(h) CREDIT FOR EMPLOYEE HEALTH INSURANCE EXPENSES OF SMALL EMPLOYERS.—No deduction shall be allowed for that portion of the premiums for qualified health plans (as defined in section 1301(a) of the Patient Protection and Affordable Care Act), or for health insurance coverage in the case of taxable years beginning in 2010, 2011, 2012, or 2013, paid by an employer which is equal to the amount of the credit determined under section 45R(a) with respect to the premiums.

[CCH Explanation at ¶ 310.]

Amendments

• **2010, Patient Protection and Affordable Care Act (P.L. 111-148)**

P.L. 111-148, § 1421(d)(1):

Amended Code Sec. 280C, as amended by Act Sec. 1401(b), by adding at the end a new subsection (h). **Effective** for amounts paid or incurred in tax years beginning after 12-31-2009 [**effective** date changed by Act Sec. 10105(e)(4).—CCH].

P.L. 111-148, § 10105(e)(3):

Amended Code Sec. 280C(h), as added by Act Sec. 1421(d)(1), by striking "2011" and inserting "2010, 2011". **Effective** as if included in the enactment of Act Sec. 1421 [**effective** for amounts paid or incurred in tax years beginning after 12-31-2009 [**effective** date changed by Act Sec. 10105(e)(4).—CCH]].

[¶5170] CODE SEC. 401. QUALIFIED PENSION, PROFIT-SHARING, AND STOCK BONUS PLANS.

* * *

(h) MEDICAL, ETC., BENEFITS FOR RETIRED EMPLOYEES AND THEIR SPOUSES AND DEPENDENTS.—Under regulations prescribed by the Secretary, and subject to the provisions of section 420, a pension or annuity plan may provide for the payment of benefits for sickness, accident, hospitalization, and medical expenses of retired employees, their spouses and their dependents, but only if—

(1) such benefits are subordinate to the retirement benefits provided by the plan,

(2) a separate account is established and maintained for such benefits,

(3) the employer's contributions to such separate account are reasonable and ascertainable,

(4) it is impossible, at any time prior to the satisfaction of all liabilities under the plan to provide such benefits, for any part of the corpus or income of such separate account to be (within the taxable year or thereafter) used for, or diverted to, any purpose other than the providing of such benefits,

(5) notwithstanding the provisions of subsection (a)(2), upon the satisfaction of all liabilities under the plan to provide such benefits, any amount remaining in such separate account must, under the terms of the plan, be returned to the employer, and

(6) in the case of an employee who is a key employee, a separate account is established and maintained for such benefits payable to such employee (and his spouse and dependents) and such benefits (to the extent attributable to plan years beginning after March 31, 1984, for which the employee is a key employee) are only payable to such employee (and his spouse and dependents) from such separate account.

For purposes of paragraph (6), the term "key employee" means any employee, who at any time during the plan year or any preceding plan year during which contributions were made on behalf of such employee, is or was a key employee as defined in section 416(i). In no event shall the requirements of paragraph (1) be treated as met if the aggregate actual contributions for medical benefits, when added to actual contributions for life insurance protection under the plan, exceed 25 percent of the total actual contributions to the plan (other than contributions to fund past service credits) after the date on which the account is established. *For purposes of this subsection, the term "dependent" shall include any individual who is a child (as defined in section 152(f)(1)) of a retired employee who as of the end of the calendar year has not attained age 27.*

* * *

[CCH Explanation at ¶220.]

Amendments

• **2010, Health Care and Education Reconciliation Act of 2010 (P.L. 111-152)**

P.L. 111-152, § 1004(d)(5):

Amended Code Sec. 401(h) by adding at the end a new sentence. **Effective** 3-30-2010.

[¶5180] CODE SEC. 501. EXEMPTION FROM TAX ON CORPORATIONS, CERTAIN TRUSTS, ETC.

* * *

(c) LIST OF EXEMPT ORGANIZATIONS.—The following organizations are referred to in subsection (a):

* * *

(9) Voluntary employees' beneficiary associations providing for the payment of life, sick, accident, or other benefits to the members of such association or their dependents or designated beneficiaries, if no part of the net earnings of such association inures (other than through such payments) to the benefit of any private shareholder or individual. *For purposes of providing for the payment of sick and accident benefits to members of such an association and their dependents, the term "dependent" shall include any individual who is a child (as defined in section 152(f)(1)) of a member who as of the end of the calendar year has not attained age 27.*

* * *

(29) *CO-OP* HEALTH INSURANCE ISSUERS.—

(A) IN GENERAL.—*A qualified nonprofit health insurance issuer (within the meaning of section 1322 of the Patient Protection and Affordable Care Act) which has received a loan or grant under the CO-OP program under such section, but only with respect to periods for which the issuer is in compliance with the requirements of such section and any agreement with respect to the loan or grant.*

(B) CONDITIONS FOR EXEMPTION.—*Subparagraph (A) shall apply to an organization only if—*

(i) *the organization has given notice to the Secretary, in such manner as the Secretary may by regulations prescribe, that it is applying for recognition of its status under this paragraph,*

(ii) *except as provided in section 1322(c)(4) of the Patient Protection and Affordable Care Act, no part of the net earnings of which inures to the benefit of any private shareholder or individual,*

(iii) *no substantial part of the activities of which is carrying on propaganda, or otherwise attempting, to influence legislation, and*

(iv) *the organization does not participate in, or intervene in (including the publishing or distributing of statements), any political campaign on behalf of (or in opposition to) any candidate for public office.*

* * *

[CCH Explanation at ¶ 220.]

Amendments

• 2010, Health Care and Education Reconciliation Act of 2010 (P.L. 111-152)

P.L. 111-152, § 1004(d)(4):

Amended Code Sec. 501(c)(9) by adding at the end a new sentence. **Effective** 3-30-2010.

• 2010, Patient Protection and Affordable Care Act (P.L. 111-148)

P.L. 111-148, § 1322(h)(1):

Amended Code Sec. 501(c) by adding at the end a new paragraph (29). **Effective** 3-23-2010.

(l) GOVERNMENT CORPORATIONS EXEMPT UNDER SUBSECTION (c)(1).—For purposes of subsection (c)(1), the following organizations are described in this subsection:

* * *

(4) *The Patient-Centered Outcomes Research Institute established under section 1181(b) of the Social Security Act.*

* * *

[CCH Explanation at ¶ 545.]

Amendments

• 2010, Patient Protection and Affordable Care Act (P.L. 111-148)

P.L. 111-148, § 6301(f):

Amended Code Sec. 501(l) by adding at the end a new paragraph (4). **Effective** 3-23-2010.

(r) ADDITIONAL REQUIREMENTS FOR CERTAIN HOSPITALS.—

(1) IN GENERAL.—*A hospital organization to which this subsection applies shall not be treated as described in subsection (c)(3) unless the organization—*

(A) *meets the community health needs assessment requirements described in paragraph (3),*

(B) *meets the financial assistance policy requirements described in paragraph (4),*

(C) *meets the requirements on charges described in paragraph (5), and*

(D) *meets the billing and collection requirement described in paragraph (6).*

(2) HOSPITAL ORGANIZATIONS TO WHICH SUBSECTION APPLIES.—

(A) IN GENERAL.—*This subsection shall apply to—*

(i) an organization which operates a facility which is required by a State to be licensed, registered, or similarly recognized as a hospital, and

(ii) any other organization which the Secretary determines has the provision of hospital care as its principal function or purpose constituting the basis for its exemption under subsection (c)(3) (determined without regard to this subsection).

(B) ORGANIZATIONS WITH MORE THAN 1 HOSPITAL FACILITY.—If a hospital organization operates more than 1 hospital facility—

(i) the organization shall meet the requirements of this subsection separately with respect to each such facility, and

(ii) the organization shall not be treated as described in subsection (c)(3) with respect to any such facility for which such requirements are not separately met.

(3) COMMUNITY HEALTH NEEDS ASSESSMENTS.—

(A) IN GENERAL.—An organization meets the requirements of this paragraph with respect to any taxable year only if the organization—

(i) has conducted a community health needs assessment which meets the requirements of subparagraph (B) in such taxable year or in either of the 2 taxable years immediately preceding such taxable year, and

(ii) has adopted an implementation strategy to meet the community health needs identified through such assessment.

(B) COMMUNITY HEALTH NEEDS ASSESSMENT.—A community health needs assessment meets the requirements of this paragraph if such community health needs assessment—

(i) takes into account input from persons who represent the broad interests of the community served by the hospital facility, including those with special knowledge of or expertise in public health, and

(ii) is made widely available to the public.

(4) FINANCIAL ASSISTANCE POLICY.—An organization meets the requirements of this paragraph if the organization establishes the following policies:

(A) FINANCIAL ASSISTANCE POLICY.—A written financial assistance policy which includes—

(i) eligibility criteria for financial assistance, and whether such assistance includes free or discounted care,

(ii) the basis for calculating amounts charged to patients,

(iii) the method for applying for financial assistance,

(iv) in the case of an organization which does not have a separate billing and collections policy, the actions the organization may take in the event of non-payment, including collections action and reporting to credit agencies, and

(v) measures to widely publicize the policy within the community to be served by the organization.

(B) POLICY RELATING TO EMERGENCY MEDICAL CARE.—A written policy requiring the organization to provide, without discrimination, care for emergency medical conditions (within the meaning of section 1867 of the Social Security Act (42 U.S.C. 1395dd)) to individuals regardless of their eligibility under the financial assistance policy described in subparagraph (A).

(5) LIMITATION ON CHARGES.—An organization meets the requirements of this paragraph if the organization—

(A) limits amounts charged for emergency or other medically necessary care provided to individuals eligible for assistance under the financial assistance policy described in paragraph (4)(A) to not more than the amounts generally billed to individuals who have insurance covering such care, and

(B) prohibits the use of gross charges.

(6) BILLING AND COLLECTION REQUIREMENTS.—An organization meets the requirement of this paragraph only if the organization does not engage in extraordinary collection actions before the organization has made reasonable efforts to determine whether the individual is eligible for assistance under the financial assistance policy described in paragraph (4)(A).

(7) REGULATORY AUTHORITY.—The Secretary shall issue such regulations and guidance as may be necessary to carry out the provisions of this subsection, including guidance relating to what constitutes reasonable efforts to determine the eligibility of a patient under a financial assistance policy for purposes of paragraph (6).

[CCH Explanation at ¶ 355.]

Amendments

• **2010, Patient Protection and Affordable Care Act (P.L. 111-148)**

P.L. 111-148, § 9007(a):

Amended Code Sec. 501 by redesignating subsection (r) as subsection (s) and by inserting after subsection (q) a new subsection (r). **Effective** for tax years beginning after 3-23-2010. For a special rule, see Act Sec. 9007(f)(2), below.

P.L. 111-148, § 9007(f)(2), provides:

(2) COMMUNITY HEALTH NEEDS ASSESSMENT.—The requirements of section 501(r)(3) of the Internal Revenue Code of 1986, as added by subsection (a), shall apply to taxable years beginning after the date which is 2 years after the date of the enactment of this Act.

P.L. 111-148, § 10903(a):

Amended Code Sec. 501(r)(5)(A), as added by Act Sec. 9007, by striking "the lowest amounts charged" and inserting "the amounts generally billed". **Effective** for tax years beginning 3-23-2010.

(s) CROSS REFERENCE.—

For nonexemption of Communist-controlled organizations, see section 11(b) of the Internal Security Act of 1950 (64 Stat. 997; 50 U. S. C. 790 (b)).

Amendments

• **2010, Patient Protection and Affordable Care Act (P.L. 111-148)**

P.L. 111-148, § 9007(a):

Amended Code Sec. 501 by redesignating subsection (r) as subsection (s). **Effective** for tax years beginning 3-23-2010.

[¶ 5190] CODE SEC. 833. TREATMENT OF BLUE CROSS AND BLUE SHIELD ORGANIZATIONS, ETC.

* * *

(c) ORGANIZATIONS TO WHICH SECTION APPLIES.—

* * *

(5) NONAPPLICATION OF SECTION IN CASE OF LOW MEDICAL LOSS RATIO.—Notwithstanding the preceding paragraphs, this section shall not apply to any organization unless such organization's percentage of total premium revenue expended on reimbursement for clinical services provided to enrollees under its policies during such taxable year (as reported under section 2718 of the Public Health Service Act) is not less than 85 percent.

[CCH Explanation at ¶ 555.]

Amendments

• **2010, Patient Protection and Affordable Care Act (P.L. 111-148)**

P.L. 111-148, § 9016(a):

Amended Code Sec. 833(c) by adding at the end a new paragraph (5). **Effective** for tax years beginning after 12-31-2009.

[¶ 5200] CODE SEC. 1401. RATE OF TAX.

* * *

(b) HOSPITAL INSURANCE.—

(1) IN GENERAL.—In addition to the tax imposed by the preceding subsection, there shall be imposed for each taxable year, on the self-employment income of every individual, a tax equal to the following percent of the amount of the self-employment income for such taxable year:

	In the case of a taxable year	
Beginning after:	And before:	Percent
December 31, 1983	January 1, 1985	2.60
December 31, 1984	January 1, 1986	2.70
December 31, 1985		2.90

(2) ADDITIONAL TAX.—

(A) IN GENERAL.—In addition to the tax imposed by paragraph (1) and the preceding subsection, there is hereby imposed on every taxpayer (other than a corporation, estate, or trust) for each taxable year beginning after December 31, 2012, a tax equal to 0.9 percent of the self-employment income for such taxable year which is in excess of—

(i) in the case of a joint return, $250,000,

(ii) in the case of a married taxpayer (as defined in section 7703) filing a separate return, ½ of the dollar amount determined under clause (i), and

(iii) in any other case, $200,000.

(B) COORDINATION WITH FICA.—The amounts under clause (i), (ii), or (iii) (whichever is applicable) of subparagraph (A) shall be reduced (but not below zero) by the amount of wages taken into account in determining the tax imposed under section 3121(b)(2) with respect to the taxpayer.

* * *

[CCH Explanation at ¶ 620.]

Amendments

• **2010, Health Care and Education Reconciliation Act of 2010 (P.L. 111-152)**

P.L. 111-152, § 1402(b)(1)(B)(i)-(ii):

Amended Code Sec. 1401(b)(2), as added by section 9015 of the Patient Protection and Affordable Care Act (P.L. 111-148), and amended by section 10906 of such Act, by striking "and" at the end of clause (i), by redesignating clause (ii) as clause (iii), and by inserting after clause (i) a new clause (ii) in subparagraph (A); by striking "under clauses (i) and (ii)" and inserting "under clause (i), (ii), or (iii) (whichever is applicable)" in subparagraph (B). **Effective** with respect to remuneration received, and tax years beginning after, 12-31-2012.

• **2010, Patient Protection and Affordable Care Act (P.L. 111-148)**

P.L. 111-148, § 9015(b)(1)(A)-(B):

Amended Code Sec. 1401(b) by striking "In addition" and inserting:

"(1) IN GENERAL.—In addition",

and by adding at the end a new paragraph (2). **Effective** with respect to remuneration received, and tax years beginning, after 12-31-2012.

P.L. 111-148, § 10906(b):

Amended Code Sec. 1401(b)(2)(A), as added by Act Sec. 9015(b)(1), by striking "0.5 percent" and inserting "0.9 percent". **Effective** with respect to remuneration received, and tax years beginning, after 12-31-2012.

[¶ 5210] CODE SEC. 1402. DEFINITIONS.

(a) NET EARNINGS FROM SELF-EMPLOYMENT.—The term "net earnings from self-employment" means the gross income derived by an individual from any trade or business carried on by such individual, less the deductions allowed by this subtitle which are attributable to such trade or business, plus his distributive share (whether or not distributed) of income or loss described in section 702(a)(8) from any trade or business carried on by a partnership of which he is a member; except that in computing such gross income and deductions and such distributive share of partnership ordinary income or loss—

* * *

(12) in lieu of the deduction provided by section 164(f) (relating to deduction for one-half of self-employment taxes), there shall be allowed a deduction equal to the product of—

(A) the taxpayer's net earnings from self-employment for the taxable year (determined without regard to this paragraph), and

(B) one-half of the sum of the rates imposed by subsections (a) and (b) of section 1401 for such year *(determined without regard to the rate imposed under paragraph (2) of section 1401(b))*;

* * *

[CCH Explanation at ¶ 620.]

Amendments

• **2010, Patient Protection and Affordable Care Act (P.L. 111-148)**

P.L. 111-148, § 9015(b)(2)(B):

Amended Code Sec. 1402(a)(12)(B) by inserting "(determined without regard to the rate imposed under paragraph

(2) of section 1401(b))" after "for such year". **Effective** with respect to remuneration received, and for tax years beginning, after 12-31-2012.

[¶ 5220] CODE SEC. 1411. IMPOSITION OF TAX.

(a) IN GENERAL.—*Except as provided in subsection (e)—*

(1) APPLICATION TO INDIVIDUALS.—*In the case of an individual, there is hereby imposed (in addition to any other tax imposed by this subtitle) for each taxable year a tax equal to 3.8 percent of the lesser of—*

(A) net investment income for such taxable year, or

(B) the excess (if any) of—

(i) the modified adjusted gross income for such taxable year, over

(ii) the threshold amount.

(2) APPLICATION TO ESTATES AND TRUSTS.—*In the case of an estate or trust, there is hereby imposed (in addition to any other tax imposed by this subtitle) for each taxable year a tax of 3.8 percent of the lesser of—*

(A) the undistributed net investment income for such taxable year, or

(B) the excess (if any) of—

(i) the adjusted gross income (as defined in section 67(e)) for such taxable year, over

(ii) the dollar amount at which the highest tax bracket in section 1(e) begins for such taxable year.

(b) THRESHOLD AMOUNT.—*For purposes of this chapter, the term "threshold amount" means—*

(1) in the case of a taxpayer making a joint return under section 6013 or a surviving spouse (as defined in section 2(a)), $250,000,

(2) in the case of a married taxpayer (as defined in section 7703) filing a separate return, ½ of the dollar amount determined under paragraph (1), and

(3) in any other case, $200,000.

(c) NET INVESTMENT INCOME.—*For purposes of this chapter—*

(1) IN GENERAL.—*The term "net investment income" means the excess (if any) of—*

(A) the sum of—

(i) gross income from interest, dividends, annuities, royalties, and rents, other than such income which is derived in the ordinary course of a trade or business not described in paragraph (2),

(ii) other gross income derived from a trade or business described in paragraph (2), and

(iii) net gain (to the extent taken into account in computing taxable income) attributable to the disposition of property other than property held in a trade or business not described in paragraph (2), over

(B) the deductions allowed by this subtitle which are properly allocable to such gross income or net gain.

(2) TRADES AND BUSINESSES TO WHICH TAX APPLIES.—A trade or business is described in this paragraph if such trade or business is—

(A) a passive activity (within the meaning of section 469) with respect to the taxpayer, or

(B) a trade or business of trading in financial instruments or commodities (as defined in section 475(e)(2)).

(3) INCOME ON INVESTMENT OF WORKING CAPITAL SUBJECT TO TAX.—A rule similar to the rule of section 469(e)(1)(B) shall apply for purposes of this subsection.

(4) EXCEPTION FOR CERTAIN ACTIVE INTERESTS IN PARTNERSHIPS AND S CORPORATIONS.—In the case of a disposition of an interest in a partnership or S corporation—

(A) gain from such disposition shall be taken into account under clause (iii) of paragraph (1)(A) only to the extent of the net gain which would be so taken into account by the transferor if all property of the partnership or S corporation were sold for fair market value immediately before the disposition of such interest, and

(B) a rule similar to the rule of subparagraph (A) shall apply to a loss from such disposition.

(5) EXCEPTION FOR DISTRIBUTIONS FROM QUALIFIED PLANS.—The term "net investment income" shall not include any distribution from a plan or arrangement described in section 401(a), 403(a), 403(b), 408, 408A, or 457(b).

(6) SPECIAL RULE.—Net investment income shall not include any item taken into account in determining self-employment income for such taxable year on which a tax is imposed by section 1401(b).

(d) MODIFIED ADJUSTED GROSS INCOME.—For purposes of this chapter, the term "modified adjusted gross income" means adjusted gross income increased by the excess of—

(1) the amount excluded from gross income under section 911(a)(1), over

(2) the amount of any deductions (taken into account in computing adjusted gross income) or exclusions disallowed under section 911(d)(6) with respect to the amounts described in paragraph (1).

(e) NONAPPLICATION OF SECTION.—This section shall not apply to—

(1) a nonresident alien, or

(2) a trust all of the unexpired interests in which are devoted to one or more of the purposes described in section 170(c)(2)(B).

[CCH Explanation at ¶ 605, ¶ 610 and ¶ 615.]

Amendments
• 2010, Health Care and Education Reconciliation Act of 2010 (P.L. 111-152)

P.L. 111-152, § 1402(a)(1):

Amended subtitle A by inserting after chapter 2 a new chapter 2A (Code Sec. 1411). **Effective** for tax years beginning after 12-31-2012.

[¶ 5230] CODE SEC. 3101. RATE OF TAX.

* * *

(b) HOSPITAL INSURANCE.—

(1) IN GENERAL.—In addition to the tax imposed by the preceding subsection, there is hereby imposed on the income of every individual a tax equal to 1.45 percent of the wages (as defined in section 3121(a)) received by him with respect to employment (as defined in section 3121(b)).

(2) ADDITIONAL TAX.—In addition to the tax imposed by paragraph (1) and the preceding subsection, there is hereby imposed on every taxpayer (other than a corporation, estate, or trust) a tax equal to 0.9 percent of wages which are received with respect to employment (as defined in section 3121(b)) during any taxable year beginning after December 31, 2012, and which are in excess of—

(A) in the case of a joint return, $250,000,

(B) in the case of a married taxpayer (as defined in section 7703) filing a separate return, ½ of the dollar amount determined under subparagraph (A), and

(C) in any other case, $200,000.

* * *

[CCH Explanation at ¶ 620.]
Amendments

• **2010, Tax Relief, Unemployment Insurance Reauthorization, and Job Creation Act of 2010 (P.L. 111-312)**

P.L. 111-312, § 601(a)-(e), provides:

(a) IN GENERAL.—Notwithstanding any other provision of law—

(1) with respect to any taxable year which begins in the payroll tax holiday period, the rate of tax under section 1401(a) of the Internal Revenue Code of 1986 shall be 10.40 percent, and

(2) with respect to remuneration received during the payroll tax holiday period, the rate of tax under section 3101(a) of such Code shall be 4.2 percent (including for purposes of determining the applicable percentage under section 3201(a) and 3211(a)(1) of such Code).

(b) COORDINATION WITH DEDUCTIONS FOR EMPLOYMENT TAXES.—

(1) DEDUCTION IN COMPUTING NET EARNINGS FROM SELFEMPLOYMENT.—For purposes of applying section 1402(a)(12) of the Internal Revenue Code of 1986, the rate of tax imposed by subsection 1401(a) of such Code shall be determined without regard to the reduction in such rate under this section.

(2) INDIVIDUAL DEDUCTION.—In the case of the taxes imposed by section 1401 of such Code for any taxable year which begins in the payroll tax holiday period, the deduction under section 164(f) with respect to such taxes shall be equal to the sum of—

(A) 59.6 percent of the portion of such taxes attributable to the tax imposed by section 1401(a) (determined after the application of this section), plus

(B) one-half of the portion of such taxes attributable to the tax imposed by section 1401(b).

(c) PAYROLL TAX HOLIDAY PERIOD.—The term "payroll tax holiday period" means calendar year 2011.

(d) EMPLOYER NOTIFICATION.—The Secretary of the Treasury shall notify employers of the payroll tax holiday period in any manner the Secretary deems appropriate.

(e) TRANSFERS OF FUNDS.—

(1) TRANSFERS TO FEDERAL OLD-AGE AND SURVIVORS INSURANCE TRUST FUND.—There are hereby appropriated to the Federal Old-Age and Survivors Trust Fund and the Federal Disability Insurance Trust Fund established under section 201 of the Social Security Act (42 U.S.C. 401) amounts equal to the reduction in revenues to the Treasury by reason of the application of subsection (a). Amounts appropriated by the preceding sentence shall be transferred from the general fund at such times and in such manner as to replicate to the extent possible the transfers which would have occurred to such Trust Fund had such amendments not been enacted.

(2) TRANSFERS TO SOCIAL SECURITY EQUIVALENT BENEFIT ACCOUNT.—There are hereby appropriated to the Social Security Equivalent Benefit Account established under section 15A(a) of the Railroad Retirement Act of 1974 (45 U.S.C. 231n–1(a)) amounts equal to the reduction in revenues to the Treasury by reason of the application of subsection (a)(2). Amounts appropriated by the preceding sentence shall be transferred from the general fund at such times and in such manner as to replicate to the extent possible the transfers which would have occurred to such Account had such amendments not been enacted.

(3) COORDINATION WITH OTHER FEDERAL LAWS.—For purposes of applying any provision of Federal law other than the provisions of the Internal Revenue Code of 1986, the rate of tax in effect under section 3101(a) of such Code shall be determined without regard to the reduction in such rate under this section.

• **2010, Health Care and Education Reconciliation Act of 2010 (P.L. 111-152)**

P.L. 111-152, § 1402(b)(1)(A):

Amended Code Sec. 3101(b)(2), as added by section 9015 of the Patient Protection and Affordable Care Act (P.L. 111-148), and amended by section 10906 of such Act, by striking "and" at the end of subparagraph (A), by redesignating subparagraph (B) as subparagraph (C), and by inserting after subparagraph (A) a new subparagraph (B). **Effective** with respect to remuneration received, and tax years beginning after, 12-31-2012.

• **2010, Patient Protection and Affordable Care Act (P.L. 111-148)**

P.L. 111-148, § 9015(a)(1)(A)-(D):

Amended Code Sec. 3101(b) by striking "In addition" and inserting:

"(1) IN GENERAL.—In addition",

by striking "the following percentages of the" and inserting "1.45 percent of the", by striking "(as defined in section 3121(b))—"and all that follows and inserting "(as defined in section 3121(b)).", and by adding at the end a new paragraph (2). **Effective** with respect to remuneration received, and tax years beginning, after 12-31-2012. Prior to amendment, Code Sec. 3101(b) read as follows:

(b) HOSPITAL INSURANCE.—In addition to the tax imposed by the preceding subsection, there is hereby imposed on the income of every individual a tax equal to the following percentages of the wages (as defined in section 3121(a)) received by him with respect to employment (as defined in section 3121(b))—

(1) with respect to wages received during the calendar years 1974 through 1977, the rate shall be 0.90 percent;

(2) with respect to wages received during the calendar year 1978, the rate shall be 1.00 percent;

(3) with respect to wages received during the calendar years 1979 and 1980, the rate shall be 1.05 percent;

(4) with respect to wages received during the calendar years 1981 through 1984, the rate shall be 1.30 percent;

(5) with respect to wages received during the calendar year 1985, the rate shall be 1.35 percent; and

(6) with respect to wages received after December 31, 1985, the rate shall be 1.45 percent.

P.L. 111-148, § 10906(a):

Amended Code Sec. 3101(b)(2), as added by Act Sec. 9015(a)(1), by striking "0.5 percent" and inserting "0.9 percent". **Effective** with respect to remuneration received, and tax years beginning, after 12-31-2012.

[¶ 5240] CODE SEC. 3102. DEDUCTION OF TAX FROM WAGES.

* * *

(f) Special Rules for Additional Tax.—

(1) In general.—In the case of any tax imposed by section 3101(b)(2), subsection (a) shall only apply to the extent to which the taxpayer receives wages from the employer in excess of $200,000, and the employer may disregard the amount of wages received by such taxpayer's spouse.

(2) Collection of amounts not withheld.—To the extent that the amount of any tax imposed by section 3101(b)(2) is not collected by the employer, such tax shall be paid by the employee.

(3) Tax paid by recipient.—If an employer, in violation of this chapter, fails to deduct and withhold the tax imposed by section 3101(b)(2) and thereafter the tax is paid by the employee, the tax so required to be deducted and withheld shall not be collected from the employer, but this paragraph shall in no case relieve the employer from liability for any penalties or additions to tax otherwise applicable in respect of such failure to deduct and withhold.

[CCH Explanation at ¶ 620.]
Amendments
• 2010, Patient Protection and Affordable Care Act (P.L. 111-148)

P.L. 111-148, § 9015(a)(2):

Amended Code Sec. 3102 by adding at the end a new subsection (f). **Effective** with respect to remuneration received, and tax years beginning, after 12-31-2012.

[¶ 5250] *CODE SEC. 4191. MEDICAL DEVICES.*

(a) In General.—There is hereby imposed on the sale of any taxable medical device by the manufacturer, producer, or importer a tax equal to 2.3 percent of the price for which so sold.

(b) Taxable Medical Device.—For purposes of this section—

(1) In general.—The term "taxable medical device" means any device (as defined in section 201(h) of the Federal Food, Drug, and Cosmetic Act) intended for humans.

(2) Exemptions.—Such term shall not include—

(A) eyeglasses,

(B) contact lenses,

(C) hearing aids, and

(D) any other medical device determined by the Secretary to be of a type which is generally purchased by the general public at retail for individual use.

[CCH Explanation at ¶ 350.]
Amendments
• 2010, Health Care and Education Reconciliation Act of 2010 (P.L. 111-152)

P.L. 111-152, § 1405(a)(1):

Amended chapter 32 by inserting after subchapter D a new subchapter E (Code Sec. 4191). **Effective** for sales after 12-31-2012.

[¶ 5260] CODE SEC. 4221. CERTAIN TAX-FREE SALES.

(a) General Rule.—Under regulations prescribed by the Secretary, no tax shall be imposed under this chapter (other than under section 4121 or 4081) on the sale by the manufacturer (or under subchapter A or C of chapter 31 on the first retail sale) of an article—

(1) for use by the purchaser for further manufacture, or for resale by the purchaser to a second purchaser for use by such second purchaser in further manufacture,

(2) for export, or for resale by the purchaser to a second purchaser for export,

(3) for use by the purchaser as supplies for vessels or aircraft,

(4) to a State or local government for the exclusive use of a State or local government,

(5) to a nonprofit educational organization for its exclusive use, or

(6) to a qualified blood collector organization (as defined in section 7701(a)(49)) for such organization's exclusive use in the collection, storage, or transportation of blood,

but only if such exportation or use is to occur before any other use. Paragraphs (4), (5), and (6) shall not apply to the tax imposed by section 4064. In the case of taxes imposed by section 4051 or 4071, paragraphs (4) and (5) shall not apply on and after *October 1, 2016*. In the case of the tax imposed by section 4131, paragraphs (3), (4), and (5) shall not apply and paragraph (2) shall apply only if the use of the exported vaccine meets such requirements as the Secretary may by regulations prescribe. In the case of taxes imposed by subchapter A of chapter 31, paragraphs (1), (3), (4), and (5) shall not apply. In the case of taxes imposed by subchapter C or D, paragraph (6) shall not apply. *In the case of the tax imposed by section 4191, paragraphs (3), (4), (5), and (6) shall not apply.*

* * *

[CCH Explanation at ¶ 350.]

Amendments

• **2012, Highway Investment, Job Creation, and Economic Growth Act of 2012 (P.L. 112-141)**

P.L. 112-141, § 40102(d)(1):

Amended Code Sec. 4221(a) by striking "July 1, 2012" and inserting "October 1, 2016". **Effective** 7-1-2012.

• **2012, Temporary Surface Transportation Extension Act of 2012 (P.L. 112-140)**

P.L. 112-140, § 1(c), provides:

(c) SPECIAL RULE FOR EXECUTION OF AMENDMENTS IN MAP–21.—On the date of enactment of the MAP–21 [P.L. 112-141]—

(1) this Act and the amendments made by this Act shall cease to be effective;

(2) the text of the laws amended by this Act shall revert back so as to read as the text read on the day before the date of enactment of this Act; and

(3) the amendments made by the MAP–21 shall be executed as if this Act had not been enacted.

P.L. 112-140, § 402(c):

Amended Code Sec. 4221(a) by striking "July 1, 2012" and inserting "July 7, 2012". **Effective** 7-1-2012. For a special rule, see Act Sec. 1(c), above.

• **2012, Surface Transportation Extension Act of 2012 (P.L. 112-102)**

P.L. 112-102, § 402(d):

Amended Code Sec. 4221(a) by striking "April 1, 2012" and inserting "July 1, 2012". **Effective** 4-1-2012.

• **2011, Surface Transportation Extension Act of 2011, Part II (P.L. 112-30)**

P.L. 112-30, § 142(d):

Amended Code Sec. 4221(a) by striking "October 1, 2011" and inserting "April 1, 2012". **Effective** 10-1-2011.

• **2010, Health Care and Education Reconciliation Act of 2010 (P.L. 111-152)**

P.L. 111-152, § 1405(b)(1):

Amended Code Sec. 4221(a) by adding at the end a new sentence. **Effective** for sales after 12-31-2012.

[¶ 5270] CODE SEC. 4375. HEALTH INSURANCE.

(a) IMPOSITION OF FEE.—*There is hereby imposed on each specified health insurance policy for each policy year ending after September 30, 2012, a fee equal to the product of $2 ($1 in the case of policy years ending during fiscal year 2013) multiplied by the average number of lives covered under the policy.*

(b) LIABILITY FOR FEE.—*The fee imposed by subsection (a) shall be paid by the issuer of the policy.*

(c) SPECIFIED HEALTH INSURANCE POLICY.—*For purposes of this section:*

(1) IN GENERAL.—*Except as otherwise provided in this section, the term "specified health insurance policy" means any accident or health insurance policy (including a policy under a group health plan) issued with respect to individuals residing in the United States.*

(2) EXEMPTION FOR CERTAIN POLICIES.—*The term "specified health insurance policy" does not include any insurance if substantially all of its coverage is of excepted benefits described in section 9832(c).*

(3) Treatment of Prepaid Health Coverage Arrangements.—

(A) In General.—In the case of any arrangement described in subparagraph (B), such arrangement shall be treated as a specified health insurance policy, and the person referred to in such subparagraph shall be treated as the issuer.

(B) Description of Arrangements.—An arrangement is described in this subparagraph if under such arrangement fixed payments or premiums are received as consideration for any person's agreement to provide or arrange for the provision of accident or health coverage to residents of the United States, regardless of how such coverage is provided or arranged to be provided.

(d) Adjustments for Increases in Health Care Spending.—In the case of any policy year ending in any fiscal year beginning after September 30, 2014, the dollar amount in effect under subsection (a) for such policy year shall be equal to the sum of such dollar amount for policy years ending in the previous fiscal year (determined after the application of this subsection), plus an amount equal to the product of—

(1) such dollar amount for policy years ending in the previous fiscal year, multiplied by

(2) the percentage increase in the projected per capita amount of National Health Expenditures, as most recently published by the Secretary before the beginning of the fiscal year.

(e) Termination.—This section shall not apply to policy years ending after September 30, 2019.

[CCH Explanation at ¶545 and ¶550.]

Amendments
• **2010, Patient Protection and Affordable Care Act (P.L. 111-148)**

P.L. 111-148, §6301(e)(2)(A):

Amended chapter 34 by adding at the end a new subchapter B [sic] (Code Secs. 4375-4377). **Effective** 3-23-2010.

[¶5280] *CODE SEC. 4376. SELF-INSURED HEALTH PLANS.*

(a) Imposition of Fee.—In the case of any applicable self-insured health plan for each plan year ending after September 30, 2012, there is hereby imposed a fee equal to $2 ($1 in the case of plan years ending during fiscal year 2013) multiplied by the average number of lives covered under the plan.

(b) Liability for Fee.—

(1) In General.—The fee imposed by subsection (a) shall be paid by the plan sponsor.

(2) Plan Sponsor.—For purposes of paragraph (1) the term "plan sponsor" means—

(A) the employer in the case of a plan established or maintained by a single employer,

(B) the employee organization in the case of a plan established or maintained by an employee organization,

(C) in the case of—

(i) a plan established or maintained by 2 or more employers or jointly by 1 or more employers and 1 or more employee organizations,

(ii) a multiple employer welfare arrangement, or

(iii) a voluntary employees' beneficiary association described in section 501(c)(9), the association, committee, joint board of trustees, or other similar group of representatives of the parties who establish or maintain the plan, or

(D) the cooperative or association described in subsection (c)(2)(F) in the case of a plan established or maintained by such a cooperative or association.

(c) Applicable Self-Insured Health Plan.—For purposes of this section, the term "applicable self-insured health plan" means any plan for providing accident or health coverage if—

(1) any portion of such coverage is provided other than through an insurance policy, and

(2) such plan is established or maintained—

(A) by 1 or more employers for the benefit of their employees or former employees,

(B) by 1 or more employee organizations for the benefit of their members or former members,

(C) *jointly by 1 or more employers and 1 or more employee organizations for the benefit of employees or former employees,*

(D) *by a voluntary employees' beneficiary association described in section 501(c)(9),*

(E) *by any organization described in section 501(c)(6), or*

(F) *in the case of a plan not described in the preceding subparagraphs, by a multiple employer welfare arrangement (as defined in section 3(40) of [the] Employee Retirement Income Security Act of 1974), a rural electric cooperative (as defined in section 3(40)(B)(iv) of such Act), or a rural telephone cooperative association (as defined in section 3(40)(B)(v) of such Act).*

(d) ADJUSTMENTS FOR INCREASES IN HEALTH CARE SPENDING.—*In the case of any plan year ending in any fiscal year beginning after September 30, 2014, the dollar amount in effect under subsection (a) for such plan year shall be equal to the sum of such dollar amount for plan years ending in the previous fiscal year (determined after the application of this subsection), plus an amount equal to the product of—*

(1) *such dollar amount for plan years ending in the previous fiscal year, multiplied by*

(2) *the percentage increase in the projected per capita amount of National Health Expenditures, as most recently published by the Secretary before the beginning of the fiscal year.*

(e) TERMINATION.—*This section shall not apply to plan years ending after September 30, 2019.*

[CCH Explanation at ¶ 545 and ¶ 550.]

Amendments

• **2010, Patient Protection and Affordable Care Act (P.L. 111-148)**

P.L. 111-148, § 6301(e)(2)(A):

Amended chapter 34 by adding at the end a new subchapter B [sic] (Code Secs. 4375-4377). **Effective** 3-23-2010.

[¶ 5290] *CODE SEC. 4377. DEFINITIONS AND SPECIAL RULES.*

(a) DEFINITIONS.—*For purposes of this subchapter—*

(1) ACCIDENT AND HEALTH COVERAGE.—*The term "accident and health coverage" means any coverage which, if provided by an insurance policy, would cause such policy to be a specified health insurance policy (as defined in section 4375(c)).*

(2) INSURANCE POLICY.—*The term "insurance policy" means any policy or other instrument whereby a contract of insurance is issued, renewed, or extended.*

(3) UNITED STATES.—*The term "United States" includes any possession of the United States.*

(b) TREATMENT OF GOVERNMENTAL ENTITIES.—

(1) IN GENERAL.—*For purposes of this subchapter—*

(A) *the term "person" includes any governmental entity, and*

(B) *notwithstanding any other law or rule of law, governmental entities shall not be exempt from the fees imposed by this subchapter except as provided in paragraph (2).*

(2) TREATMENT OF EXEMPT GOVERNMENTAL PROGRAMS.—*In the case of an exempt governmental program, no fee shall be imposed under section 4375 or section 4376 on any covered life under such program.*

(3) EXEMPT GOVERNMENTAL PROGRAM DEFINED.—*For purposes of this subchapter, the term "exempt governmental program" means—*

(A) *any insurance program established under title XVIII of the Social Security Act,*

(B) *the medical assistance program established by title XIX or XXI of the Social Security Act,*

(C) *any program established by Federal law for providing medical care (other than through insurance policies) to individuals (or the spouses and dependents thereof) by reason of such individuals being members of the Armed Forces of the United States or veterans, and*

(D) any program established by Federal law for providing medical care (other than through insurance policies) to members of Indian tribes (as defined in section 4(d) of the Indian Health Care Improvement Act).

(c) Treatment as Tax.—For purposes of subtitle F, the fees imposed by this subchapter shall be treated as if they were taxes.

(d) No Cover Over to Possessions.—Notwithstanding any other provision of law, no amount collected under this subchapter shall be covered over to any possession of the United States.

[CCH Explanation at ¶ 545 and ¶ 550.]

Amendments

• **2010, Patient Protection and Affordable Care Act (P.L. 111-148)**

P.L. 111-148, § 6301(e)(2)(A):

Amended chapter 34 by adding at the end a new subchapter B [sic] (Code Secs. 4375-4377). **Effective** 3-23-2010.

[¶ 5310] CODE SEC. 4959. TAXES ON FAILURES BY HOSPITAL ORGANIZATIONS.

If a hospital organization to which section 501(r) applies fails to meet the requirement of section 501(r)(3) for any taxable year, there is imposed on the organization a tax equal to $50,000.

[CCH Explanation at ¶ 355.]

Amendments

• **2010, Patient Protection and Affordable Care Act (P.L. 111-148)**

P.L. 111-148, § 9007(b)(1):

Amended subchapter D of chapter 42 by adding at the end a new Code Sec. 4959. **Effective** for failures occurring after 3-23-2010.

[¶ 5320] CODE SEC. 4980H. SHARED RESPONSIBILITY FOR EMPLOYERS REGARDING HEALTH COVERAGE.

(a) Large Employers Not Offering Health Coverage.—If—

(1) any applicable large employer fails to offer to its full-time employees (and their dependents) the opportunity to enroll in minimum essential coverage under an eligible employer-sponsored plan (as defined in section 5000A(f)(2)) for any month, and

(2) at least one full-time employee of the applicable large employer has been certified to the employer under section 1411 of the Patient Protection and Affordable Care Act as having enrolled for such month in a qualified health plan with respect to which an applicable premium tax credit or cost-sharing reduction is allowed or paid with respect to the employee,

then there is hereby imposed on the employer an assessable payment equal to the product of the applicable payment amount and the number of individuals employed by the employer as full-time employees during such month.

(b) [Stricken.]

[CCH Explanation at ¶ 305.]

Amendments

• **2010, Health Care and Education Reconciliation Act of 2010 (P.L. 111-152)**

P.L. 111-152, § 1003(d):

Amended Code Sec. 4980H, as added by section 1513 of the Patient Protection and Affordable Care Act (P.L. 111-148) and amended by section 10106 of such Act, and as amended by Act Sec. 1003(a)-(c) of this Act, by striking subsection (b) and redesignating subsections (c), (d), and (e) as subsections (b), (c), and (d), respectively. **Effective** 3-30-2010. Prior to being stricken, Code Sec. 4980H(b) read as follows:

(b) Large Employers With Waiting Periods Exceeding 60 Days.—

(1) In general.—In the case of any applicable large employer which requires an extended waiting period to enroll in any minimum essential coverage under an employer-sponsored plan (as defined in section 5000A(f)(2)), there is hereby imposed on the employer an assessable payment of $600 for each full-time employee of the employer to whom the extended waiting period applies.

(2) EXTENDED WAITING PERIOD.—The term "extended waiting period" means any waiting period (as defined in section 2701(b)(4) of the Public Health Service Act) which exceeds 60 days.

• 2010, Patient Protection.and Affordable Care Act (P.L. 111-148)

P.L. 111-148, § 10106(e):

Amended Code Sec. 4980H(b), as added by Act Sec. 1513(a). **Effective** 3-23-2010. Prior to amendment, Code Sec. 4980H(b) read as follows:

(b) LARGE EMPLOYERS WITH WAITING PERIODS EXCEEDING 30 DAYS.—

(1) IN GENERAL.—In the case of any applicable large employer which requires an extended waiting period to enroll in any minimum essential coverage under an employer-

sponsored plan (as defined in section 5000A(f)(2)), there is hereby imposed on the employer an assessable payment, in the amount specified in paragraph (2), for each full-time employee of the employer to whom the extended waiting period applies.

(2) AMOUNT.—For purposes of paragraph (1), the amount specified in this paragraph for a full-time employee is—

(A) in the case of an extended waiting period which exceeds 30 days but does not exceed 60 days, $400, and

(B) in the case of an extended waiting period which exceeds 60 days, $600.

(3) EXTENDED WAITING PERIOD.—The term "extended waiting period" means any waiting period (as defined in section 2701(b)(4) of the Public Health Service Act) which exceeds 30 days.

(b) LARGE EMPLOYERS OFFERING COVERAGE WITH EMPLOYEES WHO QUALIFY FOR PREMIUM TAX CREDITS OR COST-SHARING REDUCTIONS.—

(1) IN GENERAL.—If—

(A) an applicable large employer offers to its full-time employees (and their dependents) the opportunity to enroll in minimum essential coverage under an eligible employer-sponsored plan (as defined in section 5000A(f)(2)) for any month, and

(B) 1 or more full-time employees of the applicable large employer has been certified to the employer under section 1411 of the Patient Protection and Affordable Care Act as having enrolled for such month in a qualified health plan with respect to which an applicable premium tax credit or cost-sharing reduction is allowed or paid with respect to the employee,

then there is hereby imposed on the employer an assessable payment equal to the product of the number of full-time employees of the applicable large employer described in subparagraph (B) for such month and an amount equal to 1/12 of $3,000.

(2) OVERALL LIMITATION.—The aggregate amount of tax determined under paragraph (1) with respect to all employees of an applicable large employer for any month shall not exceed the product of the applicable payment amount and the number of individuals employed by the employer as full-time employees during such month.

[CCH Explanation at ¶ 305.]

Amendments

• 2011, Department of Defense and Full-Year Continuing Appropriations Act, 2011 (P.L. 112-10)

P.L. 112-10, § 1858(b)(4):

Amended Code Sec. 4980H(b) by striking paragraph (3). **Effective** as if included in the provision of, and the amendments made by, the provision of the Patient Protection and Affordable Care Act (P.L. 111-148) to which it relates [**effective** for months beginning after 12-31-2013.—CCH]. Prior to being stricken, Code Sec. 4980H(b)(3) read as follows:

(3) SPECIAL RULES FOR EMPLOYERS PROVIDING FREE CHOICE VOUCHERS.—No assessable payment shall be imposed under paragraph (1) for any month with respect to any employee to whom the employer provides a free choice voucher under section 10108 of the Patient Protection and Affordable Care Act for such month.

• 2010, Health Care and Education Reconciliation Act of 2010 (P.L. 111-152)

P.L. 111-152, § 1003(b)(1):

Amended Code Sec. 4980H, as added by section 1513 of the Patient Protection and Affordable Care Act (P.L.

111-148) and amended by section 10106 of such Act, in the flush text following subsection (c)(1)(B), by striking "400 percent of the applicable payment amount" and inserting "an amount equal to 1/12 of $3,000". **Effective** 3-30-2010.

P.L. 111-152, § 1003(d):

Amended Code Sec. 4980H, as added by section 1513 of the Patient Protection and Affordable Care Act (P.L. 111-148) and amended by section 10106 of such Act, and as amended by Act Sec. 1003(a)-(c) of this Act, by redesignating subsection (c) as subsection (b). **Effective** 3-30-2010.

• 2010, Patient Protection and Affordable Care Act (P.L. 111-148)

P.L. 111-148, § 10108(i)(1)(A):

Amended Code Sec. 4980H(c), as added by Act Sec. 1513, by adding at the end a new paragraph (3). **Effective** for months beginning after 12-31-2013.

(c) Definitions and Special Rules.—For purposes of this section—

(1) Applicable payment amount.—The term "applicable payment amount" means, with respect to any month, ½2 of $2,000.

(2) Applicable large employer.—

(A) In general.—The term "applicable large employer" means, with respect to a calendar year, an employer who employed an average of at least 50 full-time employees on business days during the preceding calendar year.

(B) Exemption for certain employers.—

(i) In general.—An employer shall not be considered to employ more than 50 full-time employees if—

(I) the employer's workforce exceeds 50 full-time employees for 120 days or fewer during the calendar year, and

(II) the employees in excess of 50 employed during such 120-day period were seasonal workers.

(ii) Definition of seasonal workers.—The term "seasonal worker" means a worker who performs labor or services on a seasonal basis as defined by the Secretary of Labor, including workers covered by section 500.20(s)(1) of title 29, Code of Federal Regulations and retail workers employed exclusively during holiday seasons.

(C) Rules for determining employer size.—For purposes of this paragraph—

(i) Application of aggregation rule for employers.—All persons treated as a single employer under subsection (b), (c), (m), or (o) of section 414 of the Internal Revenue Code of 1986 shall be treated as 1 employer.

(ii) Employers not in existence in preceding year.—In the case of an employer which was not in existence throughout the preceding calendar year, the determination of whether such employer is an applicable large employer shall be based on the average number of employees that it is reasonably expected such employer will employ on business days in the current calendar year.

(iii) Predecessors.—Any reference in this subsection to an employer shall include a reference to any predecessor of such employer.

(D) Application of employer size to assessable penalties.—

(i) In general.—The number of individuals employed by an applicable large employer as full-time employees during any month shall be reduced by 30 solely for purposes of calculating—

(I) the assessable payment under subsection (a), or

(II) the overall limitation under subsection (b)(2).

(ii) Aggregation.—In the case of persons treated as 1 employer under subparagraph (C)(i), only 1 reduction under subclause (I) or (II) shall be allowed with respect to such persons and such reduction shall be allocated among such persons ratably on the basis of the number of full-time employees employed by each such person.

(E) Full-time equivalents treated as full-time employees.—Solely for purposes of determining whether an employer is an applicable large employer under this paragraph, an employer shall, in addition to the number of full-time employees for any month otherwise determined, include for such month a number of full-time employees determined by dividing the aggregate number of hours of service of employees who are not full-time employees for the month by 120.

(3) Applicable premium tax credit and cost-sharing reduction.—The term "applicable premium tax credit and cost-sharing reduction" means—

(A) any premium tax credit allowed under section 36B,

(B) any cost-sharing reduction under section 1402 of the Patient Protection and Affordable Care Act, and

(C) any advance payment of such credit or reduction under section 1412 of such Act.

(4) FULL-TIME EMPLOYEE.—

(A) IN GENERAL.—The term "full-time employee" means, with respect to any month, an employee who is employed on average at least 30 hours of service per week.

(B) HOURS OF SERVICE.—The Secretary, in consultation with the Secretary of Labor, shall prescribe such regulations, rules, and guidance as may be necessary to determine the hours of service of an employee, including rules for the application of this paragraph to employees who are not compensated on an hourly basis.

(5) INFLATION ADJUSTMENT.—

(A) IN GENERAL.—In the case of any calendar year after 2014, each of the dollar amounts in subsection (b) and paragraph (1) shall be increased by an amount equal to the product of—

(i) such dollar amount, and

(ii) the premium adjustment percentage (as defined in section 1302(c)(4) of the Patient Protection and Affordable Care Act) for the calendar year.

(B) ROUNDING.—If the amount of any increase under subparagraph (A) is not a multiple of $10, such increase shall be rounded to the next lowest multiple of $10.

(6) OTHER DEFINITIONS.—Any term used in this section which is also used in the Patient Protection and Affordable Care Act shall have the same meaning as when used in such Act.

(7) TAX NONDEDUCTIBLE.—For denial of deduction for the tax imposed by this section, see section 275(a)(6).

[CCH Explanation at ¶ 305.]

Amendments

• 2010, Health Care and Education Reconciliation Act of 2010 (P.L. 111-152)

P.L. 111-152, § 1003(a):

Amended subsection (d)(2)(D) of Code Sec. 4980H, as added by section 1513 of the Patient Protection and Affordable Care Act (P.L. 111-148) and amended by section 10106 of such Act. **Effective** 3-30-2010. Prior to amendment, Code Sec. 4980H(d)(2)(D) read as follows:

(D) APPLICATION TO CONSTRUCTION INDUSTRY EMPLOYERS.—In the case of any employer the substantial annual gross receipts of which are attributable to the construction industry—

(i) subparagraph (A) shall be applied by substituting "who employed an average of at least 5 full-time employees on business days during the preceding calendar year and whose annual payroll expenses exceed $250,000 for such preceding calendar year" for "who employed an average of at least 50 full-time employees on business days during the preceding calendar year", and

(ii) subparagraph (B) shall be applied by substituting "5" for "50".

P.L. 111-152, § 1003(b)(2):

Amended Code Sec. 4980H, as added by section 1513 of the Patient Protection and Affordable Care Act (P.L. 111-148) and amended by section 10106 of such Act, in subsection (d)(1), by striking "$750" and inserting "$2,000". **Effective** 3-30-2010.

P.L. 111-152, § 1003(b)(3):

Amended Code Sec. 4980H, as added by section 1513 of the Patient Protection and Affordable Care Act (P.L.

111-148) and amended by section 10106 of such Act, in the matter preceding clause (i) of subsection (d)(5)(A), by striking "subsection (b)(2) and (d)(1)" and inserting "subsection (b) and paragraph (1)". **Effective** 3-30-2010.

P.L. 111-152, § 1003(c):

Amended Code Sec. 4980H(d)(2), as added by section 1513 of the Patient Protection and Affordable Care Act (P.L. 111-148) and amended by section 10106 of such Act and as amended by Act Sec. 1003(a), by adding at the end a new subparagraph (E). **Effective** 3-30-2010.

P.L. 111-152, § 1003(d):

Amended Code Sec. 4980H, as added by section 1513 of the Patient Protection and Affordable Care Act (P.L. 111-148) and amended by section 10106 of such Act, and as amended by Act Sec. 1003(a)-(c) of this Act, by redesignating subsection (d) as subsection (c). **Effective** 3-30-2010.

• 2010, Patient Protection and Affordable Care Act (P.L. 111-148)

P.L. 111-148, § 10106(f)(1):

Amended Code Sec. 4980H(d)(4)(A), as added by Act Sec. 1513(a), by inserting ", with respect to any month," after "means". **Effective** 3-23-2010.

P.L. 111-148, § 10106(f)(2):

Amended Code Sec. 4980H(d)(2), as added by Act Sec. 1513(a), by adding at the end a new subparagraph (D). **Effective** for months beginning after 12-31-2013.

(d) Administration and Procedure.—

(1) In general.—*Any assessable payment provided by this section shall be paid upon notice and demand by the Secretary, and shall be assessed and collected in the same manner as an assessable penalty under subchapter B of chapter 68.*

(2) Time for payment.—*The Secretary may provide for the payment of any assessable payment provided by this section on an annual, monthly, or other periodic basis as the Secretary may prescribe.*

(3) Coordination with credits, etc.—*The Secretary shall prescribe rules, regulations, or guidance for the repayment of any assessable payment (including interest) if such payment is based on the allowance or payment of an applicable premium tax credit or cost-sharing reduction with respect to an employee, such allowance or payment is subsequently disallowed, and the assessable payment would not have been required to be made but for such allowance or payment.*

[CCH Explanation at ¶ 305.]

Amendments

• **2010, Health Care and Education Reconciliation Act of 2010 (P.L. 111-152)**

P.L. 111-152, § 1003(d):

Amended Code Sec. 4980H, as added by section 1513 of the Patient Protection and Affordable Care Act (P.L. 111-148) and amended by section 10106 of such Act, and as amended by Act Sec. 1003(a)-(c) of this Act, by redesignating subsection (e) as subsection (d). **Effective** 3-30-2010.

• **2010, Patient Protection and Affordable Care Act (P.L. 111-148)**

P.L. 111-148, § 1513(a):

Amended chapter 43 by adding at the end a new Code Sec. 4980H. **Effective** for months beginning after 12-31-2013.

>>>→ *Caution: Code Sec. 4980I, below, as added and amended by P.L. 111-148 , applies to tax years beginning after December 31, 2017.*

[¶ 5330] *CODE SEC. 4980I. EXCISE TAX ON HIGH COST EMPLOYER-SPONSORED HEALTH COVERAGE.*

(a) Imposition of Tax.—*If—*

(1) an employee is covered under any applicable employer-sponsored coverage of an employer at any time during a taxable period, and

(2) there is any excess benefit with respect to the coverage,

there is hereby imposed a tax equal to 40 percent of the excess benefit.

(b) Excess Benefit.—*For purposes of this section—*

(1) In general.—*The term "excess benefit" means, with respect to any applicable employer-sponsored coverage made available by an employer to an employee during any taxable period, the sum of the excess amounts determined under paragraph (2) for months during the taxable period.*

(2) Monthly excess amount.—*The excess amount determined under this paragraph for any month is the excess (if any) of—*

(A) the aggregate cost of the applicable employer-sponsored coverage of the employee for the month, over

(B) an amount equal to $\frac{1}{12}$ of the annual limitation under paragraph (3) for the calendar year in which the month occurs.

(3) Annual limitation.—*For purposes of this subsection—*

(A) In general.—*The annual limitation under this paragraph for any calendar year is the dollar limit determined under subparagraph (C) for the calendar year.*

(B) Applicable annual limitation.—

(i) In general.—*Except as provided in clause (ii), the annual limitation which applies for any month shall be determined on the basis of the type of coverage (as determined under subsection (f)(1)) provided to the employee by the employer as of the beginning of the month.*

(ii) MULTIEMPLOYER PLAN COVERAGE.—Any coverage provided under a multiemployer plan (as defined in section 414(f)) shall be treated as coverage other than self-only coverage.

(C) APPLICABLE DOLLAR LIMIT.—

(i) 2018.—In the case of 2018, the dollar limit under this subparagraph is—

(I) in the case of an employee with self-only coverage, $10,200 multiplied by the health cost adjustment percentage (determined by only taking into account self-only coverage), and

(II) in the case of an employee with coverage other than self-only coverage, $27,500 multiplied by the health cost adjustment percentage (determined by only taking into account coverage other than self-only coverage).

(ii) HEALTH COST ADJUSTMENT PERCENTAGE.—For purposes of clause (i), the health cost adjustment percentage is equal to 100 percent plus the excess (if any) of—

(I) the percentage by which the per employee cost for providing coverage under the Blue Cross/Blue Shield standard benefit option under the Federal Employees Health Benefits Plan for plan year 2018 (determined by using the benefit package for such coverage in 2010) exceeds such cost for plan year 2010, over

(II) 55 percent.

(iii) AGE AND GENDER ADJUSTMENT.—

(I) IN GENERAL.—The amount determined under subclause (I) or (II) of clause (i), whichever is applicable, for any taxable period shall be increased by the amount determined under subclause (II).

(II) AMOUNT DETERMINED.—The amount determined under this subclause is an amount equal to the excess (if any) of—

(aa) the premium cost of the Blue Cross/Blue Shield standard benefit option under the Federal Employees Health Benefits Plan for the type of coverage provided such individual in such taxable period if priced for the age and gender characteristics of all employees of the individual's employer, over

(bb) that premium cost for the provision of such coverage under such option in such taxable period if priced for the age and gender characteristics of the national workforce.

(iv) EXCEPTION FOR CERTAIN INDIVIDUALS.—In the case of an individual who is a qualified retiree or who participates in a plan sponsored by an employer the majority of whose employees covered by the plan are engaged in a high-risk profession or employed to repair or install electrical or telecommunications lines—

(I) the dollar amount in clause (i)(I) shall be increased by $1,650, and

(II) the dollar amount in clause (i)(II) shall be increased by $3,450,

(v) SUBSEQUENT YEARS.—In the case of any calendar year after 2018, each of the dollar amounts under clauses (i) (after the application of clause (ii)) and (iv) shall be increased to the amount equal to such amount as in effect for the calendar year preceding such year, increased by an amount equal to the product of—

(I) such amount as so in effect, multiplied by

(II) the cost-of-living adjustment determined under section 1(f)(3) for such year (determined by substituting the calendar year that is 2 years before such year for "1992" in subparagraph (B) thereof), increased by 1 percentage point in the case of determinations for calendar years beginning before 2020.

If any amount determined under this clause is not a multiple of $50, such amount shall be rounded to the nearest multiple of $50.

(D) [Stricken.]

[CCH Explanation at ¶ 345.]

Amendments

• 2010, Health Care and Education Reconciliation Act of 2010 (P.L. 111-152)

P.L. 111-152, § 1401(a)(1)(A)-(B):

Amended Code Sec. 4980I, as added by section 9001 of the Patient Protection and Affordable Care Act (P.L. 111-148), and amended by section 10901 of such Act, by striking "The annual" in subsection (b)(3)(B) and inserting:

"(i) IN GENERAL.—Except as provided in clause (ii), the annual";

and by adding at the end a new clause (ii). **Effective** 3-30-2010.

P.L. 111-152, § 1401(a)(2)(A)-(E):

Amended Code Sec. 4980I, as added by section 9001 of the Patient Protection and Affordable Care Act (P.L. 111-148) and amended by section 10901 of such Act, by striking "Except as provided in subparagraph (D)—"in subsection (b)(3)(C); by striking "2013" in clause (i) of subsection (b)(3)(C) each place it appears in the heading and the text and inserting "2018"; by striking "$8,500" in subclause (I) and inserting "$10,200 multiplied by the health cost adjustment percentage (determined by only taking into account self-only coverage)"; and by striking "$23,000" in subclause (II) and inserting "$27,500 multiplied by the health cost adjustment percentage (determined by only taking into account coverage other than self-only coverage)"; by redesignating clauses (ii) and (iii) of subsection (b)(3)(C) as clauses (iv) and (v), respectively, and by inserting after clause (i) new clauses (ii) and (iii); in clause (iv) of subsection (b)(3)(C), as redesignated by Act Sec. 1401(a)(2)(C), by inserting "covered by the plan" after "whose employees"; and by striking subclauses (I) and (II) and inserting new subclauses (I) and (II); in clause (v) of subsection (b)(3)(C), as redesignated by Act Sec. 1401(a)(2)(C), by striking "2013" and inserting "2018"; by striking "clauses (i) and (ii)" and inserting "clauses (i) (after the application of clause (ii)) and (iv)"; and by inserting "in the case of determinations for calendar years beginning before 2020" after "1 percentage point" in subclause (II) thereof. **Effective** 3-30-2010. Prior to amendment, Code Sec. 4980I(b)(3)(C) read as follows:

(C) APPLICABLE DOLLAR LIMIT.—Except as provided in subparagraph (D)—

(i) 2013.—In the case of 2013, the dollar limit under this subparagraph is—

(I) in the case of an employee with self-only coverage, $8,500, and

(II) in the case of an employee with coverage other than self-only coverage, $23,000.

(ii) EXCEPTION FOR CERTAIN INDIVIDUALS.—In the case of an individual who is a qualified retiree or who participates in a plan sponsored by an employer the majority of whose employees are engaged in a high-risk profession or employed to repair or install electrical or telecommunications lines—

(I) the dollar amount in clause (i)(I) (determined after the application of subparagraph (D)) shall be increased by $1,350, and

(II) the dollar amount in clause (i)(II) (determined after the application of subparagraph (D)) shall be increased by $3,000.

(iii) SUBSEQUENT YEARS.—In the case of any calendar year after 2013, each of the dollar amounts under clauses (i) and (ii) shall be increased to the amount equal to such amount as in effect for the calendar year preceding such year, increased by an amount equal to the product of—

(I) such amount as so in effect, multiplied by

(II) the cost-of-living adjustment determined under section 1(f)(3) for such year (determined by substituting the calendar year that is 2 years before such year for "1992" in subparagraph (B) thereof), increased by 1 percentage point.

If any amount determined under this clause is not a multiple of $50, such amount shall be rounded to the nearest multiple of $50.

P.L. 111-152, § 1401(a)(3):

Amended Code Sec. 4980I, as added by section 9001 of the Patient Protection and Affordable Care Act (P.L. 111-148) and amended by section 10901 of such Act, by striking subparagraph (D) of subsection (b)(3). **Effective** 3-30-2010. Prior to being stricken, Code Sec. 4980I(b)(3)(D) read as follows:

(D) TRANSITION RULE FOR STATES WITH HIGHEST COVERAGE COSTS.—

(i) IN GENERAL.—If an employee is a resident of a high cost State on the first day of any month beginning in 2013, 2014, or 2015, the annual limitation under this paragraph for such month with respect to such employee shall be an amount equal to the applicable percentage of the annual limitation (determined without regard to this subparagraph or subparagraph (C)(ii)).

(ii) APPLICABLE PERCENTAGE.—The applicable percentage is 120 percent for 2013, 110 percent for 2014, and 105 percent for 2015.

(iii) HIGH COST STATE.—The term "high cost State" means each of the 17 States which the Secretary of Health and Human Services, in consultation with the Secretary, estimates had the highest average cost during 2012 for employer-sponsored coverage under health plans. The Secretary's estimate shall be made on the basis of aggregate premiums paid in the State for such health plans, determined using the most recent data available as of August 31, 2012.

(c) LIABILITY TO PAY TAX.—

(1) IN GENERAL.—Each coverage provider shall pay the tax imposed by subsection (a) on its applicable share of the excess benefit with respect to an employee for any taxable period.

(2) COVERAGE PROVIDER.—For purposes of this subsection, the term "coverage provider" means each of the following:

(A) HEALTH INSURANCE COVERAGE.—If the applicable employer-sponsored coverage consists of coverage under a group health plan which provides health insurance coverage, the health insurance issuer.

(B) HSA AND MSA CONTRIBUTIONS.—If the applicable employer-sponsored coverage consists of coverage under an arrangement under which the employer makes contributions described in subsection (b) or (d) of section 106, the employer.

(C) OTHER COVERAGE.—In the case of any other applicable employer-sponsored coverage, the person that administers the plan benefits.

(3) APPLICABLE SHARE.—For purposes of this subsection, a coverage provider's applicable share of an excess benefit for any taxable period is the amount which bears the same ratio to the amount of such excess benefit as—

(A) the cost of the applicable employer-sponsored coverage provided by the provider to the employee during such period, bears to

(B) the aggregate cost of all applicable employer-sponsored coverage provided to the employee by all coverage providers during such period.

(4) RESPONSIBILITY TO CALCULATE TAX AND APPLICABLE SHARES.—

(A) IN GENERAL.—Each employer shall—

(i) calculate for each taxable period the amount of the excess benefit subject to the tax imposed by subsection (a) and the applicable share of such excess benefit for each coverage provider, and

(ii) notify, at such time and in such manner as the Secretary may prescribe, the Secretary and each coverage provider of the amount so determined for the provider.

(B) SPECIAL RULE FOR MULTIEMPLOYER PLANS.—In the case of applicable employer-sponsored coverage made available to employees through a multiemployer plan (as defined in section 414(f)), the plan sponsor shall make the calculations, and provide the notice, required under subparagraph (A).

(d) APPLICABLE EMPLOYER-SPONSORED COVERAGE; COST.—For purposes of this section—

(1) APPLICABLE EMPLOYER-SPONSORED COVERAGE.—

(A) IN GENERAL.—The term "applicable employer-sponsored coverage" means, with respect to any employee, coverage under any group health plan made available to the employee by an employer which is excludable from the employee's gross income under section 106, or would be so excludable if it were employer-provided coverage (within the meaning of such section 106).

(B) EXCEPTIONS.—The term "applicable employer-sponsored coverage" shall not include—

(i) any coverage (whether through insurance or otherwise) described in section 9832(c)(1) (other than subparagraph (G) thereof) or for long-term care, or

(ii) any coverage under a separate policy, certificate, or contract of insurance which provides benefits substantially all of which are for treatment of the mouth (including any organ or structure within the mouth) or for treatment of the eye, or

(iii) any coverage described in section 9832(c)(3) the payment for which is not excludable from gross income and for which a deduction under section 162(l) is not allowable.

(C) COVERAGE INCLUDES EMPLOYEE PAID PORTION.—Coverage shall be treated as applicable employer-sponsored coverage without regard to whether the employer or employee pays for the coverage.

(D) SELF-EMPLOYED INDIVIDUAL.—In the case of an individual who is an employee within the meaning of section 401(c)(1), coverage under any group health plan providing health insurance coverage shall be treated as applicable employer-sponsored coverage if a deduction is allowable under section 162(l) with respect to all or any portion of the cost of the coverage.

(E) GOVERNMENTAL PLANS INCLUDED.—Applicable employer-sponsored coverage shall include coverage under any group health plan established and maintained primarily for its civilian employees by the Government of the United States, by the government of any State or political subdivision thereof, or by any agency or instrumentality of any such government.

(2) DETERMINATION OF COST.—

(A) IN GENERAL.—The cost of applicable employer-sponsored coverage shall be determined under rules similar to the rules of section 4980B(f)(4), except that in determining such cost, any portion of the cost of such coverage which is attributable to the tax imposed under this section shall not be taken into account and the amount of such cost shall be calculated separately for self-only coverage and other coverage. In the case of applicable employer-sponsored coverage which provides coverage to *retired employees, the plan may elect to treat a retired employee who has not attained the age of 65 and a retired employee who has attained the age of 65 as similarly situated beneficiaries.*

(B) HEALTH FSAS.—In the case of applicable employer-sponsored coverage consisting of coverage under a flexible spending arrangement (as defined in section 106(c)(2)), the cost of the coverage shall be equal to the sum of—

(i) the amount of employer contributions under any salary reduction election under the arrangement, plus

(ii) the amount determined under subparagraph (A) with respect to any reimbursement under the arrangement in excess of the contributions described in clause (i).

(C) ARCHER MSAS AND HSAS.—In the case of applicable employer-sponsored coverage consisting of coverage under an arrangement under which the employer makes contributions described in subsection (b) or (d) of section 106, the cost of the coverage shall be equal to the amount of employer contributions under the arrangement.

(D) ALLOCATION ON A MONTHLY BASIS.—If cost is determined on other than a monthly basis, the cost shall be allocated to months in a taxable period on such basis as the Secretary may prescribe.

(3) EMPLOYEE.—The term "employee" includes any former employee, surviving spouse, or other primary insured individual.

[CCH Explanation at ¶ 345.]

Amendments

• **2010, Health Care and Education Reconciliation Act of 2010 (P.L. 111-152)**

P.L. 111-152, § 1401(a)(4)-(5):

Amended Code Sec. 4980I, as added by section 9001 of the Patient Protection and Affordable Care Act (P.L. 111-148), and amended by section 10901 of such Act, by redesignating clause (iii) as clause (iii) in subsection (d)(1)(B), and by inserting after clause (i) a new clause (ii); and by adding at the end of subsection (d) a new paragraph (3). **Effective** 3-30-2010.

• **2010, Patient Protection and Affordable Care Act (P.L. 111-148)**

P.L. 111-148, § 10901(b):

Amended Code Sec. 4980I(d)(1)(B)(i), as added by Act Sec. 9001, by striking "section 9832(c)(1)(A)" and inserting "section 9832(c)(1) (other than subparagraph (G) thereof)". **Effective** for tax years beginning after 12-31-2017 [**effective** date changed by P.L. 111-152, § 1401(b)(2).—CCH].

(e) PENALTY FOR FAILURE TO PROPERLY CALCULATE EXCESS BENEFIT.—

(1) IN GENERAL.—If, for any taxable period, the tax imposed by subsection (a) exceeds the tax determined under such subsection with respect to the total excess benefit calculated by the employer or plan sponsor under subsection (c)(4)—

(A) each coverage provider shall pay the tax on its applicable share (determined in the same manner as under subsection (c)(4)) of the excess, but no penalty shall be imposed on the provider with respect to such amount, and

(B) the employer or plan sponsor shall, in addition to any tax imposed by subsection (a), pay a penalty in an amount equal to such excess, plus interest at the underpayment rate determined under section 6621 for the period beginning on the due date for the payment of tax imposed by subsection (a) to which the excess relates and ending on the date of payment of the penalty.

(2) LIMITATIONS ON PENALTY.—

(A) PENALTY NOT TO APPLY WHERE FAILURE NOT DISCOVERED EXERCISING REASONABLE DILIGENCE.— No penalty shall be imposed by paragraph (1)(B) on any failure to properly calculate the excess benefit during any period for which it is established to the satisfaction of the Secretary that the employer or plan sponsor neither knew, nor exercising reasonable diligence would have known, that such failure existed.

(B) PENALTY NOT TO APPLY TO FAILURES CORRECTED WITHIN 30 DAYS.—No penalty shall be imposed by paragraph (1)(B) on any such failure if—

(i) such failure was due to reasonable cause and not to willful neglect, and

(ii) such failure is corrected during the 30-day period beginning on the 1st date that the employer knew, or exercising reasonable diligence would have known, that such failure existed.

(C) WAIVER BY SECRETARY.—In the case of any such failure which is due to reasonable cause and not to willful neglect, the Secretary may waive part or all of the penalty imposed by paragraph (1), to the extent that the payment of such penalty would be excessive or otherwise inequitable relative to the failure involved.

(f) OTHER DEFINITIONS AND SPECIAL RULES.—For purposes of this section—

(1) COVERAGE DETERMINATIONS.—

(A) IN GENERAL.—Except as provided in subparagraph (B), an employee shall be treated as having self-only coverage with respect to any applicable employer-sponsored coverage of an employer.

(B) MINIMUM ESSENTIAL COVERAGE.—An employee shall be treated as having coverage other than self-only coverage only if the employee is enrolled in coverage other than self-only coverage in a group health plan which provides minimum essential coverage (as defined in section 5000A(f)) to the employee and at least one other beneficiary, and the benefits provided under such minimum essential coverage do not vary based on whether any individual covered under such coverage is the employee or another beneficiary.

(2) QUALIFIED RETIREE.—The term "qualified retiree" means any individual who—

(A) is receiving coverage by reason of being a retiree,

(B) has attained age 55, and

(C) is not entitled to benefits or eligible for enrollment under the Medicare program under title XVIII of the Social Security Act.

(3) EMPLOYEES ENGAGED IN HIGH-RISK PROFESSION.—The term "employees engaged in a high-risk profession" means law enforcement officers (as such term is defined in section 1204 of the Omnibus Crime Control and Safe Streets Act of 1968), employees in fire protection activities (as such term is defined in section 3(y) of the Fair Labor Standards Act of 1938), individuals who provide out-of-hospital emergency medical care (including emergency medical technicians, paramedics, and first-responders), individuals whose primary work is longshore work (as defined in section 258(b) of the Immigration and Nationality Act (8 U.S.C. 1288(b)), determined without regard to paragraph (2) thereof), and individuals engaged in the construction, mining, agriculture (not including food processing), forestry, and fishing industries. Such term includes an employee who is retired from a high-risk profession described in the preceding sentence, if such employee satisfied the requirements of such sentence for a period of not less than 20 years during the employee's employment.

(4) GROUP HEALTH PLAN.—The term "group health plan" has the meaning given such term by section 5000(b)(1).

(5) HEALTH INSURANCE COVERAGE; HEALTH INSURANCE ISSUER.—

(A) HEALTH INSURANCE COVERAGE.—The term "health insurance coverage" has the meaning given such term by section 9832(b)(1) (applied without regard to subparagraph (B) thereof, except as provided by the Secretary in regulations).

(B) HEALTH INSURANCE ISSUER.—The term "health insurance issuer" has the meaning given such term by section 9832(b)(2).

(6) PERSON THAT ADMINISTERS THE PLAN BENEFITS.—The term "person that administers the plan benefits" shall include the plan sponsor if the plan sponsor administers benefits under the plan.

(7) PLAN SPONSOR.—The term "plan sponsor" has the meaning given such term in section 3(16)(B) of the Employee Retirement Income Security Act of 1974.

(8) TAXABLE PERIOD.—The term "taxable period" means the calendar year or such shorter period as the Secretary may prescribe. The Secretary may have different taxable periods for employers of varying sizes.

(9) AGGREGATION RULES.—All employers treated as a single employer under subsection (b), (c), (m), or (o) of section 414 shall be treated as a single employer.

(10) DENIAL OF DEDUCTION.—For denial of a deduction for the tax imposed by this section, see section 275(a)(6).

[CCH Explanation at ¶ 345.]

Amendments

• **2010, Patient Protection and Affordable Care Act (P.L. 111-148)**

P.L. 111-148, § 10901(a):

Amended Code Sec. 4980I(f)(3), as added by Act Sec. 9001, by inserting "individuals whose primary work is long-shore work (as defined in section 258(b) of the Immigration and Nationality Act (8 U.S.C. 1288(b)), determined without regard to paragraph (2) thereof)," before "and individuals engaged in the construction, mining". **Effective** for tax years beginning after 12-31-2017 [**effective** date changed by P.L. 111-152, § 1401(b)(2).—CCH].

(g) REGULATIONS.—The Secretary shall prescribe such regulations as may be necessary to carry out this section.

[CCH Explanation at ¶ 345.]

Amendments

• **2010, Patient Protection and Affordable Care Act (P.L. 111-148)**

P.L. 111-148, § 9001(a):

Amended chapter 43, as amended by Act Sec. 1513, by adding at the end a new Code Sec. 4980I. **Effective** for tax years beginning after 12-31-2017 [**effective** date changed by P.L. 111-152, § 1401(b)(1).—CCH].

[¶ 5340] CODE SEC. 5000A. REQUIREMENT TO MAINTAIN MINIMUM ESSENTIAL COVERAGE.

(a) REQUIREMENT TO MAINTAIN MINIMUM ESSENTIAL COVERAGE.—An applicable individual shall for each month beginning after 2013 ensure that the individual, and any dependent of the individual who is an applicable individual, is covered under minimum essential coverage for such month.

(b) SHARED RESPONSIBILITY PAYMENT.—

(1) IN GENERAL.—If a taxpayer who is an applicable individual, or an applicable individual for whom the taxpayer is liable under paragraph (3), fails to meet the requirement of subsection (a) for 1 or more months, then, except as provided in subsection (e), there is hereby imposed on the taxpayer a penalty with respect to such failures in the amount determined under subsection (c).

(2) INCLUSION WITH RETURN.—Any penalty imposed by this section with respect to any month shall be included with a taxpayer's return under chapter 1 for the taxable year which includes such month.

(3) PAYMENT OF PENALTY.—If an individual with respect to whom a penalty is imposed by this section for any month—

(A) is a dependent (as defined in section 152) of another taxpayer for the other taxpayer's taxable year including such month, such other taxpayer shall be liable for such penalty, or

(B) files a joint return for the taxable year including such month, such individual and the spouse of such individual shall be jointly liable for such penalty.

[CCH Explanation at ¶ 205.]

Amendments

• **2010, Patient Protection and Affordable Care Act (P.L. 111-148)**

P.L. 111-148, § 10106(b)(1):

Amended Code Sec. 5000A(b)(1), as added by Act Sec. 1501(b). **Effective** 3-23-2010. Prior to amendment, Code Sec. 5000A(b)(1) read as follows:

(1) IN GENERAL.—If an applicable individual fails to meet the requirement of subsection (a) for 1 or more months during any calendar year beginning after 2013, then, except as provided in subsection (d), there is hereby imposed a penalty with respect to the individual in the amount determined under subsection (c).

(c) AMOUNT OF PENALTY.—

(1) IN GENERAL.—The amount of the penalty imposed by this section on any taxpayer for any taxable year with respect to failures described in subsection (b)(1) shall be equal to the lesser of—

(A) the sum of the monthly penalty amounts determined under paragraph (2) for months in the taxable year during which 1 or more such failures occurred, or

(B) an amount equal to the national average premium for qualified health plans which have a bronze level of coverage, provide coverage for the applicable family size involved, and are offered through Exchanges for plan years beginning in the calendar year with or within which the taxable year ends.

(2) MONTHLY PENALTY AMOUNTS.—For purposes of paragraph (1)(A), the monthly penalty amount with respect to any taxpayer for any month during which any failure described in subsection (b)(1) occurred is an amount equal to ¹⁄₁₂ of the greater of the following amounts:

(A) FLAT DOLLAR AMOUNT.—An amount equal to the lesser of—

(i) the sum of the applicable dollar amounts for all individuals with respect to whom such failure occurred during such month, or

(ii) 300 percent of the applicable dollar amount (determined without regard to paragraph (3)(C)) for the calendar year with or within which the taxable year ends.

(B) PERCENTAGE OF INCOME.—An amount equal to the following percentage of the excess of the taxpayer's household income for the taxable year over the amount of gross income specified in section 6012(a)(1) with respect to the taxpayer for the taxable year:

(i) 1.0 percent for taxable years beginning in 2014.

(ii) 2.0 percent for taxable years beginning in 2015.

(iii) 2.5 percent for taxable years beginning after 2015.

(3) APPLICABLE DOLLAR AMOUNT.—For purposes of paragraph (1)—

(A) IN GENERAL.—Except as provided in subparagraphs (B) and (C), the applicable dollar amount is $695.

(B) PHASE IN.—The applicable dollar amount is $95 for 2014 and $325 for 2015.

(C) SPECIAL RULE FOR INDIVIDUALS UNDER AGE 18.—If an applicable individual has not attained the age of 18 as of the beginning of a month, the applicable dollar amount with respect to such individual for the month shall be equal to one-half of the applicable dollar amount for the calendar year in which the month occurs.

(D) INDEXING OF AMOUNT.—In the case of any calendar year beginning after 2016, the applicable dollar amount shall be equal to $695, increased by an amount equal to—

(i) $695, multiplied by

(ii) the cost-of-living adjustment determined under section 1(f)(3) for the calendar year, determined by substituting "calendar year 2015" for "calendar year 1992" in subparagraph (B) thereof.

If the amount of any increase under clause (i) is not a multiple of $50, such increase shall be rounded to the next lowest multiple of $50.

(4) TERMS RELATING TO INCOME AND FAMILIES.—For purposes of this section—

(A) FAMILY SIZE.—The family size involved with respect to any taxpayer shall be equal to the number of individuals for whom the taxpayer is allowed a deduction under section 151 (relating to allowance of deduction for personal exemptions) for the taxable year.

(B) HOUSEHOLD INCOME.—The term "household income" means, with respect to any taxpayer for any taxable year, an amount equal to the sum of—

(i) the modified adjusted gross income of the taxpayer, plus

(ii) the aggregate modified adjusted gross incomes of all other individuals who—

(I) were taken into account in determining the taxpayer's family size under paragraph (1), and

(II) were required to file a return of tax imposed by section 1 for the taxable year.

(C) MODIFIED ADJUSTED GROSS INCOME.—The term "modified adjusted gross income" means adjusted gross income increased by—

(i) any amount excluded from gross income under section 911, and

(ii) any amount of interest received or accrued by the taxpayer during the taxable year which is exempt from tax.

(D) [Stricken.]

[CCH Explanation at ¶ 205.]

Amendments

• 2010, Health Care and Education Reconciliation Act of 2010 (P.L. 111-152)

P.L. 111-152, § 1002(a)(1)(A)-(D):

Amended Code Sec. 5000A(c), as added by section 1501(b) of the Patient Protection and Affordable Care Act (P.L. 111-148) and amended by section 10106, in the matter preceding clause (i) of paragraph (2)(B) by inserting "the excess of" before "the taxpayer's household income"; and inserting "for the taxable year over the amount of gross income specified in section 6012(a)(1) with respect to the taxpayer" before "for the taxable year"; by striking "0.5" and inserting "1.0" in clause (i) of paragraph (2)(B); by striking "1.0" and inserting "2.0" in clause (ii) of paragraph (2)(B); and by striking "2.0" and inserting "2.5" in clause (iii) of paragraph (2)(B). **Effective** 3-30-2010.

P.L. 111-152, § 1002(a)(2)(A)-(C):

Amended Code Sec. 5000A(c), as added by section 1501(b) of the Patient Protection and Affordable Care Act (P.L. 111-148) and amended by section 10106, by striking "$750" and inserting "$695" in subparagraph (A) of paragraph (3); by striking "$495" and inserting "$325" in subparagraph (B) of paragraph (3); and in the matter preceding clause (i) of subparagraph (D) by striking "$750" and inserting "$695"; and by striking "$750" and inserting "$695" in clause (i) of subparagraph (D). **Effective** 3-30-2010.

P.L. 111-152, § 1002(b)(1):

Amended Code Sec. 5000A, as added by section 1501(b) of the Patient Protection and Affordable Care Act (P.L. 111-148) and amended by section 10106, by striking subsection (c)(4)(D). **Effective** 3-30-2010. Prior to being stricken, Code Sec. 5000A(c)(4)(D) read as follows:

(D) POVERTY LINE.—

(i) IN GENERAL.—The term "poverty line" has the meaning given that term in section 2110(c)(5) of the Social Security Act (42 U.S.C. 1397jj(c)(5)).

(ii) POVERTY LINE USED.—In the case of any taxable year ending with or within a calendar year, the poverty line used shall be the most recently published poverty line as of the 1st day of such calendar year.

P.L. 111-152, § 1004(a)(1)(C):

Amended Code Sec. 5000A(c)(4)[(B)](i)-(ii), as added by section 1501(b) of the Patient Protection and Affordable Care

Act (P.L. 111-148), by striking "modified gross" each place it appears and inserting "modified adjusted gross". **Effective** 3-30-2010.

P.L. 111-152, § 1004(a)(2)(B):

Amended Code Sec. 5000A(c)(4)(C), as added by section 1501(b) of the Patient Protection and Affordable Care Act (P.L. 111-148). **Effective** 3-30-2010. Prior to amendment, Code Sec. 5000A(c)(4)(C) read as follows:

(C) MODIFIED GROSS INCOME.—The term "modified gross income" means gross income—

(i) decreased by the amount of any deduction allowable under paragraph (1), (3), (4), or (10) of section 62(a),

(ii) increased by the amount of interest received or accrued during the taxable year which is exempt from tax imposed by this chapter, and

(iii) determined without regard to sections 911, 931, and 933.

• 2010, Patient Protection and Affordable Care Act (P.L. 111-148)

P.L. 111-148, § 10106(b)(2):

Amended Code Sec. 5000A(c)(1)-(2), as added by this Act. **Effective** 3-23-2010. Prior to amendment, Code Sec. 5000A(c)(1)-(2) read as follows:

(1) IN GENERAL.—The penalty determined under this subsection for any month with respect to any individual is an amount equal to 1/12 of the applicable dollar amount for the calendar year.

(2) DOLLAR LIMITATION.—The amount of the penalty imposed by this section on any taxpayer for any taxable year with respect to all individuals for whom the taxpayer is liable under subsection (b)(3) shall not exceed an amount equal to 300 percent [of] the applicable dollar amount (determined without regard to paragraph (3)(C)) for the calendar year with or within which the taxable year ends.

P.L. 111-148, § 10106(b)(3):

Amended Code Sec. 5000A(c)(3)[(B)], as added by Act Sec. 1501(b), by striking "$350" and inserting "$495". **Effective** 3-23-2010.

(d) APPLICABLE INDIVIDUAL.—For purposes of this section—

(1) IN GENERAL.—The term "applicable individual" means, with respect to any month, an individual other than an individual described in paragraph (2), (3), or (4).

(2) RELIGIOUS EXEMPTIONS.—

(A) RELIGIOUS CONSCIENCE EXEMPTION.—Such term shall not include any individual for any month if such individual has in effect an exemption under section 1311(d)(4)(H) of the Patient Protection and Affordable Care Act which certifies that such individual is—

(i) a member of a recognized religious sect or division thereof which is described in section 1402(g)(1), and

(ii) an adherent of established tenets or teachings of such sect or division as described in such section.

(B) HEALTH CARE SHARING MINISTRY.—

(i) IN GENERAL.—Such term shall not include any individual for any month if such individual is a member of a health care sharing ministry for the month.

(ii) HEALTH CARE SHARING MINISTRY.—The term "health care sharing ministry" means an organization—

(I) which is described in section 501(c)(3) and is exempt from taxation under section 501(a),

(II) members of which share a common set of ethical or religious beliefs and share medical expenses among members in accordance with those beliefs and without regard to the State in which a member resides or is employed,

(III) members of which retain membership even after they develop a medical condition,

(IV) which (or a predecessor of which) has been in existence at all times since December 31, 1999, and medical expenses of its members have been shared continuously and without interruption since at least December 31, 1999, and

(V) which conducts an annual audit which is performed by an independent certified public accounting firm in accordance with generally accepted accounting principles and which is made available to the public upon request.

(3) INDIVIDUALS NOT LAWFULLY PRESENT.—Such term shall not include an individual for any month if for the month the individual is not a citizen or national of the United States or an alien lawfully present in the United States.

(4) INCARCERATED INDIVIDUALS.—Such term shall not include an individual for any month if for the month the individual is incarcerated, other than incarceration pending the disposition of charges.

[CCH Explanation at ¶ 205.]

Amendments

• 2010, Patient Protection and Affordable Care Act (P.L. 111-148)

P.L. 111-148, § 10106(c):

Amended Code Sec. 5000A(d)(2)(A), as added by Act Sec. 1501(b). **Effective** 3-23-2010. Prior to amendment, Code Sec. 5000A(d)(2)(A) read as follows:

(A) RELIGIOUS CONSCIENCE EXEMPTION.—Such term shall not include any individual for any month if such individual has in effect an exemption under section 1311(d)(4)(H) of the Patient Protection and Affordable Care Act which certifies that such individual is a member of a recognized religious sect or division thereof described in section 1402(g)(1) and an adherent of established tenets or teachings of such sect or division as described in such section.

(e) EXEMPTIONS.—No penalty shall be imposed under subsection (a) with respect to—

(1) INDIVIDUALS WHO CANNOT AFFORD COVERAGE.—

(A) IN GENERAL.—Any applicable individual for any month if the applicable individual's required contribution (determined on an annual basis) for coverage for the month exceeds 8 percent of such individual's household income for the taxable year described in section 1412(b)(1)(B) of the Patient Protection and Affordable Care Act. For purposes of applying this subparagraph, the taxpayer's household income shall be increased by any exclusion from gross income for any portion of the required contribution made through a salary reduction arrangement.

(B) REQUIRED CONTRIBUTION.—For purposes of this paragraph, the term "required contribution" means—

(i) in the case of an individual eligible to purchase minimum essential coverage consisting of coverage through an eligible-employer-sponsored plan, the portion of the annual premium which would be paid by the individual (without regard to whether paid through salary reduction or otherwise) for self-only coverage, or

(ii) in the case of an individual eligible only to purchase minimum essential coverage described in subsection (f)(1)(C), the annual premium for the lowest cost bronze plan available in the individual market through the Exchange in the State in the rating area in which the individual resides (without regard to whether the individual purchased a qualified health plan through the Exchange), reduced by the amount of the credit allowable under section 36B for the taxable year (determined as if the individual was covered by a qualified health plan offered through the Exchange for the entire taxable year).

(C) SPECIAL RULES FOR INDIVIDUALS RELATED TO EMPLOYEES.—For purposes of subparagraph (B)(i), if an applicable individual is eligible for minimum essential coverage through an employer by reason of a relationship to an employee, the determination under subparagraph (A) shall be made by reference to required contribution of the employee.

(D) INDEXING.—In the case of plan years beginning in any calendar year after 2014, subparagraph (A) shall be applied by substituting for "8 percent" the percentage the Secretary of Health and Human Services determines reflects the excess of the rate of premium growth between the preceding calendar year and 2013 over the rate of income growth for such period.

(2) TAXPAYERS WITH INCOME BELOW FILING THRESHOLD.—Any applicable individual for any month during a calendar year if the individual's household income for the taxable year described in section 1412(b)(1)(B) of the Patient Protection and Affordable Care Act is less than the amount of gross income specified in section 6012(a)(1) with respect to the taxpayer.

(3) MEMBERS OF INDIAN TRIBES.—Any applicable individual for any month during which the individual is a member of an Indian tribe (as defined in section 45A(c)(6)).

(4) MONTHS DURING SHORT COVERAGE GAPS.—

(A) IN GENERAL.—Any month the last day of which occurred during a period in which the applicable individual was not covered by minimum essential coverage for a continuous period of less than 3 months.

(B) SPECIAL RULES.—For purposes of applying this paragraph—

(i) the length of a continuous period shall be determined without regard to the calendar years in which months in such period occur,

(ii) if a continuous period is greater than the period allowed under subparagraph (A), no exception shall be provided under this paragraph for any month in the period, and

(iii) if there is more than 1 continuous period described in subparagraph (A) covering months in a calendar year, the exception provided by this paragraph shall only apply to months in the first of such periods.

The Secretary shall prescribe rules for the collection of the penalty imposed by this section in cases where continuous periods include months in more than 1 taxable year.

(5) HARDSHIPS.—Any applicable individual who for any month is determined by the Secretary of Health and Human Services under section 1311(d)(4)(H) to have suffered a hardship with respect to the capability to obtain coverage under a qualified health plan.

[CCH Explanation at ¶ 205.]
Amendments

• 2010, Health Care and Education Reconciliation Act of 2010 (P.L. 111-152)

P.L. 111-152, § 1002(b)(2)(A)-(B):

Amended Code Sec. 5000A(e)(2), as added by section 1501(b) of the Patient Protection and Affordable Care Act (P.L. 111-148) and amended by section 10106, by striking "UNDER 100 PERCENT OF POVERTY LINE" and inserting "BELOW

FILING THRESHOLD" [in the heading]; and by striking all that follows "less than" and inserting "the amount of gross income specified in section 6012(a)(1) with respect to the taxpayer.". **Effective** 3-30-2010. Prior to being stricken, all that followed "less than" in Code Sec. 5000A(e)(2) read as follows:

100 percent of the poverty line for the size of the family involved (determined in the same manner as under subsection (b)(4)).

• **2010, Patient Protection and Affordable Care Act (P.L. 111-148)**

P.L. 111-148, §10106(d):

Amended Code Sec. 5000A(e)(1)(C), as added by Act Sec. 1501(b). **Effective** 3-23-2010. Prior to amendment, Code Sec. 5000A(e)(1)(C) read as follows:

(C) SPECIAL RULES FOR INDIVIDUALS RELATED TO EMPLOYEES.—For purposes of subparagraph (B)(i), if an applicable individual is eligible for minimum essential coverage through an employer by reason of a relationship to an employee, the determination shall be made by reference to the affordability of the coverage to the employee.

(f) MINIMUM ESSENTIAL COVERAGE.—For purposes of this section—

(1) IN GENERAL.—The term "minimum essential coverage" means any of the following:

(A) GOVERNMENT SPONSORED PROGRAMS.—Coverage under—

(i) the Medicare program under part A of title XVIII of the Social Security Act,

(ii) the Medicaid program under title XIX of the Social Security Act,

(iii) the CHIP program under title XXI of the Social Security Act,

(iv) medical coverage under chapter 55 of title 10, United States Code, including coverage under the TRICARE program;

(v) a health care program under chapter 17 or 18 of title 38, United States Code, as determined by the Secretary of Veterans Affairs, in coordination with the Secretary of Health and Human Services and the Secretary [of the Treasury],

(vi) a health plan under section 2504(e) of title 22, United States Code (relating to Peace Corps volunteers); or

(vii) the Nonappropriated Fund Health Benefits Program of the Department of Defense, established under section 349 of the National Defense Authorization Act for Fiscal Year 1995 (Public Law 103–337; 10 U.S.C. 1587 note).

(B) EMPLOYER-SPONSORED PLAN.—Coverage under an eligible employer-sponsored plan.

(C) PLANS IN THE INDIVIDUAL MARKET.—Coverage under a health plan offered in the individual market within a State.

(D) GRANDFATHERED HEALTH PLAN.—Coverage under a grandfathered health plan.

(E) OTHER COVERAGE.—Such other health benefits coverage, such as a State health benefits risk pool, as the Secretary of Health and Human Services, in coordination with the Secretary, recognizes for purposes of this subsection.

(2) ELIGIBLE EMPLOYER-SPONSORED PLAN.—The term "eligible employer-sponsored plan" means, with respect to any employee, a group health plan or group health insurance coverage offered by an employer to the employee which is—

(A) a governmental plan (within the meaning of section 2791(d)(8) of the Public Health Service Act), or

(B) any other plan or coverage offered in the small or large group market within a State.

Such term shall include a grandfathered health plan described in paragraph (1)(D) offered in a group market.

(3) EXCEPTED BENEFITS NOT TREATED AS MINIMUM ESSENTIAL COVERAGE.—The term "minimum essential coverage" shall not include health insurance coverage which consists of coverage of excepted benefits—

(A) described in paragraph (1) of subsection (c) of section 2791 of the Public Health Service Act; or

(B) described in paragraph (2), (3), or (4) of such subsection if the benefits are provided under a separate policy, certificate, or contract of insurance.

(4) INDIVIDUALS RESIDING OUTSIDE UNITED STATES OR RESIDENTS OF TERRITORIES.—Any applicable individual shall be treated as having minimum essential coverage for any month—

(A) if such month occurs during any period described in subparagraph (A) or (B) of section 911(d)(1) which is applicable to the individual, or

(B) if such individual is a bona fide resident of any possession of the United States (as determined under section 937(a)) for such month.

(5) INSURANCE-RELATED TERMS.—Any term used in this section which is also used in title I of the Patient Protection and Affordable Care Act shall have the same meaning as when used in such title.

[CCH Explanation at ¶ 205.]

Amendments

• 2010 (P.L. 111-173)

P.L. 111-173, § 1(a):

Amended Code Sec. 5000A(f)(1)(A)(v), as added by section 1501(b) of the Patient Protection and Affordable Care Act (P.L. 111-148). **Effective** as if included in section 1501(b) of the Patient Protection and Affordable Care Act (P.L. 111-148) [**effective** for tax years ending after 12-31-2013.—CCH]. Prior to amendment, Code Sec. 5000A(f)(1)(A)(v) read as follows:

(v) the veteran's health care program under chapter 17 of title 38, United States Code,

• 2010, TRICARE Affirmation Act (P.L. 111-159)

P.L. 111-159, § 2(a):

Amended Code Sec. 5000A(f)(1)(A), as added by section 1501(b) of the Patient Protection and Affordable Care Act (P.L. 111-148), by striking clause (iv) and inserting a new clause (iv); by striking "or" at the end of clause (v); by striking the period at the end of clause (vi) and inserting "; or"; and by inserting after clause (vi) a new clause (vii). **Effective** as if included in section 1501(b) of the Patient Protection and Affordable Care Act (P.L. 111-148) [**effective** for tax years ending after 12-31-2013.—CCH]. Prior to being stricken, Code Sec. 5000A(f)(1)(A)(iv) read as follows:

(iv) the TRICARE for Life program,

(g) ADMINISTRATION AND PROCEDURE.—

(1) IN GENERAL.—The penalty provided by this section shall be paid upon notice and demand by the Secretary, and except as provided in paragraph (2), shall be assessed and collected in the same manner as an assessable penalty under subchapter B of chapter 68.

(2) SPECIAL RULES.—Notwithstanding any other provision of law—

(A) WAIVER OF CRIMINAL PENALTIES.—In the case of any failure by a taxpayer to timely pay any penalty imposed by this section, such taxpayer shall not be subject to any criminal prosecution or penalty with respect to such failure.

(B) LIMITATIONS ON LIENS AND LEVIES.—The Secretary shall not—

(i) file notice of lien with respect to any property of a taxpayer by reason of any failure to pay the penalty imposed by this section, or

(ii) levy on any such property with respect to such failure.

[CCH Explanation at ¶ 205.]

Amendments

• 2010, Patient Protection and Affordable Care Act (P.L. 111-148)

P.L. 111-148, § 1501(b):

Amended subtitle D by adding at the end a new chapter 48 (Code Sec. 5000A). **Effective** for tax years ending after 12-31-2013.

P.L. 111-148, § 1502(c), provides:

(c) NOTIFICATION OF NONENROLLMENT.—Not later than June 30 of each year, the Secretary of the Treasury, acting through the Internal Revenue Service and in consultation with the Secretary of Health and Human Services, shall send a notification to each individual who files an individual income tax return and who is not enrolled in minimum essential coverage (as defined in section 5000A of the Internal Revenue Code of 1986). Such notification shall contain information on the services available through the Exchange operating in the State in which such individual resides.

[¶ 5350] CODE SEC. 6033. RETURNS BY EXEMPT ORGANIZATIONS.

* * *

(b) CERTAIN ORGANIZATIONS DESCRIBED IN SECTION 501(c)(3).—Every organization described in section 501(c)(3) which is subject to the requirements of subsection (a) shall furnish annually information, at such time and in such manner as the Secretary may by forms or regulations prescribe, setting forth—

* * *

(10) the respective amounts (if any) of the taxes imposed on the organization, or any organization manager of the organization, during the taxable year under any of the following provisions (and the respective amounts (if any) of reimbursements paid by the organization

during the taxable year with respect to taxes imposed on any such organization manager under any of such provisions):

* * *

(B) section 4912 (relating to tax on disqualifying lobbying expenditures of certain organizations),

(C) section 4955 (relating to taxes on political expenditures of section 501(c)(3) organizations), except to the extent that, by reason of section 4962, the taxes imposed under such section are not required to be paid or are credited or refunded, *and*

(D) section 4959 (relating to taxes on failures by hospital organizations),

* * *

(14) such information as the Secretary may require with respect to disaster relief activities, including the amount and use of qualified contributions to which section 1400S(a) applies,

(15) in the case of an organization to which the requirements of section 501(r) apply for the taxable year—

(A) a description of how the organization is addressing the needs identified in each community health needs assessment conducted under section 501(r)(3) and a description of any such needs that are not being addressed together with the reasons why such needs are not being addressed, and

(B) the audited financial statements of such organization (or, in the case of an organization the financial statements of which are included in a consolidated financial statement with other organizations, such consolidated financial statement).

(16) such other information for purposes of carrying out the internal revenue laws as the Secretary may require.

* * *

[CCH Explanation at ¶ 355.]

Amendments

• **2010, Patient Protection and Affordable Care Act (P.L. 111-148)**

P.L. 111-148, § 9007(d)(1):

Amended Code Sec. 6033(b) by striking "and" at the end of paragraph (14), by redesignating paragraph (15) as paragraph (16), and by inserting after paragraph (14) a new paragraph (15). **Effective** for tax years beginning after 3-23-2010.

P.L. 111-148, § 9007(d)(2):

Amended Code Sec. 6033(b)(10) by striking "and" at the end of subparagraph (B), by inserting "and" at the end of subparagraph (C), and by adding at the end a new subparagraph (D). **Effective** for tax years beginning after 3-23-2010.

* * *

[¶ 5360] CODE SEC. 6051. RECEIPTS FOR EMPLOYEES.

(a) REQUIREMENT.—Every person required to deduct and withhold from an employee a tax under section 3101 or 3402, or who would have been required to deduct and withhold a tax under section 3402 (determined without regard to subsection (n)) if the employee had claimed no more than one withholding exemption, or every employer engaged in a trade or business who pays remuneration for services performed by an employee, including the cash value of such remuneration paid in any medium other than cash, shall furnish to each such employee in respect of the remuneration paid by such person to such employee during the calendar year, on or before January 31 of the succeeding year, or, if his employment is terminated before the close of such calendar year, within 30 days after the date of receipt of a written request from the employee if such 30-day period ends before January 31, a written statement showing the following:

* * *

(12) the amount contributed to any health savings account (as defined in section 223(d)) of such employee or such employee's spouse,

(13) the total amount of deferrals for the year under a nonqualified deferred compensation plan (within the meaning of section 409A(d)), *and*

(14) the aggregate cost (determined under rules similar to the rules of section 4980B(f)(4)) of applicable employer-sponsored coverage (as defined in section 4980I(d)(1)), except that this paragraph shall not apply to—

(A) *coverage to which paragraphs (11) and (12) apply, or*

(B) *the amount of any salary reduction contributions to a flexible spending arrangement (within the meaning of section 125).*

* * *

[CCH Explanation at ¶ 405.]

Amendments

• 2010, Patient Protection and Affordable Care Act (P.L. 111-148)

P.L. 111-148, § 9002(a):

Amended Code Sec. 6051(a) by striking "and" at the end of paragraph (12), by striking the period at the end of paragraph (13) and inserting ", and", and by adding after paragraph (13) a new paragraph (14). **Effective** for tax years beginning after 12-31-2010.

[¶ 5370] *CODE SEC. 6055. REPORTING OF HEALTH INSURANCE COVERAGE.*

(a) IN GENERAL.—*Every person who provides minimum essential coverage to an individual during a calendar year shall, at such time as the Secretary may prescribe, make a return described in subsection (b).*

(b) FORM AND MANNER OF RETURN.—

(1) IN GENERAL.—*A return is described in this subsection if such return—*

(A) *is in such form as the Secretary may prescribe, and*

(B) *contains—*

(i) *the name, address and TIN of the primary insured and the name and TIN of each other individual obtaining coverage under the policy,*

(ii) *the dates during which such individual was covered under minimum essential coverage during the calendar year,*

(iii) *in the case of minimum essential coverage which consists of health insurance coverage, information concerning—*

(I) *whether or not the coverage is a qualified health plan offered through an Exchange established under section 1311 of the Patient Protection and Affordable Care Act, and*

(II) *in the case of a qualified health plan, the amount (if any) of any advance payment under section 1412 of the Patient Protection and Affordable Care Act of any cost-sharing reduction under section 1402 of such Act or of any premium tax credit under section 36B with respect to such coverage, and*

(iv) *such other information as the Secretary may require.*

(2) INFORMATION RELATING TO EMPLOYER-PROVIDED COVERAGE.—*If minimum essential coverage provided to an individual under subsection (a) consists of health insurance coverage of a health insurance issuer provided through a group health plan of an employer, a return described in this subsection shall include—*

(A) *the name, address, and employer identification number of the employer maintaining the plan,*

(B) *the portion of the premium (if any) required to be paid by the employer, and*

(C) *if the health insurance coverage is a qualified health plan in the small group market offered through an Exchange, such other information as the Secretary may require for administration of the credit under section 45R (relating to credit for employee health insurance expenses of small employers).*

(c) STATEMENTS TO BE FURNISHED TO INDIVIDUALS WITH RESPECT TO WHOM INFORMATION IS REPORTED.—

(1) IN GENERAL.—*Every person required to make a return under subsection (a) shall furnish to each individual whose name is required to be set forth in such return a written statement showing—*

(A) *the name and address of the person required to make such return and the phone number of the information contact for such person, and*

(B) *the information required to be shown on the return with respect to such individual.*

(2) TIME FOR FURNISHING STATEMENTS.—The written statement required under paragraph (1) shall be furnished on or before January 31 of the year following the calendar year for which the return under subsection (a) was required to be made.

(d) COVERAGE PROVIDED BY GOVERNMENTAL UNITS.—In the case of coverage provided by any governmental unit or any agency or instrumentality thereof, the officer or employee who enters into the agreement to provide such coverage (or the person appropriately designated for purposes of this section) shall make the returns and statements required by this section.

(e) MINIMUM ESSENTIAL COVERAGE.—For purposes of this section, the term "minimum essential coverage" has the meaning given such term by section 5000A(f).

[CCH Explanation at ¶ 410.]
Amendments
• 2010, Patient Protection and Affordable Care Act (P.L. 111-148)

P.L. 111-148, § 1502(a):

Amended part III of subchapter A of chapter 61 by inserting after subpart C a new subpart D (Code Sec. 6055). **Effective** for calendar years beginning after 2013.

[¶ 5380] CODE SEC. 6056. CERTAIN EMPLOYERS REQUIRED TO REPORT ON HEALTH INSURANCE COVERAGE.

(a) IN GENERAL.—Every applicable large employer required to meet the requirements of section 4980H with respect to its full-time employees during a calendar year shall, at such time as the Secretary may prescribe, make a return described in subsection (b).

[CCH Explanation at ¶ 415.]
Amendments
• 2011, Department of Defense and Full-Year Continuing Appropriations Act, 2011 (P.L. 112-10)

P.L. 112-10, § 1858(b)(5)(A):

Amended Code Sec. 6056(a) by striking "and every offering employer" before "shall". **Effective** as if included in the provision of, and the amendments made by, the provision of the Patient Protection and Affordable Care Act (P.L. 111-148) to which it relates [effective for periods beginning after 12-31-2013.—CCH].

• 2010, Patient Protection and Affordable Care Act (P.L. 111-148)

P.L. 111-148, § 10108(j)(1):

Amended Code Sec. 6056(a), as added by Act Sec. 1514, by inserting "and every offering employer" before "shall". **Effective** for periods beginning after 12-31-2013.

P.L. 111-148, § 10108(j)(3)(A):

Amended the heading of Code Sec. 6056, as added by Act Sec. 1514, by striking "**LARGE**" and inserting "**CERTAIN**". **Effective** for periods beginning after 12-31-2013.

(b) FORM AND MANNER OF RETURN.—A return is described in this subsection if such return—

(1) is in such form as the Secretary may prescribe, and

(2) contains—

(A) the name, date, and employer identification number of the employer,

(B) a certification as to whether the employer offers to its full-time employees (and their dependents) the opportunity to enroll in minimum essential coverage under an eligible employer-sponsored plan (as defined in section 5000A(f)(2)),

(C) if the employer certifies that the employer did offer to its full-time employees (and their dependents) the opportunity to so enroll—

(i) the length of any waiting period (as defined in section 2701(b)(4) of the Public Health Service Act) with respect to such coverage,

(ii) the months during the calendar year for which coverage under the plan was available,

(iii) the monthly premium for the lowest cost option in each of the enrollment categories under the plan, and

(iv) the employer's share of the total allowed costs of benefits provided under the plan,

(D) the number of full-time employees for each month during the calendar year,

(E) the name, address, and TIN of each full-time employee during the calendar year and the months (if any) during which such employee (and any dependents) were covered under any such health benefits plans, and

(F) such other information as the Secretary may require.

The Secretary shall have the authority to review the accuracy of the information provided under this subsection, including the applicable large employer's share under paragraph (2)(C)(iv).

[CCH Explanation at ¶415.]

Amendments

• 2011, Department of Defense and Full-Year Continuing Appropriations Act, 2011 (P.L. 112-10)

P.L. 112-10, §1858(b)(5)(B)(i)-(iv):

Amended Code Sec. 6056(b)(2)(C) by striking "in the case of an applicable large employer," before "the length" in clause (i), by inserting "and" at the end of clause (iii), by striking "and" at the end of clause (iv), and by striking clause (v). **Effective** as if included in the provision of, and the amendments made by, the provision of the Patient Protection and Affordable Care Act (P.L. 111-148) to which it relates [**effective** for periods beginning after 12-31-2013.— CCH]. Prior to being stricken, Code Sec. 6056(b)(2)(C)(v) read as follows:

(v) in the case of an offering employer, the option for which the employer pays the largest portion of the cost of the plan and the portion of the cost paid by the employer in each of the enrollment categories under such option,

• 2010, Patient Protection and Affordable Care Act (P.L. 111-148)

P.L. 111-148, §10106(g):

Amended Code Sec. 6056(b), as added by Act Sec. 1514(a), by adding at the end a new flush sentence. **Effective** 3-23-2010.

P.L. 111-148, §10108(j)(3)(B)(i)-(v):

Amended Code Sec. 6056(b)(2)(C) by inserting "in the case of an applicable large employer," before "the length" in clause (i); by striking "and" at the end of clause (iii); by striking "applicable large employer" in clause (iv) and inserting "employer"; by inserting "and" at the end of clause (iv); and by inserting at the end a new clause (v). **Effective** for periods beginning after 12-31-2013.

(c) STATEMENTS TO BE FURNISHED TO INDIVIDUALS WITH RESPECT TO WHOM INFORMATION IS REPORTED.—

(1) IN GENERAL.—Every person required to make a return under subsection (a) shall furnish to each full-time employee whose name is required to be set forth in such return under subsection (b)(2)(E) a written statement showing—

(A) the name and address of the person required to make such return and the phone number of the information contact for such person, and

(B) the information required to be shown on the return with respect to such individual.

(2) TIME FOR FURNISHING STATEMENTS.—The written statement required under paragraph (1) shall be furnished on or before January 31 of the year following the calendar year for which the return under subsection (a) was required to be made.

(d) COORDINATION WITH OTHER REQUIREMENTS.—To the maximum extent feasible, the Secretary may provide that—

(1) any return or statement required to be provided under this section may be provided as part of any return or statement required under section 6051 or 6055, and

(2) in the case of an applicable large employer offering health insurance coverage of a health insurance issuer, the employer may enter into an agreement with the issuer to include information required under this section with the return and statement required to be provided by the issuer under section 6055.

[CCH Explanation at ¶415.]

Amendments

• 2011, Department of Defense and Full-Year Continuing Appropriations Act, 2011 (P.L. 112-10)

P.L. 112-10, §1858(b)(5)(C):

Amended Code Sec. 6056(d)(2) by striking "or offering employer" after "applicable large employer". **Effective** as if included in the provision of, and the amendments made by, the provision of the Patient Protection and Affordable Care Act (P.L. 111-148) to which it relates [**effective** for periods beginning after 12-31-2013.—CCH].

• 2010, Patient Protection and Affordable Care Act (P.L. 111-148)

P.L. 111-148, §10108(j)(3)(C):

Amended Code Sec. 6056(d)(2) by inserting "or offering employer" after "applicable large employer". **Effective** for periods beginning after 12-31-2013.

(e) COVERAGE PROVIDED BY GOVERNMENTAL UNITS.—*In the case of any applicable large employer which is a governmental unit or any agency or instrumentality thereof, the person appropriately designated for purposes of this section shall make the returns and statements required by this section.*

[CCH Explanation at ¶415.]

Amendments

• **2011, Department of Defense and Full-Year Continuing Appropriations Act, 2011 (P.L. 112-10)**

P.L. 112-10, §1858(b)(5)(C):

Amended Code Sec. 6056(e) by striking "or offering employer" after "applicable large employer". **Effective** as if included in the provision of, and the amendments made by, the provision of the Patient Protection and Affordable Care Act (P.L. 111-148) to which it relates [effective for periods beginning after 12-31-2013.—CCH]

• **2010, Patient Protection and Affordable Care Act (P.L. 111-148)**

P.L. 111-148, §10108(j)(3)(D):

Amended Code Sec. 6056(e) by inserting "or offering employer" after "applicable large employer". **Effective** for periods beginning after 12-31-2013.

(f) DEFINITIONS.—*For purposes of this section, any term used in this section which is also used in section 4980H shall have the meaning given such term by section 4980H.*

[CCH Explanation at ¶415.]

Amendments

• **2011, Department of Defense and Full-Year Continuing Appropriations Act, 2011 (P.L. 112-10)**

P.L. 112-10, §1858(b)(5)(D):

Amended Code Sec. 6056(f). **Effective** as if included in the provision of, and the amendments made by, the provision of the Patient Protection and Affordable Care Act (P.L. 111-148) to which it relates [effective for periods beginning after 12-31-2013.—CCH]. Prior to amendment, Code Sec. 6056(f) read as follows:

(f) DEFINITIONS.—For purposes of this section—

(1) OFFERING EMPLOYER.—

(A) IN GENERAL.—The term "offering employer" means any offering employer (as defined in section 10108(b) of the Patient Protection and Affordable Care Act) if the required contribution (within the meaning of section 5000A(e)(1)(B)(i)) of any employee exceeds 8 percent of the wages (as defined in section 3121(a)) paid to such employee by such employer.

(B) INDEXING.—In the case of any calendar year beginning after 2014, the 8 percent under subparagraph (A) shall be adjusted for the calendar year to reflect the rate of premium growth between the preceding calendar year and 2013 over the rate of income growth for such period.

(2) OTHER DEFINITIONS.—Any term used in this section which is also used in section 4980H shall have the meaning given such term by section 4980H.

• **2010, Patient Protection and Affordable Care Act (P.L. 111-148)**

P.L. 111-148, §1514(a):

Amended subpart D of part III of subchapter A of chapter 61, as added by Act Sec. 1502, by inserting after Code Sec. 6055 a new Code Sec. 6056. **Effective** for periods beginning after 12-31-2013.

P.L. 111-148, §10108(j)(2):

Amended Code Sec. 6056(f), as added by Act Sec. 1514. **Effective** for periods beginning after 12-31-2013. Prior to amendment, Code Sec. 6056(f) read as follows:

(f) DEFINITIONS.—For purposes of this section, any term used in this section which is also used in section 4980H shall have the meaning given such term by section 4980H.

[¶5390] CODE SEC. 6211. DEFINITION OF A DEFICIENCY.

* * *

(b) RULES FOR APPLICATION OF SUBSECTION (a).—For purposes of this section—

* * *

(4) For purposes of subsection (a)—

(A) *any excess of the sum of the credits allowable under sections 24(d), 25A by reason of subsection (i)(6) thereof, 32, 34, 35, 36, 36A, 36B, 53(e), 168(k)(4), 6428, and 6431 over the tax imposed by subtitle A (determined without regard to such credits), and*

(B) any excess of the sum of such credits as shown by the taxpayer on his return over the amount shown as the tax by the taxpayer on such return (determined without regard to such credits),

[CCH Explanation at ¶ 210.]

Amendments

- **2013, American Taxpayer Relief Act of 2012 (P.L. 112-240)**

P.L. 112-240, § 101(a)(1) and (3), provides:

SEC. 101. PERMANENT EXTENSION AND MODIFICATION OF 2001 TAX RELIEF.

(a) PERMANENT EXTENSION.—

(1) IN GENERAL.—The Economic Growth and Tax Relief Reconciliation Act of 2001 is amended by striking title IX.

* * *

(3) EFFECTIVE DATE.—The amendments made by this subsection shall apply to taxable, plan, or limitation years beginning after December 31, 2012, and estates of decedents dying, gifts made, or generation skipping transfers after December 31, 2012.

- **2010, Tax Relief, Unemployment Insurance Reauthorization, and Job Creation Act of 2010 (P.L. 111-312)**

P.L. 111-312, § 101(b)(1):

Amended Code Sec. 6211(b)(4)(A) to read as such provision would read if section 10909 of the Patient Protection

and Affordable Care Act (P.L. 111-148) had never been enacted. **Effective** for tax years beginning after 12-31-2011.

- **2010, Patient Protection and Affordable Care Act (P.L. 111-148)**

P.L. 111-148, § 10105(d):

Amended Act Sec. 1401(d) by adding at the end a new Act Sec. 1401(d)(3), which amends Code Sec. 6211(b)(4)(A) by inserting "36B," after "36A,". **Effective** 3-23-2010.

P.L. 111-148, § 10909(b)(2)(N):

Amended Code Sec. 6211(b)(4)(A) by inserting "36C," before "53(e)". **Effective** for tax years beginning after 12-31-2009.

P.L. 111-148, § 10909(c), provides:

(c) APPLICATION AND EXTENSION OF EGTRRA SUNSET.—Notwithstanding section 901 of the Economic Growth and Tax Relief Reconciliation Act of 2001, such section shall apply to the amendments made by this section and the amendments made by section 202 of such Act by substituting "December 31, 2011" for "December 31, 2010" in subsection (a)(1) thereof.

[¶ 5400] CODE SEC. 6416. CERTAIN TAXES ON SALES AND SERVICES.

* * *

(b) SPECIAL CASES IN WHICH TAX PAYMENTS CONSIDERED OVERPAYMENTS.—Under regulations prescribed by the Secretary, credit or refund (without interest) shall be allowed or made in respect of the overpayments determined under the following paragraphs:

* * *

(2) SPECIFIED USES AND RESALES.—The tax paid under chapter 32 (or under subsection (a) or (d) of section 4041 in respect of sales or under section 4051) in respect of any article shall be deemed to be an overpayment if such article was, by any person—

(A) exported;

(B) used or sold for use as supplies for vessels or aircraft;

(C) sold to a State or local government for the exclusive use of a State or local government;

(D) sold to a nonprofit educational organization for its exclusive use;

(E) sold to a qualified blood collector organization (as defined in section 7701(a)(49)) for such organization's exclusive use in the collection, storage, or transportation of blood;

(F) in the case of any tire taxable under section 4071(a), sold to any person for use as described in section 4221(e)(3); or

(G) in the case of gasoline, used or sold for use in the production of special fuels referred to in section 4041.

Subparagraphs (C), (D), and (E) shall not apply in the case of any tax paid under section 4064. This paragraph shall not apply in the case of any tax imposed under section 4041(a)(1) or 4081 on diesel fuel or kerosene and any tax paid under section 4121. In the case of the tax imposed by section 4131, subparagraphs (B), (C), (D), and (E) shall not apply and subparagraph (A) shall apply only if the use of the exported vaccine meets such requirements as the Secretary may by regulations prescribe. Subparagraphs (C) and (D) shall not apply in the case of any tax imposed on gasoline under section 4081 if the requirements of subsection (a)(4) are not met. In the case of taxes imposed by subchapter C or D of chapter 32, subparagraph (E) shall not apply. *In the case of the tax imposed by section 4191, subparagraphs (B), (C), (D), and (E) shall not apply.*

* * *

[CCH Explanation at ¶350.]

Amendments

• 2010, Health Care and Education Reconciliation Act of 2010 (P.L. 111-152)

P.L. 111-152, §1405(b)(2):

Amended Code Sec. 6416(b)(2), by adding at the end a new sentence. **Effective** for sales after 12-31-2012.

[¶5410] CODE SEC. 6654. FAILURE BY INDIVIDUAL TO PAY ESTIMATED INCOME TAX.

(a) ADDITION TO THE TAX.—Except as otherwise provided in this section, in the case of any underpayment of estimated tax by an individual, there shall be added to the tax under chapter 1[,] *the tax under chapter 2, and the tax under chapter 2A* for the taxable year an amount determined by applying—

(1) the underpayment rate established under section 6621,

(2) to the amount of the underpayment,

(3) for the period of the underpayment.

* * *

[CCH Explanation at ¶605.]

Amendments

• 2010, Health Care and Education Reconciliation Act of 2010 (P.L. 111-152)

P.L. 111-152, §1402(a)(2)(A):

Amended Code Sec. 6654(a) by striking "and the tax under chapter 2" and inserting "the tax under chapter 2,

and the tax under chapter 2A". **Effective** for tax years beginning after 12-31-2012.

(f) TAX COMPUTED AFTER APPLICATION OF CREDITS AGAINST TAX.—For purposes of this section, the term "tax" means—

(1) the tax imposed by chapter 1 (other than any increase in such tax by reason of section 143(m)), plus

(2) the tax imposed by chapter 2, *plus*

(3) *the taxes imposed by chapter 2A, minus*

(4) the credits against tax provided by part IV of subchapter A of chapter 1, other than the credit against tax provided by section 31 (relating to tax withheld on wages).

* * *

[CCH Explanation at ¶605.]

Amendments

• 2010, Health Care and Education Reconciliation Act of 2010 (P.L. 111-152)

P.L. 111-152, §1402(a)(2)(B)(i)-(ii):

Amended Code Sec. 6654(f) by striking "minus" at the end of paragraph (2) and inserting "plus"; and by redesig-

nating paragraph (3) as paragraph (4) and inserting after paragraph (2) a new paragraph (3). **Effective** for tax years beginning after 12-31-2012.

(m) SPECIAL RULE FOR MEDICARE TAX.—*For purposes of this section, the tax imposed under section 3101(b)(2) (to the extent not withheld) shall be treated as a tax imposed under chapter 2.*

[CCH Explanation at ¶620.]

Amendments

• 2010, Health Care and Education Reconciliation Act of 2010 (P.L. 111-152)

P.L. 111-152, §1402(b)(2):

Amended Code Sec. 6654 by redesignating subsection (m) as subsection (n) and by inserting after subsection (l) a new

subsection (m). **Effective** with respect to remuneration received, and tax years beginning after, 12-31-2012.

(n) REGULATIONS.—The Secretary shall prescribe such regulations as may be necessary to carry out the purposes of this section.

[CCH Explanation at ¶ 620.]
Amendments
• 2010, Health Care and Education Reconciliation Act of 2010 (P.L. 111-152)

P.L. 111-152, § 1402(b)(2):

Amended Code Sec. 6654 by redesignating subsection (m) as subsection (n). **Effective** with respect to remuneration received, and tax years beginning after, 12-31-2012.

[¶ 5420] CODE SEC. 6724. WAIVER; DEFINITIONS AND SPECIAL RULES.

* * *

(d) DEFINITIONS.—For purposes of this part—

(1) INFORMATION RETURN.—The term "information return" means—

* * *

(B) any return required by—

* * *

(xxii) section 6039(a) (relating to returns required with respect to certain options),

(xxiii) section 6050W (relating to returns to payments made in settlement of payment card transactions),

(xxiv) section 6055 (relating to returns relating to information regarding health insurance coverage), or

(xxv) section 6056 (relating to returns relating to certain employers required to report on health insurance coverage), and

* * *

(2) PAYEE STATEMENT.—The term "payee statement" means any statement required to be furnished under—

* * *

(EE) section 6050U (relating to charges or payments for qualified long-term care insurance contracts under combined arrangements),

(FF) section 6050W(c) (relating to returns relating to payments made in settlement of payment card transactions),

(GG) section 6055(c) (relating to statements relating to information regarding health insurance coverage), or

(HH) section 6056(c) (relating to statements relating to certain employers required to report on health insurance coverage).

* * *

[CCH Explanation at ¶ 410 and ¶ 415.]
Amendments
• 2010, Patient Protection and Affordable Care Act (P.L. 111-148)

P.L. 111-148, § 1502(b)(1):

Amended Code Sec. 6724(d)(1)(B) by striking "or" at the end of clause (xxii), by striking "and" at the end of clause (xxiii) and inserting "or", and by inserting after clause (xxiii) a new clause (xxiv). **Effective** for calendar years beginning after 2013.

P.L. 111-148, § 1502(b)(2):

Amended Code Sec. 6724(d)(2) by striking "or" at the end of subparagraph (EE), by striking the period at the end of subparagraph (FF) and inserting ", or" and by inserting after subparagraph (FF) a new subparagraph (GG). **Effective** for calendar years beginning after 2013.

P.L. 111-148, § 1514(b)(1):

Amended Code Sec. 6724(d)(1)(B), as amended by Act Sec. 1502(b)(1), by striking "or" at the end of clause (xxiii), by striking "and" at the end of clause (xxiv) and inserting "or", and by inserting after clause (xxiv) a new clause (xxv). **Effective** for periods beginning after 12-31-2013.

P.L. 111-148, § 1514(b)(2):

Amended Code Sec. 6724(d)(2), as amended by Act Sec. 1502(b)(2), by striking "or" at the end of subparagraph (FF), by striking the period at the end of subparagraph (GG) and inserting ", or" and by inserting after subparagraph (GG) a new subparagraph (HH). **Effective** for periods beginning after 12-31-2013.

P.L. 111-148, § 10108(j)(3)(E):

Amended Code Sec. 6724(d)(1)(B)(xxv), as added by Act Sec. 1514(b)(1), by striking "large" and inserting "certain". **Effective** for periods beginning after 12-31-2013.

P.L. 111-148, § 10108(j)(3)(F):

Amended Code Sec. 6724(d)(2)(HH), as added by Act Sec. 1514(b)(2), by striking "large" and inserting "certain". **Effective** for periods beginning after 12-31-2013.

[¶ 5430] CODE SEC. 9511. PATIENT-CENTERED OUTCOMES RESEARCH TRUST FUND.

(a) CREATION OF TRUST FUND.—There is established in the Treasury of the United States a trust fund to be known as the "Patient-Centered Outcomes Research Trust Fund" (hereafter in this section referred to as the "PCORTF"), consisting of such amounts as may be appropriated or credited to such Trust Fund as provided in this section and section 9602(b).

(b) TRANSFERS TO FUND.—

(1) APPROPRIATION.—There are hereby appropriated to the Trust Fund the following:

(A) For fiscal year 2010, $10,000,000.

(B) For fiscal year 2011, $50,000,000.

(C) For fiscal year 2012, $150,000,000.

(D) For fiscal year 2013—

(i) an amount equivalent to the net revenues received in the Treasury from the fees imposed under subchapter B of chapter 34 (relating to fees on health insurance and self-insured plans) for such fiscal year; and

(ii) $150,000,000.

(E) For each of fiscal years 2014, 2015, 2016, 2017, 2018, and 2019—

(i) an amount equivalent to the net revenues received in the Treasury from the fees imposed under subchapter B of chapter 34 (relating to fees on health insurance and self-insured plans) for such fiscal year; and

(ii) $150,000,000.

The amounts appropriated under subparagraphs (A), (B), (C), (D)(ii), and (E)(ii) shall be transferred from the general fund of the Treasury, from funds not otherwise appropriated.

(2) TRUST FUND TRANSFERS.—In addition to the amounts appropriated under paragraph (1), there shall be credited to the PCORTF the amounts transferred under section 1183 of the Social Security Act.

(3) LIMITATION ON TRANSFERS TO PCORTF.—No amount may be appropriated or transferred to the PCORTF on and after the date of any expenditure from the PCORTF which is not an expenditure permitted under this section. The determination of whether an expenditure is so permitted shall be made without regard to—

(A) any provision of law which is not contained or referenced in this chapter or in a revenue Act, and

(B) whether such provision of law is a subsequently enacted provision or directly or indirectly seeks to waive the application of this paragraph.

(c) TRUSTEE.—The Secretary of the Treasury shall be a trustee of the PCORTF.

(d) EXPENDITURES FROM FUND.—

(1) AMOUNTS AVAILABLE TO THE PATIENT-CENTERED OUTCOMES RESEARCH INSTITUTE.—Subject to paragraph (2), amounts in the PCORTF are available, without further appropriation, to the Patient-Centered Outcomes Research Institute established under section 1181(b) of the Social Security Act for carrying out part D of title XI of the Social Security Act (as in effect on the date of enactment of such Act).

(2) *TRANSFER OF FUNDS.—*

    (A) *IN GENERAL.—The trustee of the PCORTF shall provide for the transfer from the PCORTF of 20 percent of the amounts appropriated or credited to the PCORTF for each of fiscal years 2011 through 2019 to the Secretary of Health and Human Services to carry out section 937 of the Public Health Service Act.*

    (B) *AVAILABILITY.—Amounts transferred under subparagraph (A) shall remain available until expended.*

    (C) *REQUIREMENTS.—Of the amounts transferred under subparagraph (A) with respect to a fiscal year, the Secretary of Health and Human Services shall distribute—*

        (i) *80 percent to the Office of Communication and Knowledge Transfer of the Agency for Healthcare Research and Quality (or any other relevant office designated by Agency for Healthcare Research and Quality) to carry out the activities described in section 937 of the Public Health Service Act; and*

        (ii) *20 percent to the Secretary to carry out the activities described in such section 937.*

  (e) *NET REVENUES.—For purposes of this section, the term "net revenues" means the amount estimated by the Secretary of the Treasury based on the excess of—*

    (1) *the fees received in the Treasury under subchapter B of chapter 34, over*

    (2) *the decrease in the tax imposed by chapter 1 resulting from the fees imposed by such subchapter.*

  (f) *TERMINATION.—No amounts shall be available for expenditure from the PCORTF after September 30, 2019, and any amounts in such Trust Fund after such date shall be transferred to the general fund of the Treasury.*

[CCH Explanation at ¶ 545 and ¶ 550.]
Amendments
• **2010, Patient Protection and Affordable Care Act (P.L. 111-148)**

P.L. 111-148, § 6301(e)(1)(A):

Amended subchapter A of chapter 98 by adding at the end a new Code Sec. 9511. **Effective** 3-23-2010.

[¶ 5440] *CODE SEC. 9815. ADDITIONAL MARKET REFORMS.*

  (a) *GENERAL RULE.—Except as provided in subsection (b)—*

    (1) *the provisions of part A of title XXVII of the Public Health Service Act (as amended by the Patient Protection and Affordable Care Act) shall apply to group health plans, and health insurance issuers providing health insurance coverage in connection with group health plans, as if included in this subchapter; and*

    (2) *to the extent that any provision of this subchapter conflicts with a provision of such part A with respect to group health plans, or health insurance issuers providing health insurance coverage in connection with group health plans, the provisions of such part A shall apply.*

  (b) *EXCEPTION.—Notwithstanding subsection (a), the provisions of sections 2716 and 2718 of title XXVII of the Public Health Service Act (as amended by the Patient Protection and Affordable Care Act) shall not apply with respect to self-insured group health plans, and the provisions of this subchapter shall continue to apply to such plans as if such sections of the Public Health Service Act (as so amended) had not been enacted.*

[CCH Explanation at ¶ 540 and ¶ 555.]
Amendments
• **2010, Patient Protection and Affordable Care Act (P.L. 111-148)**

P.L. 111-148, § 1563(f) (as redesignated by P.L. 111-148, § 10107(b)):

Amended subchapter B of chapter 100 by adding at the end a new Code Sec. 9815. **Effective** 3-23-2010.

Act Sections Not Amending Code Sections

PATIENT PROTECTION AND AFFORDABLE CARE ACT

[¶ 7005] ACT SEC. 1. SHORT TITLE; TABLE OF CONTENTS.

(a) SHORT TITLE.—This Act may be cited as the "Patient Protection and Affordable Care Act".

* * *

TITLE IX—REVENUE PROVISIONS

Subtitle A—Revenue Offset Provisions

* * *

[¶ 7030] ACT SEC. 9008. IMPOSITION OF ANNUAL FEE ON BRANDED PRESCRIPTION PHARMACEUTICAL MANUFACTURERS AND IMPORTERS.

(a) IMPOSITION OF FEE.—

(1) IN GENERAL.—Each covered entity engaged in the business of manufacturing or importing branded prescription drugs shall pay to the Secretary of the Treasury not later than the annual payment date of each calendar year beginning after 2009 a fee in an amount determined under subsection (b).

(2) ANNUAL PAYMENT DATE.—For purposes of this section, the term "annual payment date" means with respect to any calendar year the date determined by the Secretary, but in no event later than September 30 of such calendar year.

(b) DETERMINATION OF FEE AMOUNT.—

(1) IN GENERAL.—With respect to each covered entity, the fee under this section for any calendar year shall be equal to an amount that bears the same ratio to $2,300,000,000 as—

(A) the covered entity's branded prescription drug sales taken into account during the preceding calendar year, bear to

(B) the aggregate branded prescription drug sales of all covered entities taken into account during such preceding calendar year.

(2) SALES TAKEN INTO ACCOUNT.—For purposes of paragraph (1), the branded prescription drug sales taken into account during any calendar year with respect to any covered entity shall be determined in accordance with the following table:

With respect to a covered entity's aggregate branded prescription drug sales during the calendar year that are:	The percentage of such sales taken into account is:
Not more than $5,000,000	0 percent
More than $5,000,000 but not more than $125,000,000.	10 percent
More than $125,000,000 but not more than $225,000,000.	40 percent
More than $225,000,000 but not more than $400,000,000.	75 percent
More than $400,000,000	100 percent.

(3) SECRETARIAL DETERMINATION.—The Secretary of the Treasury shall calculate the amount of each covered entity's fee for any calendar year under paragraph (1). In calculating such amount, the Secretary of the Treasury shall determine such covered entity's branded prescription drug

sales on the basis of reports submitted under subsection (g) and through the use of any other source of information available to the Secretary of the Treasury.

(c) TRANSFER OF FEES TO MEDICARE PART B TRUST FUND.—There is hereby appropriated to the Federal Supplementary Medical Insurance Trust Fund established under section 1841 of the Social Security Act an amount equal to the fees received by the Secretary of the Treasury under subsection (a).

(d) COVERED ENTITY.—

(1) IN GENERAL.—For purposes of this section, the term "covered entity" means any manufacturer or importer with gross receipts from branded prescription drug sales.

(2) CONTROLLED GROUPS.—

(A) IN GENERAL.—For purposes of this subsection, all persons treated as a single employer under subsection (a) or (b) of section 52 of the Internal Revenue Code of 1986 or subsection (m) or (o) of section 414 of such Code shall be treated as a single covered entity.

(B) INCLUSION OF FOREIGN CORPORATIONS.—For purposes of subparagraph (A), in applying subsections (a) and (b) of section 52 of such Code to this section, section 1563 of such Code shall be applied without regard to subsection (b)(2)(C) thereof.

(e) BRANDED PRESCRIPTION DRUG SALES.—For purposes of this section—

(1) IN GENERAL.—The term "branded prescription drug sales" means sales of branded prescription drugs to any specified government program or pursuant to coverage under any such program.

(2) BRANDED PRESCRIPTION DRUGS.—

(A) IN GENERAL.—The term "branded prescription drug" means—

(i) any prescription drug the application for which was submitted under section 505(b) of the Federal Food, Drug, and Cosmetic Act (21 U.S.C. 355(b)), or

(ii) any biological product the license for which was submitted under section 351(a) of the Public Health Service Act (42 U.S.C. 262(a)).

(B) PRESCRIPTION DRUG.—For purposes of subparagraph (A)(i), the term "prescription drug" means any drug which is subject to section 503(b) of the Federal Food, Drug, and Cosmetic Act (21 U.S.C. 353(b)).

(3) EXCLUSION OF ORPHAN DRUG SALES.—The term "branded prescription drug sales" shall not include sales of any drug or biological product with respect to which a credit was allowed for any taxable year under section 45C of the Internal Revenue Code of 1986. The preceding sentence shall not apply with respect to any such drug or biological product after the date on which such drug or biological product is approved by the Food and Drug Administration for marketing for any indication other than the treatment of the rare disease or condition with respect to which such credit was allowed.

(4) SPECIFIED GOVERNMENT PROGRAM.—The term "specified government program" means—

(A) the Medicare Part D program under part D of title XVIII of the Social Security Act,

(B) the Medicare Part B program under part B of title XVIII of the Social Security Act,

(C) the Medicaid program under title XIX of the Social Security Act,

(D) any program under which branded prescription drugs are procured by the Department of Veterans Affairs,

(E) any program under which branded prescription drugs are procured by the Department of Defense, or

(F) the TRICARE retail pharmacy program under section 1074g of title 10, United States Code.

(f) Tax Treatment of Fees.—The fees imposed by this section—

(1) for purposes of subtitle F of the Internal Revenue Code of 1986, shall be treated as excise taxes with respect to which only civil actions for refund under procedures of such subtitle shall apply, and

(2) for purposes of section 275 of such Code, shall be considered to be a tax described in section 275(a)(6).

(g) Reporting Requirement.—Not later than the date determined by the Secretary of the Treasury following the end of any calendar year, the Secretary of Health and Human Services, the Secretary of Veterans Affairs, and the Secretary of Defense shall report to the Secretary of the Treasury, in such manner as the Secretary of the Treasury prescribes, the total branded prescription drug sales for each covered entity with respect to each specified government program under such Secretary's jurisdiction using the following methodology:

(1) Medicare Part D Program.—The Secretary of Health and Human Services shall report, for each covered entity and for each branded prescription drug of the covered entity covered by the Medicare Part D program, the product of—

(A) the per-unit ingredient cost, as reported to the Secretary of Health and Human Services by prescription drug plans and Medicare Advantage prescription drug plans, minus any per-unit rebate, discount, or other price concession provided by the covered entity, as reported to the Secretary of Health and Human Services by the prescription drug plans and Medicare Advantage prescription drug plans, and

(B) the number of units of the branded prescription drug paid for under the Medicare Part D program.

(2) Medicare Part B Program.—The Secretary of Health and Human Services shall report, for each covered entity and for each branded prescription drug of the covered entity covered by the Medicare Part B program under section 1862(a) of the Social Security Act, the product of—

(A) the per-unit average sales price (as defined in section 1847A(c) of the Social Security Act) or the per-unit Part B payment rate for a separately paid branded prescription drug without a reported average sales price, and

(B) the number of units of the branded prescription drug paid for under the Medicare Part B program.

The Centers for Medicare and Medicaid Services shall establish a process for determining the units and the allocated price for purposes of this section for those branded prescription drugs that are not separately payable or for which National Drug Codes are not reported.

(3) Medicaid Program.—The Secretary of Health and Human Services shall report, for each covered entity and for each branded prescription drug of the covered entity covered under the Medicaid program, the product of—

(A) the per-unit ingredient cost paid to pharmacies by States for the branded prescription drug dispensed to Medicaid beneficiaries, minus any per-unit rebate paid by the covered entity under section 1927 of the Social Security Act and any State supplemental rebate, and

(B) the number of units of the branded prescription drug paid for under the Medicaid program.

(4) Department of Veterans Affairs Programs.—The Secretary of Veterans Affairs shall report, for each covered entity and for each branded prescription drug of the covered entity, the total amount paid for each such branded prescription drug procured by the Department of Veterans Affairs for its beneficiaries.

(5) Department of Defense Programs and Tricare.—The Secretary of Defense shall report, for each covered entity and for each branded prescription drug of the covered entity, the sum of—

(A) the total amount paid for each such branded prescription drug procured by the Department of Defense for its beneficiaries, and

(B) for each such branded prescription drug dispensed under the TRICARE retail pharmacy program, the product of—

(i) the per-unit ingredient cost, minus any per-unit rebate paid by the covered entity, and

(ii) the number of units of the branded prescription drug dispensed under such program.

(h) SECRETARY.—For purposes of this section, the term "Secretary" includes the Secretary's delegate.

(i) GUIDANCE.—The Secretary of the Treasury shall publish guidance necessary to carry out the purposes of this section.

(j) APPLICATION OF SECTION.—This section shall apply to any branded prescription drug sales after December 31, 2008.

(k) CONFORMING AMENDMENT.—Section 1841(a) of the Social Security Act is amended by inserting "or section 9008(c) of the Patient Protection and Affordable Care Act of 2009" after "this part".

* * *

[Note: The text of Act Sec. 9008, as reproduced above, does not reflect amendments made by Act Sec. 1404 of the Health Care and Education Reconciliation Act of 2010. See ¶7106.]

[CCH Explanation at ¶352.]

[¶7036] ACT SEC. 9010. IMPOSITION OF ANNUAL FEE ON HEALTH INSURANCE PROVIDERS.

(a) IMPOSITION OF FEE.—

(1) IN GENERAL.—Each covered entity engaged in the business of providing health insurance shall pay to the Secretary not later than the annual payment date of each calendar year beginning after 2010 a fee in an amount determined under subsection (b).

(2) ANNUAL PAYMENT DATE.—For purposes of this section, the term "annual payment date" means with respect to any calendar year the date determined by the Secretary, but in no event later than September 30 of such calendar year.

(b) DETERMINATION OF FEE AMOUNT.—

(1) IN GENERAL.—With respect to each covered entity, the fee under this section for any calendar year shall be equal to an amount that bears the same ratio to the applicable amount as—

(A) the covered entity's net premiums written with respect to health insurance for any United States health risk that are taken into account during the preceding calendar year, bears to

(B) the aggregate net premiums written with respect to such health insurance of all covered entities that are taken into account during such preceding calendar year.

(2) AMOUNTS TAKEN INTO ACCOUNT.—For purposes of paragraph (1), the net premiums written with respect to health insurance for any United States health risk that are taken into account during any calendar year with respect to any covered entity shall be determined in accordance with the following table:

"With respect to a covered entity's net premiums written during the calendar year that are:	The percentage of net premiums written that are taken into account is:
Not more than $25,000,000	0 percent
More than $25,000,000 but not more than $50,000,000.	50 percent
More than $50,000,000	100 percent.

(3) SECRETARIAL DETERMINATION.—The Secretary shall calculate the amount of each covered entity's fee for any calendar year under paragraph (1). In calculating such amount, the Secretary shall determine such covered entity's net premiums written with respect to any United States

health risk on the basis of reports submitted by the covered entity under subsection (g) and through the use of any other source of information available to the Secretary.

(c) COVERED ENTITY.—

(1) IN GENERAL.—For purposes of this section, the term "covered entity" means any entity which provides health insurance for any United States health risk.

(2) EXCLUSION.—Such term does not include—

(A) any employer to the extent that such employer self-insures its employees' health risks,

(B) any governmental entity,

(C) any entity—

(i)(I) which is incorporated as, is a wholly owned subsidiary of, or is a wholly owned affiliate of, a nonprofit corporation under a State law, or

(II) which is described in section 501(c)(4) of the Internal Revenue Code of 1986 and the activities of which consist of providing commercial-type insurance (within the meaning of section 501(m) of such Code),

(ii) the premium rate increases of which are regulated by a State authority,

(iii) which, as of the date of the enactment of this section, acts as the insurer of last resort in the State and is subject to State guarantee issue requirements, and

(iv) for which the medical loss ratio (determined in a manner consistent with the determination of such ratio under section 2718(b)(1)(A) of the Public Health Service Act) with respect to the individual insurance market for such entity for the calendar year is not less than 100 percent,

(D) any entity—

(i)(I) which is incorporated as a nonprofit corporation under a State law, or

(II) which is described in section 501(c)(4) of the Internal Revenue Code of 1986 and the activities of which consist of providing commercial-type insurance (within the meaning of section 501(m) of such Code), and

(ii) for which the medical loss ratio (as so determined)—

(I) with respect to each of the individual, small group, and large group insurance markets for such entity for the calendar year is not less than 90 percent, and

(II) with respect to all such markets for such entity for the calendar year is not less than 92 percent, or

(E) any entity—

(i) which is a mutual insurance company,

(ii) which for the period reported on the 2008 Accident and Health Policy Experience Exhibit of the National Association of Insurance Commissioners had—

(I) a market share of the insured population of a State of at least 40 but not more than 60 percent, and

(II) with respect to all markets described in subparagraph (D)(ii)(I), a medical loss ratio of not less than 90 percent, and

(iii) with respect to annual payment dates in calendar years after 2011, for which the medical loss ratio (determined in a manner consistent with the determination of such ratio under section 2718(b)(1)(A) of the Public Health Service Act) with respect to all such markets for such entity for the preceding calendar year is not less than 89 percent (except that with respect to such annual payment date for 2012, the calculation under 2718(b)(1)(B)(ii) of such Act is determined by reference to the previous year, and with respect to such annual payment date for 2013, such calculation is determined by reference to the average for the previous 2 years).

(3) CONTROLLED GROUPS.—

(A) IN GENERAL.—For purposes of this subsection, all persons treated as a single employer under subsection (a) or (b) of section 52 of the Internal Revenue Code of 1986 or subsection (m) or (o) of section 414 of such Code shall be treated as a single covered entity (or employer for purposes of paragraph (2)).

(B) INCLUSION OF FOREIGN CORPORATIONS.—For purposes of subparagraph (A), in applying subsections (a) and (b) of section 52 of such Code to this section, section 1563 of such Code shall be applied without regard to subsection (b)(2)(C) thereof.

If any entity described in subparagraph (C)(i)(I), (D)(i)(I) or (E)(i) of paragraph (2) is treated as a covered entity by reason of the application of the preceding sentence, the net premiums written with respect to health insurance for any United States health risk of such entity shall not be taken into account for purposes of this section.

(d) UNITED STATES HEALTH RISK.—For purposes of this section, the term "United States health risk" means the health risk of any individual who is—

(1) a United States citizen,

(2) a resident of the United States (within the meaning of section 7701(b)(1)(A) of the Internal Revenue Code of 1986), or

(3) located in the United States, with respect to the period such individual is so located.

(e) APPLICABLE AMOUNT.—For purposes of subsection (b)(1), the applicable amount shall be determined in accordance with the following table:

"Calendar year	Applicable amount
2011	$2,000,000,000
2012	$4,000,000,000
2013	$7,000,000,000
2014, 2015 and 2016	$9,000,000,000
2017 and thereafter	$10,000,000,000.".

(f) TAX TREATMENT OF FEES.—The fees imposed by this section—

(1) for purposes of subtitle F of the Internal Revenue Code of 1986, shall be treated as excise taxes with respect to which only civil actions for refund under procedures of such subtitle shall apply, and

(2) for purposes of section 275 of such Code shall be considered to be a tax described in section 275(a)(6).

(g) REPORTING REQUIREMENT.—

(1) IN GENERAL.—Not later than the date determined by the Secretary following the end of any calendar year, each covered entity shall report to the Secretary, in such manner as the Secretary prescribes, the covered entity's net premiums written with respect to health insurance for any United States health risk for such calendar year.

(2) PENALTY FOR FAILURE TO REPORT.—

(A) IN GENERAL.—In the case of any failure to make a report containing the information required by paragraph (1) on the date prescribed therefor (determined with regard to any extension of time for filing), unless it is shown that such failure is due to reasonable cause, there shall be paid by the covered entity failing to file such report, an amount equal to—

(i) $10,000, plus

(ii) the lesser of—

(I) an amount equal to $1,000, multiplied by the number of days during which such failure continues, or

(II) the amount of the fee imposed by this section for which such report was required.

(B) TREATMENT OF PENALTY.—The penalty imposed under subparagraph (A)—

(i) shall be treated as a penalty for purposes of subtitle F of the Internal Revenue Code of 1986,

(ii) shall be paid on notice and demand by the Secretary and in the same manner as tax under such Code, and

(iii) with respect to which only civil actions for refund under procedures of such subtitle F shall apply.

(h) ADDITIONAL DEFINITIONS.—For purposes of this section—

(1) SECRETARY.—The term "Secretary" means the Secretary of the Treasury or the Secretary's delegate.

(2) UNITED STATES.—The term "United States" means the several States, the District of Columbia, the Commonwealth of Puerto Rico, and the possessions of the United States.

(3) HEALTH INSURANCE.—The term "health insurance" shall not include—

(A) any insurance coverage described in paragraph (1)(A) or (3) of section 9832(c) of the Internal Revenue Code of 1986,

(B) any insurance for long-term care, or

(C) "any medicare supplemental health insurance (as defined in section 1882(g)(1) of the Social Security Act).".

(i) GUIDANCE.—The Secretary shall publish guidance necessary to carry out the purposes of this section and shall prescribe such regulations as are necessary or appropriate to prevent avoidance of the purposes of this section, including inappropriate actions taken to qualify as an exempt entity under subsection (c)(2).

(j) APPLICATION OF SECTION.—This section shall apply to any net premiums written after December 31, 2009, with respect to health insurance for any United States health risk.

* * *

[Note: The text of Act Sec. 9010, as reproduced above, reflects amendments made by Act Sec. 10905. See ¶7051. It does not reflect amendments made by Act Sec. 1406 of the Health Care and Education Reconciliation Act of 2010. See ¶7112]

[CCH Explanation at ¶543.]

TITLE X—STRENGTHENING QUALITY, AFFORDABLE HEALTH CARE FOR ALL AMERICANS

* * *

Subtitle H—Provisions Relating to Title IX

* * *

[¶7051] ACT SEC. 10905. MODIFICATION OF ANNUAL FEE ON HEALTH INSURANCE PROVIDERS.

(a) DETERMINATION OF FEE AMOUNT.—Subsection (b) of section 9010 of this Act is amended to read as follows:

"(b) DETERMINATION OF FEE AMOUNT.—

"(1) IN GENERAL.—With respect to each covered entity, the fee under this section for any calendar year shall be equal to an amount that bears the same ratio to the applicable amount as—

"(A) the covered entity's net premiums written with respect to health insurance for any United States health risk that are taken into account during the preceding calendar year, bears to

"(B) the aggregate net premiums written with respect to such health insurance of all covered entities that are taken into account during such preceding calendar year.

"(2) AMOUNTS TAKEN INTO ACCOUNT.—For purposes of paragraph (1), the net premiums written with respect to health insurance for any United States health risk that are taken into account during any calendar year with respect to any covered entity shall be determined in accordance with the following table:

"With respect to a covered entity's net premiums written during the calendar year that are:	The percentage of net premiums written that are taken into account is:
Not more than $25,000,000	0 percent
More than $25,000,000 but not more than $50,000,000.	50 percent
More than $50,000,000	100 percent.

"(3) SECRETARIAL DETERMINATION.—The Secretary shall calculate the amount of each covered entity's fee for any calendar year under paragraph (1). In calculating such amount, the Secretary shall determine such covered entity's net premiums written with respect to any United States health risk on the basis of reports submitted by the covered entity under subsection (g) and through the use of any other source of information available to the Secretary.".

(b) APPLICABLE AMOUNT.—Subsection (e) of section 9010 of this Act is amended to read as follows:

"(e) APPLICABLE AMOUNT.—For purposes of subsection (b)(1), the applicable amount shall be determined in accordance with the following table:

"Calendar year	Applicable amount
2011	$2,000,000,000
2012	$4,000,000,000
2013	$7,000,000,000
2014, 2015 and 2016	$9,000,000,000
2017 and thereafter	$10,000,000,000.".

(c) EXEMPTION FROM ANNUAL FEE ON HEALTH INSURANCE FOR CERTAIN NONPROFIT ENTITIES.—Section 9010(c)(2) of this Act is amended by striking "or" at the end of subparagraph (A), by striking the period at the end of subparagraph (B) and inserting a comma, and by adding at the end the following new subparagraphs:

"(C) any entity—

"(i) (I) which is incorporated as, is a wholly owned subsidiary of, or is a wholly owned affiliate of, a nonprofit corporation under a State law, or

"(II) which is described in section 501(c)(4) of the Internal Revenue Code of 1986 and the activities of which consist of providing commercial-type insurance (within the meaning of section 501(m) of such Code),

"(ii) the premium rate increases of which are regulated by a State authority,

"(iii) which, as of the date of the enactment of this section, acts as the insurer of last resort in the State and is subject to State guarantee issue requirements, and

"(iv) for which the medical loss ratio (determined in a manner consistent with the determination of such ratio under section 2718(b)(1)(A) of the Public Health Service Act) with respect to the individual insurance market for such entity for the calendar year is not less than 100 percent,

"(D) any entity—

"(i) (I) which is incorporated as a nonprofit corporation under a State law, or

"(II) which is described in section 501(c)(4) of the Internal Revenue Code of 1986 and the activities of which consist of providing commercial-type insurance (within the meaning of section 501(m) of such Code), and

"(ii) for which the medical loss ratio (as so determined)—

"(I) with respect to each of the individual, small group, and large group insurance markets for such entity for the calendar year is not less than 90 percent, and

"(II) with respect to all such markets for such entity for the calendar year is not less than 92 percent, or

"(E) any entity—

"(i) which is a mutual insurance company,

"(ii) which for the period reported on the 2008 Accident and Health Policy Experience Exhibit of the National Association of Insurance Commissioners had—

"(I) a market share of the insured population of a State of at least 40 but not more than 60 percent, and

"(II) with respect to all markets described in subparagraph (D)(ii)(I), a medical loss ratio of not less than 90 percent, and

"(iii) with respect to annual payment dates in calendar years after 2011, for which the medical loss ratio (determined in a manner consistent with the determination of such ratio under section 2718(b)(1)(A) of the Public Health Service Act) with respect to all such markets for such entity for the preceding calendar year is not less than 89 percent (except that with respect to such annual payment date for 2012, the calculation under [section] 2718(b)(1)(B)(ii) of such Act is determined by reference to the previous year, and with respect to such annual payment date for 2013, such calculation is determined by reference to the average for the previous 2 years).".

(d) CERTAIN INSURANCE EXEMPTED FROM FEE.—Paragraph (3) of section 9010(h) of this Act is amended to read as follows:

"(3) HEALTH INSURANCE.—The term 'health insurance' shall not include—

"(A) any insurance coverage described in paragraph (1)(A) or (3) of section 9832(c) of the Internal Revenue Code of 1986,

"(B) any insurance for long-term care, or

"(C) any medicare supplemental health insurance (as defined in section 1882(g)(1) of the Social Security Act).".

(e) ANTI-AVOIDANCE GUIDANCE.—Subsection (i) of section 9010 of this Act is amended by inserting "and shall prescribe such regulations as are necessary or appropriate to prevent avoidance of the purposes of this section, including inappropriate actions taken to qualify as an exempt entity under subsection (c)(2)" after "section".

(f) CONFORMING AMENDMENTS.—

(1) Section 9010(a)(1) of this Act is amended by striking "2009" and inserting "2010".

(2) Section 9010(c)(2)(B) of this Act is amended by striking "(except" and all that follows through "1323)".

(3) Section 9010(c)(3) of this Act is amended by adding at the end the following new sentence: "If any entity described in subparagraph (C)(i)(I), (D)(i)(I), or (E)(i) of paragraph (2) is treated as a covered entity by reason of the application of the preceding sentence, the net premiums written with respect to health insurance for any United States health risk of such entity shall not be taken into account for purposes of this section.".

(4) Section 9010(g)(1) of this Act is amended by striking "and third party administration agreement fees".

(5) Section 9010(j) of this Act is amended—

(A) by striking "2008" and inserting "2009", and

(B) by striking ", and any third party administration agreement fees received after such date".

(g) EFFECTIVE DATE.—The amendments made by this section shall take effect as if included in the enactment of section 9010.

* * *

[CCH Explanation at ¶ 543.]

HEALTH CARE AND EDUCATION RECONCILIATION ACT OF 2010

[¶ 7103] ACT SEC. 1. SHORT TITLE; TABLE OF CONTENTS.

(a) SHORT TITLE.—This Act may be cited as the "Health Care and Education Reconciliation Act of 2010".

* * *

TITLE I—COVERAGE, MEDICARE, MEDICAID, AND REVENUES

* * *

Subtitle E—Provisions Relating to Revenue

* * *

[¶ 7106] ACT SEC. 1404. BRAND NAME PHARMACEUTICALS.

(a) IN GENERAL.—Section 9008 of the Patient Protection and Affordable Care Act is amended—

(1) in subsection (a)(1), by striking "2009" and inserting "2010";

(2) in subsection (b)—

(A) by striking "$2,300,000,000" in paragraph (1) and inserting "the applicable amount"; and

(B) by adding at the end the following new paragraph:

"(4) APPLICABLE AMOUNT.—For purposes of paragraph (1), the applicable amount shall be determined in accordance with the following table:

"Calendar year	Applicable amount
2011	$2,500,000,000
2012	$2,800,000,000
2013	$2,800,000,000
2014	$3,000,000,000
2015	$3,000,000,000
2016	$3,000,000,000
2017	$4,000,000,000
2018	$4,100,000,000
2019 and thereafter	$2,800,000,000.";

(3) in subsection (d), by adding at the end the following new paragraph:

"(3) JOINT AND SEVERAL LIABILITY.—If more than one person is liable for payment of the fee under subsection (a) with respect to a single covered entity by reason of the application of paragraph (2), all such persons shall be jointly and severally liable for payment of such fee."; and

(4) by striking subsection (j) and inserting the following new subsection:

"(j) EFFECTIVE DATE.—This section shall apply to calendar years beginning after December 31, 2010.".

(b) EFFECTIVE DATE.—The amendments made by this section shall take effect as if included in section 9008 of the Patient Protection and Affordable Care Act.

* * *

[CCH Explanation at ¶ 352.]

[¶ 7112] ACT SEC. 1406. HEALTH INSURANCE PROVIDERS.

(a) IN GENERAL.—Section 9010 of the Patient Protection and Affordable Care Act, as amended by section 10905 of such Act, is amended—

(1) in subsection (a)(1), by striking "2010" and inserting "2013";

(2) in subsection (b)(2)—

(A) by striking "For purposes of paragraph (1), the net premiums" and inserting "For purposes of paragraph (1)—

"(A) IN GENERAL.—The net premiums"; and

(B) by adding at the end the following subparagraph:

"(B) PARTIAL EXCLUSION FOR CERTAIN EXEMPT ACTIVITIES.—After the application of subparagraph (A), only 50 percent of the remaining net premiums written with respect to health insurance for any United States health risk that are attributable to the activities (other than activities of an unrelated trade or business as defined in section 513 of the Internal Revenue Code of 1986) of any covered entity qualifying under paragraph (3), (4), (26), or (29) of section 501(c) of such Code and exempt from tax under section 501(a) of such Code shall be taken into account.";

(3) in subsection (c)—

(A) by inserting "during the calendar year in which the fee under this section is due" in paragraph (1) after "risk";

(B) in paragraph (2), by striking subparagraphs (C), (D), and (E) and inserting the following new subparagraphs:

"(C) any entity—

"(i) which is incorporated as a nonprofit corporation under a State law,

"(ii) no part of the net earnings of which inures to the benefit of any private shareholder or individual, no substantial part of the activities of which is carrying on propaganda, or otherwise attempting, to influence legislation (except as otherwise provided in section 501(h) of the Internal Revenue Code of 1986), and which does not participate in, or intervene in (including the publishing or distributing of statements), any political campaign on behalf of (or in opposition to) any candidate for public office, and

"(iii) more than 80 percent of the gross revenues of which is received from government programs that target low-income, elderly, or disabled populations under titles XVIII, XIX, and XXI of the Social Security Act, and

"(D) any entity which is described in section 501(c)(9) of such Code and which is established by an entity (other than by an employer or employers) for purposes of providing health care benefits.";

(C) in paragraph (3)(A), by striking "subparagraph (C)(i)(I), (D)(i)(I), or (E)(i)" and inserting "subparagraph (C) or (D)"; and

(D) by adding at the end the following new paragraph:

"(4) JOINT AND SEVERAL LIABILITY.—If more than one person is liable for payment of the fee under subsection (a) with respect to a single covered entity by reason of the application of paragraph (3), all such persons shall be jointly and severally liable for payment of such fee.";

(4) by striking subsection (e) and inserting the following:

"(e) APPLICABLE AMOUNT.—For purposes of subsection (b)(1)—

"(1) YEARS BEFORE 2019.—In the case of calendar years beginning before 2019, the applicable amount shall be determined in accordance with the following table:

"Calendar year	Applicable amount
2014	$8,000,000,000
2015	$11,300,000,000
2016	$11,300,000,000

"Calendar year	Applicable amount
2017	$13,900,000,000
2018	$14,300,000,000.

"(2) YEARS AFTER 2018.—In the case of any calendar year beginning after 2018, the applicable amount shall be the applicable amount for the preceding calendar year increased by the rate of premium growth (within the meaning of section 36B(b)(3)(A)(ii) of the Internal Revenue Code of 1986) for such preceding calendar year.";

(5) in subsection (g), by adding at the end the following new paragraphs:

"(3) ACCURACY-RELATED PENALTY.—

"(A) IN GENERAL.—In the case of any understatement of a covered entity's net premiums written with respect to health insurance for any United States health risk for any calendar year, there shall be paid by the covered entity making such understatement, an amount equal to the excess of—

"(i) the amount of the covered entity's fee under this section for the calendar year the Secretary determines should have been paid in the absence of any such understatement, over

"(ii) the amount of such fee the Secretary determined based on such understatement.

"(B) UNDERSTATEMENT.—For purposes of this paragraph, an understatement of a covered entity's net premiums written with respect to health insurance for any United States health risk for any calendar year is the difference between the amount of such net premiums written as reported on the return filed by the covered entity under paragraph (1) and the amount of such net premiums written that should have been reported on such return.

"(C) TREATMENT OF PENALTY.—The penalty imposed under subparagraph (A) shall be subject to the provisions of subtitle F of the Internal Revenue Code of 1986 that apply to assessable penalties imposed under chapter 68 of such Code.

"(4) TREATMENT OF INFORMATION.—Section 6103 of the Internal Revenue Code of 1986 shall not apply to any information reported under this subsection."; and

(6) by striking subsection (j) and inserting the following new subsection:

"(j) EFFECTIVE DATE.—This section shall apply to calendar years beginning after December 31, 2013.".

(b) EFFECTIVE DATE.—The amendments made by this section shall take effect as if included in section 9010 of the Patient Protection and Affordable Care Act.

• • *PATIENT PROTECTION AND AFFORDABLE CARE ACT, ACT SEC. 9010 AS AMENDED*————————————————————————————————

ACT SEC. 9010. IMPOSITION OF ANNUAL FEE ON HEALTH INSURANCE PROVIDERS.

(a) IMPOSITION OF FEE—

(1) IN GENERAL—Each covered entity engaged in the business of providing health insurance shall pay to the Secretary not later than the annual payment date of each calendar year beginning after *2013* a fee in an amount determined under subsection (b).

* * *

(b) DETERMINATION OF FEE AMOUNT—

* * *

(2) AMOUNTS TAKEN INTO ACCOUNT.—*For purposes of paragraph (1)*—

(A) IN GENERAL.—*The net premiums* written with respect to health insurance for any United States health risk that are taken into account during any calendar year with respect to any covered entity shall be determined in accordance with the following table:

* * *

(B) PARTIAL EXCLUSION FOR CERTAIN EXEMPT ACTIVITIES.—After the application of subparagraph (A), only 50 percent of the remaining net premiums written with respect to health insurance for any United States health risk that are attributable to the activities (other than activities of an unrelated trade or business as defined in section 513 of the Internal Revenue Code of 1986) of any covered entity qualifying under paragraph (3), (4), (26), or (29) of section 501(c) of such Code and exempt from tax under section 501(a) of such Code shall be taken into account.

* * *

(c) COVERED ENTITY.—

(1) IN GENERAL.—For purposes of this section, the term "covered entity" means any entity which provides health insurance for any United States health risk *during the calendar year in which the fee under this section is due.*

(2) EXCLUSION.—Such term does not include—

* * *

(C) any entity—

(i) which is incorporated as a nonprofit corporation under a State law,

(ii) no part of the net earnings of which inures to the benefit of any private shareholder or individual, no substantial part of the activities of which is carrying on propaganda, or otherwise attempting, to influence legislation (except as otherwise provided in section 501(h) of the Internal Revenue Code of 1986), and which does not participate in, or intervene in (including the publishing or distributing of statements), any political campaign on behalf of (or in opposition to) any candidate for public office, and

(iii) more than 80 percent of the gross revenues of which is received from government programs that target low-income, elderly, or disabled populations under titles XVIII, XIX, and XXI of the Social Security Act, and

(D) any entity which is described in section 501(c)(9) of such Code and which is established by an entity (other than by an employer or employers) for purposes of providing health care benefits.

(3) CONTROLLED GROUPS.—

* * *

If any entity described in *subparagraph (C) or (D)* of paragraph (2) is treated as a covered entity by reason of the application of the preceding sentence, the net premiums written with respect to health insurance for any United States health risk of such entity shall not be taken into account for purposes of this section.

(4) JOINT AND SEVERAL LIABILITY.—If more than one person is liable for payment of the fee under subsection (a) with respect to a single covered entity by reason of the application of paragraph (3), all such persons shall be jointly and severally liable for payment of such fee.

* * *

(e) APPLICABLE AMOUNT.—For purposes of subsection (b)(1)—

(1) YEARS BEFORE 2019.—In the case of calendar years beginning before 2019, the applicable amount shall be determined in accordance with the following table:

"Calendar year	Applicable amount
2014	$8,000,000,000
2015	$11,300,000,000
2016	$11,300,000,000
2017	$13,900,000,000
2018	$14,300,000,000.

• • *PATIENT PROTECTION AND AFFORDABLE CARE ACT, ACT SEC. 9010 AS AMENDED*

(2) YEARS AFTER 2018.—*In the case of any calendar year beginning after 2018, the applicable amount shall be the applicable amount for the preceding calendar year increased by the rate of premium growth (within the meaning of section 36B(b)(3)(A)(ii) of the Internal Revenue Code of 1986) for such preceding calendar year.*

* * *

(g) REPORTING REQUIREMENT.—

* * *

(3) ACCURACY-RELATED PENALTY.—

(A) IN GENERAL.—*In the case of any understatement of a covered entity's net premiums written with respect to health insurance for any United States health risk for any calendar year, there shall be paid by the covered entity making such understatement, an amount equal to the excess of—*

(i) *the amount of the covered entity's fee under this section for the calendar year the Secretary determines should have been paid in the absence of any such understatement, over*

(ii) *the amount of such fee the Secretary determined based on such understatement.*

(B) UNDERSTATEMENT.—*For purposes of this paragraph, an understatement of a covered entity's net premiums written with respect to health insurance for any United States health risk for any calendar year is the difference between the amount of such net premiums written as reported on the return filed by the covered entity under paragraph (1) and the amount of such net premiums written that should have been reported on such return.*

(C) TREATMENT OF PENALTY.—*The penalty imposed under subparagraph (A) shall be subject to the provisions of subtitle F of the Internal Revenue Code of 1986 that apply to assessable penalties imposed under chapter 68 of such Code.*

(4) TREATMENT OF INFORMATION.—*Section 6103 of the Internal Revenue Code of 1986 shall not apply to any information reported under this subsection.*

* * *

(j) EFFECTIVE DATE.—*This section shall apply to calendar years beginning after December 31, 2013.*

* * *

[CCH Explanation at ¶ 543.]

Topical Index